DEPLOYING WINDOWS NT 4 IN THE ENTERPRISE

James Plas

SAMS
PUBLISHING

201 W. 103rd Street
Indianapolis, IN 46290

Publisher	*Richard K. Swadley*
Publishing Manager	*Dean Miller*
Director of Editorial Services	*Cindy Morrow*
Director of Marketing	*Kelli S. Spencer*
Assistant Marketing Managers	*Kristina Perry*
	Rachel Wolfe

Acquisitions Editor
Kim Spilker

Development Editor
Jeffrey J. Koch

Software Development Specialist
Patty Brooks

Production Editor
Mitzi Foster

Copy Editor
Anne Owen

Indexer
Ginny Bess

Technical Reviewer
Jeff Shockley

Editorial Coordinator
Katie Wise

Technical Edit Coordinator
Lynette Quinn

Resource Coordinator
Deborah Frisby

Editorial Assistants
Carol Ackerman
Andi Richter
Rhonda Tinch-Mize

Cover Designer
Karen Ruggles

Book Designer
Anne Jones

Copy Writer
David Reichwein

Production Team Supervisors
Brad Chinn
Charlotte Clapp

Production
Georgiana Briggs
Lana Dominguez
Brad Lenser
Andy Stone
Becky Stutzman

Contents

Dedication

This book is dedicated to my wife Diane and my daughters Remy, Sydney, and Sam. Thank you for all of your support in this endeavor, especially for putting up with me for the past six months.

Acknowledgments

Thanks to Kim for browsing the newsgroups and giving me this great opportunity. Without you, I wouldn't be writing this today. (P.S. I'll have the movie script done in a few weeks. Can we get Leonard Nimoy to direct?)

Thanks to all of the supporting staff at Sams, especially Jeff and Mitzi. I'm sure you two were tired of my smart aleck comments halfway through author review. I appreciate the hard work.

Thank you to my good friends Greg Ledom and Dexter Burch for their infinite wisdom and never-ending supply of cabbage. The book is finally here, so please, no more questions! By the way, I'll have another Honey Brown.

Thank you to Scott Riggs for the fluff, the excellent tips on effective car waxing, and the Land Cruiser discovery adventures.

I would like to thank the cursed individual who left me with a batch of NT deployments to clean up a few years back—without you, I'd still be seeing Red.

Continuing onward, I would like to thank Steve Bush for his mentoring during the early stages of my career. Even though Steve may not know it, he was a tremendous example when I first got started in this business.

Thanks to Mom and Pop, without whom I would not be here today. Who would've guessed that the math genius could pick this stuff up?

Finally and most importantly, I would like to thank my wife and kids for their support. This was a lot of hard work for all of us, but we did it!

About the Author

James Plas

Jim Plas was recently made the Manager of Technology and Technical Operations at Output Technologies in Kansas City, Missouri. His main responsibilities will be strategic direction and the support of a 2000+ user WAN that spans most of the continental United States. Previous to this position Jim was heavily involved in the deployment of client/server technology in a wide variety of networks and enterprise types. Jim has been working with Windows NT Server since its introduction as Windows NT Advanced Server 3.1.

Tell Us What You Think!

As a reader, you are the most important critic and commentator of our books. We value your opinion and want to know what we're doing right, what we could do better, what areas you'd like to see us publish in, and any other words of wisdom you're willing to pass our way. You can help us make strong books that meet your needs and give you the computer guidance you require.

Do you have access to CompuServe or the World Wide Web? Then check out our CompuServe forum by typing GO SAMS at any prompt. If you prefer the World Wide Web, check out our site at http://www.mcp.com.

NOTE

If you have a technical question about this book, call the technical support line at 317-581-3833.

As the publishing manager of the group that created this book, I welcome your comments. You can fax, e-mail, or write to me directly to let me know what you did or didn't like about this book—as well as what we can do to make our books stronger. Here's the information:

Fax: 317-581-4669
E-mail: Dean Miller at opsys_mgr@sams.samspublishing.com
Mail: Dean Miller
        Sams Publishing
        201 W. 103rd Street
        Indianapolis, IN 46290

IN THIS PART

- **Beginning the Design Process**   3

- **Why Windows NT Server?**   13

- **The Importance of Standardization**   25

PART

Beginning the Process

Beginning the Design Process

IN THIS CHAPTER

CHAPTER 1

Windows NT Server 4.0 is in itself an expansive subject. There are so many different features and functions and means of deployment available that to attempt to address them all would do neither the operating system nor the reader justice. The purpose of this book is to set a foundation for deploying Windows NT Server as your primary Network Operating System as well as the core production system in your enterprise.

Ten years ago, network computing meant file and print sharing; today, file and print sharing is an afterthought—it's the features and functionality that enable a network operating system to act as the anchor in your distributed enterprise that attracts the savvy systems engineer. Enterprise computing has evolved so rapidly in the past 10 years that most networks today consist of multiple network operating systems, multiple client types, a variety of office automation applications, overlapping application services, and numerous communication protocols. When integrating new services or applications into an environment, the systems engineer must weigh these factors as well as those still yet to come.

As equally challenging as integrating new services into an existing environment or migrating to a new network operating system is the task of designing an entirely new enterprise. As rapidly as enterprise computing has changed in the past, the rate does not seem to be slowing in the near future. Luckily, with the mainstream advent of the Internet, many of the industry leaders have begun to comply with the long standing traditions—or standards—that those contributing to the Internet have adhered to. The Internet is beginning to become the center from which all new enterprise-level development flows. Because of the central role that the Internet is playing in today's enterprise development, it is becoming less of a task to design and manage a distributed enterprise. The challenge that remains, however, is to design or migrate to an enterprise that is open and scalable enough to allow for the rapid growth and change that the information industry undoubtedly will continue to foster.

Windows NT Server 4.0 is extremely well suited to the diverse and transitory technologies that make up enterprise computing. With its open architecture, portability, capable Domain Directory Services and robust performance and feature set, Windows NT Server is primed as the premier network operating system available today. However, simply because Windows NT Server 4.0 provides all of the tools necessary to deploy or integrate into a successful distributed environment does not mean that every deployment will be successful. This book will outline a domain deployment process as well as several managment practices designed to help you deploy the successful enterprise your users and your corporation deserve.

When designing your enterprise, there are Six Key Design Objectives to keep in mind. These objectives are crucial not only in day-to-day management and controlled growth, but also for maintaining a flexible, open, and scalable enterprise that allows for rapid change and the introduction of new technologies without harming core enterprise integrity.

- Objective One: A Central User Directory
- Objective Two: A Standard User Environment
- Objective Three: A Single Logon to All Common Resources

- Objective Four: An Open and Scalable Design
- Objective Five: Fault Tolerance
- Objective Six: A Solid Support Organization

These objectives, which will be explained in further detail, can be drawn in differing degrees to every step of enterprise design and deployment. These objectives will guide you in designing and maintaining an environment geared for not only short-term, but long-term success. Using these objectives as guidelines, you will find that Windows NT Server 4.0 is not only easy to deploy, but it is simple to manage and maintain.

As equally important as the Six Key Design Objectives is determining the needs that your enterprise must fulfill. Deploying technology simply for technology's sake rarely buys a company or the administrator anything. This chapter will briefly explore three deployment models as well as detail the Six Key Design Objectives and how they apply to enterprise design.

> **NOTE**
>
> Having been involved in the technology industry as a consultant, an integrator, a network administrator, and a systems engineer, I have seen many NOS deployments. The three recommended deployment models are built on a combination of Microsoft suggestions and the experiences I have had with not only the successful deployments of Windows NT Server (and NetWare), but also the unsuccessful deployments of NT, NetWare, and OS/2 LAN Server.

Determining Your Deployment Needs

Windows NT Server 4.0 is a very scalable operating system and therefore offers many deployment models. As this book travels the different stages of Windows NT Server deployment, you will be provided with blueprints for the three most practical deployment models. As detailed later in the book, there are far more than three possible deployment scenarios; however, the three featured herein are those that not only comply with the Six Key Design Objectives, but are also modeled after some extremely successful deployments. These models are based on a company's organizational and physical structure as well as the number of users within an organization. The three models are as follows:

- **Model Number One: The InterDepartmental Domain.** Model Number One is for a small- to medium-sized organization. This model applies to those companies with a single location and less than 250 users. Model Number One fits the needs of most organizations and through adherence to the Six Key Design Objectives, allows for the growth and scalability required by today's technology. Model One could easily move to Model Two or Model Three.

■ **Model Number Two: The InterDivisional Domain.** Model Number Two is for a medium- to large-sized corporation with multiple locations, a single support organization, and any number of users. Model Number Two works excellently in the campus environment, as well as the large WAN environment, but does not take into account providing desktop support for those users in remote locations. If you use Model Two in an organization with a good deal of geographic diversity and only one central support organization, it is assumed that you have remote support personnel in place. Model Number Two is also extremely flexible and has the potential to comfortably move to Model Three if required.

■ **Model Number Three: The InterCorporate Domain.** Model Number Three is for the medium- to large-sized corporation with any number of locations, multiple support organizations, and potentially thousands of users. This model is for the company with either enough organizational or geographic diversity to require more than one support organization. This model assumes that these support organizations realize the need to cooperate in order to truly serve the user and the company's business needs. Model Three provides all of the flexibility of Models One and Two, yet realizes the need to distribute support responsibility.

These models have many similarities in their deployment methods. What makes them different enough to detail during each significant deployment step is the complexity of organization, geography, and corporate culture. While models are very helpful in understanding the theories behind practical implementation, they are not very personal and don't provide for as much clear understanding or retention. Therefore, while this book will detail each significant step of deployment for the three different models, it will also provide a pseudo-company that fits each model. Those companies are as follows:

MODEL NUMBER ONE: THE HORTON AGENCY

The Horton Agency is an advertising agency with 120 employees and four primary departments: Creative, Accounting, Sales, and Administrative. The environment consists solely of Macintosh and Windows for Workgroups workstations. Its goal is to migrate to Windows NT Server 4.0, to eliminate its existing network operating systems, and to move the majority of its users to Windows 95, while still retaining a small percentage of its Macintosh workstations. While Model Number One will fit any small- to medium-sized, single location environment, the migration goals of the Horton Agency will cover the majority of Windows NT Server's standard features and provide a solid model to follow during a migration or a new deployment. (See Figure 1.1.)

FIGURE 1.1.

*The Horton Agency
Illustrated.*

Model Number One: The Horton Agency

User Base:	120
Departments:	Creative Accounting Sales Administrative
Network Operating System:	NetWare 3.*X* Macintosh Server
NOS Goal:	Windows NT Server 4.0
Existing Clients:	Macintosh Windows for Workgroups
Client Goal:	Windows 95 Macintosh
Enterprise Integration:	None
Existing Protocols:	AppleTalk IPX/SPX
Protocol Goal:	TCP/IP

MODEL NUMBER TWO: THE GUARDIAN INSURANCE COMPANIES

The Guardian Insurance Companies is an insurance corporation with approximately 500 employees, three divisions, and four buildings in a single metropolitan area. The three divisions—Health, Casualty, and Corporate Benefits—all share the same Human Resources and Claims departments, yet have their own individual Accounting, Marketing, and Administrative divisions. The Guardian Insurance Companies is moving from a mainframe-centric environment to a Windows NT Server–based enterprise. The NetWare Servers it currently has are departmentally segregated and provide no room for hardware expansion. Windows for Workgroups, OS/2, and DOS workstations prevail as its sole network clients. The Guardian Insurance Companies wishes to move to a single network operating system (NOS), a single user directory, and single 3270 gateway. Additionally, Guardian wants to move to Windows NT Workstation as the primary network client. (See Figure 1.2.)

FIGURE 1.2.
*An Illustration of the
Guardian Insurance
Companies.*

Model Number Two: The Guardian Insurance Companies
Four Buildings (Campus)

User Base:	500
Divisions:	Health
	Casualty
	Corporate Benefits
Shared Departments:	Human Resources
	Claims
	Information Systems
Individual Departments:	Accounting
	Marketing
	Administrative
Network Operating Systems:	NetWare 3.*X*
NOS Goal:	Windows NT Server 4.0
Existing Clients:	Windows for Workgroups
	OS/2
	DOS
Client Goal:	Windows NT Workstation
Enterprise Integration:	AS/400
Existing Protocols:	SNA
	IPX/SPX
Protocol Goal:	TCP/IP (routed
	environment)
	SNA

Guardian HQ

Guardian Health

Guardian Corporate
Benefits

Guardian Casualty

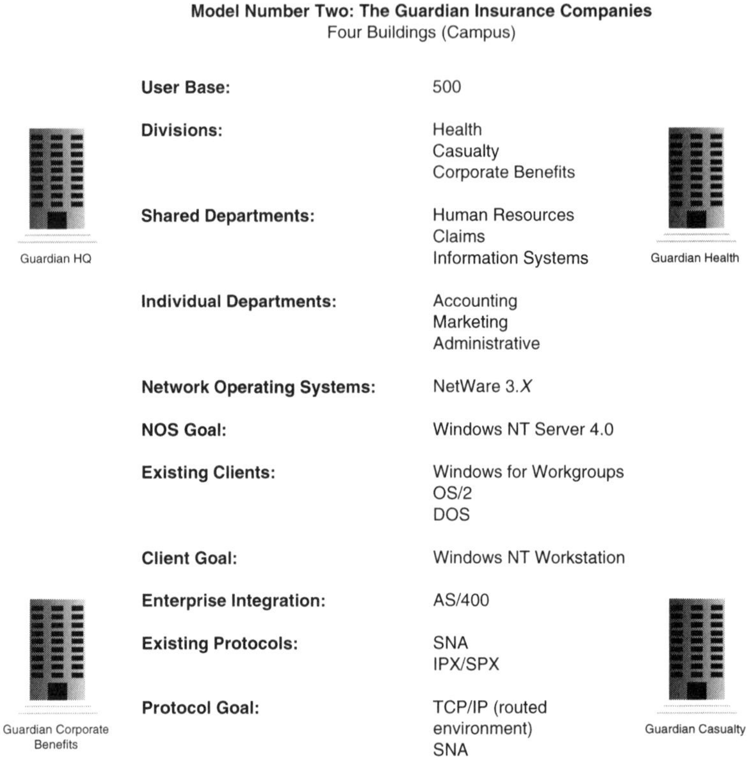

MODEL NUMBER THREE: MCMAC MINERAL, INC.

McMac Mineral is a conglomerate of four organizations: McMac Mineral, Jansen Salt, Watterson Paper, and McMac Foods. McMac Mineral was built with the mainframe as its backbone, but over the past 10 years has found the need to introduce not only UNIX, but also NetWare and LAN Server into the environment. Each division has its own support organization, but the corporation has established a Data Security department that functions as a facilitator for Human Resources and each division's Accounting department. With the help of Data Security, McMac Mineral has moved to a single mainframe user directory, but is nowhere near a single directory with any of the remaining platforms. McMac Mineral has several locations, but is based in Overland Park, Kansas. Additionally, Jansen Salt is located in Utah, Watterson Paper operates out of the state of Washington, and McMac Foods is headquartered in Kansas City, Missouri. Of the 2,000 total users, Windows for Workgroups is the primary network client at McMac Mineral, but there are some Windows 95, Windows NT, and OS/2 workstations. McMac Mineral plans to move to a single network operating system with a single user directory and single SNA gateway product.

With SNA as the exception, McMac Mineral also wants to standardize on TCP/IP as the sole network protocol. Additionally, McMac Mineral wants to move to a total Microsoft 32-bit desktop environment. (See Figure 1.3.)

FIGURE 1.3.

McMac Mineral, Inc., Illustrated.

Model Number Three: McMac Mineral, Incorporated

Watterson Paper

User Base:	2,000
Subsidiary Companies:	McMac Mineral Watterson Paper McMac Foods Jansen Salt
Shared Departments:	Human Resources Data Security Legal Public Relations R&D IS Support
Divisional Departments:	Accounting Marketing Administrative Public Relations R&D IS Support
Network Operating Systems:	NetWare 3.X OS/2 LAN Server
NOS Goal:	Windows NT Server 4.0
Existing Clients:	Windows for Workgroups Windows 95 Windows NT Workstation OS/2 DOS
Client Goal:	Windows 95 Windows NT Workstation
Enterprise Integration:	UNIX SNA (Mainframe)
Existing Protocols:	NetBIOS IPX/SPX TCP/IP SNA
Protocol Goal:	TCP/IP SNA

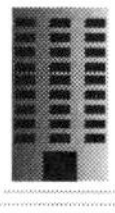

McMac Foods
Kansas City, Missouri

McMac Mineral, Inc.
Overland Park, Kansas

Jansen Salt
Salt Lake City, Utah

Beginning in Part II of this book, "The Design Basics," these models will be used to illustrate the deployment of Windows NT Server 4.0.

The Six Key Design Objectives

In each of the scenarios provided, there are multiple examples of the need to adhere to the Six Key Design Objectives. The objectives are a tool to be utilized for many purposes. First, they are a reference point for the design and implementation of your enterprise. Second, they themselves can provide justification for change or the introduction of new technologies in your environment—especially if they are used in a strategy paper that is presented to the ultimate decision makers in any organization and given their complete buy-off. Third, these objectives can help you avoid introducing any contaminating elements into your environment. If proposed technologies oppose or do not adhere to the Key Design Objectives, they should not be introduced unless there is no realistic alternative.

The Six Key Design Objectives are detailed as follows.

Objective One: A Central User Directory

A central user directory where all users and groups are created and stored allows for the efficient delivery of resource access, user creation, and a high level of security. Many organizations today have an enterprise with not only multiple network operating systems, but also varied and separate deployments of those NOSs. Sharing resources between departments and divisions is often difficult, while sharing resources between platforms can become impossible. Multiple client access packages, multiple protocols, and multiple user naming conventions create a quagmire that is often too daunting for the end user and, in the end, results in lessened productivity. A central user directory where all users are defined and from which all users are granted access to all NOS-based resources completely eliminates the difficulties traditionally dealt with in a distributed enterprise. The Central User Directory is the anchor that holds a successful enterprise.

Objective Two: A Standard User Environment

A standard user environment, including drive mappings, office applications, communication applications, server structure, and a single network protocol, as well as a single network client package per desktop, not only fosters a more accessible enterprise environment, but also reduces operating expense. The less disciplines there are to learn, the more time your users have to work, and the less time your support personnel have to spend working on issues caused by a chaotic environment. A standard user environment not only applies to the server, but also to the workstation. The more alike each workstation is in basic structure, the easier it is for users to manipulate resources and for support personnel to solve issues.

In addition to server and workstation configuration, it is also crucial to determine standard office automation packages. Each user should use the same spreadsheet, word processor, mail package, presentation creator, and database application, so as to reduce training and support costs. While it is understood that there will be certain applications required to fit the needs of certain users or departments, each user should have a common, basic tool set.

Objective Three: A Single Logon to All Common Resources

While Objective One (a central user directory) implies that all users will be logging into the same directory, it does not account for all common resources. Many environments contain gateways, communication servers, application servers, database servers, and legacy platforms that require their own logon process. While providing a central directory for all users to log into goes a long way toward creating an ease-of-access environment, it does not address the issues of legacy connectivity or services other than standard file and print sharing. Microsoft BackOffice is a series of application services that address the issues of host connectivity, database services, and Internet connectivity as well as many other features, while requiring no additional logon. Users are granted access to BackOffice products through the Windows NT Domain Directory (which will be detailed later). Additionally, many developers provide BackOffice-compatible applications that in turn provide additional services while integrating with the existing Windows NT Domain Directory. The Windows NT Server Domain Directory, in conjunction with BackOffice and BackOffice-compatible products, form a powerful foundation for a successful distributed enterprise. While it may not be possible to provide all common enterprise resources through a single logon, it is an important goal that will be achievable in the near future as more and more developers (including Microsoft) adhere to industry standards, especially those fostered by the growth of the Internet.

Objective Four: An Open and Scalable Design

Objective Four applies more to the Network Operating System than it does to the deployment of a NOS. Your Network Operating System should be an open system that provides the foundation for your enterprise services. This foundation should be portable from platform to platform, should provide the ability to easily enhance and even add to its basic feature set, and should scale to the needs of your environment without great pains. Through such features as its BackOffice program, as well as the stable and open design of Windows NT Server, Microsoft has provided the most scalable network operating system available today. Not only does Windows NT come with a comprehensive feature set, but it is easily enhanced through third-party services and applications. Windows NT Server can communicate and even integrate with every major enterprise platform available today. Due to the combination of its robust performance, expandability, open design, and strong domain directory service, there is currently no better enterprise platform available.

Objective Five: Fault Tolerance

The adage that "Time is money" is so inherent in today's business atmosphere that it truly goes without saying. The new adage that "The enterprise is the business" is becoming more and more clear as each year passes. Companies have become so dependent on their networks that if the network goes down, they not only lose immediate productivity but are often impacted for days. While data backups often keep companies from complete disasters, they are not proactive and do not prevent network outages. Network managers and executives all know that the data stored throughout the enterprise is the business, yet data fault tolerance is often the most neglected feature of the enterprise. Power conditioners and good data backups do not prevent the company from losing money—they are merely a storm shelter. With the reliance companies have on their enterprise, fault tolerance has become so crucial that it should never be questioned. There are varying degrees of fault tolerance—from simple disk duplexing to RAID technology to complete server mirroring. The severity of the importance of the data is what should drive the fault tolerance decision. Fault tolerance is as crucial to the success of an enterprise as the existence of the enterprise itself.

Objective Six: A Solid Support Organization

Without a solid support delivery system and a well-trained, well-organized support staff, the enterprise cannot function properly. Next to fault tolerance, one of the most overlooked features of the enterprise is the support organization. While this book cannot address all of the issues concerning the support organization, it will provide some guidelines, ideas, and suggestions for delivering support to the users. When designing the enterprise, not only should you keep in mind the issues of scalability, flexibility, and growth, but also the end user and the support personnel. First, without the end user the enterprise would most likely not exist. Second, in order to properly serve the end user, the support organization should be designed to meet, exceed, anticipate, and react to the user's needs. While there are a great number of excellent tools available to assist in the delivery and organization of enterprise support, not every corporation can afford them. This book will provide examples of support delivery tools that can be developed using the basic applications and features available in your enterprise today.

Summary

While one book cannot address all of the issues encountered in the deployment of Windows NT Server (or any NOS for that matter), through the use of the Six Key Design Objectives and the applicable deployment model as detailed throughout this book you should have a fighting chance. Windows NT Server 4.0 provides nearly all of the tools and capabilities necessary for a flourishing distributed enterprise—the trick is in the tactical deployment of those tools. This book will provide you with a proven blueprint for success.

Why Windows NT Server?

IN THIS CHAPTER

CHAPTER 2

Windows NT Server has been receiving a great deal of attention lately. It seems that every major hardware manufacturer is bundling NT with its servers, that every software corporation is porting its wares to Windows NT, and that every major industry player is aligning its products to NT for marketing purposes. At the same time, those who provide competing products have been doing an excellent job of explaining why their Network Operating Systems are better, how Windows NT Server lacks a "true" directory service, and claiming that Windows NT Server provides very little management functionality. Yet, Windows NT Server continues its market growth. Why? What does Windows NT offer that at once makes it so attractive to the end user and so nerve-wracking to its competitors? The answers are simple:

- A well-integrated Domain Directory
- Excellent file and print services
- Better client compatibility than any NOS available
- More inherent protocol functionality than any NOS available
- An expansive range of built-in, add-on, and third-party services for the diverse environment
- An ever-expanding BackOffice program
- The most open platform on the market today
- Intrinsic compatibility with Internet standards
- A well-designed, easily navigated front end environment

These features, plus many more, are what combine to make Windows NT Server the only Network Operating System that can easily integrate into any enterprise as the dominant production environment while still providing seamless connectivity to alternative platforms. This chapter will serve as an introduction to the feature-rich operating system in order to provide a solid understanding of why Windows NT Server is uniquely qualified to be your enterprise anchor.

The Domain Directory

The Windows NT Server Domain Directory is organized not through a tree like other directories, but through the use of domains. A *domain* is a logical grouping of users and resources that provides access to all of those resources through a single logon. The Windows NT Domain Directory is much maligned by its competitors, but in actuality provides a great deal of functionality. The Domain Directory, which is the place from which all domain resources are managed, is administered through three main tools: the user manager for domains, the server manager, and the Windows NT Explorer. At this time, there is no single tool that allows the administrator to manage each of the varied objects throughout the Domain Directory; however that is coming in the next version of Windows NT Server. Today's Domain Directory services do provide a great deal of functionality even in their segmented state and together form a tool set that contributes to Windows NT's ease of management. The items managed within the Windows NT Domain Directory Service are

- Users and groups
- File and directory permissions
- Shares and share level permissions
- Printers
- Advanced user properties
- Trust relationships
- Domain security policies
- Domain and object auditing
- Servers and workstations within local and trusted domains

The Windows NT Domain Directory is a comprehensive service that is pervasive throughout all aspects of the Windows NT enterprise.

The User Manager for Domains

The User Manager for Domains is where all users and groups throughout your domain are created and managed. It is through the User Manager for domains that you will manage user properties, assign logon scripts and profiles, manage a domain's security policies including auditing, manage advanced user rights, establish relationships with other domains, and organize your directory structure. The User Manager for Domains is an excellent tool and provides an intuitive interface that can be accessed from any Windows platform. The User Manager for Domains is where you will spend most of your time when administrative duties are required.

FIGURE 2.1.

A Typical View of the User Manager for Domains.

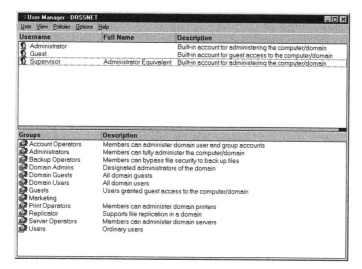

The Server Manager

The Server Manager is the tool that allows you to manage local or remote Windows NT servers and workstations within your domain as well as Windows NT machines in those domains that have previously established trust relationships. The Server Manager facilitates the following management features:

- The creation and management of shared directories including permissions
- Service management including starting, stopping, and startup modification
- The management of user connections, shared directory use, and files currently in use
- The addition and removal of Windows NT machines from the domain
- Forced domain synchronization

FIGURE 2.2.

The Windows NT Server Manager.

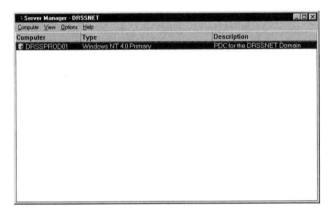

Many of the management features provided by the Server Manager are remote interfaces of those tools that exist locally on servers and workstations. The Server Manager has a well-laid-out interface that provides intuitive access to server properties.

The Windows NT Explorer

The Windows NT Explorer is the same explorer interface found in Windows 95; however, in Windows NT, the explorer provides advanced functionality. The Windows NT Explorer, as do all directory management tools, pulls permission and auditing information from the user and group directory maintained within the User Manager for Domains. With the Windows NT Explorer, you can perform the following:

- The application and manipulation of file and directory level permissions
- The management of DOS file attributes
- The creation or management of locally shared directories
- The management of object ownership

■ The auditing of files and directories

■ Remote shared printer management through the network neighborhood extension of the explorer

FIGURE 2.3.

The Windows NT Explorer Management Interface.

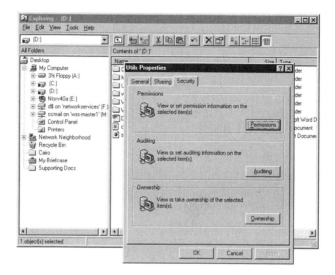

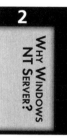

The User Manager for Domains, the Server Manager, and the Windows NT Explorer are the main tools used to manage the Windows NT Domain Directory Service; however the directory does extend beyond the NOS basics. All Microsoft BackOffice and third-party BackOffice applications pull from and integrate with the Domain Directory, adding to the comprehensive and easily managed service. The Domain Directory Service is definitely one of the many strengths found within Windows NT Server 4.0.

File and Print Services in Windows NT

When Windows NT Server was first released it was heavily criticized for providing poor performance in the area of file and print services. While this criticism was originally well founded, Windows NT Server is now not only comparable to NetWare's file and print services, it offers better client compatibility, easier manageability, and a more open resource sharing system. NTFS, the native file system for Windows NT, provides native support for not only long file names, but enhanced security and detailed auditing. Each version of Windows NT Server has provided better file and print sharing performance and 4.0 is no exception to this rule. Additionally, with DFS, or the new Distributed File System, Windows NT has exceeded anything seen in the industry yet. With DFS, a free Microsoft provided add-on, you can furnish your Windows NT 4.0 and Windows 95 clients with a shared directory structure that spans not only multiple servers, but even multiple platforms. With DFS in place, your users no longer have to navigate multiple servers to find the information they need; DFS allows you to build a custom directory structure that makes sense for your organization.

Remote Access Service

Windows NT Server provides an excellent dialup access solution with Remote Access Service (RAS). RAS provides remote node connectivity for Windows for Workgroups, Windows 95, and Windows NT clients with industry standard PPP connectivity and enhanced security features. Not only does Windows NT allow you to dial in to the network and access NT resources, but to NetWare, SNA, TCP/IP, and NetBIOS resources as well. Windows NT supports multiple communications technologies including ISDN, multi-port serial boards, and also provides LAN-to-LAN routing through RAS if necessary.

Client Compatibility

Windows NT Server supports Windows 95, Windows NT, and Windows 3.1 clients; it also provides a client package for MS DOS, Services for Macintosh, and native support for OS/2 users. Additionally, because of its open architecture, Windows NT Server supports add-on services that provide seamless connectivity to Novell NetWare Clients and UNIX workstations. The following services provide a wide variety of client compatibility:

- Services for Macintosh, which is included with Windows NT Server, provides seamless Macintosh file and print connectivity that allows the sharing of printers and data with all of your clients.
- The Internet Information Server, which ships on the Windows NT Server 4.0 CD, is a fantastic Internet platform that includes WWW, FTP, and Telnet connectivity to all client types, including UNIX. With the addition of any of the BackOffice add-ons, IIS is one of the premier Internet solutions available.
- Services for NetWare, which is an add-on product that enables your Windows NT Server to emulate a NetWare 3.*x* server so that your native Novell clients can attach to and access resources on your NT Server including printers.
- Multiple NFS solutions for Windows NT Server that, when in place, enable you to share your server's resources with UNIX clients as well as any other client type running NFS software.
- SNA Server, a BackOffice application, provides a gateway service that allows your clients to attach to legacy IBM platforms without an additional authentication process.
- TCP/IP printing, which is included with Windows NT, allows you to share printers with native UNIX workstations and attach to and share LPD/RPD printers.

Open architecture, scalable performance, and platform compatibility combine to make Windows NT Server the only platform that can anchor your enterprise by providing connectivity services to the widest variety of client types.

Multiple Protocol Support

Microsoft networking has long been associated with the NetBIOS protocol; however, Windows NT Server is protocol-independent. While NetBIOS is an integral part of the Microsoft network environment, many people are surprised to find out that Windows NT Server 4.0 defaults to TCP/IP during installation. Microsoft in many ways has positioned Windows NT Server as a chameleon (it always seems to find a way to blend in), and therefore ships NT with multiple native protocols: TCP/IP, NetBEUI(enhanced NetBIOS), IPX/SPX, DLC, PPTP, and AppleTalk. Inherent in all Windows NT protocols is the NetBIOS interface; however, it is not necessarily a pervasive element.

The NetBIOS Interface

Windows NT networking components rely on a naming convention known as NetBIOS (Network Basic Input/Output System). Windows NT Server 4.0 utilizes the NetBIOS Interface Service to provide name resolution and to establish machine-to-machine and application communications; however, the NetBIOS Interface and the NetBIOS protocol are not one and the same. The NetBIOS Interface, which is not a protocol, interacts with the differing implementations of Windows NT's protocols (NetBEUI, NWLink, NetBIOS, and WINS for TCP/IP) to provide name resolution. The NetBIOS Interface, which has no effect on physical network performance, is required for communications with Microsoft clients.

Windows NT Server 4.0 and TCP/IP

Windows NT Server provides a complete enterprise level TCP/IP solution as well as an industry standard TCP/IP stack. With the DNS, DHCP, and WINS services in place and TCP/IP installed on your client workstations, no other protocols are required for complete client/server connectivity.

- DNS, or Domain Name Service, provides static name resolution for TCP/IP clients.
- WINS, or Windows Internet Name Service, provides both browsing in the TCP/IP environment and dynamic name resolution for all Microsoft clients.
- DHCP alleviates the need to provide static addresses to each TCP/IP-based client by dynamically assigning addresses.

These three services work together to provide an easily managed enterprise-level communications solution. Windows NT Server is fully compliant with all TCP/IP standards and will work in conjunction with other DNS and DHCP solutions. While Windows NT Server's implementation of TCP/IP still requires the NetBIOS Interface in the embodiment of the WINS service, it is a truly routable, easily managed implementation of TCP/IP. WINS is not necessary for communication with non-Microsoft TCP/IP resources and is not required for access to such Internet standards as HTTP, FTP, Telnet, or SMTP services running on a Windows NT Server; rather, WINS replaces the chatty traffic usually encountered with standard Microsoft browsing services.

Microsoft NetBEUI

NetBEUI is an enhanced version of NetBIOS originally intended to allow backward compatibility with Microsoft LAN Manager and IBM LAN Server. NetBEUI is a fast, efficient protocol that is excellent in a small, non-routed environment. Unfortunately, NetBEUI cannot be routed and therefore propagates itself throughout every part of your network causing undue congestion. NetBEUI should be used only if communications with NetBIOS resources are required or if you are in a small environment with no plans to connect to other networks.

Microsoft IPS/SPX—NWLink

NWLink is Microsoft's reverse-engineered version of IPX/SPX that, in conjunction with the Gateway Service for NetWare or Services for NetWare, allows communication with both NetWare servers and NetWare clients. NWLink is implemented in two parts: IPX/SPX and NWLink NetBIOS.

NWLink IPX/SPX

IPX/SPX is used for communication with NetWare 3.*x* and 4.*x* servers and for NetWare 3.*x* emulation in conjunction with File and Print Services for NetWare. IPX/SPX is fully routable and acts nearly identical to NetWare's IPX/SPX. Without NWLink, IPX/SPX communication with NetWare resources would be impossible.

NWLink NetBIOS

NWLink NetBIOS is the Microsoft implementation of IPX/SPX and can be used as the sole mean of communication between Microsoft clients and servers. However, NWLink NetBIOS is categorized as a Type 20 protocol and proliferates itself across the network causing undue congestion. In a routed environment, Type 20 protocols must be enabled for NWLink NetBIOS to work across subnets, but in that case cause many of the same issues usually associated with NetBIOS. NWLink, therefore, should be used only for NetWare integration or in small, non-routed environments.

The DLC Protocol

The Data Link Control (DLC) protocol provided with Windows NT Server 4.0 is used primarily to communicate with network print devices, but in combination with certain applications, including Microsoft SNA Server, is used to communicate with IBM mainframes. DLC has limited functionality, but is a fully configurable protocol under Windows NT Server.

The Point-to-Point Tunneling Protocol

Point-to-Point Tunneling Protocol (PPTP) allows you to create Virtual Private Networks (VPN) to be used to connect to corporate resources securely across the Internet. PPTP enables clients using the PPTP protocol to connect to your network by dialing any Internet Service Provider or by any Internet connection type. PPTP is used in conjunction with Windows NT Server's Remote Access Server to provide a scalable and secure remote access solution that reduces costs and is easy to administer. PPTP will not be discussed in detail at any point in this book.

AppleTalk

Used in conjunction with Services for Macintosh, Windows NT Server provides a full AppleTalk solution including routing and seed routing support. Windows NT Server utilizes AppleTalk for client and printer connectivity.

Because Windows NT Server is protocol-independent, your network can be configured with only one or all of the previously mentioned protocols. Advanced binding configurations, IP/IPX routing, and DHCP relay (among other services and options) combine to make Windows NT Server a true network foundation.

A Platform for the Demanding Environment

Up to this point, this book has discussed some Windows NT Server enterprise features, but not the operating system itself. What makes Windows NT so powerful? How can Windows NT not only seamlessly communicate with native clients, but also Macintosh, UNIX, and NetWare clients, and at the same time provide application services, SNA communication, and remote access with ease? Simple. Windows NT is a multi-threaded and multi-tasking operating system that is not only processor independent, but is multi-processor–ready, has integrated fault-tolerance features, provides excellent tools for troubleshooting, and has none of the memory barriers usually associated with Microsoft or NetWare operating systems. These features combine to make Windows NT Server the most powerful operating system available today.

Architecture Independence

Windows NT Server has been designed as a portable operating system. Windows NT Server 4.0 runs on the Intel 486 and compatible processor, Intel Pentium/Pentium compatible, and Pentium Pro processor (or processors) as well as the Digital Alpha AXP, MIPS, and Power PC platforms.

In order to provide the needed portability, much of the operating system resides in the Kernel, which is processor-unspecific. What allows Windows NT to be so portable is the Hardware Abstraction Layer (HAL)—the Kernel communicates with the HAL to provide hardware specific instructions. Furthermore, many hardware vendors will provide their own HALs for Windows NT Server in order to take advantage of their proprietary hardware. Due to the relationship between the HAL and the Kernel, Windows NT Server has the ability to take advantage of new and emerging technologies rather quickly as evidenced by the recent release of Windows NT for the Power PC.

Windows NT Server was originally designed as a portable operating system in order to take advantage of more powerful hardware; however, with the rapid advance in power shown by the Intel Pentium and Pentium Pro systems, this is becoming less and less a required alternative.

Multi-Processor Support

Windows NT Server supports up to four processors out of the box, but with some vendor specific HALs can support up to 32 processors. Windows NT Server is a symmetrical multi-processing system and therefore load balances among processors. Windows NT Server scales extremely well and does not require SMP specific applications in order to take advantage of multiple processors. Due to the ability to take advantage of multiple processors, Windows NT Server rivals UNIX in application server performance and allows Windows NT Server to handle a tremendous number of production users per server.

Multi-Threaded and Multi-Tasking

Windows NT Server provides true preemptive, priority driven, time-sliced multi-tasking, which means that multiple processes and applications can run at one time and provide acceptable performance. In addition, each process or application can be multi-threaded, which means that each process or application can be conceived of a series of processes and applications, each with its own priority, time-slice, and memory. Multi-threading and multi-tasking combine to make Windows NT Server a powerful file and print server, application server, database server, and communications server.

Integrated Fault Tolerance

Even though a hardware fault-tolerance solution is more desirable, Windows NT Server provides options for those corporations unable to acquire fault-tolerant hardware. Windows NT Server provides software-driven RAID technology right out of the box; with Windows NT Server's Disk Administrator your Windows NT Server can mirror, duplex, stripe, and even deliver RAID 5 technology. In addition, Windows NT Server supports hot fixes on disks formatted with the NTFS file system and sector remapping on SCSI drives. If Windows NT finds damaged sectors on a disk, it will mark the sectors bad and move the data to a safe area, thus providing a hot fix to hardware deficiencies. Furthermore, Microsoft is developing a standard clustering technology (dubbed Wolfpack) that will work in conjunction with several third-party server clustering solutions that will allow server fail-over and load balancing between multiple servers.

Troubleshooting with the Event Log

In most cases, when an administrator finds that something has gone wrong with a system, it is too late to find an absolute cause for the issue. Windows NT Server provides an Event Log service that logs system, application, and security events. The security log tracks the auditing features you've configured, the system log tracks system events—good and bad—and the application log tracks application events—good and bad. If your server is having performance issues, communication problems, and so on, you can easily check the Event Log for any telltale signs. Additionally, if your server crashes, it is always a good idea to check the Event Log for events leading up to the system crash. The Event Log provides a way to quickly pinpoint problems and resolve issues.

Memory Like an Elephant

Comparing Windows NT's memory management to an elephant's memory is slightly misleading; you can't increase an elephant's memory size. Unlike previous Microsoft operating systems, including to a certain extent Windows 95, Windows NT is not faced with the 640KB or 1MB memory barriers. Additionally, unlike NetWare 3.*x*, the Administrator is not faced with managing memory pools to ensure that enough RAM exists to perform standard NOS tasks. Windows NT Server uses a 32-bit flat memory model that is not restricted by any particular segment size. Furthermore, Windows NT Server efficiently uses page files for demand paging and virtual memory mapping. Frequently accessed data is moved into the page file and as it is requested by the application it is moved back into physical memory. Windows NT self-manages memory and very infrequently requires administrative attention.

The Microsoft BackOffice Program

Straight out of the box, Windows NT Server provides enough enterprise services to fit into most environments. The Windows NT BackOfice program only enhances that fit. When originally released, the BackOffice suite of products consisted of SNA Server, SQL Server, MS Mail Server, and Systems Management Server. Recently, the BackOffice suite has grown to include the following products:

- Microsoft SNA Server
- Microsoft SQL Server
- Microsoft Internet Information Server
- Microsoft Index Server
- Microsoft Proxy Server
- Microsoft Content Replication Server
- Microsoft Merchant Server
- Microsoft Exchange Server
- Microsoft Systems Management Server

BackOffice applications are designed to seamlessly fit into the Windows NT Enterprise in order to eliminate many administrative and support nightmares. Applications like SNA Server integrate with the Domain Directory for user administration; others like SQL Server utilize existing operating system features and resources; and all BackOffice applications integrate with the Domain Directory for security authentication—requiring only the initial user logon for resource access. With the recent explosion of Internet technologies, Microsoft has released, and is continually releasing, a series of Internet/Intranet-based products that plug right into the operating system and take advantage of the unique services provided by Windows NT Server. Furthermore, over 1,400 applications have already been designed to meet the Microsoft BackOffice program requirements and the list is growing rapidly. Microsoft BackOffice helps in closing the gap between distributed computing and disparate functionality.

Windows NT Server 4.0 is a solid enterprise NOS. Due to its open architecture, strong ISV support, excellent performance and reliability, out-of-the-box functionality, and ease of management, Windows NT Server has the capability to be the centerpiece of your distributed enterprise. It should be noted, however, that due to all of the functionality built into Windows NT Server, combined with the very familiar Windows 95 interface, Windows NT has the ability to become deceptively simple. Windows NT Sever is a complex system designed to integrate well within a complex enterprise. The method and manner by which you introduce and integrate Windows NT Server into your enterprise is just as important as the NOS itself. Critical to your successful deployment is standardization. The next chapter will look at the importance of standardization within the Enterprise.

Summary

Windows NT Server provides a tremendous amount of functionality that, if deployed properly, will contribute to an easily managed enterprise. With its open architecture and robust feature set, Windows NT Server is easily poised to be the dominant NOS in most any enterprise.

The Importance of Standardization

CHAPTER **3**

The words standard, standardization, and convention are very common in the computer industry. *Standards* can be defined by committees (IEEE), manufacturers, developers, or service providers. Additionally, corporations may have their own standards such as standard desktops, standard applications, standard naming conventions, standard hardware, and so on. What is so important about standardization? In the end standardization is designed to help the customer. If you are a developer, developing to industry standards helps your customer integrate your product into their environment. As a systems engineer, not only deploying industry standard products, but deploying like objects with like functions in a homogenous manner helps both the end user (your customer) and the support organization. With limited disciplines to learn and limited configuration methods to memorize, support becomes leaner and more efficient, and end-user disruption becomes less severe.

There are many standards within the computer industry and those standards are defined at multiple levels. Protocol standards, database standards, hardware standards, and development standards all exist and in many different forms. Not only are there multiple standards at multiple levels, but those standards that exist today might not be standards tomorrow, or they may evolve into something different. The question then becomes, if they're always changing, are standards really important? The answer is yes. As far as the industry as a whole is concerned, standards, if even only for a short time, pull the development community together and funnel energy toward like goals. These like goals generally benefit the customer (end user). The Internet is a perfect example. Netscape, Microsoft, IBM, Lotus, Novell, and many other major industry players are advancing TCP/IP-based technology at a tremendous rate due to the booming popularity of the corporate intranet, brought about by the commercial popularity of the Internet. These major industry players are all competing for the same niche, developing products that (oddly enough) are forced to interoperate because of industry standards, and in the meantime are developing beneficial products that might not have ever been developed. Due to the fact that these Internet/intranet products interoperate on some level due to standard adherence, the corporate community truly benefits by being able to deploy best of breed products intermixed within their enterprise. Because these best of breed products interoperate, support costs are minimized and functionality is maximized.

As far as the corporate enterprise is concerned, deploying industry standard products helps minimize support costs through product interoperability. Even more so, deploying industry standard products in similar conventions throughout the enterprise helps minimize support costs even more due to the fact that once an issue is solved, the solution can generally be applied to similar objects in similar functions. Additionally, users and support personnel will require less orientation to the environment, and when changes to the environment are required, their impact is generally more uniform.

The words *standard, standardization,* and *convention* will be used almost interchangeably throughout the remainder of this book. Objective Two of the Six Key Design Objectives calls for a standard user environment and this chapter will briefly cover some core elements of this objective. The areas to be covered are

- Naming Standards
- Directory Standards
- Hardware Standards
- Application Standards
- Operating System Standards

Naming Standards

Naming standards are important for purposes of user management, enterprise organization, and user identification. Naming standards, or naming conventions, cover the following key areas:

- User Naming Conventions
- Server Naming Conventions
- Workstation Naming Conventions
- Group Naming Conventions
- Workgroup Naming Conventions
- Domain Naming Conventions

These areas are key to intuitive enterprise management and user familiarity with the enterprise as a whole.

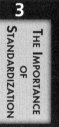

User Naming Conventions

User naming conventions are defined in terms of user name formats. Depending on the size of your organization there are several good logon name formats to choose from: last name/first initial (jacobst), first name/last initial (tomj), full initial set (tlj), last five digits of the user's social security number (16914) or employee identification number (various). Each user name format has pros and cons. With Windows NT Server, the administrator even has the ability to employ the users full name (Tom Jacobs) as the user naming convention. What is important is that an organization decide which naming convention is right for their organization and use it exclusively. The impact of user naming conventions will be explored in further detail later in the book.

Server Naming Conventions

Server naming conventions are crucial. Not only is it important that end users be able to quickly identify the servers of importance to them, it is also important (especially in a large enterprise) for support personnel to be able to identify with their servers. In today's distributed enterprise most organizations have multiple servers. Not only are server names required to be unique, they should also tell the end user something about them. For instance, if a small enterprise consisted of three servers—an office automation server (OA), a dedicated account-ing server, and a mail server—the servers might be named PROD01, ACCOUNTING1, and MAIL01. Assume, however, that your organization consists of 3,000 users. Would these names be truly functional? In the large enterprise it is helpful to name your servers after the customer base they serve. For instance, if your organization had three divisions (East, West, and South), all with several duplicate departments, you might preface all servers in the East division with the word EAST. For instance, EAST-ACCOUNTING1 or EAST-PROD01 would suffice as the OA server and the Accounting server. But what about servers that function as global re-sources? Many mail servers will serve multiple divisions and multiple departments. In that case, it is helpful to define a global preface for all divisions, such as CORP for corporate. In that case, CORP-MAIL01 would make an excellent name for a mail server.

Workstation Naming Conventions

Workstation naming conventions are more significant from an organizational standpoint than any other. While it is necessary that each workstation name be unique, it is helpful that they follow some format for identification purposes. In many cases, computer names will mirror the user name. For instance, if the user's name is JACOBST, his workstation would be named likewise. This is very handy especially in an environment that utilizes any number of desktop administration utilities that allows support personnel to manage and manipulate workstations from a remote console.

Workgroup Naming Conventions

Workgroup naming conventions are also more of an organizational tool. While Microsoft workgroups offer peer-to-peer functionality, large enterprise workgroups are more often used to sort like users. For instance, all users from the Marketing department could be put in the Marketing (or EAST-Marketing) workgroup. Sorting users in like workgroups not only helps organize the enterprise, it aids in the end user's identification with their environment. Addi-tionally, in a Microsoft network the workgroup aids in the browsing of network resources.

Domain Naming Conventions

In a single domain environment, domain naming conventions are less important. However, in an environment with multiple domains it is important that the support personnel and the end user be able to quickly identify the resources they require. Domain names for the most part should follow corporate organizational structure; however, they may vary depending on the function of the domain. Domain naming will be explored in detail later in the book.

Group Naming Conventions

When defining the User Groups within your User Directory, organization is crucial. With potentially hundreds and thousands of users, your User Groups should be easily identified.

For instance, in a small corporation, group names such as Marketing and Accounting might suffice, but in the larger organization, group names such as EAST-Accounting and WEST-Marketing are more easily identified. Additionally, groups that span global resources such as mail servers should be named accordingly (CORP-Mail). Group naming conventions, while not terribly important to the end user, are crucial to efficient end-user management.

Directory Structure

Standard directory structure, like many naming conventions, is key not only to end-user comfort and navigation, but to the efficient delivery of services. A well designed directory structure not only leads to more easily shared resources, but to end-user familiarity. Directory structure is important not only on the server, but on the workstation as well.

Server Directory Structure

The root of a drive or volume tells quite a bit about a server. If the root of a drive contains multiple directories and files, chances are the server is not being used very effectively. Have you ever been in an environment where every letter of the alphabet has been used for drive mappings (W for WordPerfect, L for Lotus, J for common data, L for the accounting department's data and so on)? A poorly organized directory structure leads to a poorly utilized server. When designing your directory structure, it is important to contemplate and categorize the applications and services you will be providing your end user. In the end, it is easier for you to manage and for your end user to utilize a well-organized server.

A data structure requires only one network share point—directory-level permissions will determine which users and groups have access to which subdirectories. All users that attach to the server can share the same mapped drive letter, yet access all of the data they need on a daily basis.

In addition to data directories, those directories that contain support utilities, client software, and applications should be designed with the fewest possible points of access while still providing an intuitive design and functional organization. Server directory structure contributes loads to the ease of management you will experience with your servers.

Workstation Directory Structure

Workstation directory structure impacts the end user less than support personnel, however, if all workstations have the same well designed structure, end users have very little trouble moving from workstation to workstation if required. Additionally, if each workstation shares the same directory structure, it is easier to plan for mass changes, provide support to a great number of people, and make environment changes through login scripts. The more your workstations look alike, the less time your support personnel will require when troubleshooting issues.

Workstation and Server Hardware

A good example of the need for corporate hardware standards is Windows 95. Imagine an environment with multiple workstation brands, multiple processor speeds, multiple memory configurations, and multiple network cards. Even as well designed as Windows 95 is there are many issues with mass upgrades. Certain network cards might conflict with certain video cards, sound boards might require new hard IRQ and I/O settings, a particular NIC driver that shipped with Windows 95 might not work properly, certain laptops might require BIOS upgrades, and the list could (and does) go on and on. Wouldn't it be better to have an enterprise consisting of perhaps only five or six various hardware configurations that could be well tested and documented before the mass deployment of Windows 95 ever took place? Imagine all of the time saved (for both regular associates and support personnel) if your technicians didn't have to spend hours a day discovering new ways for Windows 95 to fail installation. It is a common fact that most organizations do not have standard server and workstation hardware distributed throughout the enterprise; however, with the recent advancements in operating system and application development, most existing hardware is becoming obsolete. Because of these more resource-hungry developments, organizations are now being given the opportunity to purchase new hardware. With this opportunity, organizations should consider basic server and hardware configurations that allow for good performance today and expandability for the future. Following are some guidelines for hardware standardization:

- **Buy only one brand of workstation.** While it is okay to define more than one standard configuration (memory, disk space, processor speed), it is helpful to use the same manufacturer for all workstations. This helps cut down on the unexpected issues usually found in multi-vendor environments.

- **Buy only one brand of server.** Again, while you may have several different server configurations, it is helpful to have one source for hardware support. Many server manufacturers have a common feature set that can be found across all lines. Having to learn these features only once is an effective time saver

- **Use only one brand of network card.** Network cards all have their own idiosyncrasies. Even in the plug-and-play world of Windows 95, issues do arise. Again, it is okay to use different models for different configurations, but sticking to one manufacturer is a time saver.

- **Realize that technology is changing at a rapid pace—more so now than ever.** It is not necessarily a good idea to purchase –2 (Pentium 90) or –3(High-end 486) generation technology today. Three years ago the 486/66dx2 was a screamer required only by high-end users, and the 486/33dx was sufficient for almost everyone else. Today even standard office automation applications require high-speed Pentiums and large amounts of RAM. Maximize your future investment by purchasing no later than –1(Pentium 133) technology.

- **Evaluate your situation no earlier than on a six month rotating schedule.** Every six months to a year evaluate your hardware standards and see how they match up against ensuing technology. If applications and operating systems that will require more powerful hardware are on the horizon, bump up your hardware requirements. Many organizations have found that after re-evaluation at the six month marker they are able to buy nearly twice the machine for the same money.

Hardware standardization is a big subject. The key is to create an environment that is both simple to support and powerful enough to accept the inevitable changes that the near future holds.

Application Standardization

Many organizations today have multiple applications providing the same services to the end user. One department might use Lotus Smart Suite, another Corel Perfect Office, and the other Microsoft Office. Additionally, while one division might use cc:Mail, the other uses Exchange or GroupWise. Situations such as these cause headaches for users and administrators on a daily basis. The idea behind application standardization is the consolidation of support. For example, if your technicians only need to be familiar with one 3270 emulation package, your Help Desk need only support one Office Automation Suite, and your Enterprise Mail group need support only one mail application, you will see a reduction in hard and soft costs. Your users will be more satisfied because of the ability to easily share information, and your technicians and support personnel will become more focused because of the narrow support scope.

Key areas for application standardization are

- The Office Automation Suite: word processor, spreadsheet, presentation designer, data base tool, and so on
- The Mail System
- Communications Servers: SNA Gateways, Remote Access Solutions, and so on
- Communications Applications: 3270/5250 applications, X-Windows/TCP-IP Applications, and so on
- Any tool that provides a common functionality for the majority of your users

Much like hardware standardization, now is a good time to begin standardizing on core applications. Recent desktop developments have brought on a whole slew of new and more powerful applications.

Operating System Standards

Standardization truly begins with your operating system. Your desktop operating system defines many of your hardware requirements and nearly all of your application compatibility. While it might not be possible for all organizations to support only a single operating system, it is crucial that each installation of each varying operating system be nearly identical. From directory structure to office automation application and networking protocols, the configuration of your desktop determines your support needs. If you are able to deploy like workstations throughout your enterprise, you will enable your users to be more comfortable with their environment—regardless of whose workstation they're on—and you will allow your support personnel to become more focused on their daily tactical duties. Imagine an environment where every Windows 95 installation exists in the C:\WIN95 directory and every 3270 application exists in the C:\WIN32APP\3270 directory. The distribution of session updates would be as simple as the addition of six lines to your logon script:

```
IF EXIST C:\SESSION.CHK GOTO END
NET USE V: \\EAST-PROD01\SESSIONS
COPY V:\SESSION.CHK C:\
COPY V:\SESSION*.* C:\WIN32APP\3270\SESSIONS
GOTO END
:END
```

This simple batch file could (and does, by the way) save several hours of support time by automating the delivery of new 3270 session configurations to the end user. If the directory structure on each workstation were not identical, if each user weren't using Windows 95, and if each user were not using the same 3270 emulator, this scenario could never happen. Standardization as a whole allows you to provide better support and reduce time and costs.

Standardizing on a desktop operating system is not an easy task, especially with the choices provided by Microsoft today. What is clear is that the Microsoft 32-bit desktop is the best direction today. Whether you choose Windows 95, Windows NT, or both, a standard configuration and directory structure will help your end user and your support personnel tremendously.

Network Drive Mappings

Network drive mappings are sometimes a great source for humor. If you work in a large nonstandard enterprise, sit at your Help Desk one day and you'll likely hear issues such as:

"I think the J drive is down. All my files are missing!"

"How come I don't get the L drive? Bob has it and I want it!"

"I was copying a file from the M drive to the O drive—I think. Can you tell me where I put it?"

Drive mappings are key to the organizational success of an enterprise. Even if your user base is spread across distributed servers, it is helpful to designate the same driver letters to the same functions across each server. For instance, you might use O for the application share on your servers, or H for home directories. Users often don't understand that drive letters are dynamic and aren't truly hard coded to your network devices. If a user calls and says he can't get to his H drive, you'd certainly be able to deliver more efficient support if you knew automatically that he was having issues with his home directory. Standard drive mappings are another building block in the design and implementation of a standard environment.

Summary

Once again, as stated in Objective Two, standards are crucial to the success of your enterprise. The effect that non-standardization has on your enterprise can be far reaching. By standardizing almost every aspect of your environment you can consolidate your support resources, focus your energies on providing better service, and be more prepared for future changes. Standardization is a major impetus throughout this book and will be covered in almost every aspect of your enterprise deployment.

PART

IN THIS PART

The Design Basics

Designing Your Domain

IN THIS CHAPTER

CHAPTER 4

A good domain design is critical to the success of your enterprise deployment. Organizational structure, geographic diversity, number of users, and user needs are just a few of the factors to take into account in the infancy stages of your domain implementation. In order to design an effective domain directory, it is critical that you have a firm understanding of domain concepts. This chapter will first offer a modest tutorial on the Windows NT Domain framework followed immediately by user-directory principles, and will finish by providing a directory design blueprint for each deployment model endorsed by this book.

Domain Basics

A *domain* is a grouping of servers and resources that can be accessed with a single logon through a central user directory. In the domain environment, users do not log in to a server, but in to the domain. For instance, if you have a domain that consists of a production Office Automation server, an SNA server, a database server, and a data server, once your users have logged in to the domain, there is no need for further authentication. If a user has been given access to resources within the domain, regardless of which server those resources exist on, the user may freely use those resources.

In NetWare 3.*x*, users log on to one server at a time. Once a user has logged in to a server he or she has access to files, applications printers, and any additional resources that might be integrated into the system. However, if a user needs access to another NetWare 3.*x* server, he or she must go through an authentication process that is completely separate from the process he or she went through to log on to his or her original server. The end result (as seen in Figure 4.1) is that for every NetWare server a user needs to access, there must be a separate user account to maintain, not only for the user, but for the administrator as well.

FIGURE 4.1.

Mutli-Server NetWare Logon Process.

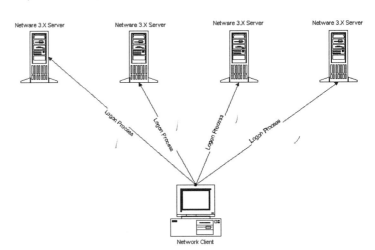

In a Windows NT domain, permissions for all domain resources are granted from within a single Domain Directory. This greatly simplifies user management and allows for easy resource expansion because the user logs in to the domain and not in to each individual server (see Figure 4.2).

FIGURE 4.2.
The Windows NT Domain Model.

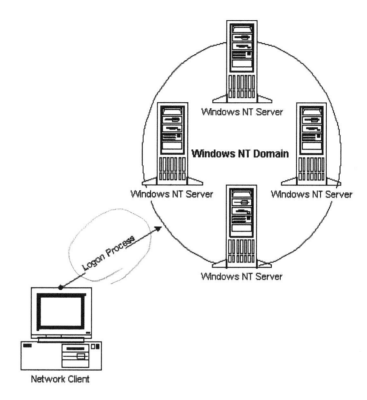

While the domain is a logical grouping of resources, the Domain Directory ties them together. The Domain Directory contains User Accounts, Group Accounts, Machine Accounts, Domain Policy, and Security Settings. In addition, the Domain Directory is where auditing, Trust Relationships, and advanced policies are maintained. The domain and the Domain Directory are integral to the Six Key Design Objectives, but particularly important to Objectives One, Three, and Four.

The Domain Directory and Objective One: A Central User Directory

A central user directory is a "must have" in today's enterprise environment. Distributed computing is becoming more and more of a reality, which in turn means that end-user resources are no longer located on one server or even one city. For the administrator, it is a management nightmare to have to maintain multiple accounts for every user. For the end user, maintaining

4

DESIGNING YOUR
DOMAIN

multiple accounts ends up in frustration and confusion. Due to the Domain Directory, it is not only possible, but also easy to maintain a single user directory for all LAN-based resources. The Windows NT Domain Directory can maintain in excess of 60,000 user accounts and, in turn, those user accounts are integrated into the rest of the Domain Directory. The Domain Directory is simply a database of objects and object properties. Those objects can be servers, workstations, users, groups, printers, shared directories, or even user environment settings. The Domain Directory is a key player in defining a standard user environment. Through the use of server naming conventions, shared resource naming conventions, user profiles, system policies, user policies, and standardization throughout your domain, you can provide an intuitive environment to your end users and support personnel.

Domain Security and Objective Three: A Single Logon to All Common Resources

When a user logs into the Domain he or she are assigned a unique Security Identifier (SID). This SID is, in essence, a security badge. Whenever a user attempts to access Domain resources, he or she presents his or her SID which in turn is referenced against the Domain Directory. If a SID carries the proper information, which often consists of not only a user's own personal account identifier but also of group membership SIDs, it is granted the designated level of access (as seen in Figure 4.3). If the SID does not carry the proper information, it is denied access. The authentication process is transparent to the end user unless access is denied.

FIGURE 4.3.

The Authentication Process.

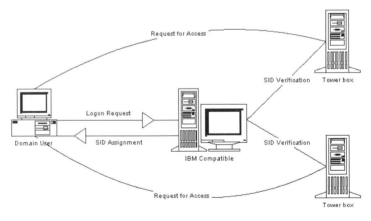

NT Servers and NT Workstations are domain members as well. In order to take advantage of the central Domain Directory, a server must be assigned a SID by joining the domain. Once a machine becomes a domain member, domain users can be granted access through the Domain Directory. This eliminates the need for additional authentication. Security is applied through a two-tiered system: Share and Directory Level security. Security will be explored in depth in Chapter 7, "Sharing and Securing Resources."

Trust Relationships and Objective Four: An Open and Scalable Design

Much like the words standards, standardization and conventions, open and scalable can mean many things.

The Windows NT Domain Directory is open and scalable due to its enormous capacity for maintaining users and objects, the capability to integrate with alternative platforms, and the capability to expand beyond a single domain and still retain manageability. At first, one might think that the Domain Directory is a closed system. It is impossible to escape the fact that for a user to have access to a server's resource without additional logon authentication, the server must be a domain member. But what if a user needs access to a server that is a member of another domain? To address this issue, Microsoft introduced the trust relationship. The trust relationship allows a domain administrator to grant users from outside domains access to internal domain resources. The trust relationship is classified as either trusting or trusted. These concepts are sometimes confusing, so it is helpful to break them out.

Trusting Domains

A *trusting domain* is a domain that allows users from other domains to access its resources. If your domain is Domain-A and your users need to access resources in Domain-B, you have two options: You can create a user account in Domain-B, or you can create a trusting relationship with Domain-B. As seen in Figure 4.4, Domain-B becomes trusting because it allows your users access to its resources without requiring an additional login process.

Trusted Domains

If you are the administrator for Domain-B and you want to allow users from Domain-A access to your resources without duplicating user accounts, you can make Domain-A a trusted domain. Users from Domain-A are trusted to use your resources without a logon ID. When you go to grant access to resources within your domain, you not only have your directory to pull users and groups from, but you can also grant rights to the users and groups in the Domain-A directory.

4

DESIGNING YOUR DOMAIN

CAUTION

Trust relationships are often antithetical to Objective One: A Central User Directory. While trust relationships are very useful in organizing your domain and often times necessary for seamless communications with other organizations, they can also become an unnecessary complicating factor. This book will explore the trust relationship in detail, and provide guidelines for their use, particularly when referring to Deployment Model Number Three.

FIGURE 4.4.
The Trust Relationship.

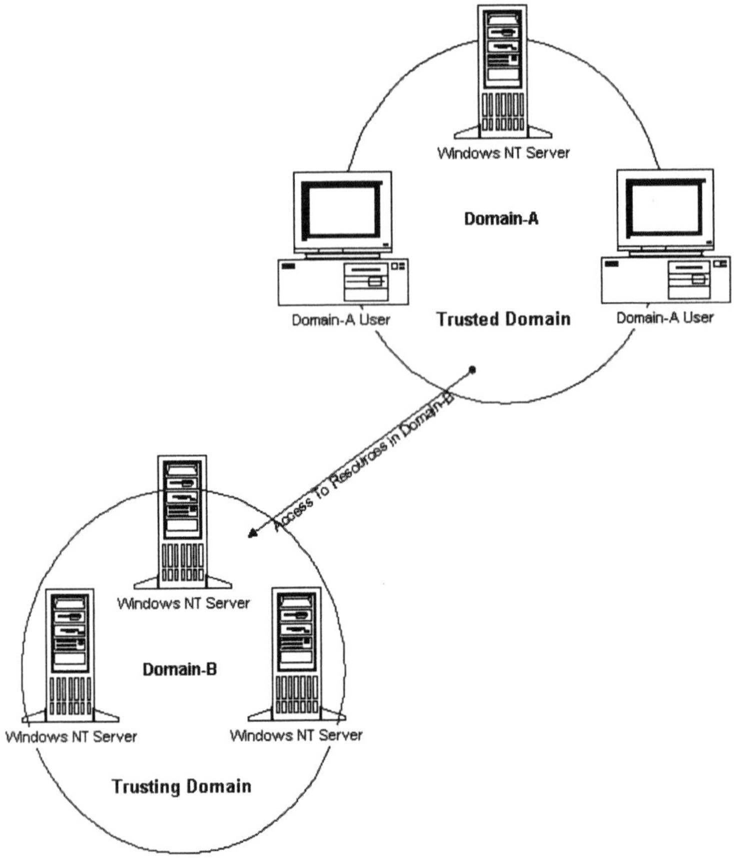

The trust relationship makes the Domain Directory both open and scalable. It is open because it allows access to resources outside of a user's home domain, and it is scalable because it allows you to grow your domain in an organized manner. Microsoft offers multiple domain models, but in reality the only models to entertain are the Single Domain Model and the Master Domain Model.

Directory Fault Tolerance and Objective Five: Fault Tolerance

There are two types of servers in a Domain: Domain Controllers and Member Servers. Domain creation begins with the installation of the Primary Domain Controller. The Primary Domain Controller (PDC) holds the master Domain Directory and is initially where all domain management flows from. Member servers are domain members that take part in domain security, but are not involved in domain management. Domain users are granted access to member servers from the Domain Directory, which adheres to Objective One: A Central User Directory. However, the member server does not hold a copy of the Domain Directory, which leads to the centrality of the PDC and the infamous single point of failure. This centrality begs the question—"What happens if my Primary Domain Controller goes down?" To answer this, Microsoft created the Backup Domain Controller. The Backup Domain Controller (BDC) provides domain directory replication and end-user logon and authentication. The BDC helps load balance user authentication and provides fault tolerance for the Domain Directory. If a BDC exists in your domain and your PDC fails, users will be logged on and authenticated through the BDC. All resources, excluding those stored on the PDC, will still be available to the end user.

Many organizations make the mistake of installing each additional domain server as a BDC. The simple act of becoming a domain controller requires somewhere in the neighborhood of 20% of a server's resources, if not more depending on the size of your domain. Good guidelines for BDC deployment is one for every 2,000 users in a single building or extremely fast WAN, or a BDC in every building. A BDC does not have to be a powerhouse machine, and, in fact, could be something as simple as a 486/66dx2 with 32MB of RAM dedicated to providing Domain Directory fault tolerance and Domain Authentication.

The domain provides the ability to implement a well-designed, easily managed enterprise of any size. Through security, expandability, integrated fault tolerance and a single directory, Windows NT Server offers a tremendous amount of flexibility. The key to an easily managed domain, however, is a well-planned Domain Directory that adheres to the Six Key Design Objectives.

Windows NT Server Domain Directory Principles

The Windows NT User Directory is managed through the User Manager for Domains. The User Manager for Domains is where users and groups are created and is the directory from which rights to network resources will be granted. The User Manager for Domains provides the administrator with the following functionality:

- The creation of users and groups
- The management of a domain's security policy
- The manipulation of user properties
- The management of groups and group membership within the domain
- Deletion, duplication, and modification of users and groups
- The management of advanced user rights
- The establishment of trusts with other domains

Due to the utility provided by the User Manager for Domains, it is important to become familiar with its basic arrangement. Whether you are using the User Manager at the server itself, a Windows 95 Workstation, a Windows NT Workstation, or a Windows for Workgroups client, the interface and functionality provided by this tool remain consistent.

4

DESIGNING YOUR DOMAIN

The User Manager Interface

As seen in Figure 4.5, the User Manager for Domains is a Windows-based tool that consists of three major sections: the Toolbar, the Users window, and the Groups window. While this interface is fairly intuitive, it provides so much domain functionality that you should be extremely familiar with its features and their use. The following section will cover the User Manager in three parts: the toolbar, the Users window, and the Groups window.

FIGURE 4.5.

The User Manager for Domains.

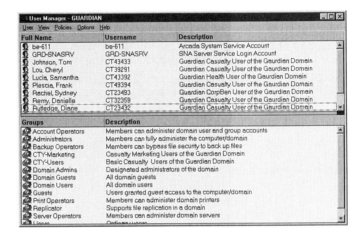

The Toolbar

The Toolbar is a text-based menu that is made up of five drop-down selections: User, View, Policies, Options, and Help.

The User Selection

The User drop-down menu on the Toolbar furnishes the administrator with the option to:

- Create new users and groups
- Copy users and groups
- Rename users (but not groups)
- Manage the properties of users and groups
- Delete users and groups
- Select users by group so that mass property changes can be made

Additionally, in a multi-domain environment, the User drop-down menu offers the ability to select and manage other domains throughout your network.

The View Selection

The View drop-down menu may not seem crucial, but in reality, is very helpful in user management. The View menu option offers the option to sort users by full name (the user's actual name) or user name (the user's logon identification). Due to the fact that the User Manager for Domains supports type-through, your chosen sort can make a substantial difference in the time it takes to find the user you're looking for, especially when you consider a single Domain Directory can support in excess of 60,000 users in NT 4. In fact, if you've used the last name, first name convention in the Full Name text box, finding users can be made terribly simple. In contrast if you're working in an environment that has less descriptive user names, such as employee ID numbers or user initials, it can become very difficult to manage users by logon ID only. Administrators are more likely to identify with their users by full name, since memorizing hundreds and thousands of user logon IDs is for most people an implausible task. Imagine a user directory consisting of user IDs ranging from 42193 to 98273, each one representing a user. As an administrator, you'll be less likely to make errors if you can manage those users by full name as opposed to some incidentally appointed number. This subject will be dealt with in detail in this chapter and in Chapter 9, "Managing Users."

The Policies Selection

The Policies menu option is where you will manage domain user account policies, advanced user rights, security auditing, and trust relationships. The Policies menu option is one that is used occasionally, but it can have significant impact on your domain when it is used.

Options and Help Selections

The Options and Help menu choices are self-explanatory. The Options pull-down menu gives you the choice to inform the system if you will be connecting to your domain through a low speed connection, provides an opportunity to turn "confirmation" on or off, and allows you to change the User Manager's font type and size. Of these three options, only the Low Speed Connection option is obscure in description. The Low Speed Connection option is meant to speed up your management capabilities over a slow link by limiting the amount of high bandwidth and GUI traffic. By choosing the Low Speed Connection option, you're limiting your management options. You can no longer see your users and groups, and you can no longer create or manage global groups. You can, however, copy, rename, manage, and delete users and local groups using the User pull-down selection and inputting the name of the user or group you wish to administer or create.

The Users Window

The Users window (see Figure 4.6) displays all of the users defined in your Domain Directory in three columns: User Name, Full Name, and Description. The User Name and Full Name columns have the capability to swap places by changing the sort order, but the Description text box remains static.

4

DESIGNING YOUR
DOMAIN

FIGURE **4.6.**

The Users Window Within the User Manager for Domains.

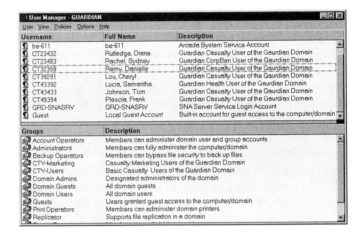

Alone, the Users window is not very functional. You can select multiple users, but only modify one at a time by double-clicking. To manage multiple user properties at once, you have two options. The following procedure provides more organized user management:

1. To ensure that no users are currently selected, select any group within the Group window by clicking once on its icon.

2. In the Toolbar, click on the Users pull-down menu. This will result in a drop-down list of management options.

3. Press Select from within the Users pull-down menu and you will be presented with a box containing all of the Local and Global groups within your domain.

4. Select the group of users you wish to manage followed by the Select option. All of the users within your selected group will now be highlighted. If you wish to manage additional users at this time, you may repeat this procedure for additional groups without deselecting the original group.

5. After selecting all of the groups that you need to manage, choose Close. The Users window will now show all of the users you've selected in black highlight.

6. To manage these mass user properties, go back to the Toolbar and select Properties. At this time, you will be presented with a User Properties box and will be able to manage all of the selected users as a group.

In addition to the preceding method, it is also possible to manage multiple users within the Users window by holding the control button on your keyboard down while selecting those users you wish to manage. Next, you may access their properties by selecting Properties in the User pull-down menu. This method is convenient for quick changes to a small group of users, but is not as efficient for managing an entire group.

The Groups Window

The Groups window, like the Users window, allows you to select and manage a single group's properties, but not multiple groups at once. Notice that there are two different icons representing groups in the Groups window (see Figure 4.7). These icons each represent a different group type: Local and Global. Local groups are represented by the icon with a computer in the background, while the Global groups are represented by the icon with the globe in the background. Group properties can be accessed in two different manners: by double-clicking on single group icon, or by selecting the group you wish to manage, and then Properties in the User pull-down menu on the Toolbar.

FIGURE 4.7.

The Groups Window Within the User Manager for Domains.

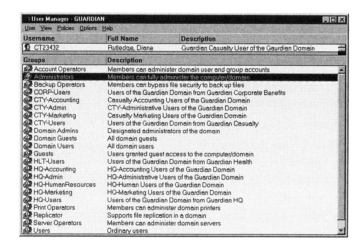

An Introduction to Built-In Users and Groups

Groups in a Network Operation System should be designed with the intent to furnish logical groupings of users based on security access, resource access, and authority delegation. After Windows NT Server is installed, there are automatically two default users and 11 default groups provided. With these groups, Microsoft has done an excellent job in developing a directory service that provides the ability to delegate support and administrative responsibilities without compromising total domain access. These groups all serve a definitive purpose, but in most cases will not have an impact on your domain organization, except where your support group is concerned. The groups are listed as follows:

- Account Operators
- Administrators
- Backup Operators
- Domain Admins

4

DESIGNING YOUR DOMAIN

- Domain Guests
- Domain Users
- Guests
- Print Operators
- Replicator
- Server Operator
- Users

The majority of these groups are designed for the disbursement of administrative tasks. However, the Users, Domain Users, Guests, and Domain Guests groups are provided as basic user groups. These groups, as discussed later, are better off ignored than used in your directory design. The following list provides a description for each default user group, excluding Guests, Domain Guests, Users, and Domain Users:

- Account Operators can create and manage user and group accounts without complete domain control.
- Administrators have complete authority (with exceptions) over the Local Domain.
- Backup Operators can bypass file- and directory-level permissions to back up and restore data.
- Domain Admins are Administrator equivalents with the capability to manage Trusting Domains.
- Print Operators can manage Domain printers.
- The Replicator group is required for directory replication (directory as in data structure, not User or Domain Directory).
- Server Operators have the capability to manage Server resources, but not Users and Groups.

While these groups are crucial to your support organization, they are not crucial to the overall design of your user directory.

As mentioned in the previous section, Windows NT Server offers two types of User Groups: Local and Global. Local Groups are Groups in a Domain that are limited to resources within their Domain, while Global Groups are Groups that can be applied to resources not only in their Local Domain, but also to resources in Trusting Domains. Local Groups are rarely used in the three deployment models endorsed by this book. Server Operators, Account Operators, Administrators, the Replicator Group, Backup Operators, Print Operators, Guests, and Users are all Local Groups.

Basic User Properties

Prior to the user deployment within your Domain, it is crucial to be familiar with all of the properties that make up a user. In the initial User Properties window there are 15 user features to manage, six of which launch property dialogs of their own (see Figure 4.8). Each of these features and properties will impact the structure and manageability of your Domain Directory which simply reinforces the need to consider the conventions and standards you will deploy throughout your Domain.

FIGURE 4.8.

The New User Properties Page.

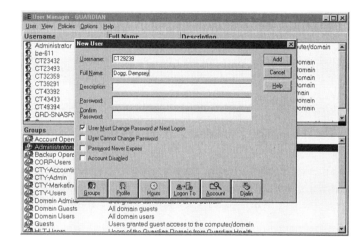

User Name

A User Name can consist of up to 20 numerical or alphabetical characters. User Names are not case sensitive, but you can enter them with any combination of upper- and lowercase characters. User-naming conventions are crucial to a successful directory design.

Full Name

The Full Name text box may not at first seem to be an important aspect of user management, however, when you take into account that the Users window can be sorted by either user name or full name, the impact becomes clear. It is more realistic for an administrator to associate a user with his or her real name rather than a user's initials or one of the last name/first name user logon ID scenarios commonly used. When entering a user's full name the last name, first name format (Benton, Tom) is most functional. While the full name property is not a required text box, it is certainly valuable.

User Description

The Description text box, like the Full Name text box, is optional, but it aids in the navigational aspect of your user directory. Even though you can't sort on this text box, it is informational when managing individual users. For instance, suppose you are in an environment with multiple member servers and those servers are each dedicated to providing production services to a particular part of your organization. If you were to place "Users of WSS-PROD01" in the

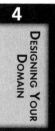

Description text box for those users whose home servers were WSS-PROD01, and "Users of WSS-PROD04" for those users whose home servers were WSS-PROD04 you are in a sense documenting your work as you create it. If you plan to use this text box to help organize your User Directory, it is important to follow a standard format for each user.

The Password and Confirm Password Options

These two fields are among the more obvious user properties. When applying or resetting a user password, it is necessary not only to enter the password, but to confirm the new password before it is reset. Once you select OK and close out of the user's properties, the password change will take affect.

User Must Change Password at Next Logon

This option can be used to manually force a user to reset his password which comes in handy when a user calls after forgetting his password. By resetting the password to something simple or even blank, and then checking this option, you do not breach any security protocols. Additionally, whenever a new user is created this option is automatically selected.

User Cannot Change Password

The User Cannot Change Password selection can be set to prevent a user from changing his password, bypassing Domain policy. This can seem to be a risky option, but if used with caution, it can come in handy. This option can be useful in service accounts; however, if used, you should never let anyone out of your administrative staff know the user ID.

Password Never Expires

Password Never Expires often works in conjunction with the previous option, User Cannot Change Password. This policy can be set to override any global password policies on an individual basis; it should, however, be used liberally. Users often disclose their passwords to others which leads to the potential of a security breach.

Account Disabled

Account Disabled is useful for vacationing employees or in the case of employee probation. When selected, this option does not allow the user access to your Domain.

Account Locked Out

If a user forgets his password and attempts to log on multiple times without success, his account will be locked out. (This option will be covered in conjunction with the section on Domain Policies.) The Account Locked Out check box can only be deselected.

Groups

The Groups button is among six buttons that pull up a completely new dialog window. When selected, the Groups button will launch the Group Memberships window (see Figure 4.9). This window is divided into two halves: The left half shows a list of groups the user is a member of, while the right column lists the groups the user does not belong to. Additionally, the top left corner provides the name of the user you are managing. In between the two windows providing group information are two buttons: Add and Remove. If you wish to add the user to any of the groups he is not a member of simply select those groups and press the Add button. If you wish to remove a user from any group membership, simply select the appropriate group, and select Remove.

FIGURE 4.9.

The Group Memberships Window.

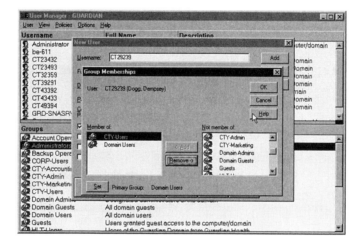

The Profile Button

The Profile button initiates a window titled User Environment Profile (see Figure 4.10). This window allows the administrator to assign a User Profile, a specific Logon Script and Home Directory. These advanced topics, which provide the ability to control your users' desktop environment, will be dealt with in detail in Chapter 9, "Managing Users."

The Hours Button

The Hours button initiates the Logon Hours window (see Figure 4.11). This window is where you will set the time that a user can no longer log in to the Domain, or in the case that your Domain policy is set to forcibly disconnect users when logon hours expire, to knock users off of all Domain resources. This option is well used if scheduled in conjunction with your network backups.

FIGURE 4.10.

The User Environment Settings.

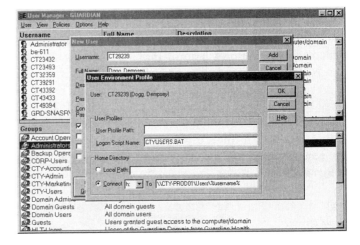

FIGURE 4.11.

Logon Hours Settings.

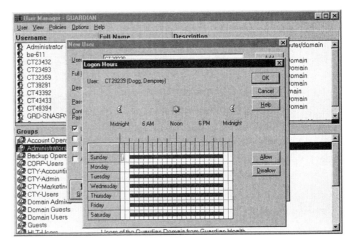

The Logon Button

The Logon button launches the Logon Workstations window (see Figure 4.12). In Microsoft Networking every machine is assigned a Netbios network name (not to be confused with the Host name in a TCP/IP environment, although the two must be the same). The options within the Logon button window allow an administrator to restrict users from logging in to the Domain by allowing their IDs to be authenticated only from certain machines . This option is helpful for Application Server Service IDs that need to log in to only specific machines on a regular basis.

FIGURE 4.12.
*Logon Workstations
Settings.*

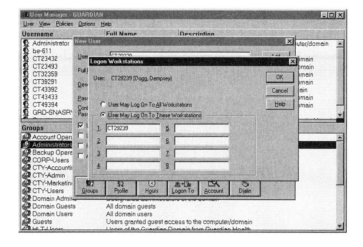

The Account Button

The Account button launches the user's Account Information window (see Figure 4.13). On the left side of the window you have the option to set an expiration date for the specific account you're working with, while the right side of the window is where you can designate a user as Local or Global. A Global User is a user that enjoys all of the benefits of being a Domain Member, while a Local user is nothing more than an access extension for a user who resides in a non-trusting/trusted Domain. Global Users can be applied to resources in Trusting Domains, but Local Users cannot. Local Users don't truly log in to the Domain, but simply attach to the Domain once they've been authenticated by their own Domain Controllers.

FIGURE 4.13.
*User Account
Information Settings.*

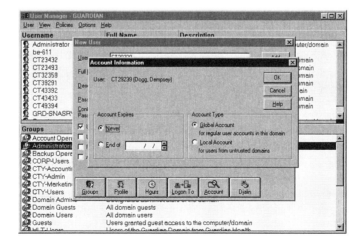

The Dialin Button

The Dialin button is a nice feature recently added with Windows NT 4.0. In previous versions of Windows NT Dialin rights, were granted only through the RAS Administrator. To grant or revoke dialin rights, go into the Dialin Information window (see Figure 4.14) by selecting the Dialin button.

FIGURE 4.14.

User Remote Access
Settings.

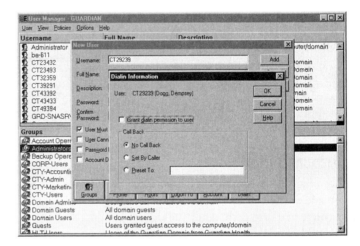

This window presents the option to grant Dialin permission to the user, which is not given by default, and to set a call back policy. The call back options are:

- No Call Back
- Set By Caller
- Preset To

The No Call Back is the simplest method for providing Dialin access. If a user with dialin rights dials in, he is authenticated and registered on the network, but can in no way reverse the call or its charges.

The Set By Caller option is helpful for mobile users. If checked, the user will dial in, thus notifying the RAS server that he wishes to establish a remote session. The server initially prompts the user for the phone number he can be reached at, disconnects from the user, then calls the number provided by the user. This is an excellent method to use when long-distance charges apply.

The Preset To option is a solid form of security that can be used to ensure that a user cannot be authenticated unless he is calling in from a preset destination. When the user dials into the network, the RAS server will disconnect the call and then dial the user back at the number predetermined by the administrator. This is a nice security feature that is also convenient for those remote users who would normally incur long-distance charges when dialing in.

Advanced User Properties

The following section will begin to cover the rudiments of more advanced user management features. These features are being presented to lay the framework for a full understanding of the concepts that will be covered in Chapter 9, "Managing Users." These features—User Profiles, Logon Scripts, and Domain Policies—are key to the administrator when considering Domain and User standardization.

Logon Scripts and Logon Script Management

Logon scripts in Windows NT are simply batch files that provide the capability to map drives to network folders or start executables each time a user logs on to the Domain. Logon scripts are not required in Domain Management, but are highly beneficial when attempting to set a standard environment, and in managing a standard environment as well.

Logon Script Basics

Logon scripts are assigned using the User Manager for Domains in the User Environment Profile page within a user's properties. By default, logon scripts are stored on the Primary Domain Controller in the \\system root\system32\repl\import\scripts directory. If you store your logon scripts there you only need to enter the script name when assigning a user a logon script. If you store your logon scripts somewhere else, you'll have to provide a complete path in order for them to run.

When a user logs in to the Domain and is authenticated, the logon script that you have assigned will process any drive mappings or executables that might be contained within. If a Backup Domain Controllers exist in the Domain, directory replication must be set up due to the fact that the scripts are pulled from whichever server processes the user's logon authentication. If directory replication is not configured, the user will receive logon scripts only when the PDC processes his authentication.

There are very few environment variables that may be incorporated into your logon scripts, and in most cases they are not very useful. Table 4.1 illustrates these variables.

Table 4.1. Windows NT Logon Script Variables.

Variable	Description	Operating System Affected
%HOMEDRIVE%	The drive letter assigned to a user's home directory	Windows 95 & Windows NT
%HOMEPATH%	The full path of the user's home directory	Windows 95 & Windows NT
%OS%	The operating system of the user's workstation	Windows 95 & Windows NT

continues

Table 4.1. continued

Variable	Description	Operating System Affected
%PROCESSOR%	The user's processor type	Windows 95 & Windows NT
%USERDOMAIN%	The user's logon domain	Windows 95 & Windows NT
%USERNAME%	The user's logon ID	Windows NT & Windows 95
/HOME	Used in conjunction with Net Use, maps a drive to the user's assigned home directory	Windows 95 & Windows NT

None of these variables apply to OS/2, Windows 3.*x*, or DOS workstations. These variables are very infrequently used and excluding the /HOME variable, remain active only during the processing of the logon script.

Logon scripts will be covered in detail in Chapter 9, including suggested scripts, idiosyncrasies for Windows 3.*x* and Windows 95, and logon scripts for OS/2 users.

Home Directories in Windows NT

Home directories in your Windows NT Domain are assigned through the User Manager for Domains. In the User Environment Profile window in a User's Properties you have two options: designation on the user's Windows NT computer or created on a network server. If the user intends to store pertinent data in his home directory, it is best to create home directories on the server. Server security is often more intense and should be backed up regularly.

Creating Home Directories

To assign a home directory to a user on his local NT computer you only have to enter the local path (that is, d:\users\jonesb). If, on the other hand, the administrator wants to assign a server-based home directory, the following procedure must be followed:

1. First, create and share the server-based home directory. For instance, D:\Users on the server HTN-PROD01 would be shared as \\HTN-PROD01\users. If this directory is not shared, the system will not be able to create the home directory.

2. Share permissions must be set at a minimum to Change for the desired group of users. If not, they will only have read access to their home directories.

3. Launch the User Manager for Domains and select the desired user. Once in the User Environment Profile page of the User Properties dialog, the administrator must choose a drive letter that the home directory will connect to and enter the path. For example, the designated drive might be H:\ and the path to the home drirectory would be \\HTN-PROD01\users\hendersonb.

4. If creating a template user (to be covered in Chapter 9, "Managing Users"), enter the variable %username% instead of a real user name. For instance, the path could be: \\HTN-PROD01\users\%username%. Each time the template is copied to create a new user, the user's home directory will be created and available.

> **NOTE**
>
> Drive letter assignments for home directories are applicable only for users of Windows NT Workstation or Server. In all other operating systems it is still required to map a drive to the USERS share in a logon script, although it does not have to map the drive assigned.

Access to User Home Directories

By default, when a home directory is created, only the user it was created for has access. Unlike other network operating systems, the Administrator, or the users in the Domain Admins or Administrator group, cannot access a user's home directory. Administrators can specifically add themselves or others to a user's home directory; however, this can become very time-consuming and usually serves no purpose.

While Administrators cannot access a user's home directory, members of the Local Group Backup Operators can. As stated in the section concerning default groups under NT, Backup Operators have the unique capability to bypass file and directory level security in order to back up files. While a Backup Operator cannot browse a user's home directory, members of this group should have no issues while performing backups.

User Profiles and Profile Management

User Profiles are used for the control of many aspects of a user's desktop environment, however, in order to take advantage of these User Profiles, a user must be using Windows 95 or Windows NT 4.0. The concepts discussed in the following section, while similar in most respects to Windows 95 profiles, are basic to Windows NT Workstation. Chapter 9 will cover both Windows 95 and Windows NT. While Windows NT and Windows 95 profiles are very similar, in nature they are not interchangeable.

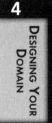

Profile Basics

Before delving too far into User Profiles, it is important to understand what makes up a user's environment in Windows NT 4.0. When a Windows NT computer is first installed, there are two separate conventions that combine to create the user's working environment: the \\system root\profiles\All Users directory structure and the Windows NT Default User profile. The very first time anyone logs in to a machine (most frequently the Administrator is the first to access a fresh install), their profile is created by combining these two features. Likewise, unless modified, each user subsequently created will receive this original environment upon initial login.

The All Users Profile

The All Users Profile is simply a directory structure made up of Common Groups and Desktop Shortcuts. In Windows NT there are two types of program groups: Common and User-specific. If a group is designated common, all users of the workstation (or server) will receive the programs contained within. If the program group is user-specific, only the user who created it will receive it when he logs in. The All Users Profile, which can only be modified by an administrator, passes along such common groups as the Startup group and the Administrative tools group. If you, as an administrator, make changes to the All Users Profile structure, every user who logs on to the machine will be affected.

CAUTION

When modifying the All Users Profile by adding Common Groups and Shortcuts, be sure that each user logging in to the workstation has access to the resource. Even though a shortcut to a network-based application might be added to the Startup menu, the end user using the workstation may not have access to the resource or may receive a different drive mapping than the administrator who added it. If either scenario is the case, the user will not receive the shortcut.

The Default User Profile

The Default User Profile is the foundation from which all new users are built. The Default User profile includes such controls as color scheme, video resolution, multiple control panel settings and instructions to include the All Users settings in each new user environment. The Default User Profile can be found in the Registry in the HKEY_USERS on Local Machine key in the root under Default (see Figure 4.15). This key, which should not be modified from within the registry, can be changed using the System Policy Editor which allows you to edit the system policy on individual workstations. The Policy editor is an advanced topic worth discussing, however, it will not be introduced until Chapter 9.

User profiles are found in the \\systemroot\profiles\%username% directory. The user may modify those settings which do not require administrative rights.

Table 4.2 lists the folders contained within a User Profile and the settings that they control.

Table 4.2. User Profile Properties.

Profile Directory	*Environment Settings*
Application Data	Application settings from profile-aware applications.
Desktop	Desktop setting such as shortcuts, folders, and files.

Profile Directory	Environment Settings
Favorites	Shortcuts to a user's favorite locations and files. Favorites are usually accessed through applications like Microsoft Office 95.
NetHood	Shortcuts to Network Resources placed in the Network Neighborhood.
Personal	Shortcuts to personal program items.
PrintHood	Shortcuts to NT Server-based network printers.
Recent Shortcuts	A list of the most recently used items provided in shortcut format.
Send To	A list of places to copy items to, that is: the floppy drive, a network drive, My Briefcase, and so on.
Start Menu	All Start menu settings including program groups and shortcuts.
Templates	Shortcuts to templates.

FIGURE 4.15.

The Default User Profile Found in the Registry.

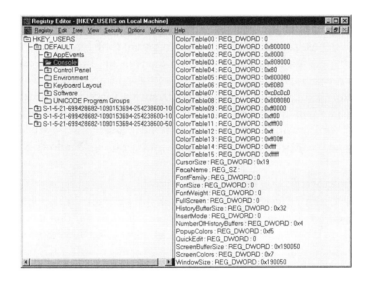

The User Profile consists of a great many elements that comprise a user's operating environment. A user may make modifications to all of his personal settings described in Table 4.2, but not those settings provided throughout the All Users directory structure.

Profile Types

Microsoft has provided for two types of User Profiles: Local and Roaming. To this point, only Local Profiles have been discussed. Local Profiles are those that exist on individual machines throughout the network, whereas Roaming Profiles are server based and follow the users wherever they go. Roaming User Profiles extend the ability to a user to log in to the Domain from any Windows NT 4.0 machine on the network and receive the same desktop environment. For instance, if a user modifies his desktop by adding a shortcut to his most frequently accessed network-based data folder, no matter whose machine they log in to, they'll receive that shortcut. Roaming Profiles can be designated simply to provide a consistent yet unique environment to each user, or can be assigned as a mandatory, unchanging environment.

Assigning User Profiles

In order for a user to take advantage of Roaming Profiles, there must be a shared Profile directory on the Primary Domain Controller of the user's logon Domain. Once this directory is shared (usually as Profiles), the administrator must create a unique Profile Directory for each user or in the case of some Mandatory Profiles, each user Group. Next, make sure that the user has been assigned a user profile directory in the User Environment Profile window within the User Manager for Domains. The next time a user logs in, a default User Profile will be created and stored in the assigned network-based directory. At this point, the user has a profile that will follow them to any NT workstation throughout the Domain.

Creating Enhanced User Profiles

Microsoft has provided the ability to assign pre-configured User Profiles to selected Domain Users or groups, or to everyone within the Domain. In order to assign a pre-configured user profile, an administrator should create a Profile Template ID and assign that ID a user profile directory using the User Manager for Domains. Once this is done, the administrator should log in to a Windows NT 4.0 machine, modify the features that are to be passed along, and log out of the Domain. After completing the Template Profile, it will be registered with the computer and may be assigned to any Domain User using Windows NT 4.0.

Assigning Specific User Profiles

In the User Manager for Domains, the administrator has the option to provide a path to store the location of a user's server-based profile directory, but this alone does not assign a specific profile to the user. Instead, this assigns a directory in which to store a Roaming User Profile. To assign specific User Profiles, the administrator must launch the Control Panel, select the System shortcut, and go to the User Profiles page in the System Properties window (see Figure 4.16). Once there, the administrator will be presented with a list of all profiles that currently exist on the machine. In order to assign a profile to a user, it is necessary to highlight the desired Profile Template and select the Copy To button. Next, you will be prompted for the user's profile directory path. Once the path is input, the Profile Template will be transferred and successfully assigned. Be sure that the path you entered for the Profile Directory is the same one that is defined in the User Environment Profile in the User Manager for Domains. The next time the user logs on he will receive the new profile.

FIGURE 4.16.
Assigning User Profiles.

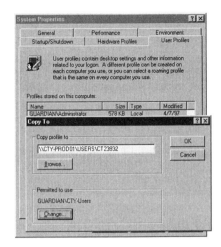

Mandatory User Profiles

As stated earlier, there are two different types of profiles: Roaming and Mandatory. While the Start Menu options, Desktop shortcuts, and network printers are contained within the Profile directory structure, the meat of the Profile is contained in a file named NTuser.dat. The NTuser.dat file is a registry extension to the registry key HKEY_LOCAL_USER on local machine. Whenever a user with a Roaming Profile logs in to the Domain from an NT 4.0 computer, the NTuser.dat file is integrated with the local registry and re-creates the desktop environment for the user. By default, a user can alter his own profile, thus any changes he makes will be reflected each time the user logs in. In many cases an administrator's intent in assigning a profile directory is to provide a uniform environment to a user no matter which machine they log in to. Furthermore, it is not uncommon to create and assign a profile that includes many standard network shortcuts and predefined network printers. In either case the end user has complete control over the profile once it is provided.

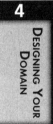

> **CAUTION**
>
> Keep in mind that just because a shortcut to a local resource contained within the Roaming Profile exists on one workstation, it doesn't mean it will exist on another. If a user moves from workstation to workstation in a non-standard environment, chances are there will be shortcuts within the Roaming Profile that don't correspond to every machine.

Profiles can be implemented for an end user's convenience. The same desktop from workstation to workstation can provide a comfort level that enhances productivity. Consider alternatively that you have a group of users whose environment needs to be identical and unwavering and, in fact, should never change. This could be achieved through the use of Mandatory Profiles. Mandatory Profiles are still Roaming Profiles, however, the end user can never make any changes. This is accomplished through renaming the NTuser.dat file to NTuser.man. The profile still follows the user wherever he goes, but any changes made will not be saved. Mandatory Profiles are the only type that could possibly be assigned to an entire group of people at a time. This would be accomplished by creating a common profile directory on the server, assigning the desired profile to the directory, and assigning the profile directory to all of the users with whom you want to share the profile. This should not be done with non-mandatory profiles because the profile will change each time a user logs on and off.

The following procedure recaps how to assign a Roaming Profile to a user:

1. Create and share a directory on your Primary Domain Controller that will contain all user profiles.

2. Create a profile directory under the share for each user you wish to assign a Roaming Profile.

3. In the User Manager for Domains, select the user or group of users you wish to assign profiles to.

4. Go to the Users pull-down menu and select Properties. Once the User Properties window is launched, open the User Environment Profile window.

5. Enter the path to the user's profile directory. For instance, if the user's logon ID is JONESB and the PDC name is ENMET the profile path will be \\HTN-PROD01\PROFILES\BAKERT. Alternately, if you are assigning a profile to multiple users at once, the path would be \\HTN-PROD01\PROFILES\%USERNAME%.

6. If your intent was simply to provide the user with a Roaming Profile, your job is done. The next time the user or users log on to the Domain, their Roaming Profiles will be created successfully.

7. If you desire to assign the user a Mandatory Profile, you must next launch the Control Panel on the Primary Domain Controller. Launch the System Properties shortcut and go to the User Profile tab.

8. Next, you will see a list of all of the profiles that exist on the PDC. Select the Profile Template you wish to assign and press Copy To.

9. You will next be prompted for the profile path. Enter the path to the user's profile directory. If you plan to apply a Mandatory Profile to a single user or to a group of users, enter the appropriate profile path. Press OK and the profile will have been successfully assigned.

10. If your intent was to assign a Mandatory Profile, be sure to go the profile directory and rename the NTuser.dat file to NTuser.man.

Policies and Security Management

Windows NT provides comprehensive security management. These settings, which are managed using the User Manager for Domains, can have a serious impact on your Domain. On the tool bar you will find a menu option titled Policies which provides four options: the management of Account Policies, User Rights, Auditing, and Trust Relationships. Each of these options is very influential in setting a standard for security in your Domain.

Account Policy

Account Policy is essentially a set of rules involving password restrictions and enforcement. There are eight options within the Account Policy window, many of which offer more than one choice (see Figure 4.17). Table 4.3 lists these options and some of their ramifications.

Table 4.3. Windows NT Domain Account Policies.

Policy	Options Ramification
Account Lockout	Lockout after XX bad attempts
Reset Account after XX Minutes	If Account Lockout is turned on, these options allow the administrator to set Lockout policies.
Forcibly Disconnect Remote Users from Server when Logon Hours Expire	Options: Yes or No. If this option is selected, users will be disconnected from all Domain resources when their logon hours expire.
Lockout Duration	Forever (Until Admin Unlocks)
Duration XX Minutes	If Forever is selected as the lockout duration, an account operator or Administrator must clear the user's account.
Minimum Password Age	Allow Changes Immediately
Allow Changes in XX days	If Allow Changes Immediately is selected, users can change passwords as often as they like.
Minimum Password Length	Permit Blank Password
At Least XX Characters	If Permit Blank Password is checked, users do not have to use passwords, but instead can enter nothing. However, when a password is required, an administrator must assign a password to every new user created.
No Account Lockout	Options: Yes or No. If not checked, user accounts will never be locked out, regardless of how many failed logon attempts occur.

4

DESIGNING YOUR DOMAIN

continues

Table 4.3. continued

Policy	Options Ramification
Password Restrictions	Password Never Expires
Password Expires in XX days	Most companies have password expiration policies. If a user is not required to change his password a security breach becomes closer to reality.
Password Uniqueness	Do Not Keep Password History
Remember XX Passwords	If a password history is not kept, a user can reuse his password as often as he likes.
Users Must Log In To Change Password	Options: Yes or No. If this option is selected, users cannot change passwords when prompted to do so, but must change their passwords after they have logged in to the Domain. If a user waits until his password expires, an Administrator must reset it for him.

FIGURE 4.17.

Account Policy Settings.

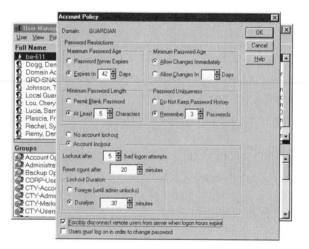

While many of these policies appear to cause inconveniences to the end user, Domain Security is of high priority. Due to the fact that most companies keep sensitive and important data on their network, security should be high at all times.

User Rights and Advanced User Rights

The User Rights Policy window is where you will go to assign basic and advanced user rights to specific users or groups of users (see Figure 4.18). Such rights as the ability to add NT Workstations to the Domain, log on as a service, back up and restore files, log on locally, or force machines to shut down over the network are administered within this window. These options are self explanatory in most cases, yet are assigned very sparingly. In most cases these rights are not granted unless a specific application requires a Service ID and that Service ID requires an advanced right or group of rights that isn't assigned to a default group. Two of the most commonly assigned rights are the ability to log on locally, and the ability to log on as a service.

Auditing

The Audit Policy window provides you with several security options, most of which simply track the use of rights throughout the Domain (see Figure 4.19). The Audit Policy tracks not only the successful use of user rights, but also the failed attempts to use rights that have and have not been assigned to a user. If the administrator chooses to turn auditing on, all events will be recorded in the Windows NT event log under the Security section.

FIGURE 4.18.

Domain User Rights Policy Settings.

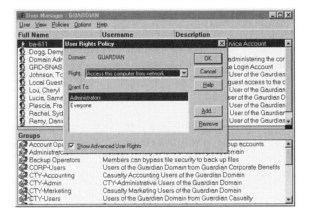

FIGURE 4.19.

The Audit Policy Window Within the User Manager for Domains.

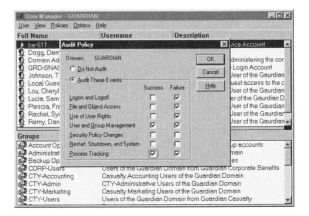

4

DESIGNING YOUR DOMAIN

Creating Users and Using User Templates

This chapter has covered many of the variables that add up to create a User Directory, but has not actually stepped through a single user's creation. This section will cover user creation and briefly touch on the use of user templates.

Creating New Users

Creating a user from scratch is a step-by-step process. The following procedure covers the basics of user creation:

1. Launch the User Manager for Domains. Select Users on the tool bar and choose New User; you will be presented with a blank New User properties page.

2. Enter the user's logon ID, and full name, last name first.

3. Enter the user description. User description will be covered in detail in Chapter 9.

4. Do not enter a password unless you have disallowed the use of blank passwords. The first time the user logs in he will be forced to change the password.

5. Select the appropriate password policies for this user if you wish to override Domain settings.

6. Initiate the Group Membership window by pressing the Groups button. Add Group memberships to the user as desired. Remember, it is possible to add more than one at a time by pressing the Ctrl button on your keyboard and selecting the necessary groups.

7. Select the Profile button after you've closed the Groups window.

8. In the User Environment Profile window, assign the user an appropriate logon script, user profile, and home directory. All of these properties are optional.

9. Close the User Environment Profile window and launch the Hours window. Once in the Logon Hours assignment box, select the logon hours you wish to assign to this user.

10. If you wish to restrict workstation access, close the Logon Hours screen and launch the Logon To window. Fill in the appropriate machine names and close the window.

11. Next, launch the Account window and choose whether the user will have an expiration date or whether the Group is Local or Global.

12. If you plan to grant Dialin rights, launch the Dialin window by pressing the Dialin button. Select the desired options and close the window.

13. After all of the properties are filled in appropriately, press Add, and your new user will be created.

Creating New Users Through the Use of User Templates

Creating users under Windows NT is not time consuming, but once the Directory begins to grow it can become difficult to keep track of which rights each new user from each different division or department requires. Windows NT allows you to copy a user's properties to a new user, which becomes quite convenient when creating User Templates that can be dedicated to individual divisions or departments within your company. Creating a User Template is no different from creating a regular user, however, there are a few points to consider.

1. Use the variable %USERNAME% when assigning non-mandatory Roaming User Profiles and User Home Directories. When a new User is copied from your template, the %USERNAME% variable will act as an instruction to create the appropriate home directory and assign the correct profile directory. If you're assigning a specific directory to a specific user, you must first create the profile directory.

2. When creating templates with Mandatory Roaming Profiles, be sure to create a User Template for each Profile Group or Type. This way, when you wish to create your users, you'll only have to copy the User Template.

3. When creating User Templates, keep in mind that these accounts will have just as much access to Domain Resources as the users that are created from them. It is common to disable the Template Account by putting a check next to the Account Disabled box.

4. Try to make the Template User Names as descriptive as possible. Additionally, follow a Templates naming convention so that they are grouped together in the User Manager for Domains. For example, use the full name of template, user, and a user name of T-Health-Admin or T-Health-Mrktg.

Creating a New User from a User Template

Creating a new user from a User Template is terribly easy. Simply select the Template ID you wish to copy, go to the Users option in the tool bar, and select Copy. You will next be presented with a User Properties box that has blank Username and Full Name text boxes. All of the User attributes you assigned to the Template exist. To finish the user creation simply enter the appropriate user name and full name, then select Add. A user with all rights required has just been created.

Creating and Managing Groups

While users use your network resources, groups are the foundation of Directory Design. It is much easier to manage a single object that contains multiple objects within it, than it is to manage multiple objects that represent only themselves.

Group Types

There are two types of groups within the Domain Directory: Local and Global. A Local Group is a group that can be added only to Local Domain resources, while a Global Group can be added to resources within your Domain and resources within Trusting Domains. (Trusting Domains are those that allow users from your Domain to access their resources without requiring an additional logon ID. Trusting Domains play a large part in the InterCorporate deployment model endorsed by this book.)

Creating New Groups

Creating new groups is very similar to creating new users; however, with groups you have the option of creating either a Local or Global Group.

To create a new Local or Global Group, follow these steps:

1. Open the User Manager for Domains.

2. Choose the Users menu on the tool bar, then New Global Group.

3. After being presented with the New Global Group window (see Figure 4.20), enter the Appropriate Group Name and Description. Press the Add button to add users to the group. An Add Users and Groups window will appear. You will now have the opportunity to add users, or in the case of a Local Group, Global Groups, as well.

FIGURE 4.20.

The New Global Group Window.

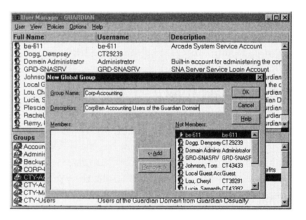

4. Once you've selected the appropriate Users and Groups, select OK until you are back at the main User Manager for Domains screen. Your new Local Group has been successfully created.

> **TIP**
>
> Before you begin the creation of your new Local or Global Group, select the Users from within the User Manager for Domains that you wish to be members of, and then select Users, followed by the New Local or Global Group option on the tool bar. The users you selected will automatically be members of your new group.

Managing Existing Groups

The User Manager for Domains does not allow you to assign groups and users to network resources, but only to manage the Directory properties. (Resources are managed through the Server Manager and the Windows NT Explore.) Once a Group has been created, the only changes that can be made to a group are Group Description and Group membership. While groups can be created, deleted, and copied, they cannot be renamed. Furthermore, if you accidentally delete a group, the Group SID will be destroyed, therefore all of its rights are gone from the entire Domain. Due to the loss of the SID, even if you recreate an identical group in every other aspect, you will still have to reapply the appropriate levels of security to network resources.

Customizing Your User Directory

The Windows NT User Directory is full of possibilities. Microsoft has provided an excellent foundation for the creation of a flexible and open enterprise. What they have not provided is any guidance in the development of a well organized directory. The remainder of this chapter is intended to help you take the basics of User management previously covered, and form your Directory into an intuitive, meaningful inventory of resources. This section will not touch on the advanced user-based topics mentioned within the first half of this chapter, however, it will aid in the designing of your directory through a well-deployed User Group foundation. User creation and management will be covered in Chapter 9.

Choosing Your Deployment Model

In Chapter 1, "Beginning the Design Process," you were introduced to three implementation models: InterDepartmental, InterDivisional, and InterCorporate. While models are helpful in planning for your deployment, they are easier to digest when provided with detailed examples. In order to provide these examples you were introduced to three companies: The Horton Agency, The Guardian Insurance Companies, and McMac Mineral, Incorporated. These companies offer enough variety to illustrate the three deployment models endorsed by this book, and should provide insight into your own deployment situation.

The following tables can be used as guidelines for choosing which implementation model you should follow.

Table 4.4. Deployment Model Number One.

The InterDepartmental Model	*The Horton Agency*
Corporate Organization	Single Company
User Base	20 to 250
Divisional Structure	Single Division
Support Organizations	Single Support Organization
Departmental Structure	Multiple Departments
Locations	Single Location

The InterDepartmental Model fits most small to medium sized, single location organizations. This model is one of the simplest to design and maintain.

Table 4.5. Deployment Model Number Two.

The InterDivisional Model	*The Guardian Insurance Companies*
Corporate Organization	Single Organization or Multiple Entities
User Base	150 to 60,000+
Divisional Structure	Single or Multiple Divisions
Support Organizations	Single Support Organization
Departmental Structure	Multiple Departments per Division or Subsidiary
Locations	Single or Multiple Location

The three biggest differences between InterDepartmental and InterDivisional Models come in the number of users within an organization, the number of entities that make up the organization, and the number of locations within the organization. An entity can be a subsidiary, sister company, related corporation, or a very large department or division within the organization, while a location can be across the street or across the country.

Table 4.6. Deployment Model Number Three.

The InterDivisional Model	*McMac Mineral, Inc.*
Corporate Organization	Single Organization or Multiple Subsidiaries
User Base	150 to 60,000+

The InterDivisional Model	McMac Mineral, Inc.
Divisional Structure	Single or Multiple Divisions
Support Organizations	Multiple Support Organizations
Departmental Structure	Multiple Departments per Division or Subsidiary
Locations	Single or Multiple Location

The InterDivisional model is very similar to the InterCorporate model in size and scale, however the biggest difference is the number of support organizations within the deployment. The InterCorporate model provides for a single and central User Directory, but allows multiple support groups to have total control over their entity's resources without harming the integrity of the Enterprise as a whole. These three models provide an excellent basis from which to design your Windows NT Server Domain in a flexible, easily managed, and scalable manner. Each of these models is based on the same Domain Directory concepts, but there are differences, the two single greatest of which are organizational structure and the number of support groups within the total enterprise.

The basis for any well designed user directory is the user group. To help develop your User Directory in a meaningful and scalable manner this book will provide five Group Classifications that are pertinent to all three deployment models. These Group Classifications are not actual requirements or options within the Windows NT Domain Directory, but have been developed from experience with multiple enterprise implementations. Each of these group types should be created as Global Groups within the User Manager for Domains. The Group Classifications are as follows:

- Basic/Divisional Groups:

    The first step in designing your user directory is the creation of the basic user group. The basic user group is the organizational foundation of the User Directory. All users, with the exception of support personnel, should be members of a Basic User group. The Basic User group will be granted access to all common resources throughout your Domain. The Basic Group is the building block for the InterDepartmental model, however is not scalable enough to provide the required functionality in the InterDivisional and InterCorporate models. The basic user group for these deployments is the Divisional Group.

- Departmental Groups:

    While basic groups are by default granted access to all common resources, Departmental Groups are designed to provide restricted access to departmentally secure resources such as data or proprietary applications. Departmental Groups are usually created for each major department within your organization.

■ Cross-Departmental Groups:

Departmental Groups are designed to secure data and applications from all but specific users within your organization, however there are times when your departments will share data or applications with one another. Most often cross-departmental data is not of a secure nature and can be shared through the use of a public or common data directory, however this is not always the case. Cross-Departmental Groups are designed to allow this intra-departmental sharing of resources in a secured manner.

■ Cross-Divisional Groups:

Cross-Divisional Groups come into play only in the InterDivisional and InterCorporate deployment models. These groups are designed to provide access to interdivisional resources, much in the same sense that Cross-Departmental groups provide secure access to resources between two groups, however it is much more common.

■ Enterprise Groups:

A corporation will often deploy an enterprise-level resource that is available to many users throughout departments and divisions, but requires restricted access. The Enterprise Group is designed for this function. The Enterprise Group is a single group dedicated to a single enterprise resource that is not bound by departmental or divisional ties (see Figure 4.21).

FIGURE 4.21.

The Group Classification Organization Chart.

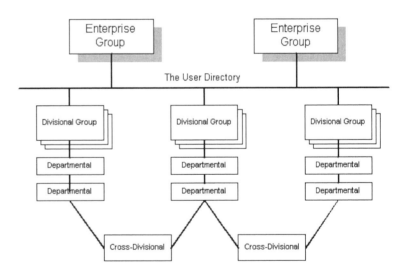

Basic Directory Design

The first stages of Domain Design are baby steps compared to the overall task of enterprise implementation, however they set the tone for the larger process. The following three factors are critical steps to take before moving forward with implementation:

1. Determine your Domain Implementation Model
2. Determine your Domain Name
3. Determine your Basic or Divisional Group Names

In addition to these three steps, it is helpful to keep the following points in mind:

■ Domain names are limited to 15 characters.

■ Group names are limited to 20 characters.

■ User names are limited to 20 characters.

■ Avoid the use of Local Groups within a Single Domain or the Master Domain of the InterCorporate model.

■ Your Directory should be modeled after your company or organization.

Basic Design for the InterDepartmental Domain

The following section will cover the initial design steps when designing the InterDepartmental Domain (see Figure 4.22).

FIGURE 4.22.
The InterDepartmental Domain Structure.

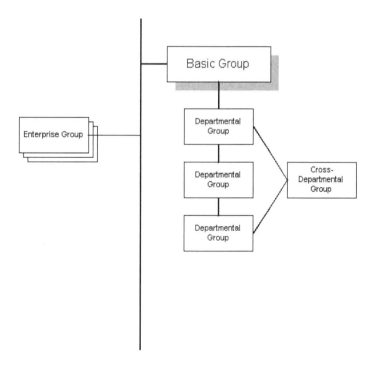

User Directory
(InterDepartmental Domain)

4

DESIGNING YOUR DOMAIN

■ Step One: Determining the Deployment Model

The first step in Domain Design is to determine the Domain model required by your organization. The Horton Agency has approximately 120 users, a single location, and four internal organizational departments. Horton does not share data or resources with outside corporations on a daily basis and does not have any internal autonomous divisions. This company is a prime candidate for the InterDepartmental Domain Deployment. (See Table 4.7.)

Table 4.7. The InterDepartmental Deployment.

The InterDepartmental Model	The Horton Agency
Corporate Organization	Single Company
User Base	20 to 500
Divisional Structure	Single Division
Support Organizations	Single Support Organization
Departmental Structure	Multiple Departments
Locations	Single Location

■ Step Two: Naming the Domain

When naming the Domain you should take into account the scale of the enterprise. Horton is interdepartmental and most likely will not grow into a multi-divisional organization in the near future. For the InterDepartmental deployment a good Domain name is a simple Domain name, therefore Horton is an excellent choice.

■ Step Three: Naming the Basic Group

The Basic Group name for the InterDepartmental Domain should not be terribly difficult to determine, however, naming conventions need to be accounted for. Even in the smallest Domains the possibility for numerous groups exists, and while the Basic Group could be something as simple as Horton Users, it is helpful for organizational purposes to have a common prefix for each group followed by a more descriptive suffix. Therefore, an excellent Basic Group name would be HTN-Users. Additionally, the Windows NT Directory provides for a group description to aid in quick identification. A solid group description for HTN-Users could be "Basic Users of the Horton Domain".

Basic Design for the InterDivisional Domain

The following section will cover the initial design steps when designing the InterDivisional Domain (see Figure 4.23).

FIGURE 4.23.

The InterDivisional Deployment.

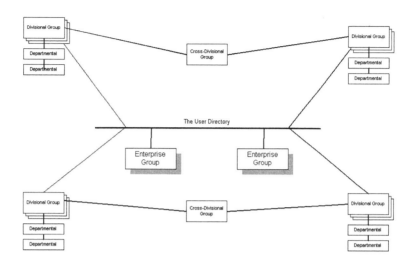

- Step One: Determining the Deployment Model

    The Guardian Insurance Companies is a complex organization when compared to the Horton Agency. Guardian has a user base of approximately 500, with three significant operational divisions and four separate buildings in a metropolitan area network. Moreover, this organization shares a Human Resources department, a Claims department, and the Information Systems department, while each division has its own Accounting, Marketing, and Administrative groups.

    Guardian is large and physically distributed, but does share a single information support group and therefore should be implemented as an InterDivisional Domain. Table 4.8 outlines the InterDivision Model for the Guardian Insurance Companies.

Table 4.8. The InterDivisional Model.

The InterDivisional Model	The Guardian Insurance Companies
Corporate Organization	Single Organization or Multiple Entities
User Base	150 to 60,000+
Divisional Structure	Single or Multiple Divisions
Support Organizations	Single Support Organization
Departmental Structure	Multiple Departments per Division or Subsidiary
Locations	Single or Multiple Location

- Step Two: Naming the Domain

    A Domain name should be something that all users within an organization can easily identify, but due to the fact that the InterDivisional Domain can consist of not only multiple divisions but multiple corporate entities as well, naming the InterDivisional Domain is not always easy. Luckily, in the case of the Guardian Insurance Companies each division shares the Guardian moniker. Therefore, Guardian is an adequate Domain name.

■ Step Three: Naming the Basic Group

The InterDivisional Domain model does not employ one single Basic Group, however, it uses a separate Divisional Group for each division or corporate entity. When designing your Divisional Groups, the prefix-suffix naming conventions become crucial to a comprehensible directory structure. In order to provide an intuitive Domain Directory, your support personnel should be able to identify which division a group belongs to as well as determine the purpose of that group simply through its name. Each division or entity should have its own dedicated group name prefix.

The four divisions inside of the Guardian Insurance Companies are Guardian Headquarters, Guardian Health, Guardian Corporate Benefits, and Guardian Casualty. Guardian Headquarters consist of top level executives, the Human Resources department, and the Information Systems department. An excellent prefix for Guardian Headquarters is HQ, making the basic Divisional Group name HQ-Users. A good prefix for Guardian Health might be HLT, therefore a good basic Divisional Group name would be HLT-Users. For Corporate Benefits a good Divisional Group name is Corp, leading to Corp-Users as the basic Divisional Group. A good prefix for Casualty could be CTY, leading to CTY-Users as their basic Divisional Group name.

Each group should follow a strict Description convention. Table 4.9 outlines the Divisional Group names and their descriptions.

Table 4.9. Divisional Groups.

Divisional Group Name	Divisional Group Description
HQ-Users	Users of the Guardian Domain from Guardian HQ
HLT-Users	Users of the Guardian Domain from Guardian Health
CORP-Users	Users of the Guardian Domain from Guardian Corporate Benefits
CTY-Users	Users of the Guardian Domain from Guardian Casualty

As the design process moves forward and the directory grows in size, these naming conventions will become crucial to efficient management of the Directory.

Basic Design for the InterCorporate Domain

The following section will cover the initial design steps when designing the InterCorporate Domain.

■ Step One: Determining the Deployment Model

McMac Mineral is a complicated environment. McMac has a user base of 2,000 people, is comprised of four separate companies, shares five corporate departments, and is spread throughout four different states. Furthermore, each company has its own Accounting, Marketing, Administrative, Public Relations, R & D departments, and IS support staff that want to maintain their own Corporations LAN. McMac Mineral is an excellent example of the InterCorporate Domain, which is based on the Master Domain model provided by Microsoft (see Figure 4.24.)

FIGURE 4.24.
The Master Domain.

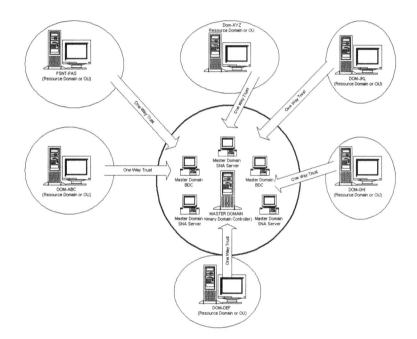

■ Step Two: Naming the Domain

The InterCorporate Domain is based on the Master Domain model. The Master Domain model is made up of multiple Resource Domains that trust a single Master Domain. This Master Domain allows each Resource Domain to share a single User Directory and still maintain control over its own Domain. All users are defined in the Master Domain, yet through trust relationships can be granted access in any of the Resource Domains. The Master Domain model is the only Domain model that implements the use of trusts in a manner that can be easily managed and maintained.

McMac Mineral is made up of four separate companies: McMac Mineral (the parent company), McMac Foods, Jansen Salt, and Watterson Paper. McMac Mineral will maintain the Master Domain, while the remaining three companies will implement pure Resource Domains. The Domains will be named as shown in Table 4.10.

4

DESIGNING YOUR
DOMAIN

Table 4.10. McMac Mineral Domain Names.

Company Name	Domain Name
McMac Mineral, Inc.	MM-Master
McMac Foods	MM-Foods
Watterson Paper	MM-Paper
Jansen Salt	MM-Salt

While corporate resources will be distributed in a dedicated manner, all users will log in to the MM-Master Domain.

> **NOTE**
>
> Resource Domains and their implementation will be discussed in further detail in Chapter 17, "Domain Documentation."

- Step Three: Naming the Basic Group

    The InterCorporate Domain calls for the use of Divisional Groups as the Basic Group for each Resource Domain. Due to the complexity of McMac Mineral, a central user directory must be highly organized. Table 4.11 outlines the divisional groups for McMac Mineral.

Table 4.11. McMac Mineral Divisional Groups.

Resource Domain Name	Divisional Group Name	Divisional Group Description
MM-Master	MMI-Users	MM-Master Domain Users
MM-Foods	MMF-Users	MM-Foods Resource Domain Users
MM-Paper	WTP-Users	MM-Paper Resource Domain Users
MM-Salt	JNS-Users	MM-Salt Resource Domain Users

Advanced Directory Groups

Departmental, Cross-Departmental, Cross-Divisional, and Enterprise Groups are all classified as advanced group types. The following table displays the advanced group types and the Deployment models they apply to.

Table 4.12. Advanced Group Types.

Deployment Type	Departmental	Cross-Departmental	Cross-Divisional	Enterprise
InterDepartmental	Yes	Yes	No	Yes
InterDivisional	Yes	Yes	Yes	Yes
InterCorporate	Yes	Yes	Yes	Yes

When initially designing your Domain Directory you will probably be aware of only very few Advanced Groups. Advanced Groups come into play over time as the relationships between divisions and departments grow and resources become more global. The following examples of advanced groups are rudimentary in nature and most likely simpler than those you will experience in your environment.

Advanced Groups and the InterDepartmental Domain

The InterDepartmental Domain will utilize Departmental, Cross-Departmental, and Enterprise Groups. While Departmental and Enterprise groups are fairly common, Cross-Departmental Groups are rare in any environment.

Designing Departmental Groups

Departmental Groups are designed to provide secure resources for the various departments throughout your company. The Horton Agency is made up of four major departments: Creative, Accounting, Sales, and Administrative. Keep in mind that the Horton Agency's Basic User Group was named HTN-Users, making the standard prefix HTN. It would then make sense to provide the following Departmental Groups and their descriptions (see Table 4.13).

Table 4.13. The Horton Domain Departmental Groups.

Department	Group Name	Group Description
Creative	HTN-Creative	Creative Users of the Horton Domain
Accounting	HTN-Accounting	Accounting Users of the Horton Domain
Sales	HTN-Sales	Sales Users of the Horton Domain
Administrative	HTN-Admin	Administrative Users of the Horton Domain

Designing Cross-Departmental Groups

While Departmental Groups help secure specific departmental resources from all Domain users, there are times when users from one group might require access to another groups resources. In most cases this can be dealt with through a well-designed directory structure, however there is the rare occasion when a new group must be created to lend the required functionality. These groups are called Cross-Departmental. Cross-Departmental groups should follow the prefix-suffix naming standard and begin with the Basic Group prefix. For example, if certain users from the Accounting department needed regular access to expense related documents maintained by the Sales department, the group shown in Table 4.14 could be created.

Table 4.14. Cross-Departmental Example.

Group Name	Group Description
HTN-SalesExpense	Accounting Users of HTN-Sales Resources

Once created, this group could be applied to the appropriate resource with the required permissions without jeopardizing all of the Sales department's private resources.

Designing Enterprise Groups

Enterprise Groups are designed for those resources that could be shared with any user in the Domain, but not necessarily all users within the Domain. For instance, the Horton Agency might have a subscription to a CD-ROM that provides a monthly compilation of major Advertising industry magazines in a searchable format. This CD-ROM would be an excellent business tool for both the Sales and Creative departments in keeping pace with industry changes, however the Accounting and Administrative groups would have no need for this access. To accommodate access to this shared CD-ROM an Enterprise group could be created. Enterprise groups should carry their own prefix followed by a descriptive suffix. For instance, all Enterprise groups within Horton might start with ENT for Enterprise. Therefore, an excellent Enterprise group name for access to the subscription CD-ROM could be ENT-Magsearch.

Advanced Groups and the InterDivisional Domain

The InterDivisional Domain will include Departmental, Cross-Departmental, Cross-Divisional, and Enterprise Groups.

Designing Departmental Groups

Departmental Groups in the InterDivisional Domain are nearly identical to those in the InterDepartmental Domain with the exception that Departmental Groups are created for each Division. In a sense, each division is treated as a unique organization and therefore, its Directory components must be organized to fit its corporate structure. Each division of the Guardian Insurance Companies has its own Accounting, Marketing, and Administrative Departments, while the Headquarters also houses Human Resources, Claims, and Information Systems. The Departmental Groups for an InterDivisional Domain might look like the ones shown in Table 4.15.

Table 4.15. InterDivisional Departmental Group Examples.

Guardian HQ	Group Name	Group Description
Accounting	HQ-Accounting	HQ-Accounting Users of the Guardian Domain
Marketing	HQ-Marketing	HQ-Marketing Users of the Guardian Domain
Administrative	HQ-Admin	HQ-Administrative Users of the Guardian Domain
Human Resources	HQ-HumanResources	HQ-Human Resources Users of the Guardian Domain
Claims	HQ-Claims	HQ-Claims Users of the Guardian Domain
Information Systems	HQ-InfoSystems	HQ-Information Systems Users of the Guardian Domain

Guardian Health	Group Name	Group Description
Accounting	HLT-Accounting	HLT-Accounting Users of the Guardian Domain
Marketing	HLT-Marketing	HLT-Marketing Users of the Guardian Domain
Administrative	HLT-Admin	HLT-Administrative Users of the Guardian Domain

Guardian Corp. Benefits	Group Name	Group Description
Accounting	Corp-Accounting	Corp-Accounting Users of the Guardian Domain
Marketing	Corp-Marketing	Corp-Marketing Users of the Guardian Domain
Administrative	Corp-Admin	Corp-Administrative Users of the Guardian Domain

Guardian Casualty	Group Name	Group Description
Accounting	CTY-Accounting	CTY-Accounting Users of the Guardian Domain
Marketing	CTY-Marketing	CTY-Marketing Users of the Guardian Domain
Administrative	CTY-Admin	CTY-Administrative Users of the Guardian Domain

4

DESIGNING YOUR
DOMAIN

Designing Cross-Departmental Groups

In addition to Departmental Domains, the InterDivisional Domain might require Cross-Departmental Groups. Cross-Departmental Groups apply only to groups within the same division. If, however, groups within different divisions need to share data, a Cross-Divisional Group should be created.

Designing Cross-Divisional Groups

Cross-Divisional Groups are extremely common in the InterDivisional Domain. Naming conventions for Cross-Divisional groups are fairly straightforward. The prefix should be the same prefix used for the group who owns the resource, followed by a descriptive suffix. For instance, if users in the Casualty Division required access to data in the Health Division, the group could be named as shown in Table 4.16.

Table 4.16. Cross-Divisional Groups.

Group Name	Group Description
HLT-Casualty	Casualty Users of Health Resources

Likewise, if users from Guardian Headquarters needed access to resources in the Corporate Benefits division, the group might be named as shown in Table 4.17.

Table 4.17. Cross-Divisional Groups.

Group Name	Group Description
Corp-HQ	Guardian HQ Users of Corporate Benefit Resources

Designing Enterprise Groups

Guardian as a whole also has a requirement for Enterprise Groups. Enterprise Groups are those groups that are applied to resources that could be accessible to any user throughout the enterprise. For instance, Guardian shares the same HR department among all of its divisions. The HR department will most likely provide resources for users throughout the Domain. For example, the HR department maintains a list of Doctors and Hospitals available through the corporate health plan. This list might be shared with all managerial staff throughout the Enterprise. Enterprise Groups should all carry the same prefix, however this prefix should be unique and dedicated solely to Enterprise Groups. For Guardian, a good enterprise prefix would be GRD. The Enterprise Group dedicated to the Benefits documentation maintained by the HR Group and shared with the managerial staff of each corporate entity could be named as shown in Table 4.18.

Table 4.18. Enterprise Groups.

Group Name	Group Description
GRD-MGRBenefits	HR Benefits Documentation to be shared with Guardian Managers

The Claims department is another Enterprise entity. Even though the Claims department is run out of Guardian Headquarters, there will be information passed between Claims and the divisional organizations. As an example, executives at each division will expect a total claims loss report on a monthly basis. These reports will be accessible through a program that exists on an application server dedicated solely to claims processing. In order for divisional executives to access this program and in turn, the loss reports, an Enterprise Group could be created. The Group is named as shown in Table 4.19.

Table 4.19. Enterprise Group Example.

Group Name	Group Description
GRD-ClaimsReports	Claims Resources to be shared with Divisional Executives

Additionally, each division stores and updates job profiles within its own Divisional Resources. Human Resources needs access to these profiles on a daily basis. In order to easily grant this access, an Enterprise Group should be created and applied to the appropriate directories on each Divisional Resource. Table 4.20 shows how this group could be named.

Table 4.20. Enterprise Group Example.

Group Name	Group Description
GRD-JobProfiles	Divisional Job Profiles to be shared with Human Resources

Enterprise resources requiring Enterprise Groups are extremely common within the InterDivisional Domain.

Advanced Groups and the InterCorporate Domain

Like the InterDivisional Domain, the InterCorporate Domain will include Departmental, Cross-Departmental, Cross-Divisional, and Enterprise Groups. In many ways the User Directory is designed identically to the InterDivisional Domain. The greatest differences between the InterDivisional Domain and the InterCorporate Domain deployments are size, the implementation of the Master Domain model, and the Support Organization.

4

DESIGNING YOUR DOMAIN

Designing Departmental Groups

Departmental Groups for the InterCorporate Domain are nearly identical to that of the InterDivisional Domain, however Departmental Groups will be created based on the Divisional Groups created and dedicated to each Resource Domain. Departmental Groups for McMac Mineral, Incorporated are as shown in Table 4.21.

Table 4.21. InterCorporate Divisional Groups.

McMac Mineral	Group Name	Group Description
Accounting	MMI-Accounting	Accounting Users in the MM-Master Domain
Marketing	MMI-Marketing	Marketing Users in the MM-Master Domain
Administrative	MMI-Admin	Administrative Users in the MM-Master Domain
Human Resources	MMI-HumanResources	Human Resources Users in the MM-Master Domain
Data Security	MMI-DataSecurity	Data Security Users in the MM-Master Domain
Legal	MMI-Legal	Legal Users in the MM-Master Domain
Public Relations	MMI-PubRel	Public Relations Users in the MM-Master Domain
Information Systems	MMI-InfoSys	Information Systems Users in the MM-Master Domain
McMac Foods	Group Name	Group Description
Accounting	MMF-Accounting	Accounting Users from the MM-Foods Resource Domain
Marketing	MMF-Marketing	Marketing Users from the MM-Foods Resource Domain
Administrative	MMF-Admin	Administrative Users from the MM-Foods Resource Domain
Public Relations	MMF- PubRel	Public Relations Users from the MM-Foods Resource Domain
Research & Development	MMF-ResDev	Research & Development Users from the MM-Foods Resource Domain
Information Systems	MMF-InfoSys	Information Systems Users from the MM-Foods Resource Domain

Watterson Paper	*Group Name*	
Accounting	WTP-Accounting	Accounting Users from the MM-Paper Resource Domain
Marketing	WTP-Marketing	Marketing Users from the MM-Paper Resource Domain
Administrative	WTP-Admin	Administrative Users from the MM-Paper Resource Domain
Public Relations	WTP-Public Relations PubRel	Public Relations Users from the MM-Paper Resource Domain
Research & Development	WTP-ResDev	Research & Development Users from the MM-Paper Resource Domain
Information Systems	WTP-InfoSys	Information Systems Users from the MM-Paper Resource Domain

Jansen Salt	*Group Name*	*Group Description*
Accounting	JNS-Accounting	Accounting Users from the MM-Salt Resource Domain
Marketing	JNS-Marketing	Marketing Users from the MM-Salt Resource Domain
Administrative	JNS-Admin	Administrative Users from the MM-Salt Resource Domain
Public Relations	JNS-PubRel	Public Relations Users from the MM-Salt Resource Domain
Research & Development	JNS-ResDev	Research & Development Users from the MM-Salt Resource Domain
Information Systems	JNS-InfoSys	Information Systems Users from the MM-Salt Resource Domain

4

DESIGNING YOUR DOMAIN

Due to the fact that the InterCorporate Domain is generally a large entity, there is a tremendous amount of groups providing basic security. More so than in any implementation model it is critical that the InterCorporate Directory be well designed.

Designing Cross-Departmental Groups
Cross Departmental Domains are rare in the InterCorporate Domain, but should follow the same rules as for the InterDepartmental and InterDivisional implementations. Cross-Departmental Groups apply only to groups within the same Resource Domain (or Master

Domain if resources are provided). Just as in the InterDivisional implementation, when groups within different Resource Domains need to share data a Cross-Divisional Group should be created.

Designing Cross-Divisional Groups

Cross-Divisional Groups are also extremely common in the InterCorporate Domain. Naming conventions for Cross-Divisional groups allow for the prefix to be the same as the prefix used for the group who owns the resource, followed by a descriptive suffix. For instance, if users in the McMac Foods Resource Domain (MM-Foods) needed access to an inventory database in the Jansen Salt Domain (MM-Salt), the group might be named as shown in Table 4.22.

Table 4.22. Cross-Divisional Example.

Group Name	Group Description
JNS-MMFInventory	Jansen Salt Database available to Users of the MM-Foods Domain

Designing Enterprise Groups

Due to the fact that McMac Mineral shares multiple departments with each of its subsidiaries, McMac will have a definite need for Enterprise Groups. Remember that Enterprise Groups should all carry the same prefix, and that prefix should be unique and dedicated solely to Enterprise Groups. A Standard Enterprise Group prefix for McMac could be MME. Enterprise Groups for McMac Mineral might be as shown in Table 4.23.

Table 4.23. Enterprise Group Example.

Group Name	Group Description
MME-Legal	Legal Resources for Users of the MM-Master Domain
MME-PubRel	Data Repository for Corporate Public Relations Material
MME-AuditRep	Data Security Audits for Corporate Executives

Directory Design is crucial. While the User Directory will obviously contain more users than groups, the focal point of user management should lie in a strong group organization. The five Group Classifications: Basic/Divisional Groups, Departmental Groups, Cross-Departmental Groups, Cross-Divisional Groups, and Enterprise Groups should offer all of the diversity required by your organization, while still providing a consistent, streamlined management interface. In conjunction with a well-designed server implementation and the application of resource security, your User Group implementation will make the management of resources throughout your enterprise intuitive and manageable. The steps outlined in this chapter are an excellent start to a well-designed Domain.

Summary

A good Domain design is critical to the success of your enterprise deployment. Organizational structure, geographic diversity, number of users, and user needs are just a few of the factors to take into account in the infancy stages of your Domain implementation. In order to design an effective Domain directory, it is critical that you have a firm understanding of Domain concepts as well as the organizational needs of your company. The three models endorsed by this book are designed to provide the scalability and expandability required in today's environment.

4

DESIGNING YOUR DOMAIN

Server Standardization, Installation, and Implementation

IN THIS CHAPTER

While the design of the User Directory is critical to your ability to manage users throughout your Domain, the installation and deployment of servers throughout your Domain plays just as large a part to your Enterprise success. Your User Directory and your Server Deployment should be extremely similar in terms of organization and convention and, in fact, should go hand in hand when considering your Domain design. This chapter will first walk you through several key pre-installation considerations, followed by step-by-step installation instructions, and will conclude with guidelines for the deployment of servers in the three deployment models endorsed throughout this book.

Pre-Installation Configuration Considerations

Before installing Windows NT Server, there are some important considerations that must be made concerning your standard Windows NT configuration. These considerations aid in adherence to the following Key Design Objectives:

- Objective Two: A Standard User Environment
- Objective Four: An Open and Scaleable Design
- Objective Five: Fault Tolerance

These issues will have implications concerning not only the scalability of your server, but server fault tolerance and your preparedness for a server failure. These factors hinge on your understanding of the following features of both Windows NT and your Enterprise Deployment:

- The Windows NT File System
- The Windows NT Boot Process
- Windows NT Disk Management Features
- Standard Volume Configurations
- Server Naming Conventions

All of the preceding factors are very influential in determining your Windows NT configuration standards. The remainder of this section will provide detailed information concerning these factors, as well as suggestions for their deployment.

The Windows NT File System

Windows NT Server 4.0 has been designed to work with two file systems: the traditional FAT file system and the more efficient and feature-rich NTFS. NTFS provides the following functionality:

- Long file names of up to 255 characters
- Multiple file extensions; for example, `homepage layout.html.doc`
- Partition sizes of up to 16 Terabytes
- File and Directory Level Security (covered in Chapter 7, "Sharing and Securing Resources")

- Case Preserving (but not case sensitive)
- Self Repairing: Constantly checks for file and directory errors
- Supports Services for Macintosh
- Supports Access and Even Auditing
- Efficient Storage: Always seeks contiguous blocks for file storage

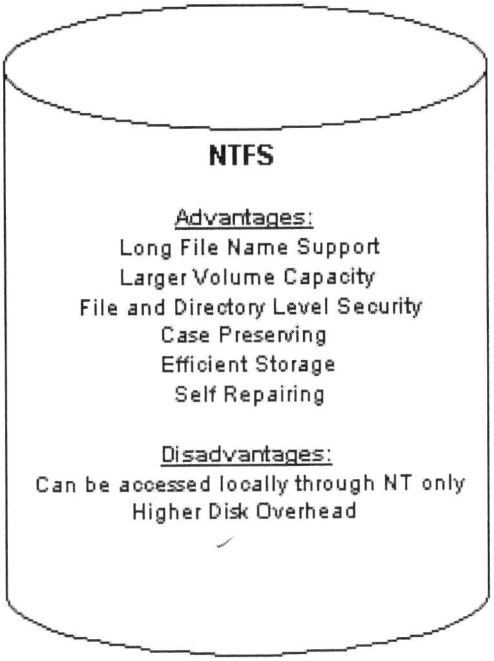

FIGURE 5.1.

NTFS versus FAT.

NTFS

Advantages:
Long File Name Support
Larger Volume Capacity
File and Directory Level Security
Case Preserving
Efficient Storage
Self Repairing

Disadvantages:
Can be accessed locally through NT only
Higher Disk Overhead

While NTFS does have its advantages, it also has its disadvantages:

- NTFS cannot be accessed locally by any other operating system.
- NTFS has higher overhead than FAT and should not be installed on a volume of less than 200 MB (NTFS uses between 1 to 5 MB of overhead depending on the volume size).
- While it is possible to make an NTFS boot disk, it is not possible to modify NTFS files unless the Operating System is active.

Windows NT Server not only supports both file systems, it also can support both on the same machine. Due to the fact that you cannot boot into and modify an NTFS file system, it is very common to install Windows NT Server with a 20 to 30 MB FAT boot partition. However, it is highly recommended that you use NTFS on any volumes that users will access on a regular basis due to its enhanced security features.

5

SERVER STANDARDIZATION

The Windows NT Boot Process

Windows NT Server boots in two stages: the boot sequence stage and the Windows NT Load Phases stage. The Boot Stage is the stage in which Windows NT gathers information about the hardware it is loading on. The Load Phases Stage is the stage in which Windows NT goes through its initiation process and ends with a complete OS load. The Boot sequence varies between platforms (RISC versus Intel), but the Load Phases are the same. The Load Phases do not truly influence your installation configuration and will not be covered in this section.

On the Intel Platform, the following files are critical to the Boot stage:

- BOOT.INI
- BOOTSECT.DOS
- NTBOOTDD.SYS
- NTLDR
- NTDETECT.COM
- NTOSKRNL.EXE

Each file performs the following specific function:

- The BOOT.INI is a read-only system file that is used to create the Boot Loader Operating Selection menu that appears on computers loaded with Windows NT. After the POST completes, the Boot Loader menu appears and shows two Windows NT Selections: Windows NT Server 4.0 and Windows NT Server 4.0 VGA Mode. Additionally, if there are multiple operating systems installed on the server, those operating systems will display in the Boot Menu as well.

- BOOTSECT.DOS contains the boot sectors of any operating systems that were installed on the server before Windows NT Server. If an operating system other than Windows NT Server 4.0 is chosen from the Boot Menu, BOOTSECT.DOS is referenced for proper initiation.

- NTBOOTD.SYS is the device driver used to initialize the SCSI controller on a server that boots from a SCSI hard disk using a controller with the BIOS disabled.

- NTLDR is the file that actually initiates the operating system load.

- NTDETECT.COM is used on Intel-based machines to detect and build a hardware list that will be passed back to the Registry later in the boot process.

- NTOSKRNL.EXE is the Windows NT Kernel.

The deletion or corruption of such files as the BOOT.INI, NTLDR, NTDETECT.COM, BOOTSECT.DOS, or NTOSKRNL.EXE can have harmful effects on your system, ranging from the inability to boot into alternative operating systems to the inability to launch Windows NT at all. While the NTFS file system is superior in terms of performance and security, it is a hindrance when any of the critical boot files are damaged or deleted due to the fact that you cannot access an NTFS volume unless Windows NT is loaded. To alleviate these issues,

Microsoft provided the Emergency Repair Disk. The Emergency Repair Disk is a critical tool in repairing a damaged Windows NT Server installation and should be updated on at least a monthly basis, and at best every time you make a major change to your server or your Domain. The Emergency Repair Disk contains valuable information about your Windows NT configuration and can be used to restore a damaged installation. The Emergency Repair Disk will perform the following functions:

- Verify your Startup Environment and repair any changes made since the time you created an ERD
- Verify that all boot files are present and replace those that are missing or corrupted
- Inspect registry files and allow you to restore individual registry hives
- In conjunction with the Windows NT Server CD-ROM, inspect system files
- Inspect your boot sector and repair if necessary

Without the Emergency Repair Disk, it becomes very difficult to repair a seriously damaged installation. While the Emergency Repair process is time consuming, it is a terrific aid in times of need.

Windows NT Disk Management Features

Once Windows NT Server is installed, you will have access to the Windows NT Disk Administrator as seen in Figure 5.2. The Disk Administrator is a powerful disk management utility that will allow you to perform the following tasks:

- Create Logical and Extended Partitions
- Delete Partitions
- Format Partitions
- Create a Stripe Set with Parity (RAID 5)
- Create a Stripe Set without Parity (RAID 0)
- Create a Volume Set
- Create a Mirror Set (RAID 1)

Many of these features are extremely helpful, while others are questionable in terms of true fault tolerance. Creating partitions, deleting partitions, and formatting partitions are all common tasks that can be performed at nearly any time by most operating systems. On the other hand, disk striping, creating mirror sets, and creating or extending volume sets are features that require consideration and do have rules. If you plan to utilize any of these features, it is important to account for them in your installation. The following section covers these extended features, as well as the rules concerning their implementation that might impact your installation configuration. This chapter will not cover the Disk Administrator or the implementation or management of its extended features. For detailed coverage of the Disk Administrator and its features, see Chapter 15, "Providing Fault Tolerance."

FIGURE 5.2.

The Windows NT Disk Administrator.

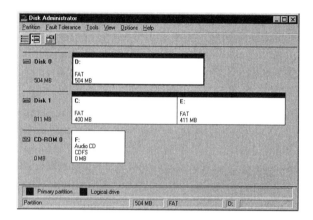

Windows NT Stripe Sets

Windows NT provides the capability to create two different types of stripe sets: RAID 0 and RAID 5. RAID, which is an acronym for a Redundant Array of Inexpensive Disks, is most often a hardware solution that can provide either extreme fault tolerance or extreme performance. RAID 0, or disk striping without parity, provides tremendous performance in terms of Disk I/O, while RAID 5, or disk striping with parity, provides extreme fault tolerance.

Striping without Parity (RAID 0)

RAID 0 is a stripe set of two or more combined disks (up to 32 in Windows NT) that behave as one drive; all space available to each drive in the stripe set combines to make one logical drive (see Figure 5.3). When data is written to the stripe set, that data is striped from disk to disk, spreading the actual file in 64 KB blocks at a time across all of the disks that combine to make that stripe set. This striping of data maximizes disk performance by utilizing each drive to read or write the same file at the same time. The performance is fantastic; however, there is one major drawback. If one of the drives in the stripe set fails, all data throughout the stripe set is lost.

The stripe set offers tremendous performance and, with the addition of multiple controllers, is an excellent performance enhancement—if adequate measures are taken to ensure that the stripe set is being backed up on a regular basis. Windows NT Server does not require the entire disk to create a stripe set but can create a set using equally sized partitions striped across multiple drives. In addition, the partition containing the systems files or the Windows NT operating system itself cannot take part in a stripe set. Stripe sets are created after Windows NT has been installed.

Stripe Sets with Parity (RAID 5)

RAID 5 at first seems very similar to RAID 1, however, in purpose is very different. RAID 5 requires at least three disks and in Windows NT can utilize up to 32 disks. RAID 5, or striping with parity, spreads files in blocks across all disks much like RAID 1, however, along with the striped file, stripes parity information concerning that file across all disks as well. This parity stripe is utilized to rebuild files and disks in case one of the disks in the stripe set fails.

With parity

FIGURE 5.3.

Stripe Set without Parity.

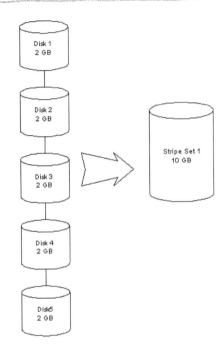

For instance, if Disk 3 in Figure 5.4 were to fail, users could still access all of the information stored across the striped set. When a file is requested, that file would be recreated using the parity information striped across the entire set. The user would never know that the drive had failed. Even nicer, RAID 5 provides the capability to re-create failed drives on the fly! If there were a spare drive installed in the system, you would simply need to instruct the Disk Administrator to rebuild the dead drive using the spare drive.

Much like RAID 0, a stripe set with parity can be built using equal sized partitions across multiple disks; however, RAID 5 does not provide a performance enhancement. Due to the fact that along with the striped data, there must be a parity stripe, you will experience a slight performance decrease with RAID 5. For the sake of fault tolerance, this decrease is very bearable. Also, unlike RAID 1, your RAID 5 does not combine all disks to create one large volume. To calculate how much storage space you will have in a stripe set, use the formula of N minus 1, N being the number of disks and 1 being one disk. In other words, if you had five 2 GB disks combined to make a RAID 5 stripe set, you would not have 10 GB of usable storage, but 8 GB. Furthermore, the partition containing the systems files or the Windows NT operating system itself cannot take part in a RAID 5 stripe set. Stripe sets are created after Windows NT has been installed.

5

SERVER STANDARDIZATION

FIGURE 5.4.

Striping with Parity (RAID 5).

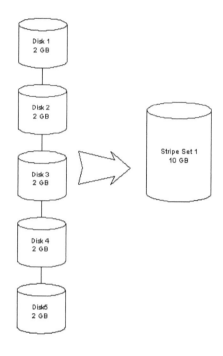

> **NOTE**
>
> Using RAID 5 as a fault tolerance solution is highly suggested. While Windows NT's software RAID solution is adequate, a true hardware-based RAID solution will provide the capability to include the system and boot partitions in the array, as well as the capability to increase the size of the stripe set on the fly. Whenever possible, use a hardware-based RAID 5 solution.

RAID 5 technology is a key contributor to Objective Five: Fault Tolerance.

Mirror Sets (RAID 1)

The mirror set, or RAID 1, is an extremely common yet expensive method of providing fault tolerance. Mirroring requires two disks and, in essence, provides what its name suggests: the mirroring of one disk to another. With a mirror set (see Figure 5.5), all data written to Disk 0 is also written to Disk 1. Therefore, if Disk 1 fails, the administrator can make a minor adjustment to the Windows NT Boot.ini, reboot the machine, and all data up to the point of failure will be intact (this will be covered in Chapter 15). Much like striping in Windows NT, mirroring can utilize two entire disks, or two equal-sized partitions on two physical disks. Unlike striping, however, it is possible to mirror any partition, including the boot or system partitions.

FIGURE 5.5.
*The Mirror Set
(RAID 1).*

> **NOTE**
>
> The fault tolerance provided by disk mirroring can be enhanced even further by utilizing a disk controller for each disk. If the controller for one of the disks fails, the other is still present. This simple addition of hardware turns Disk Mirroring into Disk Duplexing.

Like RAID 5, Disk Mirroring adheres to Objective Five: Fault Tolerance.

Volume Sets

A volume set is a set of two or more disks or areas of free space on a disk that have been combined to create a single logical drive. A volume set can consist of up to 32 disks or partitions and offers no fault tolerance whatsoever; however, it is useful when an existing drive or partition is nearly out of space. Often times a data drive or volume exceeds the expected requirements, and it is much easier to extend that drive by creating a volume set than it is to replace the drive entirely.

If you are using a hardware-based RAID 5 solution, there are no fault tolerance worries; however, one of the major drawbacks to a volume set is that if one of the drives in the volume set fails, you lose all of your data. Volume sets are extremely useful in times of emergency but should be used with caution.

Much like stripe sets, the boot or system partitions cannot take part in a volume set. Additionally, only the Windows NT installation used to create the volume set can read the volume set. DOS, Windows 3.*x*, Windows 95, or OS/2 cannot access a volume set.

Following is a summary of disk management factors and suggestions:

- Stripe sets can consist of up to 32 disks or partitions.
- RAID 0, striping without parity, provides enhanced performance.
- RAID 5, striping with parity, provides enhanced fault tolerance.
- RAID 5 requires three disks while RAID 1 requires only two.
- RAID 1, or Disk Mirroring, requires two disks.
- RAID 1 can be enhanced by using two disk controllers.
- The boot or system partitions can take part in a mirror set.
- The boot or system partitions cannot take part in a stripe set.

5

SERVER STANDARDIZATION

■ In multiboot configurations, Windows 3.*x*, Windows 95, DOS, and OS/2 are incapable of reading a volume set created by Windows NT.

■ The boot or system partitions cannot take part in a volume set.

Standard Volume Configurations

The following factors are critical considerations when designing your Windows NT Server Volume configuration:

■ NTFS cannot be accessed locally by any other operating system.

■ While it is possible to make an NTFS boot disk, it is not possible to modify NTFS files unless the Windows NT Operating system is active.

■ The Emergency Repair process is extremely time consuming.

■ The boot or system partitions cannot take part in a volume set.

As mentioned in the section titled "The Windows NT File System," it is impossible to access an NTFS volume unless Windows NT is loaded. While this is an excellent method of securing data from someone with malicious intent, it is extremely inconvenient in the case that your Windows NT installation has somehow been corrupted. Additionally, the Windows NT Emergency Repair Disk is an excellent tool in repairing a damaged installation; however, it is time consuming. If a Windows NT machine will not come up due to the corruption or deletion of one of the critical boot files, it is much easier to replace those files by simply booting to DOS than by going through the ERD process. Therefore, a DOS boot partition is extremely convenient. Furthermore, while partitions can be extended through the creation of volume sets, the boot or system partitions cannot take part in a volume set. These factors lead to the following configuration suggestions:

■ Create a boot partition.

■ Create a dedicated system partition.

Create a Boot Partition

Before installing Windows NT Server, create a 20 to 30 MB boot partition using a Windows 95 (or DOS) boot disk. Transfer the Win95 system files (`sys c:` at the command prompt), create a c:\WIN95 directory, and then copy FDISK, FORMAT, EDIT, HIMEM.SYS, EMM386.EXE, XCOPY & XCOPY32, ATTRIB, SCANDISK, and CHKDSK to the directory. Create a standard autoexec.bat and config.sys and make sure you include the drivers for your CD-ROM. When you install Windows NT Server, NT will place the following files in this partition:

■ NTLDR

■ BOOT.INI

■ BOOTSECT.DOS

- NTDETECT.COM
- NTBOOTDD.SYS

If your Windows NT installation begins to experience difficulties due to the corruption of deletion of any of these files, you will be able to boot in Win95 DOS and edit or replace these files. By creating an accessible boot partition, you can considerably reduce the amount of downtime to file corruption or accidental deletion.

> **NOTE**
>
> In Chapter 10, "Workstation Standards," the Network Client Administrator is introduced. The Network Client Administrator provides a way to install DOS-based networking software on workstations. Installing this software in the boot partition of your servers is another excellent manner to ensure that you will have access to the resources you need in case of a down server.

Create a Dedicated System Partition

Next, create a system partition of no less than 400 MB. This partition should be used for nothing other than the Windows NT Operating System itself. During installation, this is the partition where you will instruct Windows NT Setup to install system files. Windows NT will take up approximately 130 MB of space, leaving a minimum of 270 MB for additional components, DLLs, and system files that might be required for future enhancements. By creating and dedicating a system partition, you do not limit your volume creation or expansion options where your applications and data are concerned. Additionally, you protect the integrity of your system files through isolation.

By utilizing the boot partition/dedicated system partition scenario, you are ensuring your adherence to Objective Three: An Open and Scaleable Design. Additionally, by ensuring that your critical boot files are readily accessible in case of a damaged installation, you are adhering to Objective Five: Fault Tolerance.

Server Naming Conventions

In Chapter 2, "Why Windows NT Server?," group naming conventions were heavily stressed. Group naming conventions, while contributing to Objective Three: A Standard User Environment, are applicable mostly to Objective One: A Central User Directory. Server Naming conventions, on the other hand, are a very big contributing factor to Objective Three. Not only is it important that your users be able to determine the purpose of a server based on its name, but also for your support personnel to do the same. Remember, the more intuitive the Enterprise, the easier it is to navigate and manage.

5

SERVER STANDARDIZATION

Server naming conventions should closely follow your group naming conventions (see Figure 5.6). The following suggestions apply:

- In an InterDepartmental Domain, all servers should start with the same prefix as the Basic User Group, such as HTN-PROD01.

- In an InterDivisional Domain, all Divisional Servers should start with their respective divisional prefix, such as HLT-HOME1 or HQ-PROD01.

- In an InterCorporate Domain, servers in the Master Domain should use the same prefix as the Basic User Group within the Master Domain, and servers in the Resource Domains should use the same prefix as their respective Basic User Groups, such as MMI-PROD01, MMF-PROD01, WTP-PROD01, or JNS-PROD01.

- Standard Office Automation servers should share the same suffix throughout the Enterprise, such as HLT-HOME01 and CORP-HOME01, not HLT-HOME01 and CORP-PROD01.

- Like Application servers should share the same suffix throughout the Enterprise, such as JNS-INTRAWEB and MMI-INTRAWEB, not JNS-INTRAWEB and MMI-WEBSERVER.

- Enterprise Servers should share the same prefix throughout the Enterprise, such as GRD-SNA1, GRD-HRDATA04, and so on.

FIGURE 5.6.

The InterDivisional Server Naming Conventions.

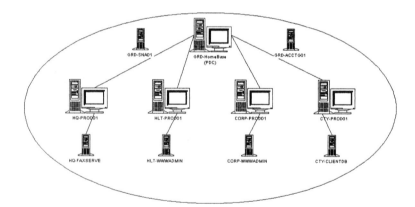

Server naming conventions are critical to Objective Two: A Standard User Environment. The importance of Server Naming conventions applies equally to the end user and your support personnel. The more similar the environment throughout the Enterprise, the easier it is to learn and navigate.

Installing Windows NT Server

For the purposes of this chapter, it will be assumed that you are installing Windows NT Server on an Intel-based platform. There are some differences in installation methods for the Alpha, MIPS, and PowerPC platforms, but not enough to change the deployment models endorsed by this book. Please refer to your hardware documentation before moving forward. Some servers require their own specific versions of Windows NT Server, while others supply their own proprietary disk and network drivers. Windows NT Server is not hard to install; in fact, in most cases it is very easy. NT Server is, however, very demanding and requires high standards in hardware compatibility. Microsoft maintains a hardware compatibility list on their World Wide Web site (go to www.microsoft.com/ntserver), which lists all of the supported hardware that has been verified to be compatible with Windows NT Server. It is always an extremely good idea to check this hardware compatibility list before beginning your installation of Windows NT Server.

Choosing Your Installation Method

There are three ways to install Windows NT Server. The first is over the network, the second is over a bootless installation, and the third is with the three installation disks provided by Microsoft. These three methods all accomplish the same thing but simply start off differently.

Network Installation

Installing over the network assumes that you have a machine with at least 150 MB of disk space partitioned and available. While installing over the network is very convenient, it is important that you have the volume structure to support a scaleable installation. The network installation is so convenient that many companies build boot disks that attach to the network, log in, and map a drive to the appropriate share. If you do this, it is important to prepare the server's partition scheme (to be detailed later in this chapter) before beginning the installation. The network installation simply copies the CD-ROM's image to your hard disk along with all of the files necessary to boot into the Windows NT installation process. Once the files are copied, you reboot the machine and are brought immediately to the installation point usually associated with the third installation disk.

To install over the network, you need to have a DOS, Windows, Windows 95, or Windows NT client attached to the network. You can either attach to a shared CD-ROM or a server-based distribution point. Once attached to either the CD-ROM or server-based distribution point, go to the I386 directory. For DOS, Windows, or Windows 95, you should run the command WINNT /B. WINNT is the Setup command for Windows NT (Server or Workstation), and the /B informs the program that you intend to do a bootless installation. If you're at a Windows NT server or workstation performing the Network Installation, you must type WINNT32 /B. This installation is slightly more interactive and can go on in the background while you perform other duties. Once Setup is started, you will be prompted to verify the location of the source files (which is always correctly displayed), and then file copying begins. Once all of the files are copied to your disk, you will restart your machine, and the installation process will begin in earnest.

The Bootless Installation

If you're like many administrators, you'll have a hard time keeping track of diskettes. Microsoft, in their infinite wisdom, was prepared for this eventuality. The Bootless Installation is identical to the Network Installation; however, it assumes that you have a working CD-ROM initiated and the Windows NT Server in that CD-ROM. Additionally, you should have your partitioning scheme in place before beginning this installation. The Bootless Installation, just like the Network Installation, requires 150 MB of free space on a FAT or NTFS volume.

To perform a bootless installation under DOS, Windows, or Windows 95, simply go to the I386 directory on your CD-ROM and type **WINNT** /**B**. If you're using Windows NT, go to the same directory but type **WINNT32** /**B**. Just as in the Network Installation, you will be prompted for the location of the source files and identically to the Network Installation as well; the Setup program will begin copying source files to your hard disk. Once the copying is complete, you will be prompted to restart your machine, and the installation process will truly begin.

Installing with the Windows NT Boot Disks

Microsoft provides three installation disks with Windows NT Server, conveniently titled Setup Disk 1, Setup Disk 2, and Setup Disk 3. To install using the Setup disks, simply insert Setup Disk 1 into your server and turn on the machine.

> **NOTE**
>
> If you've lost your installation disks and don't have either a CD-ROM to share or a network distribution point to use, you can make a set of installation disks by going to a working CD-ROM, launching a command prompt (or if you're in DOS, staying there), changing to the I386 directory, and typing **WINNT** /**OX**. This will create boot disks for the installation process. This option, too, comes in very handy from time to time.

Beginning the Installation

For the purposes of this book, assume that installation is proceeding with the use of the Windows NT Server installation boot disks. Place the first disk in the floppy drive of your server and turn it on. You will receive the message that Setup is inspecting your computer, followed by a blue screen that tells you that Setup is loading files. Depending on your hardware, this process could take some time. Once Setup has loaded, you will be prompted for the Windows NT Server Setup Disk 2. After inserting the second disk, press Enter.

You are immediately asked to wait, followed by a message in the lower-left corner that reads Setup is Loading Files. In parentheses, you will see the file types that Setup is trying to load. At this point, Setup is attempting to detect your base hardware by loading a variety of drivers. Once it's comfortable with your basic system, it loads the Windows NT Kernel and produces a blue screen with the following text:

Windows NT Server Setup

Welcome to Setup

The Setup Program for the Microsoft Windows NT operating system version 4.0 prepares Windows NT to run on your computer.

- To learn more about Windows NT Setup before continuing, Press F1.
- To set up Windows NT now, press Enter.
- To repair a damaged Windows NT version 4.0 installation, press R.
- To quit Setup without installing Windows NT, press F3.

At this point, installation is the objective, so the second option is applicable; however, the third option of repairing a damaged Windows NT installation is often very valuable. Repairing a damaged installation will be covered later in this chapter, in conjunction with a discussion concerning the Emergency Repair Disk.

After continuing with the installation, you will be told that Windows NT is about to go through a mass storage device detection routine. At this time, if you have any proprietary or hardware that was recently introduced to the market installed in your server, it is best to have the drivers at hand. You will have the option to skip hardware detection and tell Setup which drivers your server will require; however, unless you know without a doubt what hardware drivers your installation needs, allow Setup to run the detection routine. If you skip the detection routine and it turns out you don't know exactly which drivers you need, you will have to start installation over again.

Once you press Enter, Windows NT Setup will prompt you for the Windows NT Server Setup Disk 3. Place the disk in the drive and press Enter on your keyboard. If you watch the bottom left side of the screen, you will see the Setup program attempting to load a vast array of drivers. Each time Setup is successful, a message indicating that a device has been found will appear on the screen. After it has finished its routine, it will allow you to install drivers for additional mass storage devices that might have not been detected. If you have drivers, press S, and you will be presented with a list of devices to choose from, or you may use your own diskettes. At this time, you cannot access any existing files on your hard drive.

After all of the mass storage device drivers have been installed, select Enter to continue. Windows NT will now load the device drivers, including that for your hard drives and CD-ROM. If for some reason Windows NT Setup cannot detect your CD-ROM, installation will be halted. Be sure that the CD-ROM is installed correctly or that you've offered the correct drivers.

5

SERVER STANDARDIZATION

Configuring Your Disks

Once all mass storage device drivers have been loaded, you will be presented with a license agreement. After agreeing to the terms, select F8 as instructed. You will next be presented with a summary of your server's hardware. You will be asked whether this summary matches your computer and will be prompted to continue. Following hardware confirmation, you will be presented with a screen listing your server's hard disks and their existing partitions. This screen is an opportunity to partition your disk or disks before the actual installation begins. If you've already prepared your hard drives by creating not only the 20 MB boot partition, but also a minimum system partition of 130 MB (preferable 400 MB +), you can begin installation immediately. If, on the other hand, you have not prepared your disks, or you are installing over an existing operating system, you will at this time have the opportunity to reconfigure your disks as seen here:

Windows NT Server Setup

The following list shows existing partitions and spaces available for creating new partitions. Use the Up and Down arrow keys to move the highlight to an item in the list.

■ To install Windows NT on the highlighted partition or an unpartitioned space, press Enter.

■ To create a partition in the unpartitioned space, press C.

■ To delete the highlighted partition, press D.

2100 MB Disk 0 at ID 0 on bus 0 on spock

C:	FAT	30 MB <28 MB free>
D:	FAT	1746 MB <323 MB free>

From this screen, you can

■ Delete any existing partitions (excluding the boot partition or partition that holds the distribution files during a bootless or network installation)

■ Create a new partition in any unpartitioned space

■ Install Windows NT Server in the preconfigured partition of your choice

If you attempt to install Windows NT Server in a partition of less than 128 MB, you will be told immediately that the partition is too small and will be given the opportunity to go back to the configuration screen.

The bottom half of the screen consists of a rectangular box (white border, blue background) that presents your existing hard drives. Disk 0 represents the disk that Windows NT Server will place its boot files on, while any disk after that can be used to place the actual system files. To delete an existing partition, highlight that partition and press D as instructed. The screen will change and you will be presented with a screen similar to the following:

Windows NT Server Setup

You have asked Setup to remove the partition

D: FAT   1746 MB <   323 MB free>

on 2100 MB Disk 0 at ID 0 on bus 0 on spock.

■ To delete this partition, press L.

WARNING: ALL data on the partition will be lost!

■ To return to the previous screen without deleting the partition, press Esc.

To delete the partition, press L. You will immediately be taken back to the initial disk/partition configuration screen. You will notice that the partition you just deleted is now showing up as unpartitioned space. To partition unpartitioned space, simply highlight the partition of choice and press C. You will be presented with the following screen:

You have asked Setup to create a new partition on 2,100 MB Disk 0 at ID 0 on bus 0 on spock.

■ To create the new partition, enter a size below and press Enter.

■ To return to the previous screen without create the partition, press Esc.

The minimum size for the new partition is   1 megabyte <MB>.

The maximum size for the new partition is   2,100 megabytes <MB>.

Create partition of size <in MB>:   2,100.

Enter the appropriate partition size (no less than 400 MB is recommended) and press Enter. You will be brought back to the initial configuration screen. At this point, highlight the newly configured partition and press Enter to begin installation.

Once again, you will be presented with a new screen. This screen will inform you that the partition you have chosen is newly created and must be formatted. You will be given the option to format the partition using the FAT file system or Windows NT's NTFS file system. If, on the other hand, you have chosen to install over an existing partition that is currently formatted with the FAT file system, you are given the opportunity to covert it to NTFS. If you choose not to do so here, you will have the opportunity to convert it later; however, you can never return to FAT once you've converted to NTFS.

The choice between FAT and NTFS on your system partition is a tough one. For the same reasons that it's nice to have the 20 MB FAT Boot partition, it's also convenient to have a FAT system partition. And if for some reason you need to install a server as a dual boot system, no other operating system can operate on an NTFS partition. If you've created a specific System partition that will not be used for application or data storage, formatting your system partition with the FAT file system is not detrimental. If, however, you are extremely security conscious, format your system partition with NTFS.

Choosing the Install Directory

Once you've chosen the proper file system and formatted or converted your system partition, you will be presented with the following screen:

Windows NT Server Setup

Setup installs Windows NT files onto your hard disk. Choose the location where you want these files to be installed:

\WINNT

To change the suggested location, press the Backspace key to delete characters and then type the directory where you want Windows NT installed.

While the \WINNT directory is sufficient, it is not required. For those organizations that use both NT Workstation and NT Server, this directory name has the potential to become confusing. An installation directory of WINNTSRV for NT Server and WINNTWRK for NT Workstation can help eliminate any confusion. Choose a directory name of your liking, but for consistency's sake, choose a directory name that you will use in every installation of Windows NT Server.

Finalizing the DOS Portion of Setup

After entering the directory name, press Enter, and you will be brought to yet another screen informing you that Setup will examine your hard disks for corruption. This screen provides you with two choices: a standard disk scan and an exhaustive disk scan. The exhaustive disk scan can take several minutes and even hours. If you're using older hardware, this option is not a bad idea but is most likely unnecessary for new drives. To perform the exhaustive scan, press Enter; otherwise, press the Esc key and move on. The Setup program will perform a quick scan of your hard drive and then begin copying files. After all necessary files are copied to your hard disk, you will be presented with the following screen:

Windows NT Server Setup

This portion of Setup has completed successfully.

If there is a floppy disk inserted in drive A:, remove it.

Also remove any compact discs from your CD-ROM drive.

Press Enter to restart your computer.

When your computer restarts, Setup will continue.

Remove all disks, excluding the Windows NT Server CD-ROM, and press Enter. Even though Setup instructs you to remove all CD-ROMs, it still requires the Windows NT Server CD-ROM; if it is not present during Setup, it will be requested. If, however, you've done a bootless or Network installation, the CD-ROM will not be necessary.

Gathering Information

After your machine restarts and the POST completes, Setup will resume. If you chose to convert or format your System partition with NTFS, it will at this time convert to NTFS. (During installation, it formats the partition with the FAT system.) After conversion is complete, Setup will restart the machine once again. Setup will resume, but this time within Windows NT Server itself. After Setup initializes (which can take a while), it will begin copying files once again. After a small series of files is copied, you will be brought to a new screen welcoming you to the Windows NT Setup Wizard. It is on this screen that you are informed of the next three parts of Setup:

- Gathering information about your computer
- Installing Windows NT Networking
- Finishing Setup

To continue, press the Next button on the lower middle portion of this screen. Windows NT Setup will next prompt you for a name and organization. After entering the correct information, you will be prompted for a CD Key. The CD Key is a two-part code that unlocks the remainder of the Windows NT installation process. Without this key, you cannot continue Setup. This key can be found on the back side of your CD-ROM case. It is an excellent idea to write this number on the front part of your Windows NT Server CD-ROM so that it is always available. This code does not prevent you from installing from this CD-ROM multiple times on the network; however, it does prevent you from installing without the code. After entering your CD Key, select Next, and you will be brought to the Licensing Modes screen.

Licensing Options

Licensing today is a complicated issue. Microsoft has the ability to make it even more so; but in the case of BackOffice products, including Windows NT Server, it is fairly straightforward. With Windows NT, you have two licensing options: Per Server and Per Seat.

- The Per Server licensing mode is very similar to the licensing mode usually associated with NetWare. The Per Server licensing mode is a concurrent mode. In other words, you might have 50 employees that will use your server, but only about 30 of them will access it at any one time. Therefore, you need to purchase only 30 licenses. Keep in mind, however, that Per Server licenses are applied only to the server you buy them for. In other words, if you bring up a second server in the Per Server licensing mode, you would be forced to buy another round of concurrent licenses for the very same users who use your initial server.

- The Per Seat licensing mode is actually the better value. In the Per Seat licensing mode, each user is essentially assigned a Windows NT Server client access license. Once licensed, your users can access any number of NT Servers without any additional licensing. Therefore, if you are in a multiserver environment, the Per Seat licensing mode is more cost effective.

Of all the deployment models endorsed in this book, only the Departmental Model would have a legitimate chance of using the Per Server licensing mode. This mode is good only for a single server environment.

Determining Your Server Type

After choosing the appropriate licensing model, select the Next button. It is at this time that you will be prompted for a computer name. Your server name, as discussed at the beginning of this chapter, will depend on your server's purpose. Once you've selected the appropriate name, select Next. At this point, you will be prompted to choose the Server Type: Primary Domain Controller, Backup Domain Controller, or Stand-Alone Server.

> **NOTE**
>
> Stand-Alone Servers are the same as Member servers. A Stand-Alone Server has the option to join a Domain and become a Member Server, or refrain from Domain membership and become part of a workgroup.

If you select Primary Domain Controller, you will be brought to a new screen titled Administrator Account. This screen informs you that you are about to create the initial Administrator account for your Domain and that you need to enter a password of 14 characters or less. You will be required to enter this password and then confirm the password. *Do not forget the password.* If you forget the password you enter in this box, you will lose all access to your Primary Domain Controller, and you will be forced to perform an entirely new installation.

For a Backup Domain Controller, you will be prompted for an Administrator equivalent's name and password from the Domain you wish to join; for a Stand-Alone Server, you will simply be prompted for an Administrator password.

After entering the Administrator password, you will be prompted to create an Emergency Repair Disk. The Emergency Repair Disk is a critical tool in repairing a damaged Windows NT Server installation. Due to its importance, select Yes to create an Emergency Repair Disk. You will be prompted for a blank 1.44 MB floppy disk, and the disk will be formatted and then created. After the process has finished, move on to the next screen.

Next, you will have the option to select installation components. None of these components, with the possible exception of the Accessibility Options, is critical to an NT Server installation; however, many of the Accessories can become useful. Choose the components you require and select Next.

Networking Options

After the selection of installation components is complete, you will move into the second stage of the Windows NT Server Setup routine: Networking configuration. You will be presented with two networking options:

- Wired to the Network (ISDN or Network Adapter)
- Remote Access to the Network (Modem)

Remote Access installation will be covered later in this book. For the purposes of this chapter, assume you are connecting to the network via a network adapter card. Select Wired to the Network and press Next.

At this point, you will have the option to install Internet Information Server. Internet Information Server can be installed at this point or at any time after Windows NT Server has been installed. For the purposes of this chapter, assume you are either not going to install IIS or that you will install it later. Deselect this option and press Enter.

It is at this point that the installation of Network components will begin. At your prompting, Windows NT Server will begin searching for Network Adapters. Usually, Setup will find your network card immediately. However, if Windows NT does not find your adapter, you must either inform Setup which card you have or provide a driver. If you do not have a Windows NT Driver and it is not in the list of available cards, call your adapter manufacturer or check the manufacturer's Web site. If you have an updated driver or simply the required divers for a NIC that wasn't available when NT Server was shipped, choose the Select From List option. This option will list all of the available drivers plus allow you to provide your own driver through the Have Disk option. After choosing the appropriate network card, select Next.

The following screen is the Network Protocols screen. By default, Windows NT Server wants to install both TCP/IP and NwLink IPX/SPX; NetBEUI is left unchecked. Protocols will be discussed in depth in Chapter 6, "Choosing Your Protocols." For now, assume that you will install all three. Select Next, and you will be presented with the Network Services screen. The default services are

- RPC Configuration
- NetBIOS Interface
- Workstation
- Server

You also have the opportunity to select from an additional list of services that are provided with Windows NT Server. Those services include

- DHCP Relay Agent
- Gateway (and Client) Services for NetWare
- Microsoft DHCP Server
- Microsoft DNS Server
- Microsoft IIS 2.0
- Microsoft TCP/IP Printing
- Network Monitor Agent

5

SERVER STANDARDIZATION

- ■ Network Monitor Tools and Agent
- ■ Remote Access Service
- ■ Remoteboot Service
- ■ RIP for Internet Protocol
- ■ RIP for NwLink IPX/SPX compatible transport
- ■ RPC support for Banyan
- ■ SAP Agent
- ■ Services for Macintosh
- ■ Simple TCP/IP Services
- ■ SNMP Service
- ■ Windows Internet Name Service

This list of services, each of which ships with Windows NT Server at no additional cost, is what makes Windows NT such an open and scaleable system (in accordance with Design Object 4: Open and Scaleable Design).

Of this list of services, this book will discuss the Gateway (and Client) Services for NetWare, the Microsoft DHCP Server, the Microsoft DNS Server, Microsoft IIS 2.0, Microsoft TCP/IP Printing, Remote Access Service, Services for Macintosh, Simple TCP/IP Services, and the Windows Internet Name Service in conjunction with an enterprise deployment. In particular, TCP/IP is a complicated subject. This book will discuss TCP/IP in relation to Windows NT Server and those services provided by Windows NT Server, but not at the level required by infrastructure specialists.

Configuring Your Network Settings

For the purposes of this chapter, we will not be installing DHCP, DNS, or WINS at this time but simply the basic TCP/IP stack. When installing TCP/IP, it is always an excellent idea to choose the Simple TCP/IP Services, which provides such tools as Telnet and FTP. Select this option, followed by OK and Next at the initial screen. At this time, you will be informed that Windows NT is ready to install network components. You are given one last chance to go back and change any networking configurations; however, if you are comfortable with the services and protocols you have chosen, select Next. Otherwise, select Back and make the necessary selections.

After moving on, Setup will continue. In many cases you will be prompted for some sort of network card configuration. If you've installed TCP/IP, you will be asked if you wish to use a DHCP server. Briefly, a DHCP server, regardless of which platform or manufacture it is, will dynamically allocate you a TCP/IP address and all of the required configuration information including your Gateway, Subnet Mask, WINS addresses, and node type. It is not necessarily a good idea for a server to have a DHCP address, so in most cases you will select No and continue. Setup will seem to churn for a while, and next you will see all of the files required for your chosen services copied to your hard disk. Once the copy process is complete, Setup will perform a binding analysis for each protocol. If you are using NwLink, you will be prompted to provide a unique internal network number—be sure that it's not the same as any NetWare servers on your network. This number must be unique. Next, Setup will prompt you for your TCP/IP configuration. Enter the appropriate DNS, WINS, Gateway, and Subnet Mask information and continue. In most cases, your protocol configuration is complete.

You will next be brought to the bindings page. This page, which will be covered in detail in Chapter 6, will allow you to configure which protocols will bind to which network card, and in what order of precedence they will communicate. Select the default for now and move on by pressing Next. You will be informed that Windows NT is ready to start the network. Select Next, and the network will start.

Determining Your Domain

After your network has started, you will be brought to the Domain configuration page. If your server is a primary Domain controller, you will be prompted for the Domain name. Enter the name and select Next. Windows NT will then check to ensure there is not a duplicate name on the network. This may take some time depending on the size of your network.

If your server is a Backup Domain Controller, you will be prompted for the name of the Domain you will join as well as an Administrator equivalent's name and password. After entering the correct information, you will be brought to the stage of Setup titled Finishing Setup.

If your server is a member server, you will be required to either create an account in the Domain (which requires an administrator equivalent ID and password) or provide a name for a Server that has previously been added to the Domain. After the name is verified or created, you will be brought to the Finishing Setup stage.

After the network has started and you have either joined or created the appropriate Domain, you will be brought to the final part of Setup. Windows NT will create all of the appropriate Start Menu groups and then prompt you for your time, date, and time zone. Select the appropriate information and press the Close button. Next you will be prompted for your video properties. Windows NT Setup will tell you which adapter it detected and then require that you test its selection before moving on. At this time, you can accept the default selections or change them. No matter whether you accept defaults or change settings, you will be forced to test them. After choosing your video settings, move on by selecting OK.

At this point, Setup will copy more files and then set file and directory level security (on an NTFS partition) on system files. Following this, Windows NT will go through a process titled Saving Configuration, in which it builds the Registry. When this is complete, you will be presented with a screen that informs you that Windows NT Server 4.0 has been successfully installed. You are then reminded to remove all disks from the floppy and CD-ROM drives and are provided with a large Restart Computer button. Restart the computer to finish the installation. Once installation is complete and your server has restarted, you may log in and begin administering your network.

5

SERVER
STANDARDIZATION

Keep in mind that standards are critical to the success of your Enterprise. It is important that you define your server installation and naming standards before you begin your Domain deployment, and maintain those standards for as long as they are valid. Installation standards include the Server Manufacturer, the network interface card, the backup software and tape drives, the SCSI controllers, the RAID system, the CD-ROM, and even the monitor. Each of these factors can ultimately make or break the success of your Windows NT Server installation. Additionally, installation standards include the volume sizes, the directory structure, and the protocols and services you use. Your server installation should be just as well planned as your Domain as a whole. Windows NT Server, as does any sophisticated operating system, reacts either negatively or positively to the environment on which you install it. The simple act of changing the brand of SCSI controller or the model of a network card can have substantial negative impact on your installation. Before making any changes to your standards, it is crucial that you verify that those changes are matched up with products on the Hardware Compatibility List (HCL). Furthermore, once you've established a standard installation suite, it is a good idea to call the manufacturer of each product to inquire about issues with items you might be considering changing.

Finalizing Your Installation

Windows NT Server is very much a self-tuning operating system, which, as network operating systems go, is fairly unique. However, there are some settings that should be made to every server after its initial installation to ensure that it is tuned for the right type of performance. The following section will cover these settings and how they will impact the performance of both an application server and a production server.

Optimizing the Server Service

The Server service is one of the few services that can be controlled from directly within the Network configuration dialog. The Server service can be adjusted to optimize the relationship between the amount of memory used for network connections and the amount of memory used for applications running on your server. To optimize your Server service settings for the type of server you are deploying, you need to launch the Network Configuration dialog (see Figure 5.7). You can get to the Network configuration through the control panel, or by clicking your right mouse button on the Network Neighborhood icon and selecting Properties.

You will notice that there are five tabs within the Network configuration dialog: Identification, Services, Protocols, Adapters, and Bindings. Choose Services, and you will be brought to a page that lists the services currently installed on your server (see Figure 5.8).

By double-clicking on the Server service, you will bring up a dialog titled Server (see Figure 5.9). This page allows you to optimize your server's performance based on its function. The choices are

- Minimize Memory Used
- Balance
- Maximize Throughput for File Sharing
- Maximize Throughput for Network Applications
- Make Browser Broadcasts to LAN Manager 2.*x* Clients

- The Minimize Memory Used option is for those servers that will be used primarily for stand-alone processing. Choose this option if fewer than 10 users will be connecting to your server at any one time. (In this case, it is almost more sensible to employ NT Workstation, although it does have a limit of 10 inbound connections.)

- The Balance option is, in most cases, useless. It attempts to provide equal resources to intensive applications and network users at the same time. This option is not recommended for any more than 64 users.

- The Maximize Throughput for File Sharing option is an excellent choice for the standard production server. This setting is recommended for a large number of file, print, and office automation users.

- The Maximize Throughput for Network Applications option is the obvious choice for application servers. Applications such as SQL Server or SNA that do a good deal of back-end processing will require more memory and processor time, and this option provides it.

- The Make Browser Broadcasts to LAN Manager 2x Clients option instructs Windows NT Server to broadcast its presence to LAN Manager clients. This option is useful only if such clients exist on your network.

After selecting the appropriate setting for your server, select OK and close. After closing the Network Configuration dialog, Windows NT will need to restart for the changes to take effect.

FIGURE 5.7.

The Network Configuration Dialog.

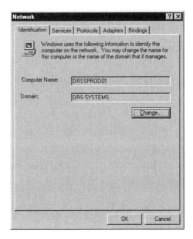

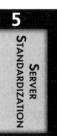

FIGURE 5.8.

*The Services Configu-
ration Page.*

FIGURE 5.9.

*The Server
Optimization
Window.*

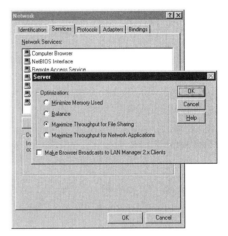

Background versus Foreground Performance

By tuning the Server service, you will focus memory and processor resources for network communications. In order to complete the tuning process, you must also determine how Windows
NT Server will balance its resources between background processes and foreground applications. This can be achieved by launching the control panel and opening the System control
panel extension, or by highlighting the My Computer shortcut on your desktop and clicking
on it with your right mouse button. Select Properties, and the System Properties dialog will
launch. You will notice it is made up of six tabs: General, Performance, Environment, Startup/
Shutdown, Hardware Profiles, and User Profiles. Select the Performance tab, and you will be
brought to the page shown in Figure 5.10.

FIGURE 5.10.

The System Properties Dialog.

You will notice that the top half of this page contains a sliding tab titled Application Performance. The left side of the tab reads None, while the right side of the tab reads Boost. This tab allows you to set the precedence of either foreground usage or background usage. If your server is a production server, you will very rarely if ever be called upon to work at the actual server; therefore, it is very unnecessary to pull any resources away from your network users simply for foreground applications. Accordingly, if your server is a server, slide the tab all the way to the left so that it can act like a server. If you need to write a document or browse the Web, use your own workstation. If, however, you decide to use Windows NT Server primarily as a workstation, slide the lever all the way to the right. This will provide more resources to running applications for the local user than for network services and back-end processing. Finally, if your server is a workgroup server that also acts as a workstation, slide the tab to the middle. This will balance performance between background and foreground processes.

Virtual Memory Management

Windows NT Server uses virtual memory constantly, regardless of how much physical memory is actually installed in your machine. In fact, the size of your server's page file increases with the amount of RAM you install. This is because Windows NT allocates half of your system's RAM to disk caching. When a process or application suddenly needs more memory than is available, Windows NT places the cached directory structures and files into the page file and gives the application physical RAM. When the resource hit passes, the cached information dynamically moves back into physical RAM until needed again. You can manage the size of your page file through the System Properties dialog (see Figure 5.11). In Figure 5.12 on the top half of the page, you will see the Application Performance control setting. The bottom half of the page tells you how much Virtual Memory is currently allocated to the system, and you are provided with a Change button. To manage your virtual memory, select Change.

FIGURE 5.11.

*The Performance Page
of System Properties
Dialog.*

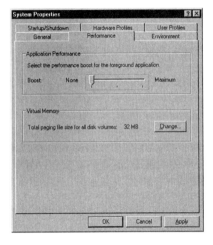

FIGURE 5.12.

*Virtual Memory
Settings.*

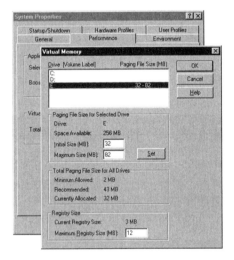

In most cases, the settings provided by Windows NT are adequate; however, there are ways of increasing or decreasing your page file performance.

- First, Windows NT can use more than one paging file; however, do not put more than one page file on a single physical disk. For instance, if you had a drive with two partitions, you could put a page file on each partition. At first, you might think this would improve performance, but what you are actually doing is putting an undue performance load on your hard drive. Windows NT seems to use all page files simultaneously; therefore, your drive would actually slow the paging process down.

- For optimum page performance, use a stripe set. A stripe set is a series of disks, or equally sized partitions on a series of disks, that are combined to appear as one volume. If you were to put your page file on a striped volume, your paging performance would increase dramatically. There is a serious drawback, however, to a stripe set. If one of the disks in your set fails, all data contained within the set is lost. Therefore, if you create a stripe set for paging, don't store any data in it.

■ Place an equally sized page file on each physical disk. Windows NT will load balance its page file use among the disks. Paging speed will increase, and data integrity will remain intact.

To modify or add a page file, simply select the disk you wish to manage in the Drive Window (see Figure 5.12). To add a page file, set the minimum size (usually the amount of physical RAM in your machine) and the maximum size. If you're using multiple page files, don't exceed twice the size of your physical RAM for the maximum size.

While tuning your Virtual Memory can help improve the performance of your server, it is not a replacement for physical memory. If your machine encounters excessive paging on a regular basis, add RAM, increase your processor speed, or even add an additional processor. Windows NT will use whatever you throw at it.

Administrative Alerts

Windows NT has the capability to alert you when it encounters problems; however, you have to instruct it to do so. In the Control Panel, you will find an extension titled Server; double-click on this shortcut, and you will be presented with the Server dialog window. (See Figure 5.13.) This utility allows you to monitor User connections, Share utilization, and files in use. Additionally, through this utility you can configure Replication and Alerts. (See Figure 5.14.)

FIGURE 5.13.

The Server Dialog.

FIGURE 5.14.

The Administrative Alerts Window.

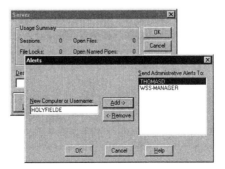

5

SERVER STANDARDIZATION

The Alerts window allows you to enter the names of users and workstations that will be alerted when a security, printing, user, or performance issue arises. To configure this service, simply enter the name of the machine or user in the text box on the left side of the window and press Add. You will see the name added to the window on the right side, titled Send Administrative Alerts To. Once you've completed your list, simply close this window, and you're done.

Deploying Servers in Your Domain

The manner in which servers are deployed varies greatly between the three deployment models endorsed in this book. Both the InterDepartmental and InterDivisional models deploy a Single Domain, while the InterCorporate Model utilizes a Master Domain deployment. All three models have to follow common ground rules, but the differences in which resources are distributed has a major impact on the number of servers in each deployment. Following is a list of common ground rules that must be followed by each model:

- Each Domain requires a Primary Domain Controller.
- If the number of users per building exceeds 2,000, two Domain Controllers are required.
- Unless in a high-speed WAN environment (45 MB or higher), each building requires a Backup Domain Controller.

The InterDepartmental Domain Deployment

The InterDepartmental Model is generally used in the small organization with somewhere between 10 to 250 users. As far as the deployment of servers is concerned, the InterDepartmental model follows the traditional Domain model: The Primary Domain Controller doubles as the standard Office Automation Production Server, application servers are deployed as needed, and a Backup Domain Controller is deployed only if the organization feels that the fault tolerance offered by Directory replication is worthwhile.

> **NOTE**
>
> If you have even one mission-critical application that is not stored on the Primary Domain Controller, it is always an excellent idea to deploy a Backup Domain Controller. Keep in mind that a BDC can be as simple as a 486/66dx2 with 32 MB of RAM and 200 MB hard drive.

Windows NT Server is a very robust operating system and, while it lends itself well to a distributed deployment, it does not require multiple servers. A single processor Pentium class or above server with a minimum of 64 MB of RAM and sufficient disk space will provide excellent performance for the InterDepartmental deployment. The InterDepartmental Domain should not require additional servers unless

- One or more departments use a mission critical application, such as a crucial accounting package or asset management application, that lends itself to a dedicated resource for fault tolerance and/or additional security.

- The deployment requires a resource intensive application such as a database or Enterprise-wide intranet server.

- The deployment calls for an enterprise communications server, such as a dial-out or fax-server. (Usually, these types of applications fit nicely on less robust or average servers.)

- One or more departments works with very large data files such as graphics, AutoCAD, or animation that might hinder the performance of the server due to excessive disk activity. Usually, a dedicated data server alleviates these issues.

The InterDepartmental Domain Example

In the case of the Horton Agency, the InterDepartmental example used throughout this book, a single office automation server that doubles as the Primary Domain Controller will be sufficient (HTN-PROD01). However, there is a definite need for one application server, and a case could be made for a second. (See Figure 5.15.)

FIGURE 5.15.

The InterDepartmental Deployment.

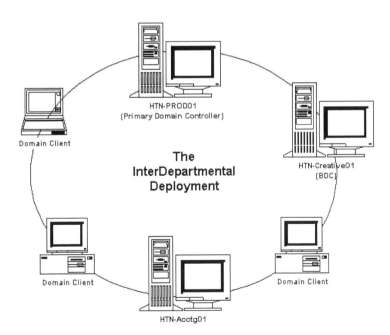

HTN-PROD01
(Primary Domain Controller)

Domain Client

The InterDepartmental Deployment

HTN-Creative01
(BDC)

Domain Client

Domain Client

HTN-Acctg01

The first application server belongs in the Accounting department. The Accounting department uses a sophisticated accounting package that not only keeps track of internal accounting, but also keeps track of project expense and customer billing. This application requires an SQL

Server back-end and has two periods during the month where heavy processing will be required. This application requires a dedicated server for two reasons:

> First, SQL Server is naturally very resource intensive and during heavy processing periods will require even more of the server's resources. This resource drain will make productivity for the non-accounting end user unbearable.

> Second, the accounting application and the information contained within are mission critical to day-to-day operations. It is important that the "single point of failure" scenario presented by leaving the application on the main production server be eliminated.

The second application server, which is more of a performance enhancement than a mission critical need, belongs to the Creative department. The Creative department works with extremely large multimedia files. These files, which will be created and accessed on a regular basis, will not only take up considerable network bandwidth but will also tax the production server's resources. The result will be a slowed response to the end-user during file reads and writes. If budget allows, a dedicated data server would reduce server-based end-user response issues, while a network ring or segment dedicated to the Creative department could help eliminate bandwidth drain to the rest of the network.

This data server, which would not require anything more than a low-end Pentium server with 48 MB of RAM, could also double as a Backup Domain Controller, thereby aiding in the fault tolerance provided by the dedicated Accounting server.

The InterDivisional Deployment

The InterDivisional Deployment is a bit more complicated than the InterDepartmental. The InterDivisional Model is used for a medium-sized organization that shares a single information systems support department and has multiple sites and/or multiple entities. (An entity can either be a very large department or division within the organization.) The InterDivisional Deployment utilizes the Single Domain Model, although on an expanded level when compared to the InterDepartmental Model. In essence, the InterDivisional Model is made up of multiple InterDepartmental Deployments that combine to share one Directory. While many of the same rules apply, the InterDivisional model allows a great deal of flexibility through the distribution of resources. Enterprise Servers, Cross-Divisional application servers, Cross-Divisional data servers, and an open environment for growth are all factors that combine to make this a well-managed environment. The following guidelines should help you in your InterDivisional Deployment:

- There should be one Office Automation Production Server for each Division.
- There must be at least one Domain Controller at each location.
- If one or more divisions share a resource intensive application, create a dedicated Cross-Divisional or Enterprise Server.

- Each Server within the Deployment should share the same core feature set (to be described in Chapter 8).

- Divisions in the same building or in a high-speed WAN environment can share a common DATA server provided adequate fault tolerance (to be discussed in Chapter 15).

The InterDivisional model is an excellent manner in which to provide a standard environment to all of your users while still creating a delineation between divisions. Not only is it easier for your users to keep track of their resources, it is also easier for your support personnel to provide good service. By providing a common feature set among all production servers no matter where your support personnel are, they will be able to assist the user with ease. Only the custom Divisional or Departmental resources will vary between divisions, minimizing the learning curve and the necessity to memorize a great deal of idiosyncrasies.

The InterDivisional Domain Example

The Guardian Insurance Companies has four major divisions. As stated above, each division should have its own office automation server. This server, called either the production or home server, should follow the same prefix-suffix naming conventions as its dedicated division or department. The production servers for the Guardian Domain could be

- HQ-PROD01 (Guardian Headquarters)
- HLT-PROD01 (Guardian Health)
- CORP-PROD01 (Guardian Corporate Benefits)
- CTY-PROD01 (Guardian Casualty)

These servers could all serve as Backup Domain Controllers, but what about the Primary Domain Controller? Due to the importance of the Directory, it is not a bad idea to have a dedicated PDC that does nothing other than act as a Domain Controller. Between replicating logon scripts and directory changes, as well as logon authentication, the PDC in a Domain the size of Guardian will be busy.

In addition to dedicated production servers, each group will most likely have its share of application servers. These application servers, which might be dedicated divisional or cross-divisional resources, should follow the same naming conventions as divisional and cross-divisional groups— the prefix should be the same prefix used for the group that owns the resource, followed by a descriptive suffix. For instance, if users in the Casualty Division required a dedicated data server, it might be named CTY-DATA. If users in the Corporate Benefits division required a financial tracking system, the server might be named CORP-Finance.

Enterprise Servers, of which Guardian will require many, should also follow the group naming conventions. The Enterprise prefix for Guardian is GRD; therefore, the Human Resources Enterprise data server might be named GRD-HRINFO, and the internal Web server might be named GRD-INTRAWEB.

The InterCorporate Deployment

As the InterDivisional Model was built upon the InterDepartmental Model, so, too, is the InterCorporate Model built upon the InterDivisional Model. The InterCorporate Model is made up of several InterDepartmental or InterDivisional Domains that share the same directory under a Master Domain. All of the deployment rules called for in the InterDepartmental and InterDivisional Models apply—however, in a much larger scale.

> **NOTE**
>
> While for the purposes of this book, the InterCorporate Model example is made up of relatively simple resource Domains, a Resource Domain can consist of multiple divisions or large departments that require their own dedicated production servers, application servers, and so on. In essence, a resource Domain can be as simple as a single InterDepartmental deployment or as complicated as an InterDivisional deployment.

McMac Industries is made up of a Master Domain and three resource Domains. By nature, each Domain will require a Primary Domain Controller, but only the Master Domain will require Backup Domain Controllers—one in each location. Much like the InterDivisional Domain, servers will follow group naming conventions. Therefore, the production servers will be named as follows:

- MMI-PROD01 (McMac Industries)
- MMF-PROD01 (McMac Foods)
- WTP-PROD01 (Watterson Papers)
- JNS-PROD01 (Jansen Salt)

Much like the InterDivisional Domain, it is a good idea to dedicate a Primary Domain Controller in the InterCorporate Domain, and there is little choice but to implement dedicated Backup Domain Controllers. The Master Domain Controllers can follow the Enterprise Naming Conventions (MME) or could have a convention of their own, just as long as they are set apart from the other servers.

Departmental, Cross-Divisional, and Enterprise Servers will also follow the same naming conventions as seen in the InterDivisional Domain.

Summary

This chapter has covered many key areas concerning the deployment of servers throughout your enterprise. The importance of configuration standardization, the consideration of fault tolerance and naming standards, and a deployment model that closely resembles your User Directory are all key factors in designing a successful enterprise. Furthermore, installation standards that provide for supportability, expandability, and growth will make a tremendous difference in the future of your deployment.

Choosing Your Protocols

IN THIS CHAPTER

CHAPTER 6

One of the many advantages of Windows NT Server is that it is to a great extent protocol independent, providing the ability to serve multiple protocols to workstations throughout your enterprise. Even though with today's 32-bit operating systems multiple protocols aren't as much of an issue as they once were, slimming down your protocol choices is good for the network, for server performance, and for communications as a whole. This chapter will very briefly touch on the best uses for each of the three primary Windows NT protocols: NetBEUI, NWLink, and TCP/IP by taking a high level look at your communications needs.

The Traditional Microsoft Network Communications Model

As mentioned in Chapter 2, "Why Windows NT Server?," Windows NT networking components rely on a naming convention known as NetBIOS (Network Basic Input/Output System). Windows NT Server 4.0 utilizes the NetBIOS Interface Service to provide name resolution and to establish machine-to-machine and application communications. This name resolution is done through network broadcasting in the form of browsing, however, the NetBIOS Interface and the NetBIOS protocol are not one in the same. The NetBIOS Interface interacts with the differing implementations of Windows NT's protocols (NetBEUI, NWLink NetBIOS, and WINS for TCP/IP) to provide name resolution, but is not in itself a protocol. In other words, the NetBIOS interface is what allows you to talk from one computer to another.

Microsoft networking has long been associated with heavy network traffic due to its NetBIOS dependencies. Even in today's high bandwidth world, browsing and broadcasting can cause undue network congestion. Unlike traditional TCP/IP clients, a traditional Microsoft Client has no idea where to go when it wants to communicate with another machine. For instance, when a UNIX client wants to talk to a UNIX host it simply queries the Domain Name Server that holds a list of machine names associated with their network address. Once the name is received, the original client knows exactly where to go to initiate communications. In contrast, when a Microsoft client needs to communicate with a Microsoft host, it begins broadcasting on its local subnet by screaming at the top of its lungs "Hey Host, where are you?". If it doesn't get an answer after a few seconds, it begins looking in other networks, still screaming "Hey Host, where are you?" until it finds the host it's looking for. When it finds its destination it initiates communications. Unfortunately when the traditional Microsoft (and IBM) protocol of NetBEUI is used, the client's broadcasts are still proliferating throughout the entire network causing unnecessary traffic.

To alleviate this situation, Microsoft invented the concept of the Master Browser. A *Master Browser*, which can be a member of a workgroup or a domain, maintains a list of all registered clients and servers on its subnet. When a Microsoft client or server first comes on to the network it registers itself with the Master Browser by making a broadcast such as, "It is I,

NetBIOS-based client JONEST and I have a MAC address of 10004F2100AB." The Master Browser then adds this name and MAC address to its browse list as long as there are no duplicates. If JONEST already existed on the network, the machine will not be able to participate in NetBIOS communications. If the name is unique and another machine on its subnet starts looking for JONEST, it now refers to the Master Browser, which hopefully points right to the desired destination.

While this works well on a single subnet, it does not alleviate browsing across networks. Therefore, if a workgroup or domain spans subnets, there will be a Master Browser on one subnet, and a Backup Browser on any additional subnets. Thus, the Master Browser (usually the PDC of a domain) will maintain the master list and the Backup Browsers will maintain a list of resources on their subnets. When the Master Browser needs to find a resource on another subnet it will first refer to the Backup Browsers. If one of the Backup Browsers know where the resource lives, the destination will be returned to the Master Browser, who will then return it to the broadcasting client. If none of the browsers know where the resource is, the client will begin broadcasting across subnets.

> **NOTE**
>
> The browsing and broadcasting process is at its most inefficient when the NetBEUI protocol is used. When NWLlnk is used, the Master Browsers and clients can at least refer to the IPX route tables held by the network routers to assist in finding clients, thus narrowing the scope of the broadcast. When NetBEUI is used, a broadcast is sent to every subnet throughout the enterprise regardless of which subnet the desired host resides on. When the WINS–TCP/IP solution is used, broadcasting very rarely happens. These topics will be covered in detail later in this chapter.

To this point, browsing can obviously help eliminate broadcasting among individual domains or workgroups, but it has not yet accounted for cross-domain or cross-workgroup communications. To address this, when a Master Browser comes on to the network it broadcasts its existence across subnets in order to register itself with other Master Browsers. Thus, each browser maintains a list of other browsers to refer to for future reference. When a client on subnet B browses the network for a resource that resides on subnet C, it is actually receiving the browse list from the Master Browser on subnet C. While this might seem efficient, it still accounts for a great deal of broadcasting and browsing—particularly when NetBEUI is used as the primary protocol. Each Master Browser and Backup Browser will announce themselves to the world every 15 minutes. Depending on how many subnets, workgroups, and domains you have, this could allow for a great deal of broadcasting.

The Environment

Of the three protocols that can be used with Windows NT for internetwork communications, all require the NetBIOS interface in one form or another. The decision for you is to determine which protocol presents the best solution for your environment. The following guidelines can be used as a starting point for your consideration:

Environmental Variables	Recommended Protocol
50 users or less and no NetWare	NetBEUI
NetWare and Non-Routed	NWLink
NetWare and Routed	TCP/IP and NWLink
Routed but no UNIX	TCP/IP with WINS only
Routed with UNIX	TCP/IP with WINS and DNS

The remainder of this chapter will tackle each recommendation, one at a time, providing brief technical or common sense reasons for the recommendation.

The 50 Users or Less and No NetWare Environment

In the small, non-routed, non-NetWare environment, the NetBEUI protocol is your easiest protocol choice. Of the three protocols available, NetBEUI is most definitely the fastest protocol in a non-routed environment, provides for the least amount of configuration, and installs on all Microsoft operating systems with ease. If you are in a small network and have no need to connect to NetWare servers, NetBEUI is your best bet.

One word of caution: If you are in a routed environment, NetBEUI is very ugly. Even with Master Browsers in place there will be a considerable amount of broadcasting, which will result in slowed network performance. Microsoft does not recommend implementing NetBEUI in an environment with more than 50 users. Due to the high network traffic caused by NetBEUI broadcasting, performance can slow considerably. Furthermore, the Microsoft implementation of NetBEUI is not as robust as the implementation of NetBEUI in OS/2 and is more prone to issues with high performance networking equipment such as token ring switching hubs.

The Non-Routed NetWare Environment

If you are in a non-routed NetWare environment and plan to use both NetWare and Windows NT Server resources on a regular basis, there is no reason to maintain multiple network protocols. The Windows NT implementation of IPX/SPX, named NWLink, allows for

Microsoft clients to connect to Windows NT with IPX only, and in conjunction with the Gateway Service for NetWare also allows for Windows NT to provide gateway services to NetWare resources. Furthermore, with the addition of File and Print Services for NetWare, native NetWare clients can attach to your Windows NT Server as if it were a NetWare server. Microsoft's NWLink is comprised of two components: NWLink IPX/SPX and NWLink NetBIOS.

- NWLink is Microsoft's reverse engineered version of IPX/SPX, which in conjunction with the Gateway Service for NetWare or File and Print Services for NetWare allows communication with both NetWare servers and NetWare clients. NWLink is implemented in two parts: IPX/SPX and NWLink NetBIOS.

- NWLink IPX/SPX is used for communication with NetWare 3.*x* and 4.*x* servers and for NetWare 3.*x* emulation in conjunction with File and Print Services for NetWare. IPX/SPX is fully routable and acts nearly identical to NetWare's IPX/SPX. Without NWLink IPX/SPX communication with NetWare resources would be impossible.

NWLink NetBIOS is the Microsoft implementation of IPX/SPX that can be used as the sole means of communication between Microsoft clients and servers. NWLink NetBIOS is categorized as a Type 20 protocol which means that unlike IPX/SPC it can proliferate itself across the network and cause undue congestion. However, unlike NetBEUI, NWLink will refer to a router's IPX Route table and in most cases broadcast for its destination host only on the correct destination subnet. NWLink is much more efficient than NetBEUI.

> **CAUTION**
>
> In a routed environment, Type 20 protocols must be enabled for NWLink NetBIOS to work across subnets. Rembember, however, Type 20 packets might cause many of the same network performance issues usually associated with NetBIOS. NWLink, therefore, is recommended, only in small routed envrionments that require NetWare cohabitation.

The NetWare and Routed Environment

There is no question that NetWare's implementation of IPX/SPX is well suited to a routed environment. There is also little question that the NetWare compatible IPX/SPX portion of the Microsoft implementation of NWLink is well suited to a routed environment. Unfortunately, the NWLink NetBIOS component of Microsoft's IPX/SPX is not so solid.

NWLink NetBIOS is very much like NetBEUI in that it relies on NetBIOS broadcasts to communicate with other NWLink computers. While there is no question that NWLink NetBIOS does not utilize as much network bandwidth as NetBEUI, it is not nearly as clean as NetWare's implementation of IPX/SPX due to the fact that it does not utilize network routing tables. Both NWLink NetBIOS and NetBEUI will broadcast across subnets on your network when looking for a resource, but only NWLink will cache NetBIOS names and their routes. NetBEUI provides for absolutely no caching, which results in broadcasting for a resource regardless of whether or not the machine was connected only minutes ago. Once an NWLink NetBIOS machine finds a resource it will remember its destination (until it is shut off).

If you are in a routed environment that includes both NetWare and Windows NT, it is your best bet to install NWLink for Windows NT Server to NetWare communication, but implement TCP/IP for Windows NT communication across your internetwork. While Microsoft's implementation of TCP/IP still requires the NetBIOS interface and name resolution, it does not require NetBIOS broadcasting. Through a NetBIOS name to TCP/IP address translation service called WINS, Windows NT can communicate across routers and on the same subnet using TCP/IP without broadcasting. The implementation of Microsoft's TCP/IP will be covered in detail in Chapter 14, "WINS, DHCP, and DNS."

CAUTION

When using NWLink for Microsoft client to Windows NT Server communications, your routers must be configured to allow Type 20 packets to pass through. If Type 20 packets are not enabled, your Windows NT Servers will not be able to communicate across subnets. What makes this extremely frustrating is that if your NT Server has Gateway Services for NetWare or File and Print Services for NetWare installed, you will be able to see your NetWare resources. This is due to the fact that Microsoft resources still require the NWLink NetBIOS interface (NWLink NetBIOS), which is in fact a Type 20 protocol.

The Routed Environment with No UNIX

If you are in a routed environment that does not also include UNIX, you are heavily encouraged to implement TCP/IP as your sole network protocol. (This statement is not meant to indicate that you wouldn't implement TCP/IP in a UNIX environment.) Windows NT Server provides a complete enterprise level TCP/IP solution that can be implemented in such a way that eliminates the need to implement any other protocols on your Windows NT network. With the DHCP and WINS services in place, your Windows resources can dynamically communicate throughout your routed environment without any NetBIOS broadcasting. This is due to WINS, or the Windows Internet Name Service. WINS is, in essence, a NetBIOS name to IP Address translator that each machine registers with when they come up on the network, and that each machine references when they attempt to attach to another Microsoft TCP/IP-based resource. It is from the WINS servers that your Master Browsers will receive their browse lists, and it is through the WINS servers that your users will be able to attach to resources across subnets. Without WINS, your Microsoft TCP/IP users would not be able to browse the network or access any NT Servers or workstations across subnets.

DHCP and WINS, which will be covered in detail in Chapter 14, while at first might seem somewhat intimidating, are actually fairly easy to implement and manage.

The Routed with UNIX Environment

In addition to the DHCP and WINS servers in Windows NT Server, Microsoft now provides a DNS server. DNS, or Domain Name Server, is required for IP to Host name connectivity in a true TCP/IP environment. Thus, if you plan to interoperate in the UNIX environment you will require a DNS Server. While Windows NT and its clients can use WINS to connect to other Microsoft-based TCP/IP resources without DNS, WINS cannot be used for connectivity to pure TCP/IP resources. Likewise, while DNS can be used for Microsoft clients (as well as UNIX, OS/2, and so on) to attach to pure IP solutions, DNS cannot be used to attach to Microsoft clients or servers unless you're running a non-NetBIOS dependent Windows NT Service.

WINS is extremely similar to DNS in that it provides host name to IP address translation, however, DNS is a much more complicated application that requires an in-depth knowledge of TCP/IP. While Chapter 14, "WINS, DHCP, and DNS," will cover the interoperability of WINS and DNS, it will not cover the DNS server in great detail. It is highly recommended that you have a firm grasp on TCP/IP and its role in your environment before you implement a DNS Server. In most cases where UNIX already exists, there will have been a previously implemented DNS Server.

Futures Caution

While it may not be stated very frequently, much of the design recommendations and guidelines presented in this book not only provide an excellent blueprint for a manageable, expandable, and easily supported network today, but also prepare you for the changes that will be made to Windows NT Server 5.0 next year. One of those major changes revolves about the new Active Directory server that will replace the existing Domain Directory with an LDAP, X.500, and Kerberos compatible directory service. A major component in this new directory service (as of April of 1996) will be integration with the TCP/IP Domain Name Server. This, of course, implies that you must be using TCP/IP as your network protocol and you must either be using DNS or be planning to use DNS. Never fear, while the Active Directory will require the Microsoft DNS Server, it does not have to be the primary DNS. While this is not mentioned to urge you to implement the Windows NT DNS server in your environment today, it is meant to provide a forewarning to the possible need for TCP/IP in your environment in the future. TCP/IP is fast becoming a universal protocol and warrants heavy investigation for your environment.

Summary

Choosing a protocol for your environment is in many cases very cut and dry: TCP/IP is the answer. While NetBEUI is excellent for the small environment and NWLink is a good choice for those networks in a small NetWare environment, TCP/IP is the protocol of the future. The sooner you begin learning the complexities of this protocol, the better, or you might end up behind the eight ball in the near future.

Sharing and Securing Resources

IN THIS CHAPTER

CHAPTER 7

The organizational design of the User Directory should be extremely similar to the manner in which you implement resources throughout your Domain—in fact, they should parallel one another. The deployment philosophy endorsed throughout this book, while based on the Six Key Design Objectives, is centered around your organizational culture as follows:

- The User Directory is designed based on your organization's divisional and departmental structure.

- The servers are deployed based on your organization's geographic or corporate diversity as well as your divisional needs.

- As you'll see in Chapter 8, "Designing Your Enterprise Resource Structure," your server's directory structure is designed around your departmental or divisional application and data needs.

- Finally, the application of security and implementation of share points are based on directory structure designed to meet your departmental and/or divisional needs.

This design philosophy was built around the strengths and weaknesses of Windows NT Server. In order to fully comprehend the implication of each design step, it is necessary to have a solid background knowledge of both File and Directory Level Permissions in Windows NT, and Network Shares and their implementation. This chapter will cover the differences and commonalties between permission types, while Chapter 8 will cover the design and deployment of resources throughout your domain.

File and Directory Level Permissions

File and Directory Level Permissions are those permissions applied directly to your server's resources. File and Directory Level Permissions work together with your server's volume and directory structure to provide the security and manageability expected in today's networking environment. Certain rules and recommendations apply to the application of these permissions:

- Managing Group access is easier than managing User access; therefore, do not apply users directly to resources.

- Groups can consist of only one user.

- If a user is a member of two groups that have been granted differing levels of access to a directory or is a member of a group with one level of access and has been applied individually with another level, the user will receive the lesser level of access.

- File and Directory Level Permissions are supported only on NTFS, not FAT or CDFS.

■ Members of the local group Backup Operators bypass File and Directory Level security in order to back up all files. This functionality negates the need to give the group Backup Operators explicit rights to any directory.

■ By default, the Administrator does not have access to all files and directories on the server. If the members of the Administrators group or Domain Admins group need access to a directory, they must either have explicit access or they may take ownership of that directory.

These guidelines are somewhat premature in the understanding of File and Directory Level Permissions; however, keep them in the back of your mind while reading the remainder of this chapter.

File and Directory Permissions Defined

File and Directory Permissions are those permissions granted to or revoked from the users or groups defined within your User Directory to specific files or directories contained on any of your domain's servers. Windows NT Server offers seven default levels of file and directory permissions and also allows the administrator to create custom permissions in the rare case that a default setting won't do (see Figure 7.1). Table 7.1 defines each permission and provides its possible consequence on user accessibility. Keep in mind that these permissions must be specifically added to a file or directory using the Windows NT Explorer.

FIGURE 7.1.

Directory Permissions.

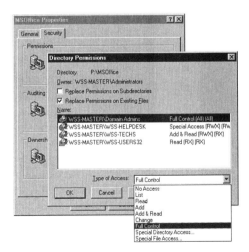

Table 7.1. File and Directory Level Permissions.

Permission	Definition	Consequence
Add	The Add permission allows the User or Group to add files and subdirectories to a directory but does not allow access to those files.	A user can add files to this directory but cannot modify them, see them, or copy them once they've been stored there. This type of security is often used for gathering data that should not be modified from its original state, such as inventory information, application response files, or personnel questionnaires.
Add & Read	Add & Read allows for the viewing of files and directories, changing to subdirectories, running applications, and adding subdirectories to a directory. It does not, however, allow for modification of existing files and directories.	Add & Read works well with applications that require the user to write files for proper operation but don't require the user to modify those files.
Change	Change allows the viewing of files and subdirectories, changing to subdirectories, running applications, adding files and directories, modification of files and directories, and the deletion of files and directories.	Change is usually applied to common or group data directories where the User or Group needs to manipulate files and directories without restriction.
Full Control	Full Control allows for the viewing of files and subdirectories, changing to subdirectories, running applications, adding files and directories, modification of files and directories, deletion of files and directories, changing file permissions, taking ownership of files and directories, and the deletion of files and directories regardless of file permissions.	Full control is usually reserved for Administrators and Support Personnel.
List	The List permission allows the viewing of files and directories as well as changing to subdirectories, but it does not allow a user to run applications, add files or directories, or delete files or directories.	List works well in a directory structure that might contain multiple subdirectories that are dedicated to different groups. For example, a Data directory has a subdirectory for Accounting,

Permission	Definition	Consequence
		Marketing, and HR. Anyone can list the directories under Data, but only specific groups have access to the subdirectories.
No Access	No Access denies access to a directory and all files underneath it. No Access overrides all other permissions.	If THOMPSONB is a member of both the HTN-USERS group and the HTN-MARKETING group, and HTN-USERS is denied access to the Marketing data directory, THOMPSONB would have no access to the Marketing directory.
Read	Read allows users to view files and directories, change to subdirectories, and run applications. It does not allow for the modification or addition of files or subdirectories.	Excellent for a directory that contains applications, common shared information such as forms or policies, and common utilities.
Special Directory Access	Can be any combination of the following rights: ■ Read ■ Write ■ Execute ■ Delete ■ Change Permissions ■ Take Ownership	Special Directory Access is used in an environment where the default permissions need to be modified at the Directory level.
Special File Access	Can be any combination of the following rights: ■ Read ■ Write ■ Execute ■ Delete ■ Change Permissions ■ Take Ownership	Special File Access, much like Special Directory Access, is utilized on a file only when the default permissions do not support the needs of the environment.

The permissions available in Windows NT Server are extremely comprehensive; however, without actually having applied them to a resource, they may seem somewhat impractical. With the list of File and Directory Permissions listed in Table 7.1 in mind, imagine a common data directory in an InterDepartmental Domain like the Horton Agency (see Figure 7.2).

FIGURE 7.2.

*An Example of a
Common Data
Directory.*

Remember that the Horton Domain contains the following groups: HTN-CREATIVE, HTN-ACCOUNTING, HTN-SALES, and HTN-ADMIN. Due to the design of the User Directory, File and Directory Level Permissions make it extremely easy to create a readily navigated data directory that contains both common and secured data, while requiring only one major network entry point. Following is a high-level introduction to applying File and Directory Level Permissions:

1. Create a subdirectory named DEPT (or Department) in the root of a directory entitled DATA.

2. Under the DEPT directory, create a subdirectory for each of your division's departmental groups.

3. At the top of the DEPT directory, using File and Directory Level Permissions, apply the Basic User group, HTN-USERS, with the LIST right. This right allows users to see only what subdirectories exist but provides no inherent access.

4. At each departmental subdirectory, apply only the appropriate Departmental Group with CHANGE Level Permissions. For instance, apply HTN-CREATIVE to the Creative directory with CHANGE Level Permissions. Once done, all users of the HTN-CREATIVE group have enough rights to create, modify, and utilize documents in the Creative subdirectory but have no access to the other departmental subdirectories.

5. Repeat the application of File and Directory Level Permissions for each departmental subdirectory, applying only the appropriate departmental group.

Because only the groups with necessary access have been given permission to their respective directories, there is no way a user could access data they were not intended to see. As you'll see in Chapter 8, minimizing major points of access using well-designed directory structures plays a key role in adhering to Objective 3: a Standard User Environment, and in turn aids in the manageability of your enterprise, as well as end-user comfort.

Administering File and Directory Level Permissions

The Windows NT Explorer is the tool used to apply and administer File and Directory Level Permissions throughout your Domain. Permissions can be managed remotely from a Windows NT computer or can be administered while physically logged on to your server. In order to remotely manage File and Directory Permissions under Windows NT 4.0, you must be attached to either an administrative share at the root of the drive or a network share point that grants you full control. Additionally, you must be using another Windows NT computer (Workstation or Server). Administrative shares will be covered later in this chapter.

In most cases, once you've completed the initial implementation of your server, you will not find it necessary to manage File and Directory Level Permissions, but knowing how to manipulate them is crucial during your initial design process. To view and/or manipulate permissions for a directory on an NTFS volume, you must first log on to your Windows NT Server as an administrator equivalent and launch the Windows NT Explorer. Once you have chosen a directory on an NTFS File System that you would like to view, there are three methods to launch its properties:

■ **Method One**

In the Windows NT Explorer, find the directory you wish to manage and click on it once with the right mouse button. A drop-down menu will launch, as shown in Figure 7.3; choose Properties.

FIGURE 7.3.

Directory Properties Example One.

▪ Method Two

Select the directory within the Windows NT Explorer that you wish to view. Go to the File option on the Explorer menu and select Properties, as shown in Figure 7.4.

FIGURE 7.4.

Directory Properties Example Two.

▪ Method Three

Select the desired directory from within the Windows NT Explorer (shown in Figure 7.5) and then choose the Properties button on the Windows NT Explorer Tool Bar.

Regardless of which method you use, you will be presented with a properties window for the directory you have chosen (see Figure 7.6).

The Directory Properties window provides you with the following information about the directory you're viewing:

- ▪ The Type of object you're viewing
- ▪ The Location of the object
- ▪ The Size of the object
- ▪ The number of files and folders contained within the directory
- ▪ The Creation Date
- ▪ The MS-DOS 8.3 name
- ▪ The MS-DOS attributes of the object

FIGURE 7.5.

Directory Properties Example Three.

FIGURE 7.6.

The Directory Properties Dialog.

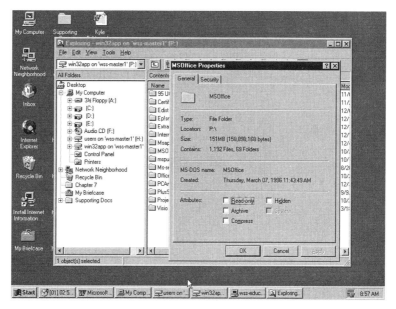

The initial Properties screen is composed of three tabs: General (the current screen), Sharing, and Security.

NOTE

If you're viewing a file or directory on a remote computer, you will not be presented with the Sharing tab. Network shares can only be created locally when using the Windows NT Explorer. Creating shares will be covered later in this chapter.

Note that in Figure 7.6, the General tab presents information about the directory you're viewing, the Sharing tab gives you the ability to create and manage network shares, and the Security tab is where you will go to manage File and Directory Level Permissions. In order to manage permissions, select the Security tab shown in Figure 7.7.

FIGURE 7.7.

The Security Window.

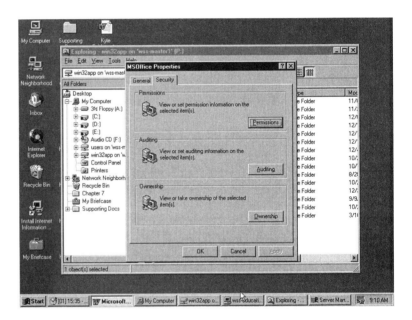

In Figure 7.7, the Security window will provide you with three management options: Permissions, Auditing, and Ownership. Each option offers different functionality:

- Auditing allows you to track a specific user or group's access to a selected object.
- Ownership will allow you to view or take ownership of an object.
- Permissions will allow you to view and manage a Directory's permissions.

In order to manage an object's access list, choose the Permissions button (see Figure 7.8). The Permissions window offers the Administrator the ability to perform the following:

- View existing permissions
- Replace permissions on subdirectories

- Replace permissions on existing files
- Change permissions for existing users or groups
- Add or remove permissions for existing users or groups

FIGURE 7.8.

The Directory Permissions Window.

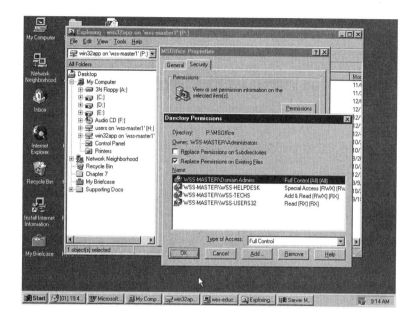

Once you've accessed the directories access list, you will need to choose the Add button in order to add, change, or revoke permissions. Once complete, you will immediately be presented with the Add Users and Groups dialog window, as seen in Figure 7.9. This window contains the list of Local and Global groups found in your Domain Directory from which you will grant permissions. To grant permissions, simply choose the group or groups desired and select the Add button. By default, you can only grant rights to Groups; however, if you want to add specific users to an object's access list, you must first choose the Show Users button. Remember that managing users separately can become convoluted and confusing and is not recommended. At this point, you may choose as many users and groups to add to this resource as desired, but notice that as you add users and groups, they all initially inherit the same level of access specified in the field titled Type of Access. This access can be modified once you are finished selecting the desired users and groups, but not at this time.

After selecting all of the necessary Groups, press the OK button, and you'll be returned to the Directory Permissions window. It is at this point that you may select each individual user or group and set the desired level of access through the Type of Access field. If you wish to apply these changes to the immediate directory only, do not select the Replace Permissions on Subdirectories option; this option will overwrite the permissions on all lower-level subdirectories, negating all settings you've applied in the past. By the same token, only choose Replace Permissions on Existing Files if you want all files in the directory structure to inherit the rights you've chosen. In the event that you do want the chosen permissions to be applied to all files and subdirectories, select the Replace Permissions on Subdirectories and Replace Permissions on Existing Files options. After choosing the OK button, the application of new rights will flash across the screen. Depending on the size of the directory and the scope of the changes you're making, this could take some time. After all changes are complete, you will be brought back to the Directory Properties window, having successfully manipulated a directory's access permissions.

Figure 7.9.

The Add Users and Groups Pop-Up Window.

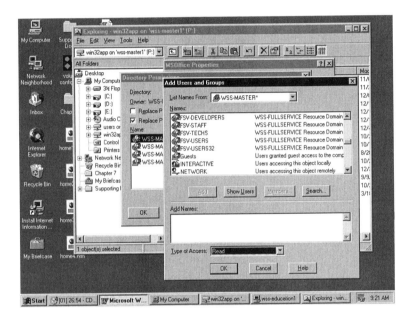

> **CAUTION**
>
> In Windows NT Server 4.0, there is no way to simply add Groups to an object's permission list using the GUI interface. If you've modified a directory's access by adding one or two groups or changing permissions, choosing the Replace Permissions on Subdirectories option does not propagate those options to lower directory levels but overwrites all subdirectory security properties. In order to edit a directory's permissions, you must use the DOS-based utility CACLS.

Default Windows NT Server Directory Permissions

When Windows NT Server is initially installed, there are a number of default directories created. Each of these directories has already been configured with the necessary default permissions. These permissions are set for optimum functionality and should not be modified; if you do modify these permissions, you could seriously impair your system's functionality.

Table 7.2 lists the default directories and their permissions.

Table 7.2. Windows NT Server 4.0 Default Directories and Their Permissions.

Directory	Default User or Group	Default Permissions
\Users\Default	Everyone	RWX
	Creator Owner	Full Control
	System	Full Control
\Users	Account Operators	RWXD
	Administrators	RWXD
	Everyone	List
	System	Full Control
\Temp	Administrators	Full Control
	Creator Owner	Full Control
	Everyone	Change
	Server Operators	Change
	System	Full Control
\\Winnt_root\ System32\Spool	Administrators	Full Control
	Creator Owner	Full Control
	Everyone	Read
	Print Operators	Full Control
	Server Operators	Full Control
	System	Full Control
\\Winnt_root\ System32\Repl\Import	Administrators	Full Control
	Creator Owner	Full Control
	Everyone	Read
	Replicator	Change
	Server Operators	Change
	System	Full Control
\\Winnt_root\ System32\Repl\Export	Administrators	Full Control
	Creator Owner	Full Control
	Everyone	Read
	Replicator	Read
	Server Operators	Change
	System	Full Control
\\Winnt_root\ System32\Repl	Administrators	Full Control
	Creator Owner	Full Control
	Everyone	Read
	Server Operators	Full Control
	System	Full Control

7

SHARING AND
SECURING
RESOURCES

continues

Table 7.2. continued

Directory	Default User or Group	Default Permissions
`\\Winnt_root\` `System32\Drivers`	Administrators	Full Control
	Creator Owner	Full Control
	Everyone	Read
	Server Operators	Full Control
	System	Full Control
`\\Winnt_root\` `System32\Config`	Administrators	Full Control
	Creator Owner	Full Control
	Everyone	List
	System	Full Control
`\\Winnt_root\System32`	Administrators	Full Control
	Creator Owner	Full Control
	Everyone	Change
	Server Operators	Change
	System	Full Control
`\\Winnt_root\`	Administrators	Full Control
	Creator Owner	Full Control
	Everyone	Change
	Server Operators	Change
	System	Full Control

This table has been provided for administrative reference. If you've modified any of these settings and are experiencing difficulties, returning the directories to the setting in Table 7.2 should alleviate your issues. It may, however, be necessary to restart you server before the changes will take effect.

Shared Directory Basics

File and Directory permissions apply strictly to the local resources contained on your server's volume and directory structure. Users cannot attach to your server until and unless you manually share a directory. A Shared Directory (often referred to simply as a Share) can be any point in a server's directory structure that you wish to advertise and make available to the network attached user. When users browse your Domain in the Network Neighborhood, the folders they see under each server are those directories that have been Shared. Much like File and Directory Level Security, users cannot access a share (see Figure 7.10) unless they've been granted explicit permissions.

FIGURE 7.10.
*Shared Folders As Seen
Through the Network
Neighborhood.*

Share Security

While volumes formatted with the FAT file system do not support File and Directory Level Security, they do support network Shares. Share Level Security (see Figure 7.11) is best used when complimenting File and Directory Level Security since the true Security on an NT Server resides at this level. It is recommended that you utilize NTFS on any volumes that will contain shared directories.

The following sections list the four levels of Share Security and their definitions.

Full Control

Full Control, when coupled with Full Control at the Directory level, allows the user to do the following:

- View files and subdirectories
- Run applications
- Change to subdirectories
- Modify files and directories
- Add files and directories
- Delete files and directories
- Change file permissions
- Take ownership of files

Although a user or group may have Full Control at the Share Level, the user or group may not necessarily have such control at the File and Directory Level. Keep in mind that the more restrictive permission level always wins out.

FIGURE 7.11.

Share Level Security.

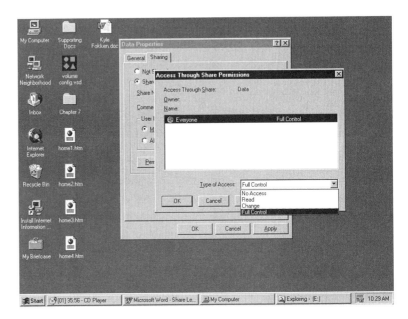

No Access

Setting No Access for a specific User or Group denies access to a Share but not necessarily to the entire directory structure beneath the Share. Since a Share can be created at any point in a directory structure, it is possible to have users that cannot access the top level of a directory through a Share but can access any number of subdirectories through alternate Shares.

Change

Change at the Share level allows the user to do the following:

- View files and subdirectories
- Run applications
- Change to subdirectories
- Modify files and directories
- Add files and directories
- Delete files and directories

Change permissions apply only if File and Directory permissions do not override them.

Read

Read is very commonly used. Read at the Share level allows users to

- View files and subdirectories
- Run applications
- Change to subdirectories

Read does not allow for the modification or addition of files or subdirectories and fits well with applications and data that should be viewed only.

When applying security, keep in mind that Share Security is always overridden by more restrictive File and Directory Level Security; however, more restrictive Share Level Security will also override more permissive File and Directory permissions. Share Level Security is crucial to good network management and will be discussed in detail in conjunction with your User Directory and domain deployment in Chapter 8.

Default Shares

When Windows NT Server is initially installed, several default Shares will be created. Much like the default directory permissions, each default share serves a purpose and should not be modified. Table 7.3 lists the default shares along with their purposes.

> **NOTE**
>
> \WINNTSRV is the recommended installation directory, often referred to as the system root.

Table 7.3. Default Shared Directories.

Default Share	Share Path	Share Purpose
REPL$	\WINNTSRV\system32\ Repl\Export	This resource is created when a server is designated as a replication export server. This Share is where all of the Logon Scripts for your Domain will originate to be replicated to other Domain Controllers are stored.
PRINT$	\WINNTSRV\\system32\spool\	This resource plays an integral drivers part in sharing printers. Print drivers are stored here, among other things.

continues

Table 7.3. continued

Default Share	*Share Path*	*Share Purpose*
NETLOGON	\WINNTSRV\\system32\Repl\	The NETLOGON Share is the share Import\ Scripts from which users receive their logon scripts. While this share can be modified, it is not recommended.
IPC$	Not Applicable	The IPC$ share, which represents Named Pipes, is used for communications between programs. IPC$ is used behind the scenes during remote administration of a Server's shared resources and program-to-program communication. This Share cannot be modified.
C$, D$, E$, etc.	The Root of a Physical Disk	This default Share allows support personnel to attach directly to the root of a physical disk to manage File and Directory Level Permissions. On a member server, only members of the Administrators or Backup Operators groups can attach to this share. However, if the machine is a Domain Controller, members of the Server Operators group can attach as well. This Share cannot be modified.
ADMIN$	\WINNTSRV\	This Share is used by the system during remote administration. On a member server, only members of the Administrators or Backup Operators groups can attach to this Share. However, if the machine is a Domain Controller, members of the Server Operators group can attach as well. This Share cannot be modified.

Creating New Shares

As you'll see in Chapter 8, there are two reasons to create a share: to facilitate the sharing of resources on a production, application or data server for its dedicated user base or to create a secured entry point for a Cross-Divisional or Enterprise group.

A share can be created through either the Windows NT Explorer or through the Server Manager; however, the Windows NT Explorer can only be used to create local shares, while the Server Manager can be used to create shares both locally and remotely. The following section will cover creating shares using both mechanisms.

Creating Shares Using the Server Manager

As mentioned in Chapter 2, "Why Windows NT Server?," the Server Manager is the tool that allows you to manage local or remote Windows NT Servers and Workstations within your Domain, as well as Windows NT machines in those Domains that have previously established Trust relationships.

The Server Manager, as seen in Figure 7.12, facilitates the following management functions:

- The creation and management of Shared Directories including share Level Permissions
- Service Management including starting, stopping, and start-up modification
- The management of User connections, shared directory use, and files currently in use
- The addition and removal of Windows NT machines from the Domain
- Forced Domain Synchronization

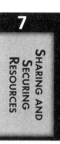

FIGURE 7.12.

The Server Manager.

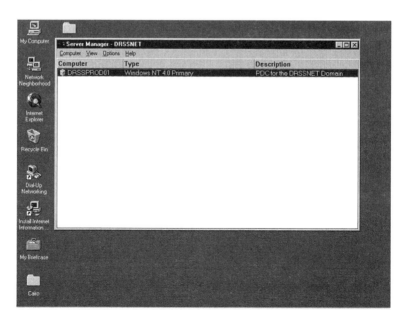

Many of the management features provided by the Server Manager are remote interfaces of those tools that exist locally on servers and workstations. The capability to create shares remotely is just one of those interfaces.

The following procedure will walk you through creating a new share using the Server Manager:

1. Go to your Windows NT 4.0 or Windows 95 Start menu, select Administrative Tools (or Windows NT Server Tools in Windows 95) in the Programs menu, and launch the Server Manager.

2. Once in the Server Manager, you will be presented with a list of Windows NT Servers and Workstations in your domain. You may choose the Windows NT Server that you wish to manage by highlighting it.

3. The Tool Bar found in the Server Manager has four pull-down options (see Figure 7.13): Computer, View, Options, and Help. For share creation, select the Computer option followed by the Shared Directories selection in the Tool Bar pull-down menu.

FIGURE 7.13.

Managing Shares through the Server Manager.

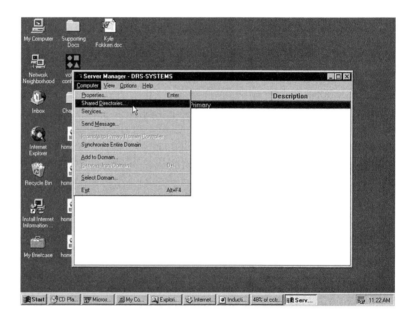

4. You will immediately be presented with a window labeled Shared Directories (see Figure 7.14). The Shared Directories window has five buttons off to the right side and displays all of the shared directories on the selected server in a subwindow. The action options in this window are: Close, New Share, Properties, Stop Sharing, and Help. In order to create a new share, click on the New Share button.

FIGURE 7.14.

The Shared Directories Window.

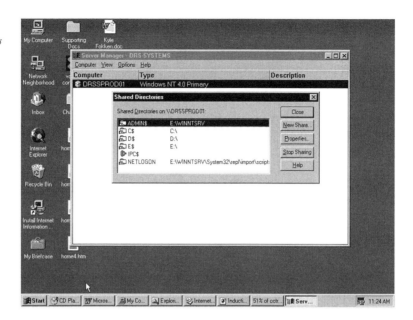

5. The New Share window contains four important text boxes (see Figure 7.15). The Share Name text box is where you enter the shared directory name, the Path text box is where you enter the physical drive and directory of the share, the Comment text box is where you place a description of the share to be viewed through the Network Neighborhood, and the User Limit option gives you the option to set a limit on how many users can actually connect to the Share at once. Once you have entered the name and path of the new share, the Permissions button becomes active.

6. Click the Permissions button, and the Access Through Share Permissions window will launch (see Figure 7.16).

7. The Access Through Share Permissions window is where you go to set permissions on the new share and, coincidentally, to manage permissions on existing shares. By default, each share has the Everyone group with Full Control applied upon creation; however, this is not a recommended setting. At this point, it is suggested that you remove the Everyone group and add the appropriate Group list by pressing the Add button.

8. You will immediately be presented with the Add Users and Groups window (as seen in Figure 7.9). Set the required permission levels and click OK until you reach the Shared Directories window. After creating a share, it is immediately available to network attached users.

FIGURE 7.15.

The New Share Window.

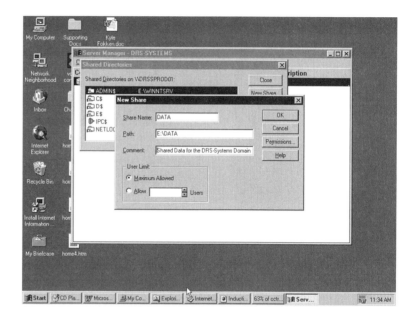

FIGURE 7.16.

Access Through Share Permissions Window.

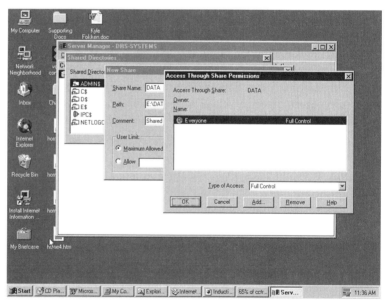

Creating Shares Through the Windows NT Explorer

When logged on locally to a machine, the Windows NT Explorer may also be used to create Shares. Creating new shares through the Windows NT Explorer is very much like administering File and Directory Level Permissions. The following procedure will walk you through creating a share using the Explorer interface:

1. Launch the Windows NT Explorer and choose the directory to which you would like to provide network access. Next, click your right mouse button to produce the default drop-down menu and select the Sharing option (see Figure 7.17).

FIGURE 7.17.

Creating a Share Through Explorer.

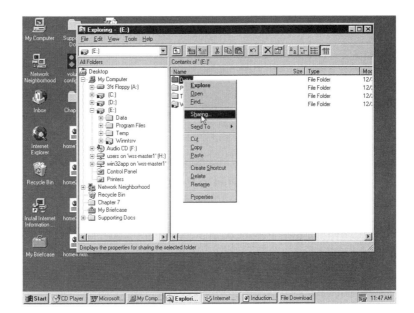

2. The Directory Properties window, as seen in Figure 7.18, will launch with the Sharing tab active. This window will appear very similar to the New Share window accessed through the Server Manager; however, when using the Explorer to create a network Share, there is no need to enter the directory path because when you selected the directory to manage, the path was automatically set.

3. Once the Sharing window is launched, creating your share is identical to the process used through the Server Manager. Click the Permissions button, and the Access Through Share Permissions window will launch (refer to Figure 7.16). The Access Through Share Permissions window is where you go to set permissions on the new share and, coincidentally, to manage permissions on existing shares.

FIGURE 7.18.

Sharing Properties Window.

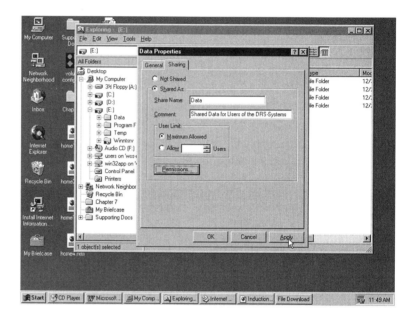

4. By default, each share has the Everyone group with Full Control applied upon creation; however, this is not a recommended setting. At this point, it is suggested that you remove the Everyone group and add the appropriate Group list by pressing the Add button.

5. You will immediately be presented with the Add Users and Groups window (as seen earlier in Figure 7.9). Set the required permission levels and click OK until you reach the Shared Directories window.

6. After setting permissions, entering a comment, and setting the User Limit (if desired), all you need to do is select Apply at the bottom of the window, and your new share will be created and accessible.

Complimenting File and Directory Permissions with Share Permissions

Sharing resources under Windows NT is not a complicated issue; however, determining what type of security levels to set can become difficult. As stated at the beginning of this chapter, Share Level Security and File and Directory Level Security should be used in a complimentary manner. By itself, Share Level Security does not provide a great deal of control; however, in conjunction with Directory Level Security, the administrator can create an extremely tight, easily managed and navigable environment.

When designing your security structure using both permission levels, you need to keep the following rules in mind:

- The lowest level of access always prevails. Therefore, if Share Level is set to Full Control for Group A, yet Directory Level is set to Read for Group A, the Group A users will have Read access to the directory and all of its subdirectories. Likewise, if Directory Level is set to Change, yet Share Level is set to No Access, the end user will be unable to connect to that directory.

- Everyone means Everyone. If you leave the Share Level permissions at their default (Everyone at Full Control), make sure you've set the appropriate Directory Level permission.

- The wrong security levels can make applications malfunction. For instance, if an application requires that the end user be able to update a database and you've set both Share and Directory levels to Read, the application most likely will not run properly.

- Share Level Security applies only to the network attached user. Those users who log on locally only have to contend with File and Directory level security.

When creating shares, keep in mind that exceeding your File and Directory Level Permissions will not affect user access; however, by setting permissions lower than those at the file and directory level, you will most likely inhibit the users functionality. Complimenting File and Directory Level Security with Share Level Permissions will be expounded upon in Chapter 8.

Hidden Shares

Up to this point, security has been discussed only in terms of explicit User or Group permissions. However, Windows NT provides one more form of security: the hidden Share. Hidden Shares provide the administrator with a level of security that at first may not seem pertinent but can become crucial to daily support operations.

To hide a share, simply add a "$" at the end of a share name. For instance, if an administrator wanted to create a hidden share to hold support utilities, the share name might be UTILS$. While no one could see the share when browsing the network, an administrator could connect by providing a path. For example:

```
Net Use K: \\HTN-PROD01\UTILS$
```

The user would then have the K:\ drive mapped to the hidden UTILS$ directory.

An excellent example for the use of a hidden share is Operating System distribution. If, as an administrator, you decided that you wanted to roll out Windows 95 to each desktop, it would be much easier to perform installations over the network rather than by attaching a CD to each workstation. Likewise, it would be extremely convenient if your support personnel could have seamless, secure access to the Windows 95 distribution files from any workstation on the network, logged in as any user in your directory. Many times, support personnel will run into a support issue that requires additional software or drivers and are grudgingly forced to close all of the end users applications, log off of the machine, and log back on with their own ID in order to access the required files. Windows 95 (as do most contemporary applications) remembers where it was installed from so a hidden share such as \\HTN-PROD01\Win95$ becomes extremely convenient when adding print drivers, network protocols, or other additional components to an existing installation. By creating a hidden share that allows all domain users to access the Win95 directory without their knowledge and by applying the appropriate security, you can make life much easier on you and your support personnel. By hiding the share, you lessen the chance that end users will find it and decide to install Windows 95 by themselves, and you provide the ability for support personnel to accomplish their tasks in less time. Additionally, by locking down access permissions on the Win95\Setup.exe file, the administrator can be sure that the source directory cannot be misused.

Administrative Shares

Each physical hard drive or volume on your server is automatically shared as an administrative share upon creation. An administrative share is set at the root of the volume and allows members of the Administrators or Domain Admins groups access. The Administrative share, which is hidden by default, cannot be seen in the Network Neighborhood but can be accessed by mapping a drive. For instance, if you happened to be remotely attached to your network and wanted to find out how much disk space remained on a certain volume, you would map a drive using the Windows NT Explorer as seen in Figure 7.19 or by typing the following at a command prompt: **Net Use I: \\DRSSPROD01\C$**. Once the drive is mapped, you may use the Windows NT Explorer to manage volume properties, including the creation of new directories, the manipulation file, and directory permissions, and you may even compress the drive. Administrative shares can be excellent tools when managing a geographically diverse enterprise.

FIGURE 7.19.

Mapping a Drive to an Administrative Share.

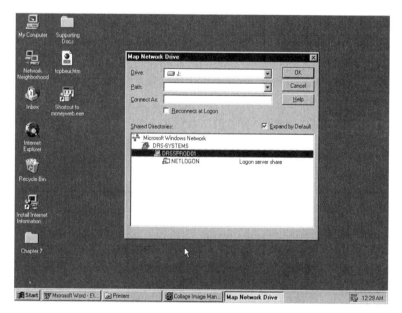

Sharing and Securing Printers

Network printing has evolved into a service that most network users and administrators now take for granted. Companies have been known to implement networks simply to save the cost of purchasing a printer for each user. Today, network printing has become so synonymous with the term "network" that the implementation and management of network printers has become an afterthought to many organizations. Luckily, Windows NT Server provides just the right combination of performance and printing features to allow users and administrators to think of printing as an afterthought. The following list identifies some of the unique print service features provided by Windows NT Server:

■ The capability to download print drivers to Microsoft clients on-the-fly

■ Direct support of printer-based Network Interface Cards

■ The elimination of the need to install print drivers on client based NT Servers and Workstations

■ A single print management interface

■ The capability to create Printer Pools for power users

■ A detailed Print Permissions interface

Basic Printer Creation

Installing printers in Windows NT Server is very similar to installing printers in Windows 95; however, there are some enhancements. Use the following procedure to create a new printer under Windows NT Server:

1. To launch the Printers folder, first go to the Start menu, select the Settings folder from the root, and choose the Printers option seen in the Setting subdirectory. Upon selection, you will be presented with the Printers window (see Figure 7.20). The Printers window has a Menu bar with the following selections: File, Edit View, and Help, followed by a standard Windows NT Tool Bar. There is also an Add Printer Wizard placed in the actual window.

2. To create a new printer, simply double-click on Add Printer. You will automatically be presented with the Add Printer Wizard (see Figure 7.21), which gives you the choice to create a local printer (My Computer) or a Network Printer Server.

3. The Network Printer Server option allows you to attach to a shared printer on another machine, while the My Computer option allows you to create a locally hosted printer. In either case, you may share the printer to users attached to your server. To attach to an existing printer server, skip to step 10, or to create a locally hosted printer, go to step 4.

4. A locally hosted printer is a printer that is not dependent on another computer to process print jobs. A locally hosted printer can be attached to a local port (serial or

parallel) or to a network attached printer with a network interface card. To install a local printer, select the My Computer option, as seen in Figure 7.21.

FIGURE 7.20.

The Printers Window.

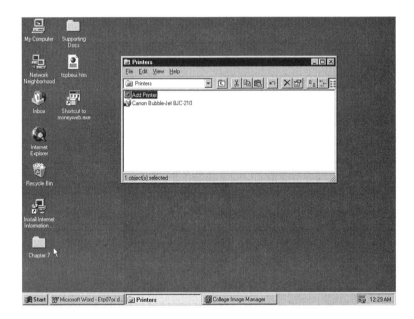

FIGURE 7.21.

The Add Printer Wizard.

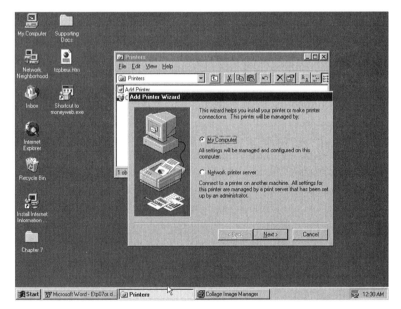

5. At this point, you will be presented with the Available Ports window as seen in Figure 7.22. The Available Ports window presents the options to connect to a currently configured port, add a new port to this computer (usually associated with a printer with a network interface card such as a JetDirect card), or configure an existing port. Using Network Interface Cards will be covered later. For the moment, assume you will install a printer to the default parallel port; therefore, select LPT1.

FIGURE 7.22.

The Available Ports Window.

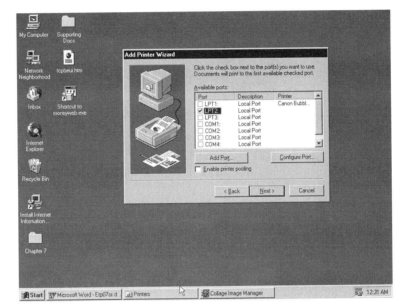

6. Once you've selected LPT1, you will be presented with a list of print drivers to choose from. This list is fairly comprehensive; however, if the printer you wish to install is not on the list of printers included with Windows NT Server 4.0, you may select the model closest to that which you have or provide the Server with the appropriate drivers. If you have the required print driver, select the Have Disk option and enter the path to the print driver. (Note that these drivers do not need to be on floppy format but can be stored locally or across the network.)

7. Once you've entered the appropriate path, you will be prompted for a printer name. As detailed on this window (see Figure 7.23), a Print Server/Printer name combination with more than 31 characters can cause issues with certain applications. A simple name, usually the name of a department or function, is appropriate.

FIGURE 7.23.

Naming a New Printer.

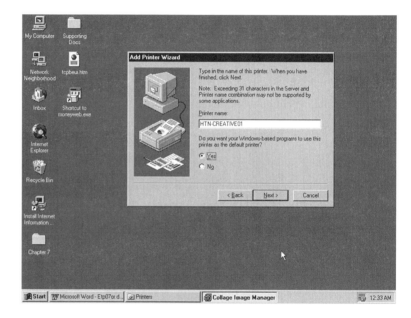

8. Once you've named your printer, you will next move to a window that provides the option to share the printer over the network. Windows NT does not assume that you plan to share every printer by default; therefore, if you don't wish to share the printer, simply move on by pressing Next. If you do plan to share this printer, simply select the Shared option as seen in Figure 7.24 and provide a name. This name, which is simply the "Shared As" name, can be different from the original name granted in Step 7. Once the name is entered, select Next.

9. Next, you will be questioned as to whether you would like to print a test page. After answering, the print drivers will be installed to the computer. Once copying has finished, the installation process for a locally hosted printer will be complete. At this point, you may begin printing.

10. When choosing to attach to an existing network print server, select the Network Print Server option. You will quickly be presented with the Connect to Printer window, as seen in Figure 7.25. Note that this window is basically nothing more than an extension of the Network Neighborhood interface; however, it only browses for Print Servers and their printers.

11. At this point, you can either wait for the browser to find all of the Print Servers in your Domain and then select the printer you need, or you may enter the UNC path of the printer. For example, if the Print Server was named HTN-PROD01 and the printer was named Creative01, the UNC path would be \\HTN-PROD01\Creative01. Once you've selected the printer you need, regardless of in which manner, select Next.

FIGURE 7.24.

Sharing the Printer.

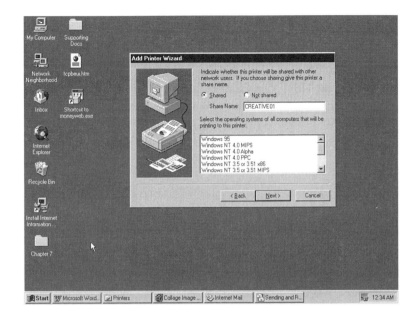

FIGURE 7.25.

The Connect to Printer Screen.

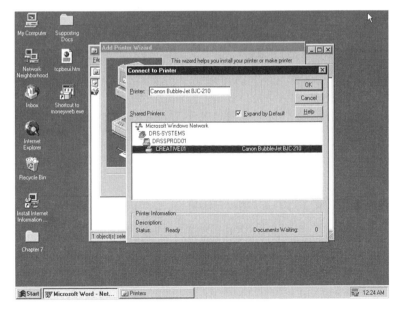

12. In most cases, when connecting to an existing Print Server, you will be forced to install a print driver on your network client. This is not the case if you happen to be using the same version of Windows NT on both your network client and your Print Server. Since the Print Server and the network client utilize the same print process and the same print driver, the Print Server needs no additional translation from the client. This is a nice feature that is unique to Windows NT.

13. If the Print Server is not hosted on a Windows NT 4.0 server, you will be informed that the Print Server does not have a suitable print driver for your workstation, and you will be given the option to install the correct software. In most cases, the Windows NT Print Server will inform you as to which type of printer you're attempting to attach to. This is significant in two ways: First, as mentioned earlier, if you are running the same version of Windows NT as the Print Server, you will not be required to install a print driver on your server. Second, due to the fact that Windows NT lends the capability to install print drivers for almost all Windows platforms on the server in such a way that print drivers can be automatically installed on the client workstation, it helps the Print Server to know which printer you're installing.

14. If the print driver is hosted on the Print Server, you will be prompted to make a decision between using the current driver or installing a new driver. Next, you will be asked if you want this printer to be your default printer. As long as the print drivers exist on the Print Server, you will be informed that the printer has been successfully installed. If, on the other hand, there is not a suitable print driver on the Print Server, you will be prompted for the location of the print driver. Once the location is provided, whether it be network based or local, the appropriate files will be copied to your workstation, and you will be asked if you want to use the printer as your default. In either case, as soon as the printer has been installed, printing may begin immediately.

> **NOTE**
>
> The printer installation process can also be launched while browsing servers in the Network Neighborhood. When browsing a server, you will also see the printers it hosts. By double-clicking on one of these printers, the installation process will be initialized. From this point on, printer installation is identical to the process listed earlier.

Managing Print Properties

Once you've installed and initially shared a printer, there are many configuration options available. To manage a printer, go to the Start menu and choose Settings, followed by Printers. Once you've opened the Printers window as seen in Figure 7.26, you will be presented with a list of printers that are locally hosted on your Windows NT Server. To manage a printer, simply launch its properties by using the drop-down menu, the Properties button, or the window's Tool Bar menu, and choose Properties. A printer's Properties window consists of six tabs. Each tab has multiple options that may or may not contribute to your environment. Those tabs, as seen in Figure 7.27, are General, Ports, Scheduling, Sharing, Security, and Device Settings.

Figure 7.26.

The Printers Window.

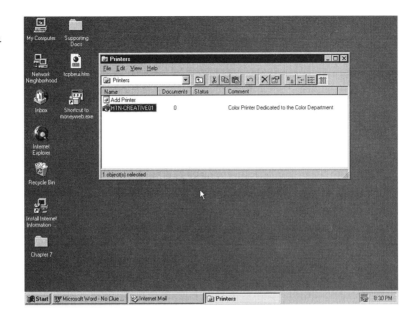

Figure 7.27.

*The Printer Properties
Windows.*

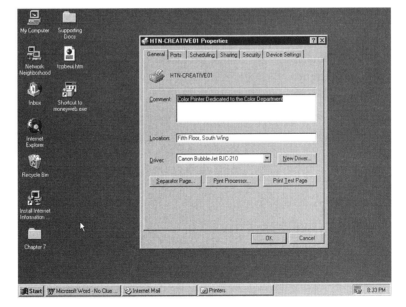

The General Tab

The General tab, as seen in Figure 7.27, provides the following options:

- Print Driver Updates or Replacements
- The modification of the print processor
- Separator page selecting
- The addition of a printer description or comment

Other than the printer description and comment fields, most options provided in the General tab will remain at their defaults. The only other option that is of any true value within this page is the capability to designate a separator page; however, even this is unusual.

The Ports Tab

The Ports tab is where you will go to manage the printer ports that your printers are connected to. The Ports window, as seen in Figure 7.28, allows you to:

- Change the port that your printer is connected to
- Add a port, including a printer with a network interface card attached
- Configure an existing port
- Set up a Printer pool

While changing a port that a printer is connected to is fairly self explanatory, Printer Pooling, Port Configuration, and Adding ports require some additional explanation.

FIGURE 7.28.

The Printer Ports Window.

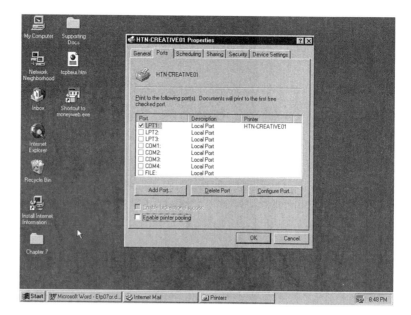

Printer Pooling

A Printer Pool is a group of printers that are hosted locally on your machine that have been shared as a single printer. For instance, if you were to install six identical printers and set them up as a pooled printer, the end user would see only one printer when browsing the network. This is an excellent tool in a high print volume environment. When the user goes to print a document, the print job will print on the first available printer, eliminating wasted time. Adding a Print Pool is fairly easy. Simply select the Enable Print Pooling option and choose the ports that your printers are connected to. After closing out the printer's properties, you will have a fully functional Printer Pool.

Adding Printer Ports

In addition to printer pooling, you may also add entirely new printer ports through this page. The Printer Ports window allows you to add a new local port or to set up a Printer Network Interface card. By default you may attach to a printer using a Digital printer NIC, a Lexmark printer NIC, or an HP JetDirect card. Each manufacturer provides the appropriate documentation for connecting to their network interface cards; however, the HP JetDirect is the most often used, so it will be covered in this chapter. There are two ways to connect to an HP JetDirect card: The first manner utilizes the services built into Windows NT, and the second is using a more advanced utility recently released by Hewlett-Packard.

DLC Connectivity

In order to connect to an HP JetDirect card using the services that are built into Windows NT Server, you must first load the DLC protocol using the Network Properties dialog. Once complete, you must run a self-test on the JetDirect card in order to produce the MAC address; however, if you are using an external model, the MAC address will be prominently labeled on the bottom. To add the port, select the Add Port button, and you will be presented with the Printer Ports window, as seen in Figure 7.29.

Choose the Hewlett-Packard Network Port, and you will be presented with the window shown in the bottom of Figure 7.29. Notice that this window provides a place to enter the Port Name as well as the Card Address. The Port Name is not necessarily the name of the printer; however, you can name it so if you like. Instead, the port name will be the name used to differentiate this port from other like network ports or the physical ports that actually exist on your server. In most cases, the window provided underneath the Card Address text box will list the MAC addresses of all of the JetDirect cards on your network. Be sure to reference the self test you printed earlier to ensure that you're connecting to the correct device. If, for some reason, your chosen device is not listed in this window, you may still connect to it by manually entering the card address.

Once you've selected the correct device, press OK, followed by Close on the previous window. Once the port is added, the Port Name will be added to the list of ports in the Ports window (see Figure 7.30). At this point, you may treat this port as if it were a locally installed device.

FIGURE 7.29.

*Adding a DLC-Based
HP JetDirect Device.*

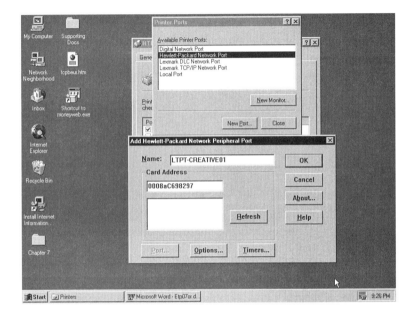

FIGURE 7.30.

*The Updated Ports
List.*

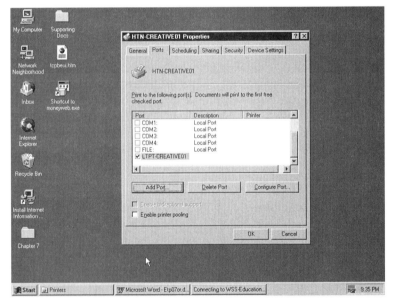

The Scheduling Tab

Following the Ports tab is the Scheduling tab seen in Figure 7.31, which provides advanced multiple options to the administrator. From the Scheduling tab, you may perform the following:

- Set the time availability for your printer
- Set the default priority of documents that enter the print queue
- Determine whether or not to spool print jobs or print them immediately as they enter the queue
- Decide whether or not to hold documents that have been assigned mismatched print size and page setup
- Choose whether to print spooled documents before those coming in
- Choose whether to keep documents in the queue after they have been printed

FIGURE 7.31.

The Scheduling Page of a Printer's Properties.

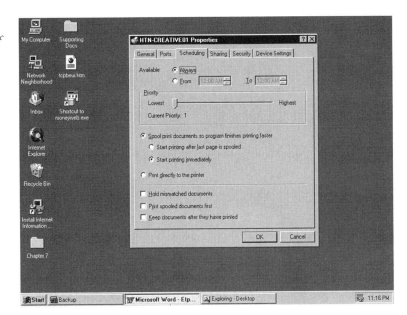

This page is one that is very rarely modified; however, if you decide that any of these settings are pertinent to your environment, you will most likely set them once and not modify again.

The Sharing Tab

The Sharing tab (see Figure 7.32), while at first may not seem to offer much in the way of functionality, can actually have a considerable impact on the productivity of your support personnel. From the Sharing tab, you may perform the following three things:

- Share an existing locally hosted printer
- Stop sharing an existing locally hosted printer
- Install and host print drivers for multiple Microsoft platforms

FIGURE 7.32.

The Sharing Page of a Printer's Properties.

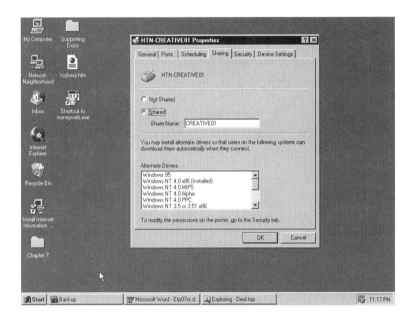

Sharing a printer with the Printer properties dialog is identical to the process used when initially creating a printer; simply check the Shared option and enter a printer name. To stop sharing a printer, you must only check the Not Shared option on this page. Once complete, your printer will no longer be broadcast on the network, nor will it be available to the end user.

The more advanced and time-saving feature available on this page is the capability to host print drivers for Windows 95 and previous versions, and optional platforms of Windows NT. These print drivers will automatically be made available to all end users who connect to your printer. For example, if you install a new HP LaserJet printer that was released after your standard desktop operating system came out, your technicians would normally have to carry those print drivers with them in order to properly install the new printer on your user's desktop. Using the Print Driver hosting feature of Windows NT, your server will store those print drivers in such a way that when your end user or support personnel go to connect to the new printer, they will have the option to allow Windows NT to install the print drivers for them. This is a feature unique to Windows NT Server and is a tremendous help in everyday support situations.

Installing these alternative print drivers is fairly simple. In the Alternate Drivers window of the Sharing properties page, there is a list of the operating systems for the platforms for which print drivers can be hosted. To install the necessary print drivers for download to your workstations, simply highlight each required platform one at a time and select OK. You will be prompted for the path of the alternative print drivers. Once given, they will be installed in such a way that when a client computer attempts to attach to your Print Server for the first time, they will be given the opportunity to install the print drivers directly.

Printer Security

The Printer Security tab as seen in Figure 7.33 is much like the Security properties tab utilized to manage permissions for files and directories. Through this page, print permissions can be managed, printer use can be audited, and printer ownership can be manipulated.

FIGURE 7.33.

The Printer Security Page.

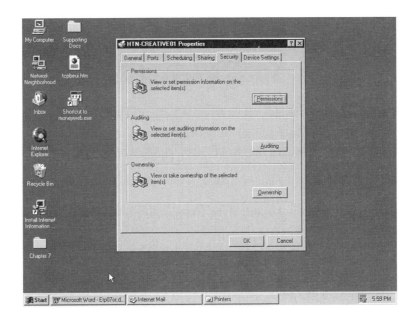

Printer Auditing

Printer use auditing is very similar to that of File and Directory use auditing. To audit a printer's use, simply select the Auditing button, and you will be presented with a window like that in Figure 7.34.

In order for Auditing to be enabled, a User or Group must be added to this page. You may track the success or failure of the following actions: printing documents, the use of Full Control rights, the use of Delete Rights, the use of Change Permissions rights, and the use of Take Ownership rights. It is important to note, however, that any time an event you have chosen to audit occurs, it will be logged in the Security portion of the Event Log. If you do not set your Event Log file size up properly, you will constantly be faced with an Event Log full message.

Figure 7.34.

Printer Auditing Configuration.

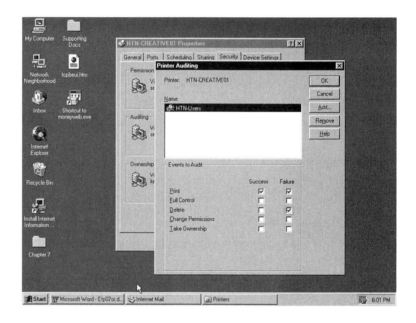

Printer Security

Print Permissions are similar to network Share Level Permissions in that they are fairly basic. Print Permissions can be managed by pressing the Permissions button as seen in Figure 7.33. Print permissions in Windows NT are as follows:

- **No Access**

    When set for a user or group, denies access to the printer.

- **Print**

    When set for a user or group, allows them to print to a printer.

- **Manage Documents**

    Allows a user or group to control job settings, pause, restart a print jobs and delete a document.

- **Full Control**

    Allows a user or group to control job settings, pause, and restart a print job, delete documents, purge the printer, change printer permissions, and delete a printer altogether.

If you desire to restrict print permissions to certain users, simply press the Add button, as seen in Figure 7.35, and you will be presented with the very familiar Add Users and Groups window. Simply choose the required groups and set the desired security levels. Once you close out of the permissions window, security settings will have changed.

The following permissions are granted to each printer by default:

Group/Object	Permission
Administrators	Full Control
Creator/Owner	Manage Documents
Everyone	Print
Print Operators	Full Control
Server Operators	Full Control

FIGURE 7.35.

Default Printer Permissions.

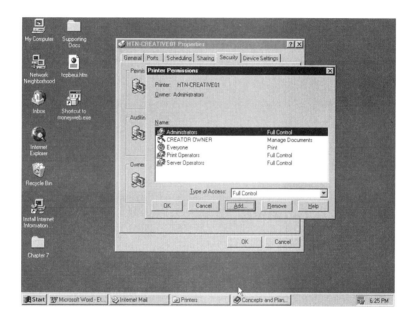

Device Settings

The final tab of the Printer Properties dialog is the Device Settings page. This page contains settings that are pertinent only to the printer you are managing. For instance, if your printer can handle 11×17 paper, you would specify which tray it is contained in, or you might set the default resolution of all documents. All of the settings you define through this tab will be passed along to any Windows NT Workstation or Server that connects to your Print Server.

Remote Management

You can manage a local or remote Print Server from any Windows NT or Windows 95 client on the network, as long as you are a member of the Print Operators, Administrators, Server Operators, or Account Operators group. Additionally, if you are not a member of those groups but have been granted Full Control to a printer, you will be able to manage local or remote printers. Keep in mind that in order to manage a remote Windows NT Printer, it is required that you be running Windows NT or Windows 95 on your desktop. As mentioned earlier in the chapter, you can manage remote printers by selecting a Print Server through the Network Neighborhood, opening the Printers folder, and clicking on the desired printer. You can manage all aspects of a printer from a remote Windows NT workstation, excluding port configuration.

Summary

This chapter covered the basic concepts concerning File and Directory Level Permissions, Shares, and Share Permissions, the relationship between File, Directory Level, and Share Level Permissions, as well as the concepts behind creating and managing shared printers. Chapter 8 will expand on the information provided in this chapter by providing implementation philosophies and concepts in conjunction with the three deployment models endorsed throughout this book.

Designing Your Enterprise Resource Structure

IN THIS CHAPTER

CHAPTER

8

A key factor in Design Objective Two: A Standard User Environment is a well-designed infrastructure in which to share resources with the end user. The manner in which you share resources throughout your enterprise not only is significant to the supportability of your deployment, but also has a tremendous impact on end-user productivity. In order to provide structure not only for your support personnel, but more importantly for your end user, it is critical that you share resources from server to server in a consistent manner. The standardization of resource sharing involves such factors as

- Directory Structure
- Directory Naming Conventions
- Share Points
- Share Naming Conventions
- Printer Sharing
- Printer Naming Conventions
- The Application of User Security

Each of these factors, if deployed properly, will combine to create a standard look and feel to your environment across domains and throughout your enterprise that not only enhances productivity, but also improves supportability. This chapter will discuss the issues involved with each of these factors and provide examples throughout using the three Deployment Models endorsed by this book. This chapter will tie together the User Directory concepts discussed in Chapter 4, "Designing Your Domain," the server deployment models advocated in Chapter 5, "Server Standardization, Installation, and Implementation," and the resource-sharing and security concepts discussed in Chapter 7, "Sharing and Securing Resources."

Standard Directory Structure

The goal in resource sharing should be to provide the least number of access points for the most common resources while maintaining a high level of security. This goal is achieved through a well-designed server directory structure. There are five steps in determining the best directory structure for your environment:

1. You must categorize the types of server-based resources you will share with your end users.
2. You must determine a standard directory structure based on your categorizations.
3. You must set Directory and Share naming conventions to be observed from server to server.
4. Based on the end-user need, you must apply the appropriate levels of Share and File and Directory level security.
5. You must keep this structure consistent throughout your enterprise.

Resource Categorization

In most companies, server-based resources can be placed in eight categories: office automation applications, development applications, critical applications, common data, secured data, project data, personal directories, and support resources. These categories are defined as follows:

■ **Office Automation Applications**

Office Automation applications are those applications that are required by the basic user to perform their job duties. These applications include such items as word processors, spreadsheets, terminal emulators, e-mail, and database applications.

■ **Development Applications**

Development applications include packages like C++, Visual Basic, Java, SmallTalk, FrontPage, and JavaScript. These tools are used primarily in the development of proprietary applications or those applications to be sold.

■ **Critical Applications**

Critical Applications are applications like SNA Server, SQL Server, DHCP or DNS Server, Platinum Enterprise Manager, or some such application that could potentially affect more than just those users who attach to a server for standard production resources. Critical applications should generally have their own dedicated server.

■ **Common Data**

Common data is that data which is not necessarily sensitive that can be shared from department to department in a common data structure. Common data, while important to the end user, does not require an intense security environment.

■ **Secured Data**

Secured data is departmentally sensitive data that requires the utmost in security. While it is possible to provide intense security within the common directory structure, those groups that require secured data often feel better if this data is somehow segregated.

■ **Project Data**

Project data is data that is related to a specific project or group. Project data can be in a common directory or structure but is often segregated for much the same reasons that sensitive data is segregated.

■ **Personal Directories**

Personal directories are end-user home directories that are provided for the sole usage of storing personal files in a secure manner.

■ **Support Resources**

Support resources are those resources required by your support personnel to perform their daily tactical functions. Support resources are often troubleshooting utilities, configuration tools, printer and network card drivers, client software packages, and knowledge resources. Support resources are accessed only by your support personnel.

A good way to drive home the importance of resource categorization and directory structure standardization is to provide an illustration of a bad deployment. The InterDepartmental representative, the Horton Agency, is a prime example of a badly planned deployment. As it exists today, the Horton Agency is using a NetWare server to provide common production resources to the end user. As is the case in many organizations, when the server was originally deployed, it was brought in for the sole purpose of printing, storing data, and running basic applications such as Lotus and WordPerfect. The original data structure, which initially worked well, appeared as in Figure 8.1.

FIGURE 8.1.

Original NetWare Directory Structure.

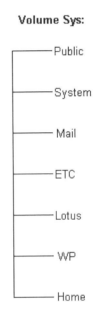

Volume Sys:

- Public
- System
- Mail
- ETC
- Lotus
- WP
- Home

During initial deployment, the server had only one volume, and the administrator provided only four standard mapped drives:

L:\ for Lotus

W:\ for WordPerfect

H:\ for Home

P:\ for Public

This structure was very easy to manage and easily navigated by the end user. However, as the environment and needs at the Horton Agency began to change, the frailty of this structure shone through. The move to additional applications was slow; therefore, a cluttered structure crept into the Horton Environment. Users began to request departmentally specific applications and secured DATA Volumes and proprietary services. As a result, after a few years the Horton Environment consisted of the following volume and directory structure as seen in Figure 8.2.

FIGURE 8.2.

The Horton Agency's Existing NetWare Volume Structure.

Volume Sys:
- Public
- System
- Mail
- ETC
- Lotus
- WP
- Home
- Paradox
- HG
- MRKTG
- Peach

Volume Sys1:
- WP60
- Excel
- Apps
- Dept
- Training

Volume Sys2:
- Autocad
- MacData
- HR
- CCMail

Due to the disorganization of the volumes, data, and applications, the end user was stuck with an environment that provided no standardization. While the original implementation had only four drive mappings that were consistent from user to user, the final implementation consisted of somewhere between 10 and 14 mappings for each user, with multiple variations and very little commonality. As a result, both the end user and the support personnel were easily confused when troubleshooting issues and new user orientation to the environment became a month-long process.

This example, while at first might seem slightly extreme, can be seen in multiple implementations of not only NetWare, but also OS/2 LAN Server, MS LAN Manager, and Windows NT as well. This disorganized environment was brought on by the rapid changes in technology and the services offered by applications. Today, while technology is moving at an even faster pace, we have the benefit of hindsight when designing our directory structure.

When designing directory structure, it is important to keep in mind not only the standard resources you wish to provide to your end users, but also the simplicity in which you wish to provide those resources. The number of mapped drives should be kept to a minimum, and their drive letters should provide consistent resource types from server to server throughout your enterprise.

Today at the Horton Agency, resources would be categorized as follows:

■ **Office Automation Applications**

Microsoft Office, Novell GroupWise, Project Manager, TeamManager 97, Internet Explorer, Graphics/Animation Applications, and Desktop Publishing applications.

- **Development Applications**

  None.

- **Critical Applications**

  SQL-based Accounting/Billing application.

- **Common Data**

  Nonsecure, common data to be shared cross-departmentally.

- **Secured Data**

  Departmentally secure or sensitive data, as well as administrative information.

- **Project Data**

  Data sorted by specific clients and current jobs in production for those clients.

- **Home Directories**

  End-user secured home directories.

- **Support Resources**

  Desktop Operating systems and support utilities.

Scalablity is a crucial component of directory structure design. A critical lack of scalability is evident in the existing NetWare deployment at Horton. This lack of growth potential is not due to the operating system; however, it is due to the lack of foresight when the original deployment was made. Keeping in mind that while the current breadth of applications and resources could potentially expand the way the original resources expanded, the directory structure you implement should be prepared for this growth. Through resource categorization, you should be able to create a scalable directory structure. For example, you might utilize the directory structure as shown in Figure 8.3.

As you can see, this directory structure has only four entry points, providing access to the most common resources you will provide your end users. These entry points, which are a direct result of the categorization of resources, allows for easy navigability and expansion. For instance, under Applications there are three subdirectories: Win32app, Win16app, and Devapps. These subdirectories are provided as a device for not only dividing development applications from general production applications, but also to segregate 32-bit applications from 16-bit applications. This type of segregation goes a long way in avoiding any confusion and helping to eliminate configuration mistakes. If a new 32-bit application your corporation requires is released, it is not necessary to create a new directory structure simply for that application; you only need to place it in the appropriate subdirectory under the Applications directory. Additionally, when 64-bit applications arrive on the market, a simple addition to this structure (Win64app) will provide the scalability required by an ever-changing enterprise. In combination with File and Directory Level Security, this directory structure provides excellent manageability for the support personnel, as well as easy access and intuitive orientation for the end user.

FIGURE 8.3.
A Scalable Directory Structure.

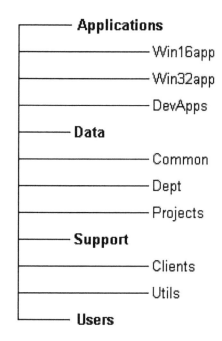

Applications
—— Win16app
—— Win32app
—— DevApps
Data
—— Common
—— Dept
—— Projects
Support
—— Clients
—— Utils
Users

The Application of File and Directory Level Security

By design, the recommended directory structure simply allows for the elimination of multiple major entry points to resources by categorizing resource types under major headings; however, under those major headings, or primary directories, it would seem that anyone could access any applications or data. It is through a combination of an efficient directory structure, well-placed network shares, and File and Directory Level permissions that you can apply strict controls while still retaining your easily managed and navigated directory structure. File and Directory Level Permissions, which were covered in Chapter 7 are a critical part of a successful deployment. The following section of this chapter will discuss the design and implementation of volume and directory structure, in conjunction with File and Directory Level Permissions and a well-designed User Directory for each of the three recommended deployment models.

The InterDepartmental Deployment

Before a successful deployment of resources can be made, it is important that you have developed and implemented your basic User Directory structure and determined how you will deploy servers in your domain. In Chapter 4, the basic user directory for the Horton Agency was determined, and in Chapter 5, the basic domain deployment was outlined. Following is a review of the Horton Domain's design to this point.

The Basic User Directory

The following list is a reminder of the Horton Domain's directory design:

Basic User Group:

> HTN-Users   Basic Users of the Horton Domain

Departmental Groups:

> HTN-Creative   Creative Users of the Horton Domain
>
> HTN-Accounting   Accounting Users of the Horton Domain
>
> HTN-Sales   Sales Users of the Horton Domain
>
> HTN-Admin   Administrative Users of the Horton Domain

Remember, the Basic User Group is the organizational foundation of the User Directory. All users, with the exception of support personnel, should be members of the Basic User group. The Basic User group will be granted access to all common resources throughout the Domain, while the Departmental Groups are designed to provide restricted access to departmentally secure resources such as data or departmental applications.

InterDepartmental Support Personnel Considerations

In NetWare, being granted Supervisor equivalency automatically overrides all file and directory restrictions; however, in Windows NT, no such entity exists. While being granted membership in the Domain Admins or Administrators group gives a user the ability to manage a server's resources, including the User Directory, such membership does not override file- and directory-level permissions. In most organizations, the support group will be granted more file and directory privileges than the basic users; however, keep in mind that if THOMPSONJ is a member of the Domain Admins group as well as a member of the basic user group, and both groups are given access permission to a directory structure, THOMPSONJ will receive the lower level of access. For this reason, there are several suggestions when designing your deployment of resources:

- Do not grant Domain Administrators membership in any group other than Domain Admins or Administrators.

- Create a separate group for your tactical support technicians (such as HTN-Support).

- If you have differing levels of support technicians and wish to stratify their access, create a group for each tier.

- Unless you specifically desire to limit their permissions to those of a basic, departmental, or enterprise group, do not add your support technicians to any additional groups.

- When applying security to a directory structure, remember that you must add the Domain Admins, the Administrators group, and any support group to any directory you wish for those users to have access to.

Keeping these guidelines in mind, the Horton Agency determined that it was necessary to create a two-tiered support structure. The first tier, Domain Admins, consisted of two individuals that provided high-level desktop, NOS, and infrastructure support, as well as strategic enterprise management. The second tier, named HTN-Support, is made of the three individuals that provided desktop, application, and basic infrastructure support to the end user. Many organizations also employ a help desk with advanced yet limited access when compared to desktop technicians. If this is the case, an additional group will be required.

InterDepartmental Server Deployment

Server deployment in the InterDepartmental Domain (see Figure 8.4) generally consists of one or two production servers and often has the potential for additional application servers. For the Horton Agency, it was determined that a single office automation server (HTN-PROD01) doubling as the Primary Domain Controller was sufficient. However, it was also decided that two application servers would be required to meet the performance and fault tolerance needs of the organization.

FIGURE 8.4.

The InterDepartmental Deployment.

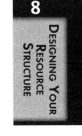

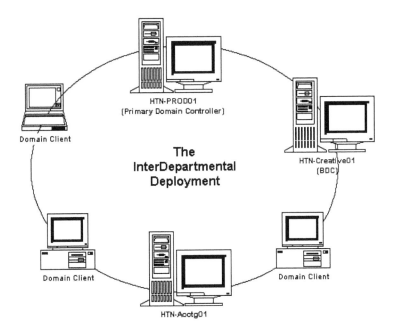

The first application server, HTN-ACCTG01, belongs to the Accounting department. The Accounting department uses a sophisticated accounting package that keeps track not only of internal accounting, but also keeps track of project expense and customer billing. This application requires an SQL Server back-end and has two periods during the month where heavy processing will be required.

The second application server, HTN-CREATIVE01, which is more of a performance enhancement than a mission critical need, belongs to the Creative Department. The Creative department works with extremely large multimedia files that will be created and accessed on a regular basis. These files not only will take up considerable network bandwidth, but also will tax the production server's resources as reads and writes occur. If these files remained on the production server, the result would be a slowed response to the end user.

InterDepartmental Directory Structure

Once the Directory and the Server Deployment have been determined, you should evaluate the types of resources you plan to share with the end user and create a sensible categorization scheme. In most cases before you begin your resource categorization, you will know which applications will require dedicated servers and which will fit just fine on your Office Automation production server. It is possible that once you've categorized your shared resources, you will find that you require an application server you didn't originally anticipate. While this type of discovery happens infrequently, it is just another benefit of resource categorization.

Once you've determined your categories, you should design an appropriate directory structure. In most organizations, the categories of office automation applications, development applications, critical applications, secured data, common data, project data, and support resources are sufficient; however, it is possible that more are required for your deployment. As it stands today, the Horton Agency does not have a categorized Volume and Directory structure. Earlier in this chapter, the Horton Agency's resources were categorized as follows:

- **Office Automation Applications**

    Microsoft Office, Novell GroupWise, Project Manager, TeamManager 97, Internet Explorer, Graphics/Animation applications, and Desktop Publishing applications.

- **Office Automation Applications**

    Microsoft Office, Novell GroupWise, Project Manager, TeamManager 97, Internet Explorer, Graphics/Animation Applications, and Desktop Publishing applications.

- **Development Applications**

    None.

- **Critical Applications**

    SQL-based Accounting/Billing application.

- **Common Data**

    Nonsecure, common data to be shared cross-departmentally.

- **Secured Data**

    Departmentally secure or sensitive data, as well as administrative information.

- **Project Data**

    Data sorted by specific clients and current jobs in production for those clients.

■ **Home Directories**

End user secured home directories.

■ **Support Resources**

Desktop Operating systems and support utilities.

Keeping the Server deployment model in mind, it has been determined that the sole critical application, the Accounting Package, will exist on its own dedicated application server, and a good portion of the multimedia files pertaining to projects will reside on a dedicated data server. The following section will detail a solid directory structure design for each of the servers deployed within the Horton Domain.

HTN-PROD01: The Production Server

The main production server for the Horton Domain, HTN-PROD01, consists of four main directory structures: Application, Data, Support, and Users.

FIGURE 8.5.

High-Level Overview of the Suggested Directory Structure for the Horton Agency.

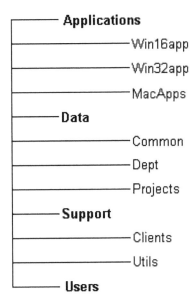

8

DESIGNING YOUR RESOURCE STRUCTURE

Applications

Notice that under the Applications directory structure, the subdirectory of MacApps has been added to the suggested structure earlier in this chapter. This simple subdirectory addition is an easy way to expand the directory structure without creating an alternative entry point into the server's resources or cluttering the root of the volume. In addition to MacApps, the Applications directory contains the subdirectories of Win16apps and Win32apps. While the Horton Agency plans to move away from a 16-bit desktop and thus toward 32-bit applications, there may be a need for some 16-bit applications during migration to the new server or for legacy purposes. By creating this separation between 16-bit and 32-bit applications, the administrator can control access to 16-bit apps on an as-needed basis.

Data

The Data directory is the root of many pitfalls. Traditional deployments, dating back to the first LAN Manager and NetWare installs, contained a Public or Common data directory structure. Soon, departments began to request segregated directory structures. Because no one really knew how the use of the file server would expand, those volumes and directory structures grew into convoluted support nightmares. Data, much like all shared resources, should be categorized and organized. Once categorized, the Horton Agency's Data structure was organized as in Figure 8.6.

FIGURE 8.6.

The Data Directory Structure for HTN-PROD01.

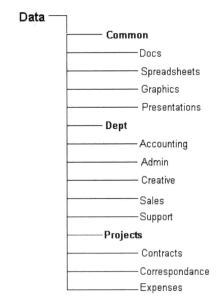

The Common subdirectory is where common data will be stored. The departmental (Dept) directory has a subdirectory for each major department within the organization. This structure is where secured data will be stored. The Projects directory will be used to organize and store documents pertaining to current and ongoing projects and campaigns. This structure will allow a single entry point into all of the most frequently accessed data within the organization.

Support

The Support directory structure is fairly simple. It is a central, yet segregated, location to store all of your support utilities, tools, applications, and operating systems. A solid support directory structure might look like the one in Figure 8.7.

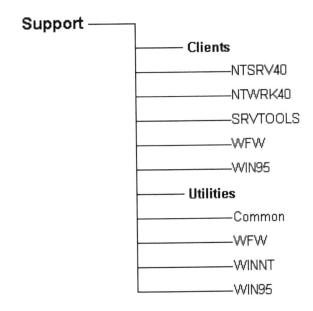

FIGURE 8.7.
*Suggested Support
Directory Structure.*

The Clients directory would be a central point for the distribution of operating systems, while the Utilities directory would be organized for operating system-specific utilities, tools, and drivers, as well as provide for common items.

Users

The Users directory is relatively simple and will be common among all production servers in any environment. The Users directory is for the end user's home directories. Any files that should not be viewed by anyone other than themselves, or files that are in pre-production, should be stored in the user's home directory. As you'll see in Chapter 9, "Managing Users," each time a user is created they will be assigned a secured home directory.

HTN-CREATIVE01: The Data Server

The HTN-CREATIVE01 server will hold the multimedia files for every campaign that the Horton Agency works on. There will not only be a great deal of account specific information, but there will also be a tremendous amount of common source files as well. Therefore, it makes sense to create one major directory structure that is broken up into two divisions: Campaign and Common (see Figure 8.8).

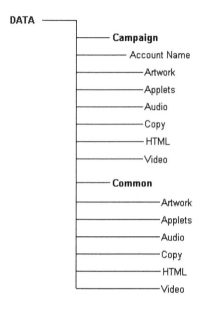

FIGURE 8.8.

The HTN-CREATIVE01 Directory Structure.

NOTE

This server will take constant large files hits. Even though it will be dedicated solely to serving these files to a small group of people, it is a good idea to either install two high-performance network cards in the server or to place this server and its dedicated users on a high-speed or switched network segment.

Campaign

The Campaign directory structure will be broken down on an account-by-account basis. Each account will have the same directory structure: Artwork, Appletts, Audio, Copy, HTML, and Video. This will lend a great deal of familiarity to the process of storing and retrieving multimedia files, making the server more navigable for the end user and easier to support for the network technicians.

Common

The Common directory structure will be similar to the Campaign directory structure in that all files will be broken down into the subdirectories of Artwork, Appletts, Audio, Copy, HTML, and Video. The major difference between the Common subdirectory and the Campaign subdirectory is that the files in Common are not account specific, however, they can be utilized from account to account and campaign to campaign.

HTN-ACCTG01: The Application Server

The HTN-ACCTG01 application server will not be used for anything other than the corporate accounting system. The application, which will build its own predetermined directory structure, will be installed in a directory named Accounting. Additionally, SQL Server will be installed in the SQL directory. Other than those directories created during the Windows NT Server installation, no other directories will exist on the HTN-ACCTG01 server.

File and Directory Level Permissions in the InterDepartmental Deployment

Once you have determined your directory structure, it is time to consider not only the application of permissions, but also the volume structure you will deploy. In Windows NT Server 4.0, there is no way to limit a user's use of disk space; therefore, when implementing your directory structure, it is important that you take into account storage needs. The following guidelines should be used when implementing your directory structure:

- As suggested in Chapter 5, create separate boot and system partitions. The boot partition is useful in supporting Windows NT Server, while the System Partition will ensure room for OS growth.

- Create separate volumes for your Data structure and your Applications structure to ensure one won't inhibit the immediate needs of the other.

- When creating your Applications Volume, estimate the space currently required by your applications and double it. You can count on future versions of applications being larger than in their current form.

- Do not allow users to write to your Application Volume unless absolutely necessary. This ensures that you will always have space for upgrades and new applications.

- Do not allow users to write to the volume containing your system files. There are two reasons for this limitation: first, you cannot expand the size of your system partition; and, second, if you take up too much of the system partition, your server's performance will slow considerably and possibly crash.

- If the server will also be used as a central store for all support tools and utilities, create a separate Support Volume. This will inhibit the possibility of limiting growth in any other volumes as operating systems get larger and utilities change.

> **NOTE**
>
> The next version of Windows NT Server, code named Cairo, is rumored to have built-in support for end user disk quotas. As it stands today, there are at least two companies that provide disk quota, add-on services for Windows NT Server; however, it is not known if the next version of Windows NT will coexist with their products.

8

DESIGNING YOUR RESOURCE STRUCTURE

Using the guidelines provided, the remainder of this section will outline the application of file- and directory-level permissions on each server in the Horton Domain. These guidelines are basic to all deployment models; however, the scale of the InterDivisional and InterCorporate models is much larger.

HTN-PROD01: The Production Server

HTN-PROD01, as seen in Figure 8.9, is the major production server for the Horton Domain. This server will be relied upon daily to provide office automation production to over 100 people. The application of permissions and a scaleable directory structure are crucial to the success of this server.

FIGURE 8.9.

HTN-PROD01—The Horton Agency's Main Production Server.

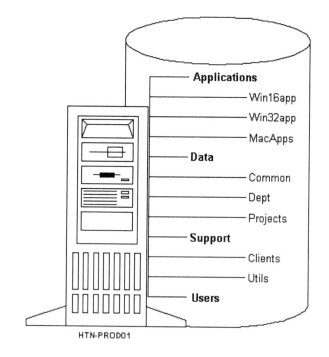

HTN-PROD01

Applications

The Horton Agency has decided to segregate their applications from their data by creating a three Gigabyte Applications Volume and a two Gigabyte DATA Volume. In the Applications Volume, they will create a directory structure consisting of a root directory entitled Applications, and the subdirectories of Win16app, Win32app, and MacApps. All users will have access to both the Win32app and MacApps directories; however, only those users that have not yet been migrated to a Win32 desktop, or that require access to a 16-bit application, will have access to the Win16app directory structure. Remember that by default, all new directories will provide Full Control access to the Everyone group, which is counteractive to true security. To accomplish the desired level of access control, the following steps must occur:

1. First, launch the Windows NT Explorer and select the Applications directory. Open the properties dialog and select the Security tab.

2. Set access permissions as follows: HTN-Users = Read, HTN-Support = Read, and Domain Admins = Full Control. This will allow all users of your support group and basic users group to view directories and run applications but not write in the root directory.

3. If you desire to allow your support personnel to add files, directories, and applications in the root of your Applications directory, simply provide them with Change level access.

4. Choose the Replace Permissions on Existing Directories and Replace Permissions on Existing Files options. Once complete, you will have set the correct basic level of access for both the Win32app and MacApps directories (see Figure 8.10).

FIGURE 8.10.

Permissions for the Root Applications Directory.

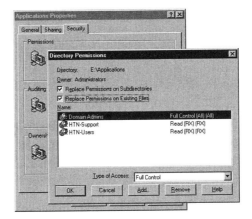

8

DESIGNING YOUR RESOURCE STRUCTURE

CAUTION

Remember that propagating permissions throughout a directory structure using Windows NT Explorer does not augment but replaces existing permissions. If you plan to propagate similar changes to an existing directory structure, make sure that you know if there are any application directories that will require your end user to modify or delete files or directories. Additionally, if you plan to make such changes during production hours, it is suggested that you do not propagate permissions to all files and directories, yet make changes one directory at a time to ensure that you do not accidentally knock people out of open application sessions.

> **NOTE**
>
> Due to the fact that Administrators in the Horton Domain wish to control the use of 16-bit applications, it is necessary to create a new Enterprise Group - ENT-Win16app. (Remember that ENT was chosen as the prefix for Enterprise Groups within the Horton Domain.) Select the Win16app directory and change permissions as follows: HTN-Support = Read, ENT-WIN16APP = Read, and Domain Admins = Full Control. Propagate these permissions throughout the directory structure. Once complete, only the support personnel and those users in the ENT-WIN16APP group will have access to the Win16app directory. All applications installed in this directory structure will inherit these permissions.

Once the base permissions for the Win16app, Win32app, and MacApps directories have been set, it is necessary to determine which applications require the end user to have Change level access. For instance, in Microsoft Office Professional versions 4.3 and 7.0, the end user must be able to modify files in the Workdir directory, which exists as a subdirectory in the root of the MSOffice directory. All applications installed in the three major subdirectories, Win16app, Win32app, and MacApps, will inherit their root permissions; thus, upon installation, Access won't work properly. In order to remedy this situation, set Workdir permissions as follows: HTN-Users = Change, HTN-Support = Change, and Domain Admins = Full Control. Once these changes are complete, Access will work properly.

Data

After securing the Applications directory structure, it is time to move to the DATA Volume. As stated earlier in the chapter, the Horton Domain will employ a basic data directory structure as follows: DATA for the root, Common for all low-security shared files, and DEPT for departmentally secure documents. To implement the appropriate security level, there are eight steps to follow:

1. Using Windows NT Explorer, the Everyone Group must be removed from the root of the DATA directory and should be replaced with the HTN-USERS group. Grant HTN-Users Read level access. This denies members of the HTN-Users group the ability to write anything to the root of the DATA structure.

2. Grant the HTN-Support group Change level access and Domain Admins Full Control access to the Data directory.

3. Before making these Permission changes, be sure to select both the Replace Permissions on Subdirectories and Replace Permissions on Existing Files options as seen in Figure 8.11. This will ensure that the permissions are propagated to all existing subdirectories and that all new subdirectories will inherit them as well.

FIGURE 8.11.

Applying Security to the Data Directory.

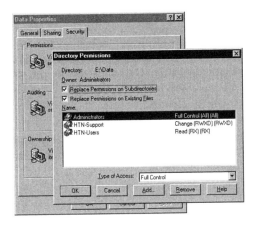

4. Either change to or create the DEPT subdirectory. Note that by default, the access permissions on this directory will be identical to set at the root directory, Data. Using Windows NT Explorer, set the access permissions for the DEPT directory as follows: HTN-USERS = List, HTN-Support = Add & Read, and Domain Admins = Full Control. This allows for all members of the HTN-USERS group to see what directories exist under DEPT, for all HTN-Support personnel to add but not modify directories and files, and continues to provide full access control to members of the Domain Admins group. Do not replace permissions on existing files or directories.

5. Create subdirectories under the subdirectory DEPT (as seen in Figure 8.12) for the major departments: Accounting, Administrative, Creative, and Sales.

FIGURE 8.12.

Security Settings for the DEPT Directory.

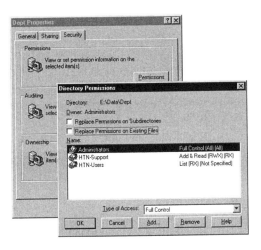

6. Select the Accounting subdirectory and, using Windows NT Explorer, modify the access permissions as follows: Remove HTN-Support, HTN-Users, and Domain

8

DESIGNING YOUR RESOURCE STRUCTURE

Admins. Add HTN-Accounting with Change level access and propagate these permissions to all files and directories. Once complete, only HTN-Accounting members will have access to this directory structure.

7. Follow this procedure for each departmental subdirectory, providing access only to the group owning the directory. Once complete, your departmental data structure is completely secure as seen in Figure 8.13.

Figure 8.13.

Security at the Departmental Level.

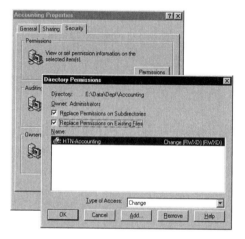

8. From the root of the DATA directory structure, select the Common subdirectory. Using Windows NT Explorer, modify the permissions as follows: HTN-Users = Change, HTN-Support = Change, and Domain Admins = Full Control. Propagate these permissions to all files and subdirectories (refer to Figure 8.14). Once complete, all users will have the ability to read, write, delete, and modify files in the Common directory.

Figure 8.14.

Permissions for the Common Directory.

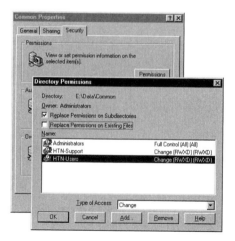

Support

The Support directory structure will be a relatively easy one to secure, due to the fact that the only users allowed to access this directory are those in the support organization. The only real question is whether Horton administrators want their support personnel to have the ability to write to the Support Volume. The Horton Agency has determined that at the Utilities level, they do want their tactical support personnel to be able to add files and directories; however, at the Clients level, they want stricter control. To accomplish these levels of security, follow these steps:

1. Launch the Windows NT Explorer and go to the Support Volume as seen in Figure 8.15. At the root of the Support directory structure, set the following permissions: Domain Admins = Full Control and HTN-Support = Read. Be sure to propagate these rights to all existing files and subdirectories. This will set the desired rights on both the root of the Support structure and the Clients subdirectory.

FIGURE 8.15.

Support Volume Permissions.

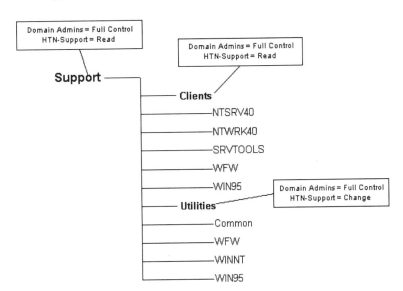

2. Go to the Utilities subdirectory and modify the permissions level as follows: Domain Admins = Full Control and HTN-Support = Change. Once complete, propagate these permissions, and the permissions will be set as desired.

Users

The Users Directory is terribly simple. As you'll see in Chapter 9, "Managing Users," each time you create a new user, a dedicated user directory will be created. By default, the only object given access to a user's home directory is the user. All an administrator needs to do to allow this to happen is create a Users Directory and provide Read-level access for the basic user and technical staff groups, and, if desired, Full Control to the Domain Admins group. By default, the administrator or administrator equivalents have no access to any home directory but their own.

HTN-CREATIVE01

HTN-CREATIVE01 will have only one major directory structure as seen in Figure 8.16. Due to the fact that this Data Server is to be used solely by the HTN-Creative group, no groups other than Domain Admins and HTN-Creative will have access to its files. As you can see in Figure 8.17, members of the HTN-Creative group cannot add files or create directories in the root of the structure, nor can they add files or create directories in the root of the major subdirectories. However, they do have the capability to manipulate all data underneath the major subdirectories. This is a fairly typical scenario for a Data Server.

FIGURE 8.16.

HTN-CREATIVE01—The Dedicated Data Server.

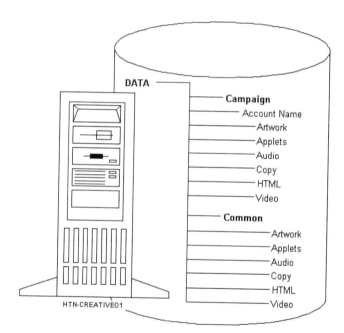

HTN-ACCTG01

Other than the standard volume structure, the accounting application server will have two volumes: one for the actual application and one for the SQL Server. Permissions to this server will be granted only to the HTN-Accounting group and only as instructed by the application developer. Nothing other than the accounting application will be stored on this server.

FIGURE 8.17.
Permissions for the HTN-CREATIVE01 Data Structure.

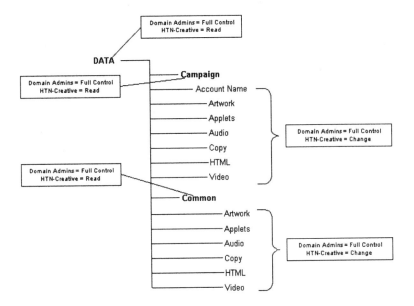

The InterDivisional Deployment

For any of the three endorsed Deployment models, it is important to have developed your basic User Directory structure and to have determined your OA server deployment throughout your Domain. In Chapter 4, the basic user directory for the Guardian Companies was determined, and in Chapter 5, the basic domain deployment was outlined. Following is a review of the Guardian Domain's design to this point.

The User Directory

Unlike the Departmental Domain, the InterDivisional Domain model does not employ one single Basic Group. However, it requires a separate Divisional Group for each division or corporate entity. Thus, the Divisional Group should be treated much like a Departmental Group. The four divisions inside of the Guardian Insurance Companies are Guardian Headquarters, Guardian Health, Guardian Corporate Benefits, and Guardian Casualty. The Divisional Groups are as follows:

HQ-Users	Users of the Guardian Domain from Guardian HQ
HLT-Users	Users of the Guardian Domain from Guardian Health
CORP-Users	Users of the Guardian Domain from Guardian Corporate Benefits
CTY-Users	Users of the Guardian Domain from Guardian Casualty

Departmental Groups in the InterDivisional Domain are nearly identical to those in the InterDepartmental Domain, with the exception that Departmental Groups are created for each

Division. In a sense, each division is treated as a unique organization, and, therefore, its Directory components must be organized to fit its corporate structure. Each division of the Guardian Insurance Companies has its own Accounting, Marketing, and Administrative Departments, while the Headquarters also houses Human Resources, Claims, and Information Systems. The Departmental Groups for the Guardian Insurance Companies are as follows:

Accounting	HQ-Accounting	HQ-Accounting Users of the Guardian Domain
Marketing	HQ-Marketing	HQ-Marketing Users of the Guardian Domain
Administrative	HQ-Admin	HQ-Administrative Users of the Guardian Domain
Human Resources	HQ-HumanResources	HQ-Human Users of the Guardian Domain
Claims	HQ-Claims	HQ-Claims Users of the Guardian Domain
Information Systems	HQ-InfoSystems	HQ-Information Systems Users of the Guardian Domain
Accounting	HLT-Accounting	HLT-Accounting Users of the Guardian Domain
Marketing	HLT-Marketing	HLT-Marketing Users of the Guardian Domain
Administrative	HLT-Admin	HLT -Administrative Users of the Guardian Domain
Accounting	Corp-Accounting	Corp-Accounting Users of the Guardian Domain
Marketing	Corp-Marketing	Corp-Marketing Users of the Guardian Domain
Administrative	Corp-Admin	Corp-Administrative Users of the Guardian Domain
Accounting	CTY-Accounting	CTY-Accounting Users of the Guardian Domain
Marketing	CTY-Marketing	CTY-Marketing Users of the Guardian Domain
Administrative	CTY-Admin	CTY-Administrative Users of the Guardian Domain

Keep in mind that as the Basic User Group is the User Directory's organizational foundation for the InterDepartmental Domain, the Divisional Group is the foundation for the

InterDivisional Domain. All users, with the exception of support personnel, should be members of a Divisional Group. Each respective Divisional Group will be granted access to all common resources throughout its division; and much like in the InterDepartmental Domain, the Departmental Groups are designed to provide restricted access to each division's departmentally secure resources, such as data or protected applications.

InterDivisional Support Personnel Considerations

In the previous section concerning the InterDepartmental deployment, there were several suggestions made concerning the application of permissions for support personnel. Due to the complexity of the InterDivsional model, it is a good idea to review the following list, which includes the original suggestions as well as additional guidelines. The suggestions are as follows:

- Do not grant Domain Administrators membership in any group other than Domain Admins or Administrators.
- Create separate groups for your tactical support technicians. If you have personnel dedicated to specific divisions, create divisional support groups.
- If you have differing levels of support technicians and wish to stratiate their access, create a group for each tier.
- Unless you specifically desire to limit their permissions to those of a basic, departmental, or enterprise group, do not add your support technicians to any additional groups.
- When applying security to a directory structure, remember that you must add the Domain Admins or Administrators group if you wish for those users to have access.

With these suggestions in mind, the Guardian Insurance Companies have implemented the following support group structure:

GRD-HelpDesk	Guardian Enterprise Help Desk Personnel
HQ-PCTech	Guardian HQ Divisional Support Team
HLT-PCTech	Guardian Health Divisional Support Team
Corp-PCTech	Guardian Corporate Benefits Divisional Support Team
CTY-PCTech	Guardian Casualty Divisional Support Team

As follows, by looking at this group distribution, there is a central Help Desk that will serve the entire organization, as well as individual support teams for each division.

InterDivisional Server Deployment

The Guardian Insurance Companies have four major divisions, and each division has its own dedicated production server that will also serve as a backup domain controller. These servers are named as follows:

- HQ-PROD01 (Guardian Headquarters)
- HLT-PROD01 (Guardian Health)
- CORP-PROD01 (Guardian Corporate Benefits)
- CTY-PROD01 (Guardian Casualty)

Additionally, each group will have their share of application servers that could be dedicated to enterprise, divisional, or cross-divisional resources that might be intranet, data, or application servers. Furthermore, Guardian will have several Enterprise servers that will provide remote access, faxing, dial-out, Internet, and intranet functions.

InterDivisional Directory Structure

Much like in the InterDepartmental deployment, resource categorization is the best place to start when creating a server's directory structure; however, the task is larger considering that it will have to be repeated for each division. The challenge in an InterDivisional domain is to take each division's categories and create a standard directory structure that can be utilized throughout all divisions.

After having categorized all of the major common resources throughout each division, Guardian's network Administrators have settled upon a standard server directory structure for all Office Automation servers as shown in Figure 8.18.

FIGURE 8.18.

Guardian Insurance Companies Standard Production Server Directory Structure.

- **Applications**
  - Win16app
  - Win32app
- **Data**
  - Common
  - Dept
  - Users
- **Support**
  - Clients
  - Utils
  - Drivers

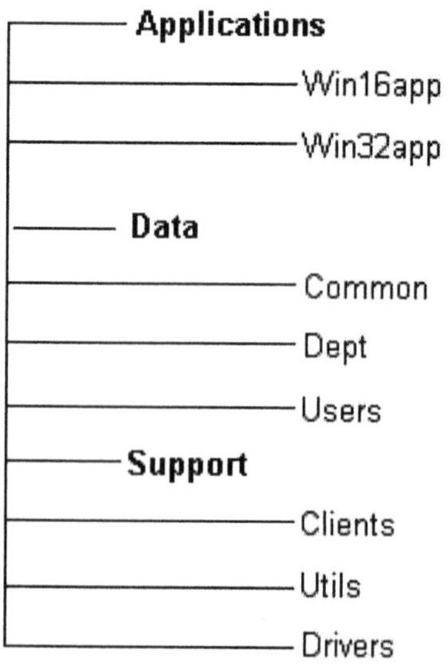

As you can see, this structure has fewer major entry points for the common user than that of the InterDepartmental deployment. The Users directory, which contains the user home directories, has been moved into the Data structure, thus eliminating an entry point. From an organizational sense, this is good; however, it will take more thought on the end user's part. Traditionally, the end user is used to having one drive letter designated for corporate common data and another drive letter dedicated to their home directory. While the proposed directory structure might make sense to the Administrators, it will take some getting used to, not only for the end user, but also for the support personnel.

As stated, each production server throughout the enterprise will share the same directory structure. Furthermore, each Divisional deployment will also share the same common application feature set (Office suite, 3270 emulator, Web Browser, mail package, and so on). The major differences between divisional production servers will be the data subdirectories and the application of security. Take Guardian Health, for example: Their data structure will be designed as seen in Figure 8.19.

The application of security to this structure will be very similar to that of security in the InterDepartmental domains. All divisional users will change access to the Common directory, and departmental directories will be secured on a departmental level. Each divisional server will be nearly identical, differing only in terms of data directory structure; however, the conventions will remain the same. By providing continuity, you will help yourself to deliver better customer service and support.

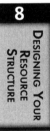

File and Directory Level Permissions in the InterCorporate Deployment

The concepts used in applying File and Directory level permissions in the InterDivisional Domain are nearly identical to those used in the InterDepartmental Domain. The greatest difference is the scope. For instance, while the InterDerpartmental Domain has only one or two production servers and only one basic user group, the InterDivisional group can have both multiple production servers and multiple basic user groups. CORP-PROD01, the production server for the Corporate Benefits division of Guardian, and HLT-PROD01, the production server for the Health Division of Guardian, will have similar directory structures, but there are differences. The only groups that will be applied to the Applications directory structure on CORP-PROD01 will be those groups beginning with the CORP prefix, and, likewise, the only groups being applied to the Applications directory structure on HLT-PROD01 will be those beginning with the HLT prefix.

These types of security differences will be seen in each major entry point on each production server, effectively dedicating resources to a specific Division. There will be many cases, however, where users from one division will need access to files or applications in other divisions. It was for this purpose that the Cross-Divisional Group was designed. For example, Guardian Corporate Benefits maintains a directory with updated collateral concerning their benefits package in the \\CORP-PROD01\Data\Common directory structure. Since the benefits packages offered to Guardian Employees are managed through Guardian Corporate Benefits, the Human Resources department from Guardian Headquarters is very interested in having access to this directory. Therefore, the Cross-Divisional Group named CORP-HQBenefits has been created. This group, which will include only users from the Headquarters division, will be applied to the appropriate resources as seen in Figure 8.20.

FIGURE 8.19.

An Example of Divisional Security Differences.

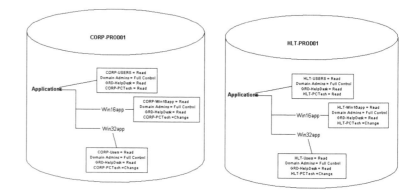

FIGURE 8.20.

Cross-Divisional Security.

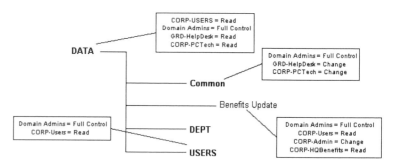

Enterprise resources, which are very similar to Cross-Divisional Resources, are also extremely common in the InterDivisional deployment. Enterprise Resources are those resources that are shared with users throughout the Domain, regardless of their group or Division membership. An excellent example of an Enterprise resource is a server dedicated to serving Computer Based Training to all employees. While providing such services to multiple locations would require a high-speed WAN, it is not uncommon. Such a resource, GRD-CBT Server, exists in the Guardian Headquarters as seen in Figure 8.21.

Notice the complicated directory structure. Due to application restrictions, in order to have access to run the CBTs, a user must not only have access to the server, but must also have an ID in the CBT system. The Human Resources department has elected to maintain which CBTs a user may have access to, and, as a result, they have been given access to the directory containing the program's administrative utilities (CBTAdmin). Since the program was designed such that each time a user is created, an account record must be added to the administrative directory, the CBT Administrators (HQ-HumanResources) must have the ability to write to the directory. Furthermore, the application requires that the Logon facility (stored in CBTMenu), the student directories (CBTStudents), and the application files (CBTClasses) must all be stored in separate directories as well. Once this security has been properly applied, in order for a user to be granted access to the CBTs, two things must happen. First, their ID must be created in the applications administrative facility, and, second, the user must be granted access to the GRD-CBTUsers group. Once complete, the user only needs to run the CBT Menu application, and they will be presented with a list of available CBTs.

FIGURE 8.21.

GRD-CBTServer—An Enterprise Resource.

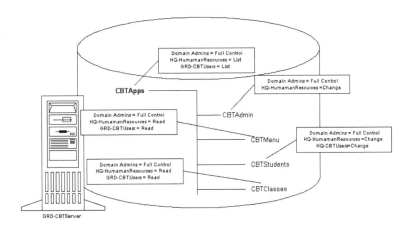

The majority of the concepts seen in the InterDepartmental Domain such as application servers and data servers will stay consistent in the InterDivisional Domain. The greatest difference between the InterDivisional and the InterDepartmental deployments is in the scope of users and the number of servers that must be managed.

The InterCorporate Domain

The concepts of resource management as seen in the InterDepartmental and InterDivisional deployment models are all present in the InterCorporate deployment. The greatest difference found in the InterCorporate Domain, as was the case when moving from the InterDepartmental Deployment to the InterDivisional Deployment, is the scale of the implementation. However, the scale factors in the InterCorporate Domain go beyond simple size due to the implementation of the Master Domain Model and the fact that each Resource Domain will maintain its own resources.

InterCorporate Support Personnel Considerations

The InterCorporate Domain brings on some interesting support issues. In many cases, there will be no central support group for the InterCorporate Domain, which can cause problems where standards management is concerned. Due to the fact that the InterCorporate Domain is based on the Master Domain Model (to be discussed in detail in Chapter 16, "Advanced Trust

8

DESIGNING YOUR RESOURCE STRUCTURE

Relationships"), the potential exists for each Resource Domain to be administered in a completely unique manner while still sharing the central user directory provided by the Master Domain. In the case of McMac Minerals, the support groups for each McMac corporate entity have formed a committee to determine deployment standards to be used throughout the enterprise. It has been determined that each group will maintain control of their respective resource domain while the user directory will be maintained by a nontechnical entity, the Data Security department. The Data Security department, which has a seat on the Standard Committee at McMac, will adhere to the conventions set by the support personnel. The InterCorporate model can be an extremely complex environment; however, if standards and conventions are adhered to closely, it is extremely convenient for the end user. The following list of suggestions builds on those provided with the sections concerning the InterDerpartmental and InterDivisional deployments:

- Limit your number of Domain Administrators. As you will see in Chapter 17, one does not have to be a Domain Administrator in the Master Domain to manage a resource Domain.
- Create separate groups for each resource domain's tactical support technicians.
- If you have differing levels of support technicians and wish to stratify their access, create a group for each tier in each resource domain.
- While adding your support personnel to basic or departmental groups dedicated to their Resource Domain can inhibit their access unnecessarily, membership in Cross-Divisional or Enterprise groups should have no bearing on their ability to support their respective domain.
- If you do not want the Master Domain's Domain Administrators to have administrative access to your resource domain, do not apply them to domain resources.

In Chapter 17, you will find that each resource domain has its own User Directory by default; however, in most cases, only service accounts and computer accounts will be maintained within the directory. When a domain joins a Master Domain, the group Domain Admins automatically becomes a member of the resource domain's local Administrators group, effectively granting all members of the Master Domain's Domain Admins group supervisory control of every Resource Domain. Due to this fact, the McMac Standards committee has determined that only one person from each division should become a member of the Master Domain's Domain Admins group. However, in order to allow resource domain Administrators the capability to manage their respective domains, it is necessary to create a new group class, the Resource Domain Admins Group. These groups were created for McMac Industries as follows:

MMI-Admins	MMI-Master Resource Domain Administrators
MMF-Admins	MM-Foods Resource Domain Administrators
WTP-Admins	MM-Paper Resource Domain Administrators
JNS-Admins	MM-Salt Resource Domain Administrators

Each of these groups will be granted membership in the Account Operators and Server Operators groups in the Master Domain. Remember that the Account Operators group can manage all Domain user account properties (excluding those of users that have membership in the following groups: Administrators, Domain Admins, Server Operators, or Account Operators), and the Server Operators group can manage all domain servers. These groups will provide the Resource Domain Administrators with the ability to manage servers and users in the Master Domain, but since both of these groups are local, they will not provide them any automatic rights in the resource domains. In order to provide these Resource Domain Admins supervisory rights in the appropriate resource domains, they must be added to the respective local Administrators groups as follows:

- The MMI-Admins group will be granted membership in the MM-Master's Administrators group.

- The MMF-Admins group will be granted membership in the MM-Foods Administrators group.

- The WTP-Admins group will be granted membership in the MM-Paper Administrators group.

- The JNS-Admins group will be granted membership in the MM-Salt Administrators group.

Once complete, the groups will have enough rights to successfully perform their jobs, without comprising security or authority in their companion resource domains.

In addition to domain administrators, each resource domain will have its own group of dedicated network technicians, while all support organizations will share the same help desk. The support groups have been created as follows:

MME-HelpDesk	MM-Master Enterprise Help Desk Personnel
MMI-NetTech	MM-Master Domain Network Technicians
MMF-NetTech	MM-Foods Resource Domain Network Technicians
WTP-NetTech	MM-Paper Resource Domain Network Technicians
JNS-NetTech	MM-Salt Resource Domain Network Technicians

InterCorporate Server Deployment

The InterCorporate Model is made up of one Master Domain and several Resource Domains that are actually independent InterDepartmental or InterDivisional Domains. Each of these domains shares the same directory under the Master Domain, which in turn makes resource sharing a simple process. All of the deployment rules called for in the InterDepartmental and InterDivisional Models apply—however, in a much larger scale. McMac Industries is made up of a Master Domain and three resource Domains. By nature, each Domain will require a

8

DESIGNING YOUR
RESOURCE
STRUCTURE

Primary Domain Controller, but only the Master Domain will require Backup Domain Controllers—one in each location. The production servers have been named as follows:

- MMI-PROD01 (McMac Industries)
- MMF-PROD01 (McMac Foods)
- WTP-PROD01 (Watterson Papers)
- JNS-PROD01 (Jansen Salt)

Additionally, each Resource Domain will have its share of application servers that could be dedicated to enterprise, divisional, or cross-divisional resources.

InterCorporate Directory Structure

Categorization of resource should be the first step in each of the three deployment models. Once all of the major common resources throughout each division have been categorized, it is time to prepare a standard directory structure. In an effort to minimize each domain's major entry points, the McMac Standards group has come up with a structure very similar to that of the Guardian Industries. Figure 8.22 illustrates the directory structure.

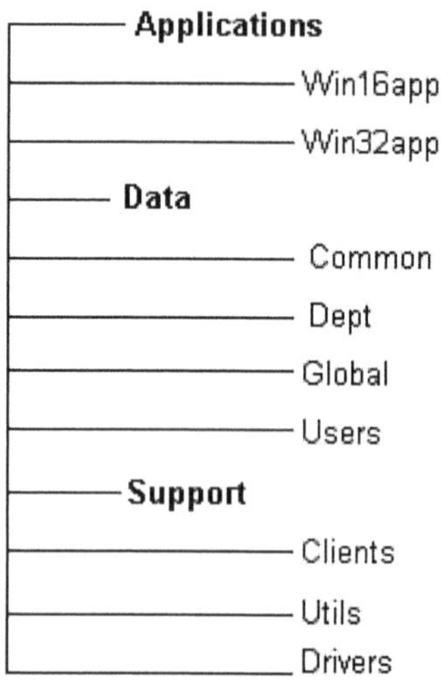

FIGURE 8.22.

*McMac Industries
Standard Production
Server Directory
Structure.*

As you can see, this structure has the same amount of major entry points for the common user as does the InterDepartmental deployment. The major difference is the addition of the \Data\Global subdirectory. This subdirectory will be used to store cross-departmental or Enterprise resources, segregating such items from the common or secured data.

File and Directory Level Permissions in the InterCorporate Deployment

The concepts used in applying File and Directory level permissions are identical throughout each deployment model—however, with the InterCorporate model, they become more detailed. The major change is in the application of support personnel. For instance, take MMF-PROD01 and compare it to JNS-PROD01 in terms of File and Directory Level Permissions (see Figure 8.23). Through group naming conventions, we know that each resource can be accessed by like groups; however, there is not one group applied to these resources that can access both servers. These types of security differences will be seen in each major entry point on each resource domain's production server. Not even the Domain Admins group will be applied to resources within the domains. However, just like with the other two deployment models, it is not uncommon for users from one resource domain to need access to files or applications on the production server in another resource domain. It was for this purpose that the Cross-Divisional Group was designed. Take, for instance, an inventory database maintained by Jansen Salt. Jansen Salt contracted a firm to create a small Access application that pulls inventory data from a more sophisticated ODBC compliant application and places it in an easy-to-read, up-to-date format. This application is now used to share inventory information with sales people from both Jansen Salt and McMac Foods. While McMac Foods sales people pull Access from their production server, and Jansen Salt sales people pull Access from their production server, both groups of users pull the database from the JNS-PROD01 production server. The Directory structure and security application are shown in Figure 8.24.

FIGURE 8.23.

*Security in the
InterCorporate
Environment.*

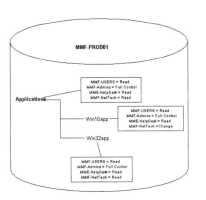 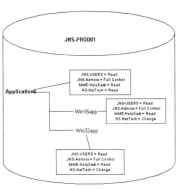

As you can see, the only directory that will allow access to users from outside the Jansen resource domain (MM-SALT) is the \Global\Marketing\SALESDB directory; and even though access has been granted to the Cross-Divisional Group (which contains users from both Jansen Salt and McMac Foods), due to the security constraints in the upper directories, only Jansen users will have access to this directory from the Data entry point. The only way that McMac salespeople will be able to access this resource is through a network share. Determining share points will be covered later in this chapter.

FIGURE 8.24.

Cross Divisional Security.

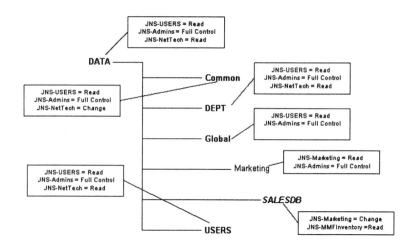

The remainder of the concepts seen in the other deployment models, such as application servers and Enterprise servers, will stay consistent in the InterCorporate Domain. The greatest difference comes in the scope of users, the number of servers, and the manner in which security must be applied.

Sharing Network Resources

The process of resource categorization has two objectives: first, to develop a directory structure that logically groups resources for the end user and, second, to minimize the number of major entry points required to gain access to those resources. Both of these objectives work hand-in-hand when considering the implementation of Network Shares. Remember that even though you've designed and implemented your standard directory structure and secured your resources using File and Directory level permissions, you still haven't made those resources available to the end user.

End users, in most cases, don't want to think about what drive letter they need to access in order to launch an application or open a document. Instead, they want their environment to offer the resources they need through an intuitive structure that requires little forethought. By minimizing the number of drive mappings it takes to access those resources, you accomplish much of your goal. However, the only way to minimize drive mappings is to provide a minimal number of required share points—for example, the resource categorization performed when designing your directory structure. The most commonly used shared resources are data and office automation applications. Most users will simply access the data and standard applications provided on their production server; however, there are those that will require access to Cross-Divisional or Enterprise resources as well. The remainder of this chapter will cover basic resource sharing only. The topics of Enterprise and Cross-Divisional resources, as well as network printers, will be addressed in Chapter 9.

Basic Resource Sharing in the InterDepartmental Domain

Due to the fact that in most cases there will be only one production server in the InterDepartmental Domain, it is perhaps the easiest deployment model in which to determine your share points. The Horton Domain is an excellent example. Their production server, HTN-PROD01, has a directory structure that consists of four major entry points: Applications, Data, Support, and Users. The majority of the users will have access to all of the resources they will need through the Applications, Data, and Users entry points, while only the Support personnel will need access to the Support directory structure. The following share points have, therefore, been created for HTN-PROD01:

- The Applications structure was shared as Apps.
- The Data structure was shared as Data.
- The Users structure was shared as Users.
- The Support structure was shared as SUPPORT$.

As for share level permissions, each share is slightly different. Remember that upon creation, a new share has default permissions of Everyone at Full Control. Even though the directory structures on HTN-PROD01 were locked down tight using file- and directory-level permissions, it is always a good idea to complete that security with share permissions. Table 8.1 lists the permissions applied on each share.

Table 8.1. Shares and Permissions for HTN-PROD01.

Share Name	*Group*	*Group Permission*
Apps	HTN-USERS	Change
	HTN-Support	Change
	Domain Admins	Full Control
Data	HTN-USERS	Change
	HTN-Support	Change
	Domain Admins	Full Control
SUPPORT$	HTN-Support	Change
	Domain Admins	Full Control
Users	HTN-USERS	Change
	HTN-Support	Change
	Domain Admins	Full Control

8

DESIGNING YOUR
RESOURCE
STRUCTURE

One can easily assume that the majority of all users will receive standard drive mappings connecting them to the Apps, Data, and User directories, while only support personnel will have access to the hidden SUPPORT$ directory (standard drive mappings will be covered in Chapter 9). Due to the fact that all resources were categorized beforehand and placed in a volume/directory structure that can handle even the most drastic changes, these share points should suffice for quite some time to come.

In addition to HTN-PROD01, users in the Creative department will need to access their data server, HTN-CREATIVE01. Remember that this server contained only one major entry point, the Data directory. In order to prevent any end-user confusion, the share name of this directory will be CREATIVE. Share level permissions for the CREATIVE share are shown in Table 8.2.

Table 8.2. Shares and Permissions for HTN-CREATIVE01.

Share Name	*Group*	*Group Permission*
CREATIVE	HTN-Creative	Change
	HTN-Support	Change
	Domain Admins	Full Control

Once complete, these network shares will provide access to all required network resources through a minimum of three shares per user. On the upper end, there will be a maximum of four shares per user, leaving a fairly intuitive and uncomplicated network environment for the end user. The importance of a standard user environment has been addressed throughout this book in some detail—however, it will be one of the main subjects in Chapter 9.

Basic Resource Sharing in the InterDivisional Domain

Sharing resources in the InterDivisional Domain becomes slightly more complicated than in the InterDepartmental Domain—however, only in terms of sheer numbers. Due to the fact that each division will have its own production server that will not only host divisional resources, but also Cross-Divisional resources, determining where to create shares can become a difficult task.

Much like the InterDepartmental Domain, each server in the InterDivisional Domain will host shares based upon their directory structure. For example, the Guardian Insurance Companies have determined that their directory structure will be categorized under the following major headings: Applications, Data, and Support . Since each divisional production server will contain the same directory structure, it makes it easy to standardize on a Share structure throughout the divisions. Those share points are listed as follows:

■ The Applications structure will be shared as Apps.

■ The Data structure will be shared as Data.

■ The Support structure will be shared as SUPPORT$.

Notice that this structure has one less standard entry point than the InterDepartmental Domain. Looking at Figure 8.20 (the InterCorporate directory structure), and comparing it to Figure 8.5 (the InterDepartmental directory structure), you can see that the Users directory was consolidated underneath the Data directory. This was done due to the fact that there will be many Cross-Divisional and Enterprise resources throughout a domain the size of Guardian. Because of these various resources, the administrators felt it would be helpful from an end-user point of view to minimize the access points for daily production resources.

Share level security for the standard shares on each of the four production servers in the Guardian Domain are shown in Tables 8.3 through 8.6.

Table 8.3. Shares and Permissions for HQ-PROD01.

Share Name	Group	Group Permission
Apps	HQ-USERS	Change
	HQ-PCTech	Change
	GRD-HelpDesk	Change
	Domain Admins	Full Control
Data	HQ-USERS	Change
	HQ-PCTech	Change
	GRD-HelpDesk	Change
	Domain Admins	Full Control
SUPPORT$	HQ-PCTech	Change
	Domain Admins	Full Control

8

DESIGNING YOUR RESOURCE STRUCTURE

Table 8.4. Shares and Permissions for HLT-PROD01.

Share Name	Group	Group Permission
Apps	HLT-USERS	Change
	HLT-PCTech	Change
	GRD-HelpDesk	Change
	Domain Admins	Full Control

continues

Table 8.4. continued

Share Name	Group	Group Permission
Data	HLT-USERS	Change
	HLT-PCTech	Change
	GRD-HelpDesk	Change
	Domain Admins	Full Control
SUPPORT$	HLT-PCTech	Change
	Domain Admins	Full Control

Table 8.5. Shares and Permissions for CORP-PROD01.

Share Name	Group	Group Permission
Apps	CORP-USERS	Change
	CORP-PCTech	Change
	GRD-HelpDesk	Change
	Domain Admins	Full Control
Data	CORP-USERS	Change
	CORP-PCTech	Change
	GRD-HelpDesk	Change
	Domain Admins	Full Control
SUPPORT$	CORP-PCTech	Change
	Domain Admins	Full Control

Table 8.6. Shares and Permissions for CTY-PROD01.

Share Name	Group	Group Permission
Apps	CTY-USERS	Change
	CTY-PCTech	Change
	GRD-HelpDesk	Change
	Domain Admins	Full Control

Share Name	Group	Group Permission
Data	CTY-USERS	Change
	CTY-PCTech	Change
	GRD-HelpDesk	Change
	Domain Admins	Full Control
SUPPORT$	CTY-PCTech	Change
	Domain Admins	Full Control

As you can see, only a user from the Corporate Benefits Division (CORP-USERS, CORP-PCTech) can access the standard shares on the Corporate Benefits production server (CORP-PROD01). This situation is identical for each divisional group. While they can access only their server, each user will receive the same drive letter and share name combinations to access like resources. In other words, users accessing the HLT-PROD01 server will receive the same drive letters per share name that users accessing the CORP-PROD01 server receive. As you will see in Chapter 9, this share standardization will be important for several reasons, not the least of which is consistency across divisions.

Due to the tight security enforced not only by share level resources, but also that applied at the File and Directory level, users will not be able to access Cross-Divisional or Enterprise resources through standard shares. Therefore, it will be necessary to create a share point for each Cross-Divisional and Enterprise resource. While at first this might seem to lead to a disorganized environment, keep in mind that the majority of all resources required by the end user will be provided by their production server. Thus, while a user might need to access a directory in each resource domain, he or she will only need three drive mappings to access all standard resources in their own domain.

8

DESIGNING YOUR RESOURCE STRUCTURE

> **NOTE**
>
> After the Windows NT Server 4.0 hit the market, Microsoft released a new service, the Directory File System. DFS, which will be covered in Chapter 9 and Chapter 11, allows you to create a virtual directory structure spanning multiple share points from server to server that is accessible to the end user from a single share. This service, which can be accessed only from Windows NT 4.0 or Windows 95, will allow you to create a DFS share, such as GRD-Marketing, that will span all Cross-Divisional marketing resources but provide a single connection point to the end user.

Basic Resource Sharing in the InterCorporate Domain

Whereas sharing resources in the InterDivisional Domain became more complicated than the InterDepartmental Domain due to the size of the implementation, sharing resources in the InterCorporate Domain became more complicated due to both size and the tiered structure of the support groups. While in the InterDivisional deployment, each division will have its own production server; the InterCorporate deployment holds the possibility for multiple InterDivisional implementations within each resource Domain. Therefore, maintaining standards in directory structures, permissions application, and share implementations are crucial to success.

Just like the other deployment models, the InterCorporate Domain will host shares based upon a server's directory structure. Since each divisional production server will contain the same directory structure, it follows that Share placement should be identical from server to server. Production Servers in the MM-Master Domain and all of its resource domains will host the following standard shares :

- The Applications structure will be shared as Apps.
- The Data structure will be shared as Data.
- The Support structure will be shared as LanAdmin$.

Share level security for the standard shares on each production server within each resource domain are shown in Tables 8.7 through 8.10.

Table 8.7. Shares and Permissions for MMI-PROD01.

Share Name	Group	Group Permission
Apps	MMI-Users	Change
	MMI-NetTech	Change
	MMI-Admins	Full Control
	MME-HelpDesk	Change
Data	MMI-Users	Change
	MMI-NetTech	Change
	MMI-Admins	Full Control
	MME-HelpDesk	Change
LanAdmin$	MMI-Users	Change
	MMI-NetTech	Change
	MMI-Admins	Full Control

Table 8.8. Shares and Permissions for MMF-PROD01.

Share Name	Group	Group Permission
Apps	MMF-Users	Change
	MMF-NetTech	Change
	MMF-Admins	Full Control
	MME-HelpDesk	Change
Data	MMF-Users	Change
	MMF-NetTech	Change
	MMF-Admins	Full Control
	MME-HelpDesk	Change
LanAdmin$	MMF-Users	Change
	MMF-NetTech	Change
	MMF-Admins	Full Control

Table 8.9. Shares and Permissions for WTP-PROD01.

Share Name	Group	Group Permission
Apps	WTP-Users	Change
	WTP-NetTech	Change
	WTP-Admins	Full Control
	MME-HelpDesk	Change
Data	WTP-Users	Change
	WTP-NetTech	Change
	WTP-Admins	Full Control
	MME-HelpDesk	Change
LanAdmin$	WTP-Users	Change
	WTP-NetTech	Change
	WTP-Admins	Full Control

8

DESIGNING YOUR
RESOURCE
STRUCTURE

Table 8.10. Shares and Permissions for JNS-PROD01.

Share Name	Group	Group Permission
Apps	JNS-Users	Change
	JNS-NetTech	Change
	JNS-Admins	Full Control
	MME-HelpDesk	Change
Data	JNS-Users	Change
	JNS-NetTech	Change
	JNS-Admins	Full Control
	MME-HelpDesk	Change
LanAdmin$	JNS-Users	Change
	JNS-NetTech	Change
	JNS-Admins	Full Control

Similar to the situation in the other deployments, users will not be able to access Cross-Divisional or Enterprise resources through standard shares due to the tight security enforced through both share level and file and directory level permissions. Therefore, Cross-Divisional and Enterprise resources will require their own share points.

Summary

This chapter has taken the concepts discussed throughout Chapters 4, 5, and 7 concerning User Directory, Server Implementation, and the application of security, and presented real-world examples as to their interrelationships and application. Chapter 9 will further the concepts brought forward in this chapter with more specific user implementations and a broader focus on the impact your implementation will have on user management.

PART

IN THIS PART

Deploying Users

Managing Users

CHAPTER 9

Most people who excel in the network support business have a serious interest in industry technology and have learned to deploy that technology in a sensible, scaleable, and cost-effective manner. Today's industry is changing so rapidly that the challenges associated with staying on top are taking a greater toll than ever. Anticipating industry trends, forecasting corporate needs, staying on top of current technologies, and ensuring that your existing Enterprise provides the infrastructure necessary for growth take a minimum of 40 hours per week. When the end user comes into the picture, your week gets even longer.

One of the main goals of the network design endorsed by this book is to effectively take the administration out of the network. By designing every component of your network based on Divisional, Departmental, Cross-Divisional, and Enterprise needs, each component becomes a piece in a complete puzzle. Growth and expansion become easy, based on a well organized deployment of resources. However, to this point in the design model, the user has not been directly addressed—and, in fact, on an individual basis never should be. This is due to the fact that, as far as the Enterprise is concerned, the user is nothing more than a collection of needs:

- The user needs a logon ID.
- The user needs a password.
- The user needs to access standard office automation resources.
- The user needs to access Divisional resources.
- The user needs to access Departmental resources.
- The user needs to access Cross-Divisional resources.
- The user needs to access Enterprise resources.
- The user needs to print.

As long as you've designed your Enterprise appropriately, managing users is as simple as grouping their needs. If you've designed your deployment using the techniques endorsed by this book, you have a tremendous advantage, due to the fact that the foundation of your user directory is your corporate organization. The basic element of your Directory is the corporate division, under the division there are departments, between the departments there are Cross-Divisional groups, and beyond the divisions there is the Enterprise. Each one of your users belongs to a division or basic user group, and under that division there is a finite number of variations in terms of the number of collections of needs. Due to the structure of your User Directory and consequent resource deployment, you will find that there are often no more than four or five different collections of user needs per division, with the occasional variation (that variation in most cases being a rare Cross-Divisional or Enterprise resource). By effectively categorizing each division's user types and creating user templates based on each category, you can make a major stride in reducing the time it takes to accomplish daily management tasks. In addition, by being able to create and manage your users in terms of user types, you take out the micromanagement required without such categorization. Keep in mind, however, that while the danger in managing your Enterprise on an individual-by-individual basis is an inefficient use of time, the danger in managing your Enterprise in terms of categorization can be the failure to meet all of your users' needs. It is important to realize that there will be exceptions to your standard user types. The trick is in minimizing those exceptions without providing too little or too much control.

This chapter will cover two tools that can be used to control and organize your user environment: User Templates and User Profiles.

User Design

There are several elements to consider when designing your user types, each of which will impact the ease with which you manage your environment. These elements are as follows:

- User Name/Full Name Conventions
- User Description Conventions
- Individual Password Policies
- Group Membership
- Logon Scripts
- Home Directories
- Logon Hours
- Logon Restrictions
- Account Type/Expiration
- Dialin Permissions
- Printers
- Cross-Divisional and Enterprise Resources

These elements or user needs can be categorized and structured much like the process used to categorize end user resource requirements and create a standard directory structure. Once all of the elements are categorized, you can develop definitive user types, which in turn translate to User Templates.

When categorizing your users to create User Types, the idea is to come up with four or five cookie cutter patterns that meet the vast majority of your user needs. These patterns, which will change as your Enterprise changes, will eventually become your User Templates. User Templates, which are nothing more than dummy users to be copied in order to create true functional users, do not have any official creation rules. There is nowhere to go in the User Manager for Domains to kick off template creation, nor is there any tool provided to form these patterns. Templates provide the following advantages:

- You will ensure that all users will be created according to predetermined standards.
- You will provide a fast, time-saving technique to create users.

9

MANAGING
USERS

- You will have the ability to delegate user creation without requiring a great deal of administrative knowledge (for example, a non-technical person within your organization such as a secretary or Data Security employee).

As you will see, many of the elements that combine to make up a user template will remain static from user to user. It follows then that the differences in your templates are very few; however, they are significant in terms of security and the resources each user will access by default. When categorizing your user types, it is best to first define the elements that will remain static from user to user, then determine the differences that will define your user types.

Static User Elements in the InterDepartmental Domain

The following elements will remain static from user to user in the Horton Domain, the InterDepartmental example used throughout this book:

- User Name/Full Name Conventions
- User Description Conventions
- Individual Password Policies
- Home Directories
- Logon Restrictions
- Account Type/Expiration
- Printers

Each of these elements, as seen in Chapter 4, "Designing Your Domain," is managed through the User Manager for Domains, unless otherwise specified.

User Name/Full Name Conventions

The User Name and Full Name of a user are determined in the User Properties window in the User Manager for Domains (see Figure 9.1). As discussed in Chapter 3, "The Importance of Standardization," user naming conventions are defined in terms of user name formats. Depending on the size of your organization, there are several good logon name formats to choose from: last name/first initial (jacobst), first name/last initial (tomj), full initial set (tlj), last five digits of the user's Social Security number, the entire Social Security number, or employee identification number. With Windows NT Server, the administrator even has the ability to use the user's full name as his logon ID. The InterDepartmental Domain is usually a fairly small deployment (anywhere between five and 150 users), so any of these naming standards will work; however, there is always the possibility that when using initials or full names for logon IDs, duplicates can crop up. When the Horton Agency initially deployed their NetWare network, they utilized the users' initials for logon IDs. As their organization grew, more and more duplicates cropped up. Therefore, with the introduction of Windows NT Server in the environment, they have elected to move forward with a Last Name/First Initial format. Therefore, Tom Jacobs' User ID will be JACOBST.

In addition to the User Name text box, the User Manager also provides a field for the user's full name (see Figure 9.1). For sorting purposes, the Horton Agency has elected to standardize on a Last Name/First Name (Jacobs, Tom) format.

Figure 9.1.

The User Properties Window.

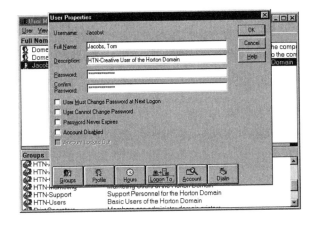

Each user that is created in the Horton Domain will be assigned these naming formats.

User Description Conventions

In Chapter 4, during the creation of the Departmental group, a standard format for group descriptions was determined (see Table 9.1). In addition to Group Descriptions, the administrator also has the ability to provide individual User descriptions using the User Manager for Domains (see Figure 9.1). To the architect of a domain, User Descriptions may not be that helpful; however, for the purposes of inherent documentation, it is an excellent idea to provide a standard user description for each user type. This description will be extremely useful for new support personnel.

Table 9.1. Departmental Groups within the Horton Domain.

Department	Group	Description
Creative	HTN-Creative	Creative Users of the Horton Domain
Accounting	HTN-Accounting	Accounting Users of the Horton Domain
Sales	HTN-Sales	Sales Users of the Horton Domain
Administrative	HTN-Admin	Administrative Users of the Horton Domain
Network Support	HTN-Support	Support Personnel in the Horton Domain

The Administrators of the Horton Domain have determined that the best use of the User Description field would be to provide an obvious description of the user's primary departmental association.

It is important to stress that User Descriptions are an excellent aid for those support personnel who are either new to your environment or not familiar with your user directory.

Password Policies

In a user's Properties window in the User Manager for Domains, you have three password options (see Figure 9.1):

- User Must Change Password at Next Logon
- User Cannot Change Password
- Password Never Expires

When a user is first created, the User Must Change Password at Next Logon option is always checked. The other two options are used at the discretion of the administrator or account operators.

Home Directories

All home directories in the Horton Domain will be created in the \\HTN-PROD01\USERS directory. Home directories are an odd resource. Many users never use theirs, and then there are those who store almost everything in the home directory. Each user in the Horton Domain will be assigned a home directory. As stated in Chapter 4, home directories are assigned and often created in the User Environment Profile in the User Manager for Domains (see Figure 9.2).

FIGURE 9.2.

The User Environment Profile.

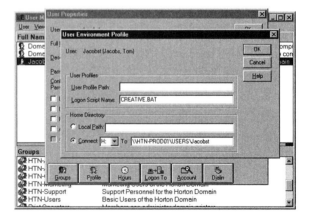

Logon Restrictions

While there may be individual cases (such as with temporary employees) when restricting a user to a specific workstation would aid in security or management, in most cases there is no need for such restriction. The Horton Agency has determined that this is an unnecessary restriction for its users, especially in light of the fact that many of its creative personnel still use Macintosh workstations. Workstation restrictions are set in the User Manager for Domains (see Figure 9.3).

FIGURE 9.3.

Logon Workstation Restrictions.

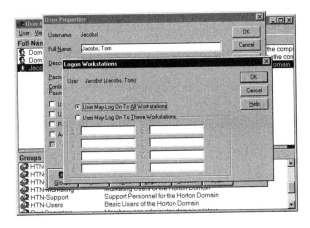

Account Type and Account Expiration

The Account Type and Account Expires settings, as seen in Figure 9.4, are managed through the User Manager for Domains, although they are rarely used in the InterDepartmental Domain. The Horton Agency has elected to ignore these options during their categorization of users.

FIGURE 9.4.

The Account Information Window.

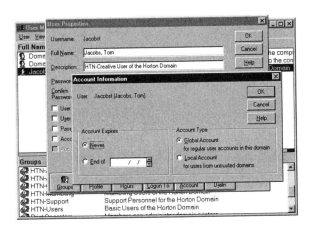

Printers

Printers in a Windows NT Server environment are generally deployed during the initial workstation deployment; however, due to the driver-hosting facility, as discussed in Chapter 7, "Sharing and Securing Resources," printers are easily added at a later date. In most cases, users will access those printers that are closely located near their work area. Due to the ease of printer connectivity provided by the Network Neighborhood in conjunction with the printer-hosting facility on NT Servers, printers are rarely a management concern.

Non-Static User Elements in the InterDepartmental Domain

The following user elements are those that will vary from user to user. While some of these elements require more thought than the static elements, it is the number of variations found in these elements that usually determines the number of User Templates you will create.

- Logon Hours
- Group Membership
- Dialin Permissions
- Enterprise Resources or Application Servers
- Logon Scripts

The manner in which you categorize and control these elements is key to the success of your Enterprise management.

Logon Hours

Many companies simply don't want their users to have the ability to log into their network after hours. While this may be an excellent form of security for organizations with a more migratory or shift-driven type of staff, most organizations don't have this type of concern. In most cases, logon hour restrictions are set to coincide with a nightly backup, to ensure that there are no open files. Administrators of the Horton Domain have decided to set restrictions on all users, excluding those members of the HTN-Support and Domain Admins groups. Users will be unable to log in during the hours of 11:00 pm to 1:00 am. They have elected not to forcibly disconnect users who are logged in during these hours. (See Chapter 4 for an explanation of this option.)

By determining that there will be variations in this setting, the Horton Domain Administrators have already created a minimum of two user types: those with logon hour restrictions and those without.

FIGURE 9.5.
The Logon Hours Window.

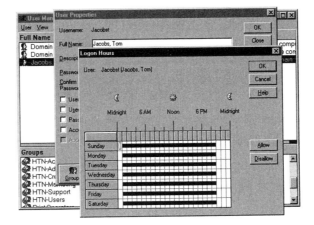

Group Membership

By defining Departmental Groups, you have already gone a long way in determining your user types. If in your InterDepartmental User Directory you have five Departmental Groups, chances are there will be very few more than five user types. Table 9.1 lists the Horton Domain's departmental groups. These departmental groups by default create five preliminary user types:

- Creative Users
- Accounting Users
- Sales Users
- Administrative Users
- Support Personnel

These departmental groups will be used as the basic building blocks of the Horton Domain's user types and user templates.

Dialin Permissions

Dialin permissions, which were briefly discussed in Chapter 4, have a direct correlation to the Windows NT Remote Access Service. RAS, which is a built-in service, provides remote node dialin for users of all Windows platforms. Access to this service, which will be explained in detail in Chapter 11, "Alternative Platform Connectivity," is not provided by default to all users (see Figure 9.6).

After careful consideration, administrators of the Horton Domain have determined to provide RAS access only to support personnel. Due to the size of the files the Creative department works with, a remote node solution would be impractical, and the remainder of the users would be able to gain very little functionality from dialin.

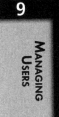

FIGURE 9.6.

The Dialin Informa-
tion Window.

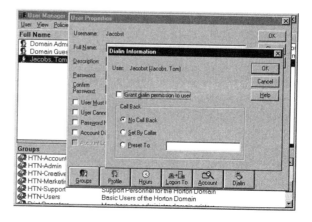

Enterprise Resources and Application Servers

Due to the nature of the InterDepartmental domain, there will be no Cross-Divisional resources; however, there are Enterprise Resources and Application servers that not all users will have access to. The Horton Domain has two dedicated application servers: the HTN-CREATOVE01 and the HTN-ACCTG01. While having group membership in the HTN-Creative and HTN-Accounting group provides automatic access to the respective resources of the Creative and Accounting departments, they will not have an automatic connection. Access to application resources should be categorized for reference when considering Logon Script design.

In addition to application servers, Enterprise resources should be considered as well. As mentioned in Chapter 4, the Creative and Sales departments will both access a monthly CD that provides current information on advertising trends and resources. To access this resource, users will need membership in the ENT-MagSearch group. By default, all users in both the Creative and Accounting categories should have membership in this group.

Logon Scripts

Logon scripts in the InterDepartmental Domain are fairly simple to maintain. Logon scripts, which are stored in the \\system root\system32\repl\import\scripts directory, are assigned to a user in the User Environment Profile window of a user's properties (see Figure 9.2).

NOTE

As a user attempts to logon to a Domain in which more than one Domain Controller exists, they will be authenticated by the DC that is either least busy or closest in proximity. Instead of making the administrator manually copy logon scripts to the Netlogon share of each Domain Controller, the administrator may set up directory replication to automatically replicate logon scripts. Once configured, any changes to the master copy of the logon scripts, usually stored on the Primary Domain Controller, will be replicated to each DC automatically. Directory Replication will be discussed in detail in Chapter 15, "Providing Fault Tolerance."

Logon scripts in Windows NT are simply batch files that provide the capability to map drives to network folders or start executables each time a user logs onto the Domain. Logon scripts are not required in Domain Management but are highly beneficial when attempting to set a standard environment. When a user logs into the domain and is authenticated, the logon script you have assigned will process any drive mappings or executables that might be contained within. In the InterDepartmental Domain, chances are that all users will need access to all major shares. Therefore, the basis for all logon scripts in the Horton Agency would begin as follows:

> Net Use H: \\HTN-PROD01\Users
>
> Net Use I: \\HTN_PROD01\DATA
>
> Net Use J: \\HTN-PROD01\Apps

It is important that all end-users receive the same drive mapping for the same resources. For instance, if some of your users received the letter L:\ in their logon scripts for the Apps share while others received J:\ for the same resources, confusion between end-users and support personnel would be inevitable. Standard drive mappings are a crucial part of a well organized environment for any domain deployment.

While all users will receive drive mappings to the primary shares, Users, DATA, and Apps, there are shares in the Horton Domain that are departmentally specific. For instance, only Support personnel will receive drive mappings to the Support$ share, only Accounting employees will receive drive mappings to the HTN-ACCTG01 server, and only Creative employees will receive drive mappings to the HTN-CREATIVE01 server.

Thus, Logon Scripts will be created and assigned as follows:

Administrative	*BASIC.BAT*
Net Use H:	\\HTN-PROD01\Users
Net Use I:	\\HTN_PROD01\DATA
Net Use J:	\\HTN-PROD01\Apps

Accounting	*ACCTG.BAT*
Net Use H:	\\HTN-PROD01\Users
Net Use I:	\\HTN_PROD01\DATA
Net Use J:	\\HTN-PROD01\Apps
Net Use K:	\\HTN-ACCTG01\ACTTGAPP

9

MANAGING USERS

Support	*SUPPORT.BAT*
Net Use H:	\\HTN-PROD01\Users
Net Use I:	\\HTN_PROD01\DATA
Net Use J:	\\HTN-PROD01\Apps
Net Use S:	\\HTN-PROD01\Support$

Creative	*CREATIVE.BAT*
Net Use H:	\\HTN-PROD01\Users
Net Use I:	\\HTN_PROD01\DATA
Net Use J:	\\HTN-PROD01\Apps
Net Use L:	\\HTN-CREATIVE01\Creative
Net Use M::	\\HTN-PROD01\MagSearch*

Sales	*SALES.BAT*
Net Use H:	\\HTN-PROD01\Users
Net Use I:	\\HTN_PROD01\DATA
Net Use J:	\\HTN-PROD01\Apps
Net Use M::	\\HTN-PROD01\MagSearch*

*MagSearch is an Enterprise resource that is shared in a CD-Tower connected to HTN-PROD01. The only group with access to this resource is an Enterprise group named ENT-MagSearch.

> **NOTE**
>
> Unfortunately, Windows NT does not provide for assigning Logon Scripts to specific groups, but through the use of User Templates, you can ensure that users are assigned the appropriate scripts upon creation. Additionally, by using the User Manager for Domains, you can select all members of a specific group and edit their properties to include the same logon script. This type of mass-user management was covered in Chapter 4, "Designing Your Domain."

Creating User Templates

Using the information gathered from defining your static user elements and categorizing your user types, you have enough information to create user templates. User templates, as mentioned earlier, are nothing more than dummy users created simply to be copied when creating real users. As in nearly every aspect of domain management, it is extremely helpful to have template-naming conventions in place. One of the nice advantages to user template-naming conventions is their place in the directory. If every user template were to have the Full Name of Template, User, and a Username (such as T-Creative), all templates would be sorted together, regardless of which sort order you had chosen in the User Manager for Domains.

To create a User Template, use the following procedure:

1. Launch the User Manager for Domains and select New User from the User option on the top menu.

2. Provide the appropriate Username, Full Name, and user Description (see Figure 9.7).

FIGURE 9.7.

Creating a User Template.

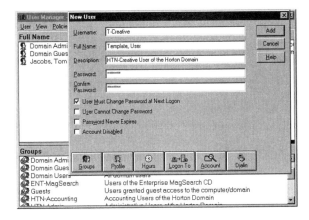

3. Select the Group button and add the appropriate group memberships (see Figure 9.8). For instance, for Creative Users in the Horton Domain, add the HTN-Users, HTN-Creative, and ENT-MagSearch groups.

FIGURE 9.8.

Template Group Membership.

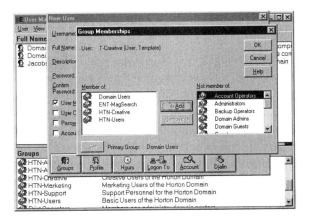

9

MANAGING USERS

4. Next, select the Profile button and enter the appropriate Logon Script Name and Home Directory. Use the %Username% variable when assigning a home directory. This will ensure that any user created when copying this template will have an appropriate home directory assigned (see Figure 9.9).

FIGURE 9.9.

Assigning Logon Scripts and Home Directories.

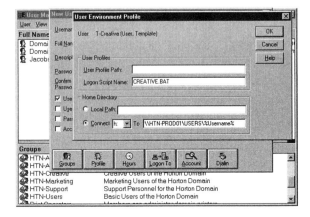

5. Finally, set the appropriate Logon Hours, Account Type information, and Dialin rights. Once complete, check the Account Disabled box on the front page of the New User window (this will ensure that no one can log on using your user templates) and select Add. Your user template will be created and added to the User Directory.

Once you complete the creation of your User Templates, creating new users is as simple as selecting the appropriate template, going to the User menu option, and selecting Copy. You will be required to enter a Username, Full Name, and in the case of a Domain where blank passwords are not permitted, an initial password; however, once complete, due to the component design of your network, your job is done. With the exception of daily desktop support, user management takes up the majority of an administrator's support time. Once your users are templated, user administration becomes almost a null issue. Furthermore, once you integrate Domain Directory-aware applications such as SNA Server to provide access to legacy and Enterprise applications, your Enterprise nearly manages itself.

User Types in the InterDivisional Domain

The process utilized for creating user types and eventually user templates in the InterDivisional Domain is identical to the process used in the InterDepartmental domain. The greatest difference, as always, is the scale of the implementation. Since many of the static elements in the InterDepartmental Domain will be static in the InterDivisional Domain, only those elements that are being addressed differently will be covered in this section.

User Name and Full Name Conventions

Most organizations will choose the Last Name/First Name conventions for full names. The Guardian Insurance Companies have done no differently. Additionally, Guardian has chosen to use their employees' Social Security numbers for user IDs. Thus, Roger Thompson's user profile will appear as in Figure 9.10.

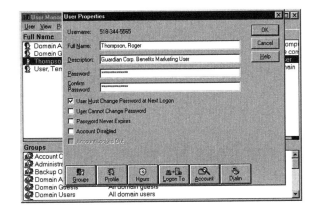

User Description Conventions

User Descriptions can become slightly more complicated in a Divisional domain. Documentation is critical in any deployment and will be covered in Chapter 17, "Domain Documentation;" however, it's not always available when required. If used effectively, the User Directory can provide a great deal of documentation; therefore, the User Description field is crucial. The administrators of the Guardian Domain have elected to categorize their users as follows:

- Accounting Users of the Corp. Benefits Division
- Accounting Users of the HQ Division
- Accounting Users of the Health Division
- Accounting Users of the Casualty Division

This convention will apply to all major departments in each division, providing anyone administering users enough information to determine their Divisional alignment and basic function in the organization.

Home Directories

Home directories in the InterDivisional deployment become slightly more complicated. Each Division has its own Production server; therefore, not all users in the User Directory will share

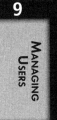

the same home directory path. The following will outline the home directory path for each division:

Guardian HeadQuarters	`\\HQ-PROD01\Data\Users\%username%`
Guardian Health	`\\HLT-PROD01\Data\Users\%username%`
Guardian Corporate Benefits	`\\CORP-PROD01\Data\Users\%username%`
Guardian Casualty	`\\CTY-PROD01\Data\Users\%username%`

While home directories may differ from division to division, each user in the Casualty division will have his/her home directory on the same server, each user in the HQ division will have his/her home directory on the same server, and so on.

The rest of the static elements in the InterDivisional Domain will remain very similar to those elements in the InterDepartmental Domain.

Non-Static User Elements in the InterDivisional Domain

Many of the organizational concepts will remain the same from deployment model to deployment model. The following non-static user elements are those that require additional consideration when compared to the InterDepartmental Domain; otherwise, the concepts and processes remain the same.

Logon Hours

Logon Hours are settings to be utilized to keep people off the network during certain hours for one of two reasons: to complete backups uninterrupted or to keep users off the network in an unattended environment. While none of the divisions in the Guardian Domain had security concerns, they were conscious of the need for good backups. Each division has determined to set a minimum of five hours of down time and has furthermore determined to forcibly disconnect users when their logon hours expire (see Chapter 4). For instance, Guardian Health will restrict access from 10 pm to 3 am each night, while Guardian Casualty has restricted access from 11 pm to 6 am. Each division will restrict logon hours based on the length of time it takes to complete backups. No other time restrictions have been deemed necessary.

Group Membership

In the InterDepartmental Domain, the number of Departmental groups usually determines the number of user types you will define and, therefore, it follows that they will also correlate to the number of User Templates that will exist in your User Directory. In the InterDivisional Domain, the number of user types/User Templates will also have a direct relationship to the total number of departmental groups within each division. For instance, Guardian HQ has six departmental groups, while Guardian Corporate Benefits, Guardian Casualty, and Guardian Health each have three departmental groups. Thus, if it follows that the number of departmental groups that exist in your domain relates to the number of User Templates you define, there will be a minimum of 15 User Templates in the Guardian Domain's User Directory.

Dialin Permissions

Dialin access will be explored further in Chapter 11; however, as far as the Guardian Domain is concerned, very few people will have dialin rights. All support personnel and some executives will be provided with remote access permissions; but even so, the only users who will be categorized as remote access users are members of the support groups within the Enterprise. Dialin permission is one of the few user needs that becomes difficult to pin down to a group level.

Enterprise Resources, Cross-Divisional Resources, and Application Servers

Cross-Divisional and Enterprise resources are inevitable in the InterDivisional Domain. With any luck, there will be a sense of order to the manner in which Cross-Divisional resources are deployed so that they may be directly associated to an entire division or at least certain departments within a division. If this is the case, users can have automatic connections to their Cross-Divisional Resources through their departmental logon scripts. If not, the administrator has three choices: First, he can increase the number of user types/user templates per division, which also requires an increased number of logon scripts per department; second, he can minimize the number of templates by adding membership to Cross-Divisional and Enterprise groups after the user is created and manually map drives during a desktop visit; or third, if he's in a pure Windows NT 4.0 and Windows 95 environment, he can deploy a new feature provided with Windows NT called the Distributed File System. DFS, which will be covered in Chapter 11, will allow you to create a virtual file system that allows your users to access all application servers and Cross-Divisional and Enterprise resources through a single mapped drive.

In reality, the administrator will most likely strike a balance between these three options, but still, time spent performing standard user administration will be cut by more than half when compared to conventional administrative techniques.

Logon Scripts

While logon scripts in the InterDepartmental Domain are fairly simple to maintain, they can become more difficult in the InterDivisional Domain. Much like there are basic elements common to all logon scripts in the InterDepartmental deployment, there will be common elements

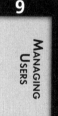

9

MANAGING
USERS

in each division's departmental logon scripts. For instance, all users in the Guardian Health division will have the following mappings in their logon scripts:

> Net Use H: \\HLT-PROD01\Data
>
> Net Use I: \\HLT-PROD01\Apps

Just like in the InterDepartmental deployment, it is important that all end-users receive the same drive mapping for the same resources from division to division. For instance, if a user in the Casualty division calls the Help Desk to inquire about problems with his I:\ drive, that Help Desk representative will know automatically that the I:\ drive is where all applications are stored—regardless of which division the user is from. While all users will receive drive mappings to the primary shares DATA and Apps, there will be departmentally specific resources, as well as Cross-Divisional or Enterprise resources that are not common to all fellow departmental members. As mentioned in the preceding section, the administrator has traditionally had two ways to address this: manually mapped drives or an increased number of logon scripts to manage. With the advent of the Directory File System, you will be able to create a virtual directory structure that will span these resources, whether they be NT, NetWare, or OS/2 LAN Servers. DFS, which will be covered in detail in Chapter 11, is accessible only by Windows NT 4.0 and Windows 95 workstations. Using DFS, you can create a directory structure per division that will provide access to all required Cross-Divisional or Enterprise resources with the simple addition of one mapped drive per logon script. However, it is still helpful to use logon scripts to map drives to departmentally specific resources or application servers for end user identification purposes.

Luckily, the Guardian Insurance Companies have elected to move to Windows NT 4.0 Workstation as the standard desktop. Thus, each division will host its own DFS structure to provide Cross-Divisional and Enterprise resource access. An example of the variety of logon scripts follows:

HQ/Claims	*HQ-CLAIMS.BAT*
Net Use H:	\\HQ-PROD01\DATA
Net Use I:	\\HQ-PROD01\APPS
Net Use J:	\\HQ-CLAIMS1\ClaimsApp
Net Use O:	\\HQ-PROD01\HQ-DFS1
Health/Administrative	*HLT-ADMIN.BAT*
Net Use H:	\\CTY-PROD01\DATA
Net Use I:	\\CTY-PROD01\APPS
Net Use O:	\\CTY-PROD01\CTY-DFS1

Corporate Benefits/Accounting	*CORP-ACCT.BAT*
Net Use H:	\\CORP-PROD01\DATA
Net Use I:	\\CORP-PROD01\APPS
Net Use J:	\\CORP-ACCTG01\MMAN
Net Use O:	\\CORP-PROD01\CORP-DFS1

Casualty/Marketing	*CLT-MRKT.BAT*
Net Use H:	\\CTY-PROD01\DATA
Net Use I:	\\CTY-PROD01\APPS
Net Use O:	\\CTY-PROD01\CTY-DFS1

Creating User Templates in the InterDivisional Domain

User templates are created in the InterDivisional domain just as they are for the InterDepartmental domain. Once you've categorized your static and non-static user elements and struck a balance between creating a user template for each major user variation and manual adjustment, you are ready to begin template creation. Naming convention is just as important in the InterDivisional domain as it is in the InterDepartmental; however, it can be more complicated. For instance, each division should have its own prefix for identification purposes; however, each template name should also be created so that they will be sorted together in the directory, regardless of which order is chosen. The following template names might be used by administrators in the Guardian Domain:

HQ/Claims	T-HQ-Claims
Health/Administrative	T-HLT-Admin
Corporate Benefits/Accounting	T-CORP-Acctg
Casualty/Marketing	T-CLT-Marketing

Much like with all objects in the User Directory, a naming standard that follows preconceived conventions and a description that provides intuitive documentation are keys to success.

User Types in the InterCorporate Domain

When compared to the InterDivisional domain, there is very little difference in the InterCorporate domain in terms of categorization, the definition of user types, and the creation of user templates. The greatest overall differences between the InterDivisional and the InterCorporate deployments are in the implementation of the Master Domain Model in the InterCorporate domain (covered in Chapter 17), and the sheer number of user types and templates. Naming conventions, drive letter standardization, and a well designed implementation of DFS technology are extremely important to this and all domain models.

Profiles

Chapter 4 discusses the creation of user profiles for Windows NT clients and briefly identifies implementation possibilities. As mentioned in this chapter, there are two different types of profiles: Roaming and Mandatory. Remember that whenever a user with a Roaming Profile logs in to the domain from an NT 4.0 computer, his profile becomes integrated with the local registry and re-creates the desktop environment for the user, no matter which NT 4.0 computer he/she logs in to. By default, a user can alter his/her own profile; therefore, any changes made will be reflected each time the user logs in. This method of profile deployment, while intriguing, can present difficulties in a large environment; this is due to the fact that just because a shortcut to a local resource contained within the Roaming Profile exists on one workstation, that doesn't mean it will exist on another. If a user moves from workstation to workstation in a non-standard or even an extremely large yet divisionally standardized environment, chances are there will be shortcuts within the Roaming Profile that don't correspond to every machine. This can cause confusion for the end user and, in many cases, for first line support personnel.

While Roaming Profiles can cause unnecessary support issues, Mandatory Profiles can provide a level of control that may be necessary in certain environments. While Mandatory Profiles are still Roaming Profiles, the end-user cannot change the predetermined environment. The profile still follows the user wherever he/she goes, but any changes made will not be saved.

Chapter 4 discussed the creation of user profiles for Windows NT computers only. Profiles, both Roaming and Mandatory, can also be created for Windows 95 machines. The remainder of this chapter will cover the creation of Roaming and Mandatory user profiles, as well as provide a solid example of how Mandatory profiles can result in reduced support headaches.

Creating User Profiles for Windows 95 Workstations

A Windows 95 User Profile will contain everything in the Hkey_Current_User section of the registry, including the following:

- Control Panel settings, including desktop background, desktop layout, fonts, and colors
- Shortcuts on the desktop and in the Start Menu
- Registry-aware application settings and accessory settings
- Menu and toolbar configurations

When user profiles are enabled on Windows 95, each user will have his significant settings stored in his own Profiles directory. These settings, such as the USER.DAT file, the Desktop Folder, and the Start Menu Folder, will be unique for each user who logs into the Windows 95 machine.

In order for either type of profile, Roaming or Mandatory, to take affect, it is necessary to enable Profiles on the Windows 95 machine. To do so, you must launch the Control Panel and select the Password extension, as seen in Figure 9.11. The Password Properties window consists of two tabs: Change Passwords and User Profiles. Select User Profiles and you will be presented with a window, as seen in Figure 9.12.

FIGURE 9.11.

*The Password
Extension in the
Windows 95 Control
Panel.*

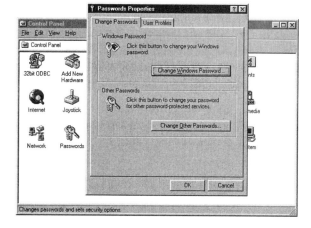

FIGURE 9.12.

*The User Profiles
Properties Page.*

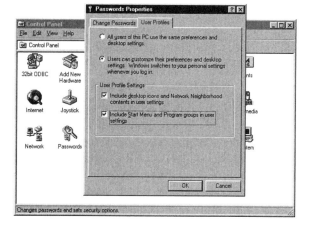

Notice that the top half of this page contains two pertinent settings: The first states that each user will share the same preferences and desktop settings, while the second designates that Windows 95 will maintain a separate profile for each user. Select this setting to enable Windows 95 Profiles.

On the second half of the screen, there are also two choices: One designates that all desktop icons and Network Neighborhood settings will be retained for each user, and the second determines that Start Menu and Program group settings will be retained for each user. To properly implement Windows 95 profiles, select both options. Select OK, and the machine will prompt you to restart the machine.

At this point, as long as the user has a properly configured Windows NT Server-based home directory and Client for Microsoft Networks is designated as the Primary Network Logon, the first time a user logs in and out of her Windows NT Server, a copy of her profile will be stored in her home directory. This profile will follow the user to whichever Windows 95 machine she logs into. Remember, however, that even though the Desktop Shortcuts and Start Menu items might follow the user, they will only work if the target workstation is configured identically to the workstation from which the user's profile was created. Obviously, in a standard environment, this will not be an issue. Chapter 10, "Workstation Standards," will provide an excellent method through which to deploy standard workstations.

To implement Mandatory profiles for your users, you will follow a procedure similar to that with Windows NT. Log on to a standard Windows 95 workstation as a Template user, create the desktop and Start menu settings you want your users to have, and log off the Windows 95 Workstation.

Next, go to the Template user's home directory and rename the USER.DAT file USER.MAN. At this point, you will have successfully created a user profile that cannot be changed. In order to apply it to your target users, you must now copy it to their home directories. It is highly recommended that you set file level security on the USER.MAN file to ensure that the end-user cannot delete it. The first time the user logs on, he will receive the new mandatory desktop. This desktop cannot change, unless you rename the USER.MAN back to USER.DAT.

Implementing User Profiles

User profiles can be an excellent tool, especially in an environment where there is a great deal of diversity in terms of user expertise. In fact, user profiles are an excellent tool to deploy for the less savvy user or in a department with high turnover. Guardian Casualty has an extremely large Claims department that requires a great deal of consistency. Most often when a user leaves the company, his workstation has been left in a state that would not lend itself well to a new user. Therefore, it becomes necessary to reconfigure a machine each time an associate joins the company. The domain administrators have determined that the implementation of user profiles will reduce support time in the Claims department and alleviate the need to reconfigure a workstation each time an employee leaves. Remember that Guardian has decided to deploy Windows NT Workstation as the sole desktop operating system; therefore, by creating and defining a standard Claims department profile, users will not be able to make any desktop or application changes to their workstations. In addition, by deploying these workstations with the NTFS file system and locking down file and directory permissions, they become virtually bulletproof. Through the combination of Windows NT profiles and directory level security, these workstations will not need reconfiguration each time a user leaves. In fact, it will not even be necessary to visit the desktop to prepare it for a new user.

Summary

The deployment models endorsed by this book not only provide for an expandable, easily navigated, and standard environment, they also result in low administration overhead. In combination with User Templates and tactfully deployed user profiles, your network in many cases will administer itself. Standardization and categorization are keys to successful domain management.

Workstation Standards

CHAPTER 10

The deployment models endorsed by this book provide a sense of stability and familiarity not only for the support personnel but also for the end user. One of the major benefits of a standard back-end environment is the lack of intrusion your enterprise management will have on the end user. In reality your end users shouldn't care what your Network Operating Systems are, nor should they care what it takes for you as an administrator to manage their resources. Up to now the focus of this book has been on an efficient back-end deployment; however, it has not yet accounted for the deployment of workstations. In order to truly provide a streamlined, efficient environment your workstations must be deployed in such a manner as to avoid intrusion into your user's daily lives. Through the topics of desktop standardization, automated deployment of workstations, and the use of the logon script as a tool, this chapter provides a good deal of information that will contribute to a well-managed desktop.

Desktop Standards

In most environments the majority of all support time is spent at the user's desktop. Unfortunately, it is not unusual for a support technician to walk from desktop to desktop and never see a similar configuration. Much like servers, it is important to standardize the desktop environment. Desktop standardization will assist not only your support personnel, but also your end user in becoming comfortable and productive in your networked environment. The desktop operating system, workstation naming conventions, application standards, directory structure, and protocols are all crucial to defining your standard desktop environment.

Operating System

As the person responsible for delivering support to your end users it is crucial that you minimize the points of failure in your environment. One of those points of failure (and unfortunately it seems to fail often) is the desktop computer and its operating system. By having multiple desktop operating systems in your environment you only increase the number of points of failure within your enterprise. Familiarity with the environment can never be overstated. The more familiar your end users are with the conventions of your enterprise, the easier it is for them to operate. Likewise, the more familiar your support technicians are, the easier it is for them to resolve issues. For these reasons it is crucial that your desktop operating systems adhere to as many standards and conventions as your network operating systems. If you can minimize the number of operating systems in your environment, you can also minimize the number of problems there will be to resolve.

In today's computing world there are very few operating systems that make sense as a strategic direction in the corporate environment. With a strong foothold on the industry, Microsoft and its 32-bit operating systems have fast become the de facto corporate standards. Luckily, as you'll see later in this chapter, Microsoft has been sensitive to the difficulties associated with standardization by providing ways to distribute its operating systems in an efficient manner.

No matter which deployment model your enterprise fits under, there may be some confusion as to whether Windows 95 or Windows NT Workstation is right for you. Many organizations have the luxury of deciding upon only one of these operating systems, while others will require both or possibly even additional operating systems. When determining your standard operating system there are many determining factors:

- Hardware Requirements
- Software Requirements
- End-User Needs
- Future Strategic Direction
- Software/Hardware Costs

Any one of these factors can determine your desktop direction. Following is a quick rundown of these factors.

Hardware Requirements

Minimum hardware guidelines as suggested by this book are based upon acceptable performance levels with shrink-wrapped office automation software. While both Windows 95 and Windows NT will run on lesser machines, productivity will be affected considerably. These requirements are based on the performance of the operating system in conjunction with the applications you need to run.

The minimum recommended hardware requirements for both Windows NT Workstation 4.0 and Windows 95 are based on realistic corporate situations. In other words, it is much easier to set standards that will affect only a portion of your current inventory, versus setting standards that immediately place all of your hardware on the endangered list. (For every government official that likes to think corporate money flows like water, there are one hundred network administrators that know better.) Table 10.1 suggests the absolute minimum level of existing hardware to be utilized during a migration to a 32-bit desktop.

Table 10.1. Absolute Minimum Hardware Requirements for Windows 95 and Windows NT Workstation 4.0.

Component	Windows 95	Windows NT Workstation 4.0
CPU	486/66 DX/2	Pentium 60
RAM	16MB	32MB
Hard Drive	210MB	300MB
Graphics Card	1MB SVGA	1MB SVGA

Again, it should be reiterated that these requirements are the bare minimum suggested. For instance, if you were to load a Windows 95 machine with a workstation install of Office 95

10

WORKSTATION
STANDARDS

and Lotus Notes on the hardware platform listed above, you would be left with somewhere between 20 and 25 MB of free hard drive space—this is barely enough for the swap file.

Keep in mind that the trend in software development has been toward larger and hungrier applications. Developers don't develop for the bare minimum requirements of any operating system. Instead, they develop for the platforms of the future. An excellent strategy, as mentioned in Chapter 3, "The Importance of Standardization," is the acquisition of Minus One generation technology. For instance, if during your purchase cycle the Pentium 166 is the new processor on the block, purchase a machine with the Pentium 133. You'll save money, have more than acceptable levels of performance, and chances are during your next buying cycle you'll be able to move to the Pentium 166 with no price increase. While it might seem savvy to purchase the 100Mhz machines at closeout prices, you'll be paying for their performance in the next 8 to 12 months.

If money were no object and you had the opportunity to replace all of the hardware in your enterprise that you felt would soon be obsolete, the configurations in Table 10.2 would be best utilized as the minimum hardware requirements.

Table 10.2. Realistic Minimum Hardware Requirements for Windows 95 and Windows NT Workstation 4.0.

Component	Windows 95	Windows NT Workstation 4.0
CPU	486 DX4 100	Pentium 90 or better
RAM	32MB	32MB or better
Hard Drive	500MB	1GB
Graphics Card	1MB SVGA	2MB SVGA

It is important to note that when performing standard office automation functions you won't see significant performance improvements on a Windows 95 machine when comparing a high-end Pentium processor with a low-end Pentium processor—memory is the key to performance in Windows 95 in the Pentium class machines. Windows NT, on the other hand, seems to be able to utilize whatever you throw at it—processor or memory. Depending on the function of your Windows NT 4.0 Workstation, hardware requirements might be greater.

Software Requirements

A quick way to determine whether or not your organization requires Windows NT Workstation is to look at the standard software that will be utilized in your environment. In most cases if your organization only utilizes standard shrink-wrapped office automation software, Windows NT Workstation is unnecessary in your environment. If, on the other hand, your corporate direction hinges on any of the advanced management features inherent to NT Workstation, NT 4.0 will be your direction. Additionally, such tasks as software development, graphic design, network administration, and workstation processing usually associated with UNIX operating systems are better left to NT Workstation.

End-User Needs

As mentioned previously, if your users only require shrink-wrapped standard office automation software such as MS Office and Lotus Notes, Windows 95 is an excellent desktop choice. Windows 95 is superior to Windows NT in many ways, including the many support advantages offered by Plug-and-Play and the tremendous amount of development support. The networking features, open platform, and improved interface are all benefits of Windows 95.

On the other hand, Windows NT Workstation is excellent in terms of multitasking and stability. Windows NT Workstation on a high-end workstation offers many advantages over Windows 95, including true multitasking, more robust networking, and a tremendous amount of administrative control.

There are two major drawbacks to Windows NT Workstation that should be noted. First, the hardware requirements are prohibitive to many organizations, and second, the development community does not support Windows NT with as much fervor as it does Windows 95. While much of the existing code for the Windows 3.1 base can be easily modified to take advantage of Windows 95, the same is not true for Windows NT Workstation. Additionally, Windows NT does not provide the same amount of multimedia support as does Windows 95. Microsoft's own MSN software is a key example: As of the writing of this book, there is no version of MSN that will run on Windows NT. Furthermore, while it does not necessarily pertain to business computing, very few of the more advanced Windows-based games will run on Windows NT. This is not to suggest that Windows NT is not suited for prime time. On the contrary, Windows NT is a superior platform for most developers and support personnel due to its stability and powerful multitasking.

Future Strategic Direction

Many companies are making their desktop decisions based on Microsoft's strategic direction which would appear to be toward Windows NT Workstation. However, there are those that feel this may not be the wisest decision for all organizations. Although it is true that the direction that Microsoft is taking with Windows is leading toward a more robust OS-like NT Workstation, Microsoft has offered no evidence that a migration from Windows NT as it stands today to the next generation of NT Workstation will be any easier than an upgrade from Windows 95. On the contrary, both versions of Windows today rely heavily upon the NetBIOS interface for network connectivity, whereas the stated direction for Cairo, or NT 5.0, is markedly away from NetBIOS. In fact, NetBIOS support will be supplied only for backwards compatibility with Windows 95, Windows NT 3.5x and 4.0, and Windows for Workgroups. In effect, this puts Windows 95 and Windows NT on an even playing field. When the next version of NT Workstation is released, assuming that a Windows 95 upgrade with the new networking components is not also available, then it will be time to move toward the more robust desktop. If your organization does not have the current hardware infrastructure to support Windows NT and it does have a specific need for the advanced security within NT Workstation or performance of Windows NT, basing your desktop deployment on Microsoft's

10

WORKSTATION STANDARDS

potential strategic direction does not necessarily make sense. However, if you do require the more robust features and performance of Windows NT, it is an excellent operating system choice.

Software/Hardware Costs

It is the subject of cost that helps many organizations determine which desktop operating systems should be deployed as standard. Obviously, Windows NT will require the more expensive hardware platform. In terms of the sheer size of the operating system and the memory and processor requirements, Windows NT is a more expensive operating system. Furthermore, Windows NT Workstation costs between fifty and one hundred dollars more than Windows 95. In any deployment, these costs can be prohibitive.

While it might seem that this chapter stacks the deck against deploying Windows NT Workstation, that is not the intention. Windows NT Workstation is a superior operating system. Once you've used Windows NT Workstation and experienced the powerful multitasking and amazing response time under 32-bit applications, you'll not want to return to Windows 95. What should be gathered from reading this chapter is that there is no clear direction—either from Microsoft or from the industry as whole—as to which operating system you should choose as your standard. What seems to be successful in many environments is departmental or user type standardization. For instance, if you have a department full of developers who require the more robust features of Windows NT, then Windows NT should be the departmental standard. What is of the utmost importance is that like users use like operating systems. This helps not only the interactivity between users, but also the efficiency of your support staff.

Applications

A standard set of applications is just as important as a standard operating system deployment. Your end users' time is precious, as is that of your support personnel. By providing a single set of office automation applications for all users throughout your enterprise, you will cut down on the confusion and complications that result from the distribution of multiple applications that perform the same function. This book will not endorse any particular office automation applications, but will provide categorizations. Applications that should be the same among all of your users are as follows:

- Electronic Mail
- Word Processor
- Spreadsheet
- Presentation Builder
- Database
- 3270/5250 Emulation
- Communication Packages
- Internet Navigator

- Internet Mail (if not integrated with your standard e-mail)
- Groupware (such as Lotus Domino, Microsoft Exchange, or the Netscape suite of products)

If you were to look at a Help Desk call summary of any medium to large enterprise you would find that the majority of the support calls taken revolve around these application types. By eliminating any duplicate-function applications, you will reduce the number of support calls and increase the efficiency of support provided. By limiting the number of products that both your end users and support staff need to learn, you streamline your delivery of enterprise support and therefore reduce your support costs.

Protocols

Even though today's 32-bit operating systems are capable of handling multiple communications protocols, by utilizing more than one you increase your chances of failure. Chapter 6, "Choosing Your Protocols," discusses the pros and cons of the three primary protocols supported by Windows NT. In today's sophisticated environment a simple change in a router's configuration can have a domino effect on your network. In short, choose only the protocols you require and no more. If your users don't require access to a NetWare server, don't use IPX, or if your users do require NetWare connectivity but not NetBIOS resources, use only IPX. If, on the other hand, you have no communications requirements consider the implementation of TCP/IP only. The point is that even though the operating system can easily handle multiple network protocols, your network might not be so lucky. By choosing and standardizing on as few protocols as possible you lessen the possibility of future complications.

Directory Structure

The importance of your servers' volume and directory structure has been discussed in detail throughout this book. Expandability, scaleability, and navigability were all key concerns when designing your back-end directory structure. Just as important as your server directory structure is your workstation directory structure and for many of the same reasons: familiarity, growth potential, and organization. It is critical, not only for the end user, but even more so for your support personnel to be able to sit down at any workstation and know exactly where all applications have been installed. In the section concerning workstation deployment you will see several examples of how a standard directory structure can be used as a support tool.

A simple directory structure is one that mirrors your servers. The following table lists a recommended directory structure for both Windows 95 and Windows NT Workstation in an environment that utilizes the following products: Microsoft Office 95, SNA Server, Extra for SNA Server, Lotus Notes for Groupware, and cc:Mail for electronic mail.

| Operating System | \Win95 | \Winntwrk |
| Microsoft Office 95 | \Win32app\Office95 | \Win32app\Office95 |

SNA Server Client	\Win32app\SNA-95	\Win32app\SNA-NT
Extra! for SNA Server	\Win32app\Epsna32	\Win32app\Epsna32
Lotus Notes	\Win32app\Notes	\Win32app\Notes
cc: Mail	\Win16app\ccMail	\Win16app\ccmail

Notice that the only difference is the directory utilized for the operating system. This directory structure has many advantages:

- First, one can easily tell which operating system is being utilized.

- Second, 16-bit applications cannot be confused for their 32-bit counterparts (or vice versa).

- Third, if utilized properly, it will provide a sense of familiarity for all support personnel.

As mentioned above, many of the benefits of a standard directory structure will be covered in the following section.

Deploying Workstations

Your best opportunity to enforce standardization is during your initial workstation deployment. Luckily, Microsoft has supplied two excellent tools for deploying its premier desktop operating systems that will aid not only in standardization but also in deployment efficiency. For Windows 95 there is Windows Batch Setup 2.0 and for Windows NT Workstation 4.0 there is the Windows NT Setup Manager. These tools provide the foundation for a solid rollout strategy that includes the use of similar tools for your standard applications as well as the Windows NT logon script as a key deployment tool.

Windows 95 Batch Installations

Windows 95 naturally lends itself to a consistent standard configuration as well as an easily managed central distribution. Using Batch Setup 2.0 and a network distribution point a standard Windows 95 configuration can be installed to any workstation on your network with very little human interaction. In short, an installation batch file is created using the Batch Setup. Once this batch file is created, a Windows 95 installation or upgrade can be performed on any workstation connected to the network by going into a Windows 95 distribution directory and typing **Setup msbatch.inf** where *msbatch* is the name of the standard installation batch file. Automating the installation of Windows 95 ensures that all workstations will be configured alike, which results in improved support performance by the help desk and the network technicians.

Writing Batch Files for Automated Windows 95 Installations

In previous versions of Windows it was possible to tailor certain files within a network-shared directory so that all installations of Windows would be alike; however, these capabilities were not inherent nor easy to manage. With Windows 95, Microsoft has met a long outstanding need. Using the Batch Setup program, you will be able to design any number of batch files to meet the needs of each of your departments, divisions, or user types within your enterprise.

Batch Setup 2.0 can be retrieved from the Microsoft Web site by searching for BATCH20.EXE. Once downloaded this file can be installed on either a Windows 95 or Windows NT workstation. In order to create a batch installation file it is important to have a basic understanding of the Windows 95 operating system, as well as to be familiar with its networking features and available accessories.

After you've installed the application in order to create a batch installation file, simply launch the program by clicking on the Windows Batch Setup shortcut that you'll find in your Start menu. The first screen presented asks for user name, company name, computer name, workgroup name, and computer description, as shown in Figure 10.1. Due to the fact that these fields will be included within the response file, it is an excellent idea to use some generic answers. As will be described later in this chapter, it is an easy matter to customize an INF file for each individual user. Notice that in addition to the naming options there are five other options, three of which follow under the heading of Setup options. The most noticeable option is grayed out unless you happen to be running Windows 95—Click Here to Retrieve Settings from the Registry. If you're lucky enough to be working at a Windows 95 workstation configured exactly as you want others to be installed, click this option and all of the batch settings will be filled in automatically. If you're not at a Windows 95 machine or if your current workstation does not meet your desired requirements, there are four remaining pertinent buttons: Network options, Installation options, Optional components, and Done.

FIGURE 10.1.

The Windows 95 Batch Setup 2.0.

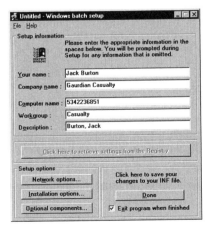

After filling in the pertinent naming information, select the Network options button and you will immediately be presented with a screen entitled Windows batch setup network options (see Figure 10.2).

FIGURE 10.2.

Windows Batch Setup Network Options.

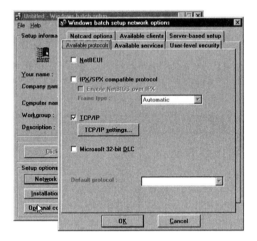

This screen has six available tabs: Netcard options, Available clients, Server-based setup, Available protocols, Available services, and User-level security. On this page you may select NetBEUI, IPX/SPX, TCP/IP, DLC, or all four protocols. Additionally, if you plan to utilize more than one you may also choose your default protocol. Note that the TCP/IP option allows you to specifically configure the TCP/IP settings or to enable DHCP configuration. Following is a quick rundown of the remaining available network configuration options:

- **Available Services:** This option allows you to determine whether you will use File and print sharing for Windows networks, for NetWare networks, or whether you will refrain from using File and print sharing (see Figure 10.3).

- **User-Level Security:** This page allows you to determine whether or not your Windows 95 workstation will allow remote administration and management (see Figure 10.4). If you decide to allow remote administration of your workstations, Windows 95 has the capability to pull security information for a Windows NT Domain, Windows NT Server (stand alone), or NetWare Server. In effect, User-level security uses an existing NOS deployment as pass-through security provider. If User-level security is chosen using a Windows NT Server or Domain, users from the Administrators group will be able to remotely manage the workstation by default. Likewise if a NetWare Server is chosen as the security provider, the NetWare Supervisor and its equivalents will be able to remotely manage the workstation. Remote management of a Windows 95 Workstation is covered in detail in *The Windows 95 Resource Kit.*

Figure 10.3.

The Available Services Page.

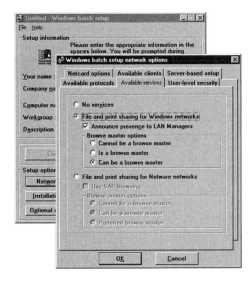

Figure 10.4.

The User-Level Security Page.

■ **NetCard Options:** This page gives you the choice of either ignoring any detected network cards during installation(which will result in Windows 95 Setup prompting you for the card type), or requiring a problem resolution wizard be launched if the card isn't found (see Figure 10.5).

■ **Available Clients:** This option allows you to select from the Microsoft Windows and Microsoft designed NetWare Clients for your workstations. Additionally, if you choose both you may choose the default client type (see Figure 10.6).

FIGURE 10.5.

*The NetCard Options
Page.*

FIGURE 10.5.

*The NetCard Options
Page.*

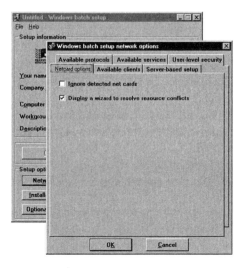

FIGURE 10.6.

*The Available Clients
Page.*

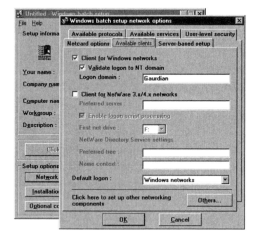

■ **Server-Based Setup:** This page allows you to determine if you wish to install Windows 95 to run from your network server. If you want to run a shared installation you will have the option of allowing Windows 95 to boot using a boot disk, local connectivity software, or a remote boot network card (see Figure 10.7).

Once your network configuration is complete, select OK at the bottom of the Windows 95 batch setup network options page, and you will be brought back to the original screen (refer back to Figure 10.1). Next, select the Installation options button and you will be presented with the screen seen in Figure 10.8.

FIGURE 10.7.
The Server-Based Setup Page.

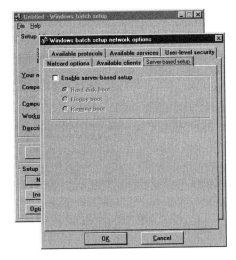

FIGURE 10.8.
The Windows Batch Installation Setup Options Page.

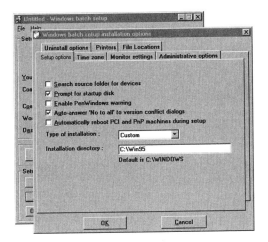

The Windows batch installation options page has seven tabs: Setup options (the default), Time zone, Monitor settings, Administrative options, Uninstall options, Printers, and File Locations. These tabs may be utilized as follows:

■ **Setup Options.** The Setup options page (see Figure 10.8) allows you to specify several options; however, two are critically important. First, the installation directory defaults to c:\windows. If you do not already have a considerable amount of Windows 3.*x* workstations in place this is acceptable; however, if you do it is recommended that you change this to c:\Win95. Second, you may at this time choose whether you wish to perform a Typical, Compact, Portable, or Custom installation. If you choose anything other than Custom you will have no control over the optional components to be installed.

■ **Time Zone.** The Time zone page allows you to set the default time zone for your installed workstations. This is one of the few pages with a single option available (see Figure 10.9).

FIGURE 10.9.

The Time Zone Page.

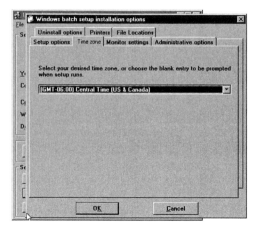

■ **Monitor Settings.** The Monitor settings page allows you to set the default screen settings for each workstation you deploy—both color depth and resolution. This is a setting best left to default unless you know your hardware's capability (see Figure 10.10).

FIGURE 10.10.

The Monitor Settings Page.

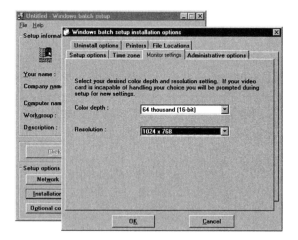

■ **Administrative Options.** This page allows you to set when and if Windows 95 will pause during installation (see Figure 10.11). Unless you plan to manually edit and create an INF file for each workstation in your environment, it is best to set this option to stop during the Network Settings portion of setup. This will allow your technicians to ensure a unique workstation name and to make any network-specific changes to your networking configuration.

FIGURE 10.11.

The Administrative Options Page.

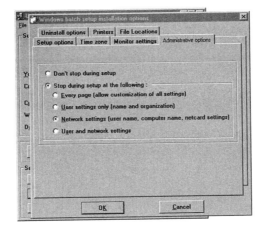

■ **Uninstall Options.** This page is pertinent only in an upgrade situation. If you think that you might find a need to uninstall Windows 95 and return the workstation to its previous state, you should force the installation to create an uninstall directory (see Figure 10.12). However, if you are not upgrading a workstation, this option should be left at its default.

FIGURE 10.12.

The Uninstall Options Page.

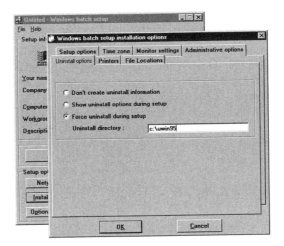

■ **Printers.** This page allows you to specify whether you want to install any printers during installation, and if so whether you want to install a specific printer, or whether you want to launch the Printer Creation Wizard (see Figure 10.13).

10

WORKSTATION
STANDARDS

FIGURE 10.13.
The Printers Page.

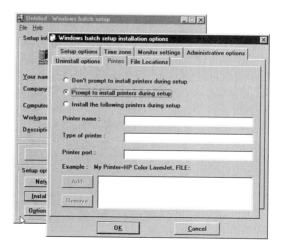

■ **File Locations.** This page allows you to specify three possible locations for Windows 95 source files (see Figure 10.14). For instance, if you installed Windows 95 from \\CTY-PROD01\SUPPORT$\Clients\Win95, then the next time the desktop required a file the server wasn't available it would search for the required files on the other two servers. This option is only helpful in the case that you keep your distribution files on more than one server.

FIGURE 10.14.
The File Locations Page.

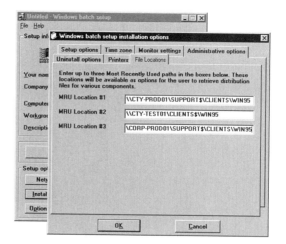

Once you've finished configuring your installation options you will be brought back to the original screen. The last remaining button, the Optional components button (see Figure 10.1), will bring up a window that will allow you to go through each component category and choose which options you wish to install (see Figure 10.15). Once you are finished with your batch file configuration choose the button marked Done on the first page and you will be asked to name the file. As soon as you save the file in the root of your Windows 95 distribution directory you will be ready to begin automated installations of Windows 95.

Figure 10.15.

The Optional Components Page.

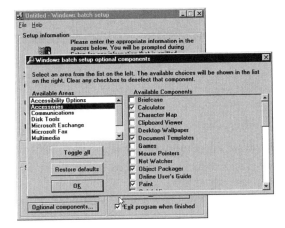

Performing Automated Installations of Windows 95

Once the basic INF file is created, it is simple to customize for individual users. The Windows Batch Installation Program stores these INF files in text format, and each option given within each screen in the Batch Setup application is presented line by line. For those options that require only a checkmark to install, there is either a 0 or a 1. For instance, the line that reads `"Dial-Up Networking"=0` indicates that Dial-Up Networking will not be installed. If the network technician performing the installation knows that the user has a modem and will be dialing into the network, all that is required is that the technician open the INF file with any text editor and next to `"Dial-Up Networking"` change the 0 to a 1. In addition, the technician could go to the line which reads `"Name="USERNAME"` and quickly change it to `"Name=Bob Smith"`. Once all necessary changes are made, the file can be saved in the Windows 95 shared directory as BSMITH.INF. At this point the technician can go to the workstation, connect to the network drive, and type `Setup BSMITH.INF`. Once setup is initiated, it will install Windows 95 in the specified directory, detect all hardware, and be configured for the appropriate connectivity options.

While Windows 95 goes a long way toward automated installation, it is not completely hands-off. Once the installation is complete, it is still necessary to install and configure applications. What the Windows 95 automation process does offer is time. If a technician can begin the installation process knowing that he or she will not be prompted for information or be required to configure anything after the initial five minutes of installation, then that technician can either initiate another (or several) automated installation(s), or work on other problems while Windows 95 is installing itself. As you'll see later in this chapter, it is possible to provide installation boot disks for almost all machines. These boot disks are designed to start the operating system, load network drivers, connect and log into the network, and finally initiate a Windows

95 installation. In combination with installation boot disks and Batch installation files, Windows 95 represents a solid time savings from traditional operating system deployment methods.

Windows NT Workstation Batch Installations

With the release of Windows NT 4.0, Microsoft has provided a batch setup utility very similar to that of Windows 95s. The Windows NT Setup Manager can be found in the root of your Windows NT Server 4.0 or Windows NT Workstation 4.0 CD-ROM in the \Support\deptools\ directory. This utility provides much the same functionality as does Batch Setup 2.0, but includes more NT-specific settings.

There are three options available on the main application window (see Figure 10.16): General Setup, Networking Setup, and Advanced Setup. If you select the General Setup button you will launch a page with seven tabs: User Information, General, Computer Role, Install Directory, Display Settings, Time Zone, and License Mode.

Figure 10.16.

The Windows NT Setup Manager.

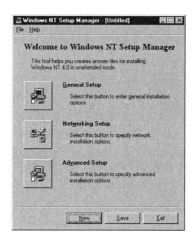

The default tab, User Information, is very similar to the very first page of the Windows 95 Batch Setup program. However, there is an additional field: Product ID. With the advent of Windows NT 4.0, it is now necessary to enter a product identification number in order to install the operating system. Luckily, Microsoft had enough foresight (either that or made a significant error) to realize that it wouldn't always be convenient for those deploying workstations to carry around a list of valid product ID codes. By simply entering 111-1111111 in the Product ID text box you will not be prompted for a code. Likewise, even when you're not performing an automated install and you're prompted for the product ID number, you may use 111-1111111.

NOTE

Keep in mind that much like in the Windows 95 .INF files, the Windows NT response files are simply text files that can be edited. The subjects of user name and computer name will be addressed in more detail in the "Automated Rollout" section of this chapter.

The next tab is the General page, shown in Figure 10.17. This page allows you to configure the following options:

■ Whether or not you wish to confirm the hardware detected during setup.

■ If you are performing an upgrade and, if so, in what manner you would like to upgrade the existing installation.

■ If you would like to launch an additional program during setup and, if so, you are allowed to enter the path, filename, and any command line options.

FIGURE 10.17.

The General Page of the Windows NT Setup Manager.

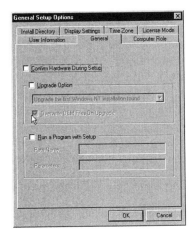

Unless you are installing Windows NT on a workstation on which you know Setup will have trouble with component detection, it is usually unnecessary to confirm hardware.

Following General is the Computer Role tab. This page also has three options: Computer Role, Domain Name, and Computer Account (see Figure 10.18). The Computer Role text box provides several options to choose from: Workstation in a Workgroup, Workstation in a Domain, Server in a Workgroup, Server in a Domain, Primary Domain Controller, and Backup Domain Controller. Depending on which option you choose you will be required to fill in different information. If you are planning to add a workstation to a domain, select the second option in the drop-down list, Workstation in a Domain. At this time you will be required to enter the domain name, but do not enter any information in the Computer Account text box. This field (which is labeled for test purposes only) would accept the computer account's SID number; however, it is unnecessary in any event.

FIGURE 10.18.

The Computer Role Page of the Windows NT Setup Manager.

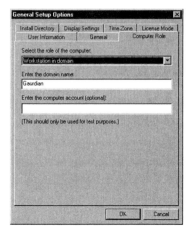

The next tab, Install Directory (see Figure 10.19), allows you to predetermine which directory NT will be installed in by selecting the default or entering an optional directory. It also allows you to have Setup prompt the user for the proper directory.

FIGURE 10.19.

The Install Directory Page of the Windows NT Setup Manager.

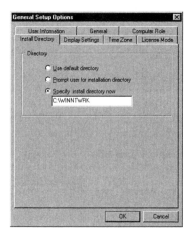

Following Install Directory is the Display Settings tab, shown in Figure 10.20. This tab allows you to manually set the display properties during installation or allows you to instruct Setup to configure display settings at logon. The default settings on this page will work with most work-stations; however, configuring at initial logon is the suggested response.

The remaining tabs in the General Setup section are Time Zone and License Mode. The Time Zone tab is fairly self explanatory; it is in this page that you set the time zone for the workstation, while the License Mode page is for server installations only— it allows you to determine whether the server will follow the per seat or per server licensing mode.

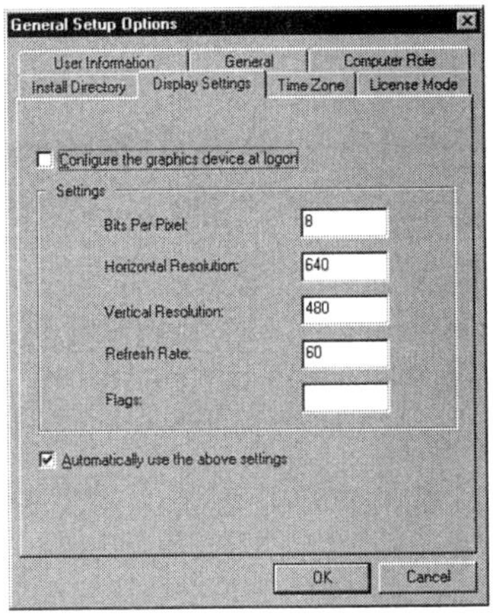

FIGURE 10.20.

The Display Settings Page of the Windows NT Setup Manager.

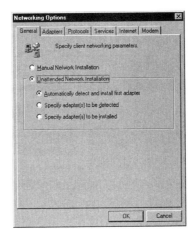

Once you've finalized your settings in the General Setup section, select OK and you will be brought back to the initial page. The next button is the Networking Setup button. Select this button and you will be presented with configuration options as seen in Figure 10.21.

FIGURE 10.21.

The Network Options Page of the Windows NT Setup Manager.

The initial screen allows you to make the following choices:

- Manual Installation which will require intervention
- Unattended Installation using the first detected adapter
- Unattended Installation using a specified number of adapters
- Unattended Installation using a specific adapter

If you choose Manual Installation you will not be required to configure any networking information at all. If, on the other hand you choose any of the unattended installation options, you

10

WORKSTATION
STANDARDS

will need to configure the remaining portions. By choosing the first unattended option, "Automatically detect and install first adapter," you will not have the option to move to the Adapter page. By choosing either of the two remaining options, you will be required to configure at least some information.

The remaining tabs, which are Protocols, Services, Internet, and Modem are fairly simple. The Protocols tab (see Figure 10.22) allows you to determine which protocols will be installed, while the Services tab allows you to install Client Services for NetWare, Remote Access Service, or the SNMP agent in addition to the default network services. Finally, the Internet tab can only be configured if you are installing a server, and the Modem tab can only be configured if you've installed RAS.

FIGURE 10.22.

The Protocols Page of the Windows NT Setup Manager.

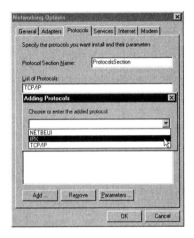

Once you've configured the desired networking options, select OK and you'll be brought back to the original page.

The final button, Advanced Setup, will bring you to a page with eight tabs: General, File System, Mass Storage, Display, Keyboard, Pointing Device, Boot Files, and Advertisement, shown in Figure 10.23.

Many of these tabs require advanced knowledge of the Windows NT Setup routing; however, those that do not are extremely useful.

■ **General.** This page (see Figure 10.23) provides you with the ability to specify your HAL (Hardware Abstraction Layer), allows you to determine a specific keyboard, provides the ability to make the system reboot after the initial text portion of setup or after the GUI portion, allows you to skip the "Welcome" page, and finally allows you to skip the question concerning the administrator password. If you choose not to enter the administrator password it will initially be left blank.

FIGURE 10.23.

The Advanced Setup Page of the Windows NT Setup Manager.

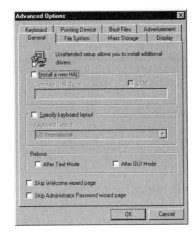

If you set the installation program to boot after the initial text portion of setup, you are effectively stopping the final configuration of your machine. If you choose to do so, upon reboot you can copy all of the files and directories installed during setup to a distribution point and copy them down to any like machine that contains a suitably sized FAT system partition. Once these machines are rebooted, you will automatically enter the final stages of Windows NT Setup.

■ **File System.** This page (see Figure 10.24) allows you to determine whether you want to convert the installation partition to NTFS and also allows you to inform Setup if you are installing on a driver larger than 2 GB.

FIGURE 10.24.

The File System Page of the Windows NT Setup Manager.

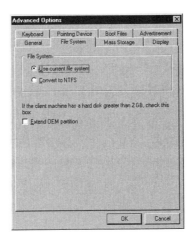

10

WORKSTATION STANDARDS

■ **Mass Storage, Display, Keyboard, Pointing Device, & Boot Files.** These pages all allow you to utilize device drivers that were not initially included in the Windows NT Workstation 4.0 source files. These options are advanced options and require in-depth knowledge of the naming conventions required by the Windows NT Setup program. The Microsoft Windows NT Resource Kit provides instructions on the utilization of these options in conjunction with a non-GUI–based form of the Windows NT Setup Manager.

■ **Advertisement.** This page (see Figure 10.25) allows you to specify a banner that will be presented during the GUI portion of NT Setup, as well as allowing you to determine a specific logo file and background to be displayed. These options are advanced, yet don't provide much functionality.

FIGURE 10.25.

The Advertisement Page of the Windows NT Setup Manager.

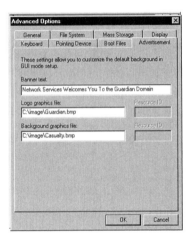

Once you've completed configuring the Advanced Setup options, select OK at the bottom of the page and you will be brought back to the original page. Select File in the upper left-hand corner of the application, followed by Save. Name the file appropriately and store it in your network distribution point for future use.

Performing Automated Installations of Windows NT

Much like the INF response files of Windows 95, the response files for Windows NT can be easily modified after creation as well. The Windows NT Setup Manager stores its response files in TXT format, which obviously can be edited by using any text editor. Therefore, if you wanted to determine user name and computer name before each installation, you could easily open the file and edit the following lines:

```
[UserData]
FullName = "Username"
OrgName = "Guardian"
ComputerName = Install
```

To utilize the response file it is necessary only to enter the following command string:

```
winnt /b /s: \\CTY-PROD01\SUPPORT$\CLIENTS\NTWRK40\i386 /u: a:\ctynt.txt
```

The /b option informs setup that you are running a bootless installation (see Chapter 5, "Server Standardization, Installation, and Implementation"), the / s: \\CTY... option informs Setup where the source files are located, and the /u option informs Setup to use a specific response file. Automated installations will also run from within Windows NT by using the winnt32.exe command with the same options.

The Network Client Administrator

The Network Client Administrator (see Figure 10.26) is probably one of the most underused utilities provided by Windows NT Server. It is, however, an extremely useful tool that can be utilized during the deployment of workstations. The Network Client Administrator has three functions:

- It can create DOS-based Network Client Installation Startup Disks.
- It can create DOS-based Network Client Installation Media.
- It can automatically create a server-based share that contains the distribution files for Windows 95, NT Server Tools, and DOS-Based Network Client source files.

When deploying workstations there are many advantages to maintaining a network-based central source for the distribution of Windows 95 and Windows NT: First, the network distribution can be updated so that all newly deployed workstations receive service packs upon installation; second, both Windows NT and Windows 95 can be updated to include any up-dated device drivers upon installation; and third, if shared properly, enhancements and additional options can be installed on workstations seamlessly across the network.

FIGURE 10.26.

The Network Client Administrator.

The first time you go to use the Network Client Administrator (NCA) to create either a DOS client installation disk set or DOS Client startup disk you will be prompted to use one of the following (see Figure 10.27):

- Share the Clients directory on your Windows NT Server CD-ROM.
- Copy the CD-ROM's Clients directory structure to a server and share it.
- Use an existing shared Clients directory (such as on another server).

Figure 10.27.
The Share Network Client Installation Files Page.

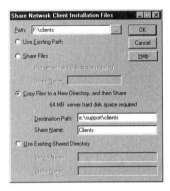

The Clients directory on your Windows NT Server CD-ROM contains the following software:

\LanMan	DOS Client Version 2.2c
\Laman.os2	OS/2 Client Version 2.2c
\Msclient	DOS Client Version 3.0
\RAS	DOS & Windows 3.1 RAS Client Software
\Rpl	Remote Boot Service for Windows NT Server
\Srvtools	Windows NT Server Tools for Windows 95 & Windows NT clients
\Support	Information concerning the NCA and distribution of Windows NT source files
\Tcp32wfw	TCP/IP-32 for Windows for Workgroups
\Update.wfw	WFW Updates
\Win95	Windows 95 Cab Files

> **NOTE**
>
> The Windows 95 directory on the Windows NT Server CD-ROM contains the Windows 95 CAB files. While Windows 95 can be successfully installed from this directory it is not as useful as a true network distribution installation of Windows 95. To create a network distribution run you must run either SETUP /A from the root of your Windows 95 CD-ROM or NETSETUP in the ADMIN directory of your Windows 95 CD-ROM. Either of these methods (depending on your source media) will create a fully expanded distribution source for Windows 95 that can be updated with new drivers and service packs for proper installation.

If you feel that all of these clients and tools are necessary for your deployment, make sure that the "Copy Files to a New Directory, and then Share" option is selected and enter the correct path and share name. Select OK and all of these files will be copied to your local server and then automatically shared for network access.

It is possible to customize your own Clients directory structure that would include only those tools you need, as well as a fully revisable Windows 95 and Windows NT distribution. To create such a structure that will be fully compatible with the NCA, you must do the following:

1. Create a Clients directory whereever desired on your server (For instance, Administrators of the Guardian Domain would create a Clients subdirectory in the root of their SUPPORT$ share)

2. Using Windows NT Explorer, select the desired components from the Clients directory on your Windows NT Server CD-ROM and copy them to your server's Client directory. In most cases the following components will suffice:

   ■ Msclient (Required to make client and startup installation disks)

   ■ Srvtools (This directory contains the Windows NT Server administration tools for Windows 95 and Windows NT.)

The Lanman and Lanman.os2 components are generally of no use. As you'll see in Chapter 11, "Alternative Platform Connectivity," OS/2's native client software is much easier to work with.

3. To create distribution points for Windows NT Server and Windows NT Workstation that will work with the NCA, go to your Clients directory and create two subdirectories: WINNT and WINNT.SRV. Under each of these subdirectories create a NETSETUP directory. For Windows NT Workstation, copy all of the files and directories under the i386 subdirectory from your CD-ROM to the \Clients\WINNT\NETSETUP subdirectory. For Windows NT Server, copy all of the files and directories under the i386 subdirectory from your NT Server CD-ROM to the \Clients\WINNT.SRV\NETSETUP subdirectory.

4. To create a distribution point for Windows 95 that will work with the NCA, using the NETSETUP or SETUP /A options, install Windows 95 in the \Clients\WIN95 directory.

5. Copy the Ncadmin.inf file from the root of the Clients directory on your Windows NT Server CD-ROM to the root of your server-based Clients directory. The Network Client Administrator requires this file to be present in order to work.

6. Finally, once at the Share Network Client Installation Files screen of the NCA (see Figure 10.27), enter the appropriate path in the Path text box and enter the desired share name in the Share text box. (Most organizations share this structure as Clients; however, for security reasons CLIENTS$ is preferable.)

Once complete, you will have a fully operational Network Client administrator. To create a set of DOS Network Client diskettes, launch the NCA and select "Make Installation Disk Set". You will be brought to the Make Installation Disk Set window as seen in Figure 10.28.

10

WORKSTATION
STANDARDS

FIGURE 10.28.

*The Make Installation
Disk Set Window.*

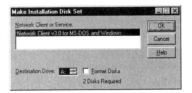

Select OK and you will be prompted to enter disks as required. Once complete, you will have the necessary disks to install the DOS Network Client on most machines.

In order to create an Installation Startup Disk, create a blank bootable disk using either MS-DOS or Windows 95 and select the Make Installation Startup Diskette option, followed by OK. You will be brought to the Target Workstation Configuration Window as seen in Figure 10.29.

FIGURE 10.29.

*The Target Worksta-
tion Configuration
Window.*

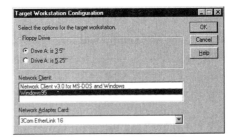

This option allows you to create a boot disk that when used will attach you to the network and initiate the installation of the chosen operating system or network client. Select the appropriate option and the required network card, then choose OK. You will then be brought to the Network Startup Disk Configuration page as seen in Figure 10.30.

FIGURE 10.30.

*The Network Startup
Disk Configuration
Page.*

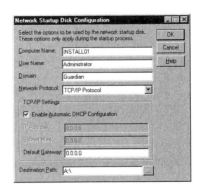

Enter the appropriate information (Machine Name, User Name, Protocol and Domain Name). Once you enter a disk the NCA will copy the necessary files. After copying is complete you will have a fully functional network-enabled boot disk that will not only attach you to the network, but also initiate the installation of the chosen operating system or network client.

> **NOTE**
>
> If you plan to utilize specific response files (such as the INF files for Windows 95 or the TXT files for Windows NT) it will be necessary for you to manually edit the Autoexec.bat on your newly created startup disks to include the appropriate command-line switches.

The Logon Script as a Tool

Many organizations have the benefit of using such tools as Microsoft's SMS, IBM's Tivoli TME 10 (formerly NetView DM/2), Symantec's Norton Administrator for Networks, Computer Associates UniCenter TNG, or Intel's LANDesk Manager, to ensure the easy, standard distribution of workstations and their required software. These tools, which all merit investigation, perform multiple functions such as

- Automated network hardware and software inventory
- Remote workstation control and support
- The automatic distribution and upgrade of software to the desktop across the network
- The automatic distribution and upgrade of operating systems across the network
- Early Warning System and Performance Monitoring

These tools are a tremendous asset to the network administrator, but unfortunately in most cases, are not readily available. In the absence of such tools, the Windows NT Logon Script can be used for several things:

- To aid in the deployment of standard desktops throughout your enterprise
- To aid in the distribution of software throughout your enterprise
- To aid in the distribution of configuration changes to workstations throughout your enterprise
- The distribution of policy and messages to users

The Automated Rollout User

Unfortunately, Windows NT Server does not have any built-in software distribution facility to use when rolling out new workstations, but with a little ingenuity you can fabricate a suitable replacement. Through a combination of the Network Client Administrator, Operating System and Application response files, the Windows NT Logon Script, a shareware utility named

ShutDown, and a fairly simply batch file process, you can deploy workstations in a fast and orderly fashion. This process saves time and ensures a standard desktop configuration. Its efficiency shines when rolling out multiple desktops, and it saves the technician time on single installations as well. This process, dubbed The Automated Rollout User, requires the following components:

- A dedicated Automatic Rollout User for each User Type, including a dedicated logon script
- A hidden share on each divisional production server for the storage of batch files and utilities
- A Network Boot Disk for each network card in your enterprise
- A working knowledge of your desktop standards
- An operating system response file (Windows 95 or Windows NT)
- Application Response files and/or knowledge of your standard applications installation process

The process, in essence, begins with the installation of your operating system using a network boot disk created through the NCA and a response file created through either the Windows 95 Batch Setup 2.0 program or the Windows NT Setup Manager. Once the OS is installed, the technician will log on to the network as an Automatic Rollout User. An Automatic Rollout User is a user that has been created simply for the installation of workstations. It is helpful if the Rollout User has no password; therefore, it is important to limit its access. For instance, in the Guardian Domain they have created a Rollout group for each division. The group CTY-SETUP has been applied to the hidden share CTY-SETUP$, the CCMAIL share and the standard share of APPS to allow for READ access only. The group CTY-SETUP, whose sole member is a user also named CTY-SETUP, does not have access to any other resources throughout the domain. Therefore, if a tech is installing several workstations for Guardian Casualty, he would log on as CTY-SETUP. The user CTY-SETUP has a dedicated logon script entitled CTYSETUP.BAT. Upon logon this script would initiate as follows:

```
NET USE M: \\CTY-PROD01\CCMAIL
NET USE O: \\CTY-PROD01\APPS
NET USE U: \\CTY-PROD01\CTY-setup$
EXPLORER
```

Notice that in addition to mapping drives, the logon script also launches the Explorer. Due to the fact that the logon script will begin the installation of applications before the logon script process terminates normally, it is necessary to launch the Explorer manually; otherwise, the process won't work.

After mapping the drives, the first section in the logon script runs as follows:

```
@ECHO CHECKING FOR PREVIOUSLY INSTALLED SOFTWARE
IF EXIST C:\CCMAIL.CHK GOTO SNA32
@CALL U:\CCMAIL.BAT
CLS
```

```
@ECHO AFTER INSTALL PRESS SPACE BAR TO REBOOT MACHINE
pause
COPY U:\CCMAIL.CHK C:\
u:\ShutDown /restart /force
GOTO EXIT
```

As you can see, the first line of the batch process is looking for the existence of another file. If this file, named CCMAIL.CHK exists, the process will skip to the next section of the logon script. Upon first use, this file will not exist, so the logon script will continue by calling an additional batch file.

> **CAUTION**
>
> It is necessary to use the @CALL string before calling another batch process from within the Windows NT logon script. If you do not, you will not be returned to the logon script upon completion of the second batch process.

The additional batch file, CCMAIL.BAT, is contained in the hidden setup directory CTY-SETUP$. Once called, CCMAIL.BAT begins the installation process for Lotus cc:Mail. While cc:Mail does not provide a response file process, you can edit the INI files within the Network Distribution to include the post office directory. The cc:Mail installation will require the technician to enter the local application directory, but that is all.

Notice that once the CCMAIL batch file is called, the logon script screen is cleared (CLS) and PAUSE is initiated. Once installation of the application is complete, the technician will hit any key and a file named CCMAIL.CHK will be copied to the root of the C:\ drive on the target workstation. This CHK file, which if you recall was the first thing the logon script searched for after the drives were mapped, is utilized to determine where the workstation is in the entire process. After the CHK file is copied, ShutDown will be launched. ShutDown is a shareware utility created by Chris Bluethman that can be found on multiple Internet sites. ShutDown will initiate a clean restart of the operating system, ensuring that any changes made to the Registry or INI files will be initiated prior to the next product installation. Notice that immediately after shutdown is called, the script is informed to GOTO EXIT. EXIT appears as follows:

```
:EXIT
EXIT
```

This line simply ensures that the logon script process will close cleanly therefore eliminating the possibility of a hung system restart (this is applicable mostly to Windows for Workgroups).

Once the machine restarts, the technician will log on again as the setup user (in this case CTY-SETUP) and the logon script will begin again. Drives will be mapped and CHK files will be searched for. Recall the first two lines after the drive mappings:

```
@ECHO CHECKING FOR PREVIOUSLY INSTALLED SOFTWARE
IF EXIST C:\CCMAIL.CHK GOTO SNA32
```

10

WORKSTATION
STANDARDS

Since the CCMAIL.CHK file was copied to the target workstation, the process will immediately go to the next section of the script: SNA32.

```
:SNA32
IF EXIST C:\SNA32.CHK GOTO EXTRA
@CALL U:\SNA32.BAT
CLS
@ECHO AFTER INSTALL PRESS SPACE BAR TO REBOOT MACHINE
pause
COPY U:\SNA32.CHK C:\
u:\ShutDown /restart /force
goto exit
```

As you can see, this section performs the exact same functions of the cc:Mail installation section. Once the Microsoft SNA client is installed, the machine will restart, map drives, and continue as follows:

```
@ECHO CHECKING FOR PREVIOUSLY INSTALLED SOFTWARE
IF EXIST C:\CCMAIL.CHK GOTO SNA32
:SNA32
IF EXIST C:\SNA32.CHK GOTO EXTRA
```

:EXTRA, or Attachmate Extra! For SNA Server, is the first product in this logon script that utilizes response files. However, its section looks no different than the others:

```
:EXTRA
IF EXIST C:\EXTRA.CHK GOTO OFFICE95
@CALL U:\EXTRA.BAT
CLS
@ECHO AFTER INSTALL PRESS SPACE BAR TO REBOOT MACHINE
pause
COPY U:\EXTRA.CHK C:\
u:\ShutDown /restart /force
goto exit
```

Once the EXTRA.BAT batch file is called two things happen: First, Extra installation is initiated utilizing a response file; and second, due to the fact that Extra uses session configuration files that can be moved from one installation to another, upon completion, the appropriate session files are copied to the session directory and session shortcuts are placed on the desktop (for Windows 95 C:\Win95\Desktop and for Windows NT C:\Winntwrk\Allusers\Desktop). Once installation is complete and the session files are copied to the desktop, the technician hits any key to revoke the PAUSE in the script, the CHK file is copied, and the machine is rebooted. This process is repeated for as many applications as required. Once the last application has been installed, the batch file runs as follows:

```
NET USE M: \\CTY-PROD01\CCMAIL
NET USE O: \\CTY-PROD01\APPS
NET USE U: \\CTY-PROD01\CTY-setup$
EXPLORER
@ECHO CHECKING FOR PREVIOUSLY INSTALLED SOFTWARE
IF EXIST C:\CCMAIL.CHK GOTO SNA32
:SNA32
IF EXIST C:\SNA32.CHK GOTO EXTRA
:EXTRA
IF EXIST C:\EXTRA.CHK GOTO OFFIC95
```

```
:OFFICE
IF EXIST C:\OFFICE95.CHK GOTO END
:END
CLS
@ECHO STANDARD APPS HAVE BEEN INSTALLED
PAUSE
:EXIT
EXIT
```

This process has several advantages over manual installation. First, it streamlines the deployment of new workstations by initiating the orderly installation of standard applications. Second, it saves time for the technician by performing many of the standard installation functions, and third it allows your technicians to work on multiple workstations at once, as well as perform multiple functions at once. While this process is somewhat robotic in function, it is extremely efficient. It is not uncommon using this process to complete the deployment of upwards of 15 or 20 workstations within a two-hour time frame. Obviously, this process must be customized for each user type in your domain, and for each major operating system in your enterprise. However, if you do not have the good fortune of owning a systems management tool like those mentioned at the beginning of this section, it is well worth the time spent developing the logon scripts.

Software Distribution

Office 97 is among a new generation of applications that have been enabled for silent software distribution. It is now possible through the use of logon scripts to install software on your users' desktops upon their initial startup in the morning. For instance, you could include the following string in your logon scripts:

```
EXPLORER
IF EXIST C:\OFFICE97.CHK GOTO END
COPY O:\WIN32APP\OFFICE97\OFFICE97.TXT C:\
NOTEPAD C:\OFFICE97.TXT
@CALL O:\WIN32APP\OFFICE97\AUTO.BAT
END
```

The first line is obviously checking for an indication that this process has been run previously. If the CHK file does not exist, the file OFFICE97.TXT will be copied to the root of the C:\ drive and opened using Notepad. This text message will inform the users that for the next 15 minutes or so Office 97 will be installed on their workstation and request that they do nothing until the machine restarts.

Once the text file is launched, a batch file containing the proper Office 97 command line and command strings will launch, and installation will begin. Due to advanced functionality within Office 97, the installation will complete without requiring any end-user interaction and the OFFICE97.CHK file will be copied to the C:\ drive. The machine will restart itself and the user will log in now having the latest version of Microsoft Office installed on their desktop.

This type of process can be utilized in a variety of ways depending on the functionality of the application. It is even possible to send instructions to the end user before the installation of an application begins, therefore requiring some user interaction.

10

WORKSTATION
STANDARDS

Configuration Changes Through Logon Scripts

The logon script can be used to distribute simple configuration changes to your workstations. It is important to note, however, that to use this functionality with any success you must have a common desktop configuration.

One example of this functionality has been already provided. For applications such as Attachmate Extra! that do not use the Registry or detailed INI files for configuration information, it is possible to distribute configuration changes through logon scripts. What is important in these cases is that directory structure be the same for each workstation you plan to distribute these changes. For example, if you wish to distribute a new NORMAL.DOT file that includes new corporate Word templates to all of your Office 95 users you could add the following to your logon scripts:

```
IF EXIST C:\NORMAL.CHK GOTO END
COPY O:\WIN32APP\OFFICE97\DOT\*.DOT C:\WIN32APP\OFFICE95\TEMPLATES
COPY O:\WIN32APP\OFFICE97\DOT\NORMAL.CHK C:\
END
```

This type of scenario can be used in many cases to reduce the number of desktop visits required to incorporate necessary changes throughout your enterprise.

End-User Communication

The logon script can also be used to communicate changes, updates or new information to the end user. As shown in the example concerning the distribution of Office 97 to the end user, you can copy files to your users' hard drives and then launch applications such as Notepad that will fall under the workstation's search path. For instance, if you wanted to inform your users that a certain server would be down for a specified period of time over the weekend you could do the following:

```
EXPLORER
IF EXIST C:\SRVDOWN.CHK GOTO END
COPY I:\COMMON\SRVDOWN.TXT TO C:\
NOTEPAD C:\SRVDOWN.TXT
COPY I:\COMMON\SRVDOWN.CHK TO C:\
END
```

While some users might be irritated with messages popping up on their desktop, this is an excellent method of communication.

Summary

Through the use of Windows 95 and Windows NT Setup Managers, the Network Client Administrator, and the logon script as a tool, desktop management can be increasingly simplified. These tools, which require an in-depth knowledge of your enterprise, when used properly will not only save you support time, but also aid in the deployment of a standard enterprise environment.

IV

PART

IN THIS PART

Integration and Alternative Platforms

Alternative Platform Connectivity

CHAPTER

11

Windows NT Server offers a great deal of connectivity options out of the box that are not offered by any other enterprise operating system. These options, such as Remote Access Service or RAS, the new DFS (Distributed File System), Gateway Services for NetWare, File and Print Sharing for NetWare, Services for Macintosh and OS/2, and UNIX compatibility combine to make Windows NT Server the best choice as the anchor for your enterprise. This chapter will explore these topics and provide examples for their deployment as successful tools in the enterprise.

Remote Access Service

The Windows NT Server Remote Access Service provides remote node access to your network for the following clients: Windows 3.*x*, Windows 95, Windows NT, and standard PPP clients. RAS, which supports TCP/IP, NetBEUI, and IPX/SPX traffic, is extremely easy to install and configure. By dialing into a RAS server, a remote client has access to all of the resources normally available to a network node, including UNIX resources, NetWare servers, Windows NT resources, and peer-to-peer clients.

Remote Node Connectivity

RAS offers what is known as Remote Node connectivity. When you dial into a RAS server and connect to the network, your workstation is essentially a normal network client, with one exception: Dialing in to your network through a modem is considerably slower. With Remote Node, it is not very likely that you'll launch any executables across the wire, and if you do, they'll either be very small or you'll be very patient. There is a great deal of functionality to be had from RAS, however. Depending on your RAS configuration, you can access almost all resources throughout your enterprise, including TCP/IP-based Internet connections. The most effective manner in which to utilize a Remote Node solution is to have all of the applications you require reside on your remote workstation so that when you access your required resources (such as a Word document or a Notes Database), you'll only have to worry about passing data back and forth across the line. RAS is an extremely valuable tool for the mobile user and is a great asset to support personnel.

Network Protocol Support

RAS provides remote users with the following protocol support:

- NetBEUI (NetBIOS)
- TCP/IP
- NetBIOS over TCP/IP
- IPX/SPX
- NetBIOS over IPS/SPX

Therefore, users dialing in can access nearly all resources throughout your enterprise. Additionally, in conjunction with an SNA server, your users can also remotely access SNA resources. Windows NT SNA Server will be covered in Chapter 12, "SNA Connectivity."

Installing RAS on Your Server

To install RAS, either right-mouse click on your Network Neighborhood shortcut and select properties, or launch the Control Panel and open the Network extension. At this time, you will be presented with the Network configuration page. Across the top of the Network configuration page are five tabs: Identification, Services, Protocols, Adapters, and Bindings. Select the Services tab and you will be presented with a screen similar to that in Figure 11.1.

FIGURE 11.1.
The Services Configuration Page of the Network Properties Dialog.

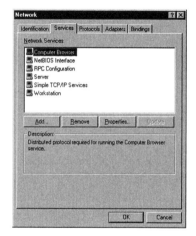

Select the Add button that is placed underneath the installed Network Services window and you will be shown a list of available Network Services (see Figure 11.1). Select Remote Access Service and press OK. You will next be prompted for the location of the Windows NT source files.

Once the correct path is entered, select Continue and the appropriate files will be copied to your server. If there are no modems installed on your server, once the files are copied you will be questioned as to whether you would like to invoke the Modem Installer. If you wish to install any modems, select Yes and you will be presented with the Install New Modem dialog, as seen in Figure 11.2.

If you know beyond a doubt which modem (or modems) you have installed, you may select the Don't detect my modem box and select your modem from a list of available drivers. If you're not sure, simply select the Next button, and Windows NT will attempt to detect your modem or modems.

FIGURE 11.2.

The Install New Modem Dialog.

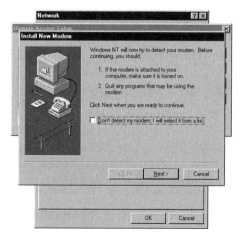

NOTE

If you are using a Digiboard or any other multi-port device to increase the number of available modems, it is necessary that you have already installed and configured the device before you attempt to detect any modems. Otherwise, the Modem Installer will not find your modems.

Once your modem is detected and installed, you will be presented with the Remote Access Setup screen, as seen in Figure 11.3.

FIGURE 11.3.

The Remote Access Setup Screen.

By default, RAS is configured to allow incoming calls using each of the protocols that are currently installed on your server. If you wish to use this server for both dial-out (local users only—

there is no modem sharing inherent to RAS) and remote access, you must manually configure it to do so. Select the Configure button at the bottom of the Remote Access Setup screen and you will be presented with the Configure Port Usage screen, as seen in Figure 11.4.

FIGURE 11.4.

The Configure Port Usage Screen.

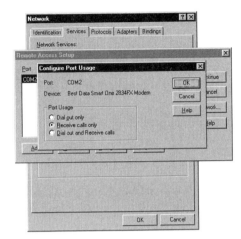

Notice that you can configure each individual modem differently. The configuration choices you have are

■ Dial out only
■ Receive calls only
■ Dial out and Receive calls

If you think that you'll ever need to use your server for dial-out connectivity, now is a good time to enable it. Once RAS is installed, the only way to configure a modem for dial-out is to go back into the Services portion of Network Properties, change the configuration, and reboot the machine.

Once you've chosen your port configuration properties, it is time to configure your network connectivity options. At this point you have two choices: You may select Continue in the upper-right corner of the Remote Access Setup window, or you may press the Network option two buttons down. If you select the Continue button, you will be prompted to configure each remote access protocol one at a time. On the other hand, if you select the Network option, you will be presented with the Network Configuration dialog, as seen in Figure 11.5.

Notice that the top half of the Network Configuration page is dedicated to Dial-Out configuration only. If you plan to connect to the Internet, be sure to select the TCP/IP option. Otherwise, select only those protocols you will need when dialing out. The middle half of the screen, titled Server Settings, allows you to configure the dial-in protocols you wish to provide through your RAS server. Your options are NetBEUI, TCP/IP, and IPX. Each protocol is configured differently.

FIGURE 11.5.
The RAS Network Configuration Dialog.

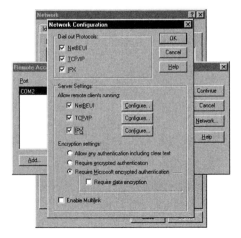

If you choose to provide access through the NetBEUI protocol, you have two choices (see Figure 11.6): You may allow NetBEUI clients to have access to the entire network, or you may limit NetBEUI clients to the RAS server only.

FIGURE 11.6.
RAS Server NetBEUI Configuration.

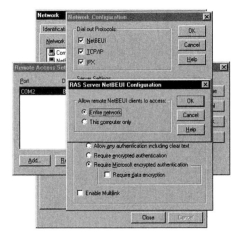

This is an all-or-nothing setting—unfortunately you cannot limit individual users to one setting or the other. In most cases, the administrator allows access to the entire enterprise.

The TCP/IP configuration is the most complex of all three protocols. Much like NetBEUI, you have the ability to limit connectivity, but you also have the following options:

- Use a DHCP server to assign remote TCP/IP addresses
- Use a static address pool assigned by the RAS server
- Allow remote clients to request a predetermined IP address

FIGURE 11.7.
*The RAS Server
TCP/IP Configuration.*

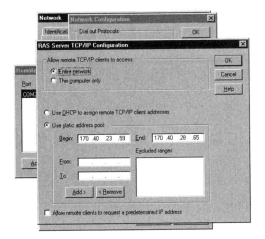

If there is a DHCP server present and operational, it is simplest to use the DHCP server option. However, many organizations do not utilize DHCP or place their RAS servers on their WAN backbone (which in most cases is set to ignore DHCP broadcasts), so the static address pool option is quite handy. Either way, TCP/IP connectivity is easily managed.

Finally, the IPX configuration properties (see Figure 11.8) are similar to both protocols in that you can limit network access, but you can also

- Allocate IPX numbers automatically
- Allocate specific IPX numbers
- Assign the same IPX number to all remote clients
- Allow remote clients to request a predetermined IPX number

FIGURE 11.8.
*The RAS Server IPX
Configuration.*

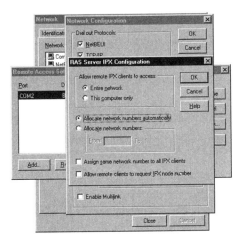

These options, much like the TCP/IP settings, are quite functional at their default values. It is important to note that if you plan to provide access to NetWare resources via RAS, IPX must be enabled.

Once you've configured your remote access protocols, Encryption settings and Multilink remain.

The available encryption settings, as seen in Figure 11.5. include

- Allow any authentication including clear text
- Require encrypted authentication
- Require Microsoft-encrypted authentication
- Require Microsoft-encrypted authentication and data encryption

The Allow any authentication including clear text option permits connections using any authentication requested by the client, including MS-CHAP, SPAP, and PAP. This option, which is not recommended for an environment with a high security concern, is useful if you have RAS clients using non-MS or Shiva client software.

The Require encrypted authentication option permits connections using any authentication requested by the client except PAP. This option, which is slightly more secure than the first, requires encrypted passwords from all clients.

The Require Microsoft encrypted authentication option permits connections using only the MS-CHAP authentication. In addition, you can also select the Require data encryption option so that all data sent over the wire is encrypted. Windows NT RAS provides data encryption using the RSA Data Security Incorporated RC4 algorithm, which is widely held as very secure.

The final option, Enable Multilink, is new to Windows NT Server 4.0. This option allows Windows NT computers dialing in to connect to multiple modems on the RAS server and synchronize those sessions to create a larger pipe. Theoretically, if you were to connect to a RAS server with two 28.8 modems, you would be able to transfer data at a rate of 56.6 KB, excluding any enhancements gained through compression. This is an excellent option if ISDN is not available in your area, or if it is not cost effective.

Once you've completed your networking configuration, select Continue. Your new network bindings will be configured and, if necessary, you will be prompted to the Windows NT CD-ROM or source files. If you've chosen IPX as one of your remote access protocols, you will be presented with a dialog box, as seen in Figure 11.9.

As mentioned in Chapter 6, "Choosing Your Protocols," Microsoft's implementation of IPX/SPX used for connectivity with Windows NT servers is in reality not a very clean protocol. Due to the NetBIOS overhead, NWLink is classified as a Type 20 packet. If you have implemented NWLink for NetWare connectivity only, there is no need to enable RIP for NWLink. On the other hand, if you use NWLink as your primary means of communication, you will not be able to access other NT servers without it. As stated in Chapter 6, if you are in

a routed network, it is highly recommended that you stay away from NWLink on your network. Instead, you should implement TCP/IP, which will be covered in detail in Chapter 14, "WINS, DHCP, and DNS."

FIGURE 11.9.

RIP for NWLink IPX Configuration.

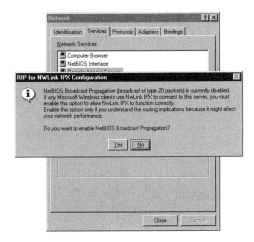

After making the appropriate response to the RIP for NWLink question, RAS configuration is complete, and you will be returned to the Network Services configuration page. To initiate your changes, press the Close button. Bindings will be reconfigured, and you will be prompted to restart your machine.

After your machine restarts, your RAS server will be fully functional. Remember, as described in both Chapter 4, "Designing Your Domain," and Chapter 9, "Managing Users," dialin permissions are set in the User Manager for Domains.

Configuring Windows 95 and Windows NT for RAS Connectivity

The Dial-Up Networking component in Windows 95 and Windows NT is all you need to connect to a RAS server. To configure Dial-Up Networking in Windows NT, go to the Start Menu, followed by Accessories. Select the Dial-Up Networking option, and you will be presented with the New Phonebook Entry dialog screen, as seen in Figure 11.10.

This page has five tabs: Basic, Server, Script, Security, and X.25. To create an entry for a RAS server, simply enter the entry name, a comment if desired, and the phone number. Notice the Alternates button off to the side of the Phone number text box: Here you can enter multiple phone numbers to be cycled through in case a busy signal is encountered. In addition to the phone numbers, you may also set certain modem features.

The most significant page in an entry's configuration is the Server page, as seen in Figure 11.11. It is here that you select the server type and the protocol settings. For a RAS server, the default setting (PPP: Windows NT, Windows 95 Plus, Internet) is correct. In configuring the protocols, simply choose the required protocols and, if necessary, configure TCP/IP. Once you've completed configuring this page, you've entered enough information to connect to a RAS server.

FIGURE 11.10.

New Phonebook Entry Dialog.

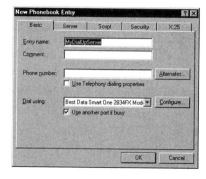

FIGURE 11.11.

Server Configuration Dialog.

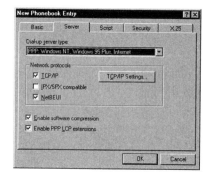

Configuring a Windows 95 RAS connection is very similar. Using the Start Menu, go to Accessories and select Dial-up Networking. Once the Dial-Up Networking window is open, double-click on the Make New Connection Shortcut. You will next be presented with the Make New Connection dialog, like that in Figure 11.12.

FIGURE 11.12.

The Make New Connection Dialog Box.

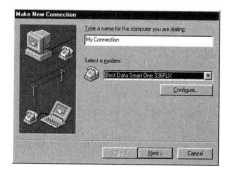

Name the entry appropriately and select the Next button on the lower portion of the screen. At this point you will be prompted to enter the phone number. Once complete, select Next once again. At this point you will be informed that you have successfully configured your Dial-Up Networking session. Select Finish and return to the Dial-Up Networking program box.

Even though Setup informed you that your configuration was complete, that's not always the case. Select the entry you just created and launch its properties by using either the mouse right-click method or the tool bar. You will be presented with your entry's general properties, as seen in Figure 11.13.

FIGURE 11.13.

A Dial-up Networking Entry's General Properties (Windows 95).

The Configure button beneath the phone number can be used to fine-tune your modem's settings. The Server Type button, much like in Windows NT, is the important option when configuring connectivity. Select the Server Type button and the Server Types window will launch (see Figure 11.14).

FIGURE 11.14.

The Server Types Configuration Page.

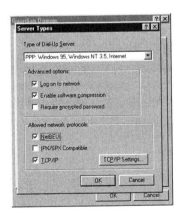

This page has three pertinent areas: the Type of Dial-Up Server drop-down box, the Advanced options section, and the Allowed network protocols section. First, the default choice of PPP: Windows 95, Windows NT 3.5, and Internet is correct for RAS connectivity. Second, under Advanced options, the default settings of Log on to network and Enable software compression are correct; however, if your RAS server requires an encrypted password, check the Require encrypted password option. And finally, choose only those protocols necessary for connection to your RAS server. The TCP/IP configuration, much like Windows NT's option, allows you to configure the protocol for DHCP or enter static addresses. Once your required configurations are complete, select OK at the bottom of the page and close out of your entry's properties. You are now ready to connect to your Windows NT RAS server.

Distributed File System

Shortly after the release of Windows NT Server 4.0, Microsoft released a new service called the Distributed File System. The Distributed File System can be used to create a virtual directory tree that spans shared volumes on multiple servers and workstations via one logical network connection. A DFS tree, which can be accessed only using Windows 95 or Windows NT 4.0 clients, can be used in two crucial ways: first, to provide organized connectivity to the end user in a disorganized environment, and second, to provide seamless connectivity to cross-divisional resources, enterprise resources, and application servers. Both of these methods for DFS use will be explored in detail following the topics of DFS Server Installation and DFS Management. Furthermore, Windows NT and Windows 95 connectivity issues will be in this section.

DFS Installation

DFS did not ship on the Windows NT Server CD-ROM and therefore must be downloaded from the Microsoft Web site—you'll have your choice of an Intel, PowerPC, or Alpha version, so be sure that you choose the correct one. DFS is downloaded as a self-extracting executable, currently titled dfs-v40-i386.exe. You can launch this executable from anywhere on your system without fear of a messy expansion—upon execution, the DFS file will expand itself in your system root under \System32\DFS. Once it's been expanded, in order to install DFS you must launch your Network configuration properties by double-clicking on the Network extension in your Control Panel or using the mouse right-click/properties sequence on your Network Neighborhood shortcut. Once the Network properties configuration window has launched, select the Service tab, followed by the Add button at the bottom of the Service page and, finally, Have Disk. Next, you will be prompted for a path to the updated or unlisted service. Unless otherwise specified, enter your `\%systemroot%\system32\DFS` and you will be presented with the DFS installation screen, as seen in Figure 11.15. Select OK and the DFS service will be added to your machine.

Once files are copied, you will be presented with the Configure Dfs window, as seen in Figure 11.16.

At this point you now have the option to create your DFS tree root, but for the purposes of this section, simply select OK without creating a DFS root. Upon completion, the Distributed File System will be added to your list of services. It is necessary to close your Network properties dialog and restart your machine in order to initialize the DFS service.

FIGURE 11.15.
Installing the DFS Service.

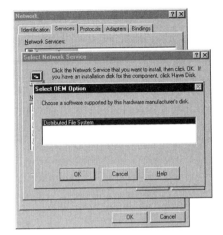

FIGURE 11.16.
The Configure Dfs Window.

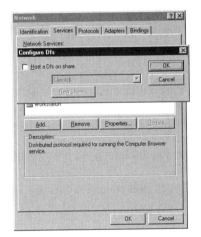

DFS Explained

Many of the most powerful networking tools seem to have the ability to confuse even the most technical person quite easily—Microsoft's DFS service is no exception. To wholly comprehend the DFS service, it is helpful to see an example of its creation and its potential use. Therefore, this section will begin with the creation of a simple DFS tree for use in the Guardian Domain.

Situation

Users in the HR department of the Guardian Domain need access to the \Data\ Common\HRProfiles directory on each production server throughout the Guardian Domain. These directories will be accessed on a daily basis, so it becomes necessary to map a drive to each server for each HR user. Even though drive mappings have been limited to three standard drives Domain-wide, there are additional resources that will be accessed on a fairly regular basis, which will also require drive mappings. The addition of four permanent drives to the standard three can confuse even the most savvy user.

Solution

Instead of adding multiple drive mappings to the HQ-Human Resources users' logon script, the administrators of the Guardian Domain have elected to host a DFS tree on the HQ-PROD01 server. With DFS, users in the HR department will be able to access the data directories on multiple servers throughout the enterprise, using one mapped drive. What's more, the users navigating the DFS share will have no idea that they're actually accessing shares on remote servers, helping to eliminate potential confusion.

Implementation

The administrators of the Guardian Domain have chosen to name the HQ-PROD01 hosted DFS tree HQ-DFS1. When designing their DFS tree, the Guardian administrators kept the following rules in mind concerning the deployment of a DFS structure:

- A DFS tree can only be hosted on a Windows NT 4.0 server.
- Each server can host only one DFS structure.
- There is no limit to the number of DFS structures that can be hosted per domain.
- Each leaf under the DFS root is referred to as a DFS volume.
- Any standard shared folder on any server can be a volume in a DFS tree, including NetWare, NT 3.5x, LAN Manager, LAN Server, and NFS volumes.
- In order to access a DFS volume, a user must have rights to the network share and must be currently logged in to the server or domain hosting that share.
- One DFS tree can be nested inside another DFS tree as an additional volume.
- No matter where the volume is located or what file system is used, users can transparently browse through a DFS tree.
- Adding an existing share as a volume in a DFS tree has no ill effect on the share.
- Only Windows NT Workstation 4.0 and Windows 95 clients can access a DFS tree.

Keeping these rules in mind, the Guardian administrators decided to add a DFS leaf volume to their DFS root, named HR. The HR leaf volume would provide access to the data directories on each production server via one mapped drive. For instance, by mapping a drive to \\HQ-PROD01\HQ-DFS1\HR, all HR user, would have access to the \Data\Common\HRProfiles directories on each server. The following procedure is a step-by-step process that can be used to create any DFS volume:

1. Launch the Network properties dialog, using either the Control Panel or by using the right-mouse click/properties method on the Network Neighborhood shortcut.

2. Once in the Network properties, move to the Services tab and select the Distributed File System listing, then press Properties at the bottom of the Services listing window.

3. The Configure DFS window will be presented, as seen in Figure 11.16. Select the New Share option and enter the appropriate path. (For HQ-DFS1, the path is E:\HQ-DFS1; see Figure 11.17.) Once entered, select Create Share.

FIGURE 11.17.

Creating a New DFS Root.

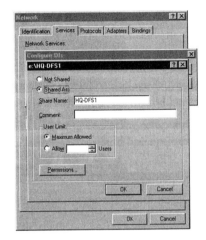

4. When you add a leaf volume to a DFS tree, a blank folder is automatically created in the root volume directory. This blank folder serves as a junction point to the leaf volume. Since in most cases the directory won't currently exist, the system will ask for creation confirmation. Answer Yes, and upon creation the system will present a standard New Share dialog, as seen in Figure 11.18. Enter the Share name and the Share description and select OK. The system will now revert back to the Configure Dfs screen, but this time the new share will appear in the Host a DFS on share text box. Select OK and then close the Network properties window. In order to initialize the DFS root, it is necessary to restart the machine at this time.

5. Once the server has been restarted, the DFS root will have been initialized. In order to manage the DFS root, it is necessary to launch the DFS Administrator, found in the Start Menu under the Distributed File System folder.

6. In essence, a DFS leaf volume acts as a gateway to the actual shared resource to which you wish to provide access. In Figure 11.19 you will see the root volume of your DFS tree. At this point the root acts just like a normal share. However, if anyone were to access the root, he would receive an empty folder. To provide access to a distributed resource, simply select either the folder with the hand underneath it or DFS on the tool bar followed by the Add To Dfs menu option.

FIGURE 11.18.

The New Share Dialog Window.

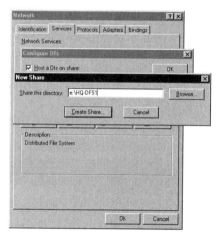

FIGURE 11.19.

The Add To Dfs Window.

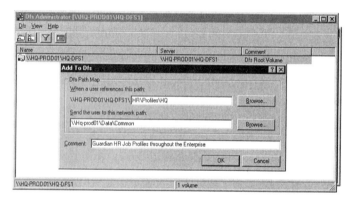

7. Once you've chosen the Add To Dfs option, you will be presented with the Add To Dfs window, as seen in Figure 11.19. Notice the text box titled When a user references this path. The UNC path next to the text box shows a standard \\%servername%\share path. Since the Guardian administrators wish to create an HR-centric leaf volume in the DFS root, they will begin with a path of \\HQ-PROD01\HQ-DFS1\HR. Under the leaf volume of HR it is possible to organize distributed resources even further. For instance, to organize the HRProfiles directories under the HR leaf volume, they will create a secondary volume (called a junction) named Profiles. Under Profiles they will provide access to the HRProfiles directory on each server. If, in addition to the need for HRProfiles, the HR department needed to access a directory named Compensation on each production server throughout the enterprise, they would create a secondary volume under HR called Comp. To provide DFS access to the HRProfiles directory on the HQ-PROD01 server, the administrator will enter \Profiles\HQ in the When a user references this path text box.

NOTE

You can extend a leaf volume no further than two directories. For instance, while \\HQ-PROD01\HQ-DFS1\HR\PROFILES is a legal structure, \\HQ-PROD01\HQ-DFS1\HR\PROFILES\1996 is not.

8. Underneath the When a user references this path text box you will find the Send the user to this network path text box. This is the actual path to which the DFS leaf object \\HQ-PROD01\HQ-DFS1\HR\HQ will send a user. The HRProfiles directory resides under the HQ-PROD01\DATA share in the DEPT\HR subdirectory. Enter the full path of HQ-PROD01\DATA\DEPT\HR\HRProfiles in this text box. Enter an appropriate comment and select OK. You will immediately be presented with a message such as the one in Figure 11.20. Select Yes and the DFS volume will be created.

FIGURE 11.20.

DFS Volume Confirmation.

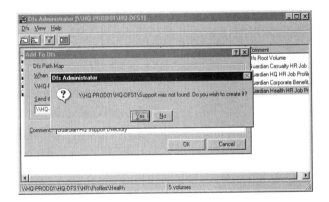

9. Once the volume creation is complete, you will see a new entry in the Dfs Administrator. At this point, when a user accesses the \\HQ-PROD01\HQ-DFS1\HR\HQ path they will be taken immediately to the \\HQ- \DATA\DEPT\HR\HRProfiles directory. Once the administrators repeat steps 7 and 8 to create DFS leaf volumes for the CTY-PROD01, HLT-PROD01, and CORP-PROD01 HRProfiles directories, the HR\Profiles portion of the DFS volume will be complete. (See Figure 11.21.)

Once volumes have been added to your DFS root, a user can navigate its structure, seamlessly moving from server to server without requiring any detailed path knowledge. With the simple addition of a drive mapping such as NET USE T: \\HQ-PROD01\HQ-DFS1, the HR users will have easy access to all required cross-divisional resources.

FIGURE 11.21.

The DFS Administrator View of the HR Volume.

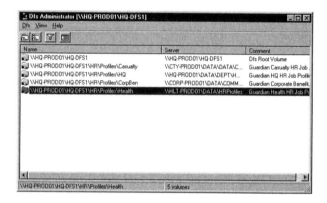

DFS Client Connectivity

While the DFS root share can be viewed by users of all Microsoft Networking-compliant operating systems, only users of Windows NT 4.0 and Windows 95 can access DFS resources. Luckily, Windows NT 4.0 ships with the DFS client built in. However, it is necessary to install an additional service for Windows 95 workstations to access DFS shares.

You can obtain the Windows 95 client in two ways: First, when you expand the server version of the executable, it places the Windows 95 client software in the \%systemroot%\ system32\dfs\win95 directory. Second, you can specifically download the Windows 95 client from the Microsoft Web site.

Either way, to install the Windows 95 DFS client is fairly simple. First launch the Network configuration properties by either using the Control Panel Network extension or the right-mouse click/Properties method on the Network Neighborhood. You will immediately be presented with the Windows 95 Network configuration page (see Figure 11.22).

FIGURE 11.22.

The Windows 95 Network Configuration Page.

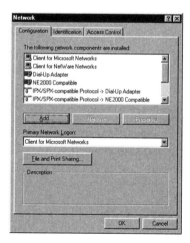

Select the Add button beneath the window displaying the installed network components. You will be presented with the Select Network Component Type window seen in Figure 11.23.

FIGURE 11.23.
The Select Network Component Type Window.

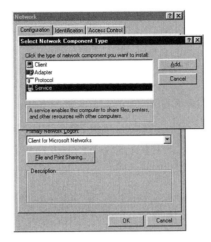

Highlight the Service option and press Add, followed by Have Disk. You will now have the opportunity to enter the path of your new service, in this case the DFS software. Once you've entered the path, select OK, and a window confirming your choice of the DFS client software will pop up. Select OK and the necessary files will be copied. Once complete, the listing of DFS Services for Microsoft Networking Client will appear in your Network Components list and DFS will be installed. In order to initialize the DFS service, it is necessary to bounce your workstation.

> **NOTE**
>
> There is no visible difference between a standard share and a DFS root when browsing either the Network Neighborhood or the DFS Host server. During its beta stage there were several rumors concerning the DFS service, mostly dealing with a DFS icon appearing in the root of every domain structure. Unfortunately, these rumors did not pan out to be true—at least not in Windows NT 4.0. To the network client, a DFS share appears identical to a standard share.

DFS as an Organizing Agent

The Distributed File System is an excellent tool that provides a great deal of flexibility in enterprise connectivity. Due to its recent introduction, there is not a great deal of history associated with a service of this type so in a sense those deploying DFS will be pioneers. There is no doubt that DFS will play a large part in the upcoming Active Directory service to be released with Windows NT 5.0. However, its potential is yet to be explored.

OS/2 in the Domain

If you spend any time in the Windows NT Internet newsgroups, you're bound to run across people wondering if OS/2 can log into and access resources on a Windows NT domain. The answer is yes; however, there are differences, both when compared to Microsoft platforms logging into an NT domain and when compared to OS/2 clients logging in to a LAN Server Domain. The questions concerning OS/2 in a Windows NT domain are generally centered around the topics of Logon Assignments, MPTS configuration, NetBEUI, NetBIOS over TCP/IP, Logon Scripts, Printers, and the Windows NT Master Domain model.

Logon Assignments

OS/2 clients logging on to a LAN Server Domain can receive what are referred to as logon assignments. These assignments, such as printers, public applications and aliases, do not have any true equivalent in Windows NT. While aliases (shares in Windows NT) and printers can be assigned through Logon Scripts, the management interface that exists in OS/2 LAN Server does not exist in Windows NT. Logon assignments are found only in OS/2 LAN Server.

MPTS

While Microsoft does provide an OS/2 client on the Windows NT Server CD, this client offers very little functionality. Instead, OS/2's MPTS (Multi-Protocol Transport Server) should be used for Windows NT connectivity. There are no unusual considerations to account for when configuring an OS/2 workstation to log into a Windows NT Domain. The only configuration required is the correct Domain name in the IBMLAN.INI and an /S added to the command string following LOGON.EXE. (/S simply quiets the Home Directory error message encountered when logging in.) Other than that, OS/2 has no issues logging into a Windows NT Domain.

Protocols

OS/2 can log into a Windows NT Domain using either the NetBEUI protocol or NetBIOS over TCP/IP. For NetBEUI there is absolutely no configuration necessary. As long as NetBEUI is installed on your Windows NT server, OS/2 can log in without any issues whatsoever. NetBIOS over TCP/IP on the other hand is another issue. OS/2's implementation of NetBIOS over TCP/IP in conjunction with Windows NT Server will be covered in detail in Chapter 14.

NET Commands

Many of the standard OS/2 networking NET commands will work with Windows NT Server, including NET USE and NET VIEW. Anything pertaining to OS/2 LAN Server proprietary services such as public applications and logon assignments will not work. In addition, while in

Alternative Platform Connectivity

CHAPTER 11

297

11

ALTERNATIVE
PLATFORM
CONNECTIVITY

OS/2 LAN Server an OS/2 client can NET USE to a modem, this functionality does not exist in Windows NT Server.

Logon Scripts

Windows NT Logon Scripts work extremely well in OS/2. However, all logon scripts to be utilized by OS/2 users must have the CMD extension rather than the standard BAT extension. Additionally, when logon scripts run on OS/2 clients, they do so in the background. Unlike in Microsoft clients, you will not see a logon script processor. Once you've been informed that logon was successful, simply go to an OS/2 window and type NET USE to see a list of drives processed.

Printers

OS/2 clients can attach to Windows NT printers simply by using the NET USE command. For instance, if an OS/2 user needed to access a printer on the CTY-PROD01 server, NET USE LPT1 \\CTY-PROD01\Q-CASUALTY1 would suffice. All that is required is that the printer driver be previously installed. Printer mappings can be set up in the STARTUP.CMD command directly following or preceding the NET START REQUESTER line.

Dual Citizenship and the Master Domain

For an OS/2 client to access both a Windows NT Domain and an OS/2 LAN Server Domain, it is helpful for the end user to have the same user ID and password on both domains. However, it is not necessary. Unfortunately, neither Microsoft nor IBM offers a utility to synchronize domain directories or user accounts. In the case of the Master Domain model (such as the InterCorporate Domain), if a user needs to access both an OS/2 LAN Server Domain and an NT Server Resource Domain, the user must log into the Master Domain and then map drives to resources in the LAN Server Domain. This is due to the trust relationships that allow users from the Master Domain to access Resource Domains. When a user is authenticated by an OS/2 LAN Server Domain and then attempts to access a Windows NT Resource Domain, the Resource Domain will check to see if the user is logged into the Master Domain. Since it is not possible that the user be logged into both the OS/2 LAN Server Domain and the Windows NT Master Domain at the same time using the same MAC address, the user will not be validated by the Master Domain. Therefore, access to the Resource Domain will be denied. On the other hand, trust relationships do not exist in the OS/2 LAN Server world, so if a user logs into a Windows NT Domain and then attempts to access an LAN Server Domain, there will be no complications.

OS/2 and DFS

At this time there is no DFS support for OS/2, and, unfortunately for some organizations, chances are there will not be an OS/2 client for DFS unless a third-party developer creates one.

NetWare Integration

Microsoft offers two ways to interact with the NetWare world: Gateway Service for NetWare and File and Print Sharing for NetWare. Both of these tools provide excellent features that can be utilized when migrating to a Windows NT environment or even for daily enterprise interactivity.

Gateway Service for NetWare

Gateway Service for NetWare is a service that was originally provided by Microsoft to relieve many of the issues involved with maintaining two network client packages on the same desktop computer. Prior to Windows NT 4.0 and Windows 95, those organizations using both NT Server and NetWare often experienced difficulty in configuring a single workstation for connectivity to both NetWare and Microsoft networks, due to the memory limitations, protocol conflicts, and resource allocation issues frequently experienced under DOS and Windows 3.1. By providing a transparent way to share NetWare Resources with Windows NT Server clients, Microsoft helped to alleviate these issues and provided an excellent tool for migration from NetWare.

Gateway Service for NetWare allows your clients to attach to NetWare servers without loading the NetWare client on each workstation. Gateway Service essentially maps a drive to a NetWare Server and in turn routes users connected to your NT server through that drive to NetWare resources. This service is so transparent to the end user that those users logging into your Windows NT Domain have no idea that they're accessing a NetWare server.

GSNW is installed as a service, much the same way that the DFS is installed. Go to the Control Panel and select Network. Once the Network properties have launched, select Services and then Add. You will soon be presented with a list of available services. Select Gateway (and Client) Service for NetWare, followed by OK, and you will be prompted for the location of your Windows NT Server source files. Enter the correct path and again select OK. Files will be copied and, if it wasn't already installed, NWLink will be added to your list of protocols. Additionally, if you have RAS installed, you will be asked if you would like to support NWLink connections. Once the service is installed, you will need to select Close at the bottom of the Network configuration page. Bindings will be reset, and it will be necessary to restart your machine before the service will be initialized.

Gateway Service for NetWare Explained

When sharing NetWare resources with your Windows NT Domain clients through Gateway Service for NetWare, there is no need to create an individual NetWare account for each user to access your NetWare Server. Instead, you need only create one NetWare account that will provide access to your NetWare resources for any user in your Domain Directory. GSNW can be a tremendous benefit for organizations with multiple users and a small NetWare user license.

For instance, NetWare is licensed in terms of the number of users who access each server. If Guardian Casualty has a NetWare server with a 25 user license count, when the 26th user attempts to logon he will be denied access. If there is a resource on this NetWare server that can't be immediately moved to an NT server (for instance, it requires a specific NetWare NLM) but more than 25 users require access, the GSNW connection will take up only one NetWare client access license. In turn, any number of users can access the NetWare server's resources through the Gateway.

NetWare Security Differences

NetWare security implementation is slightly different from Windows NT's security model. In NetWare, users and groups are granted Trustee Directory Rights to directories on volumes. These rights are applied at the directory level on each NetWare volume, much like Directory Level Permissions are applied in Windows NT. Clients cannot access directories on NetWare servers unless they have specifically been granted Trustee Directory Rights or are a member of a group that has been granted Trustee Rights. Much like in Windows NT, due to the fact that managing rights for each individual user can become very difficult, Trustee Directory Rights are generally managed on a group-by-group basis.

Unlike Windows NT Server, directory level security is the only form of security on a NetWare server (other than user account and password, of course). Furthermore, users do not connect to shares on NetWare servers, but instead connect to the entire NetWare volume. Similar to Windows NT, a volume can be a single physical disk or multiple disks that present themselves as a single directory structure. Users can attach to the root of a volume (unlike in NT, unless it is specifically shared to the end user) and navigate to the resources to which they have been granted Trustee Directory Rights. If a user does not have rights to a specific directory, he will not see the directory.

Implementing GSNW

The following list provides an overview of the necessary steps to follow when implementing a GSNW drive:

- Create a group named NTGATEWAY on each NetWare server you plan to access.
- Grant the NTGATEWAY group Trustee Directory Rights to the NetWare resources your users will access.
- Create a NetWare user that is a member of the NTGATEWAY group on each server your users will access. Additionally, there must be an identical user in your Windows NT Domain.
- Using the GSNW interface, you must map a drive (or drives) to the NetWare resources your users will access.
- Apply the appropriate share level security to each Gateway drive to provide user access.

Years ago, Guardian Casualty developed a database application that requires a NetWare server. While at this time they are in the process of porting it to VB and SQL Server, there is a definite need for multiple users to access the data. The GSNW service is an excellent way to provide this access. In preparation for the GSNW connection, the Guardian Casualty NetWare administrator has done the following:

- Created the NTGATEWAY group as suggested by Microsoft.
- Created a user called GATEWAY in both the NetWare Server's user directory and the Guardian Domain's user directory. (On the NT side, the GATEWAY user must have Administrator rights to initiate the connection.)
- Granted the NTGATEWAY group the appropriate Trustee Directory Rights on the SYS volume, in the directory APPS\CASDB.

Assume that you are an administrator in the Guardian Domain. To successfully create the GSNW connection, you must log on to CTY-PROD01 as GATEWAY and perform the following functions:

1. Launch the Control Panel and select the Gateway Service for NetWare shortcut. The opening screen is shown in Figure 11.24.

FIGURE 11.24.

The Initial Gateway Service for NetWare Window.

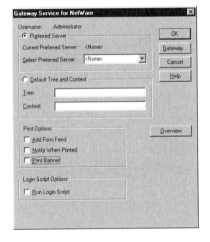

2. On a Windows NT Server 4.0 the Gateway Service also doubles as a NetWare client. Therefore, the first screen seen is that of the NetWare Client Configuration. If the server is a NetWare 3.*x* server and the NT server will not be used as a NetWare Client (it is not recommended to use your server as any type of client), this window will be left at its default configuration. On the other hand, if the NetWare server is of the 4.*x* variety, Preferred Server and Default Tree and Context must be set. The Guardian NetWare server version is 3.12, therefore this page will be left blank. Select the Gateway button to move on.

3. The next window you will be presented with is the Configure Gateway window. This is where the Gateway user account will be entered and Gateway drives will be created. To enable NetWare connectivity, it is necessary to enter the Gateway Service account and its password in the required text boxes. For Guardian, the user name is GATE-WAY and the password is 312Drive.

> **NOTE**
>
> The Gateway user account is in essence a Windows NT service account. Once the Gateway service is established and drives have been mapped, no matter who logs in locally to the server (if anyone at all) , your GSNW drives will provide constant service to the end users.

4. Next, to create Gateway drives you must select the Add button on the right side of the screen. The New Share dialog box (see Figure 11.25) will now launch. This dialog box consists of five fields: Share Name, Network Path, Comment, Use Drive, and User Limit. The Share Name is just like that of an ordinary share—in order for your users to access the Gateway drive, it must be shared. The Network Path is the path to the resource you plan to share and the Comment can be anything you like. The Use Drive field allows you to choose which drive on your local server you wish to use, and the User Limit selection allows you to limit the number of users who can access the Gateway drive at once. The path to the NetWare resource must be entered in UNC, so SERVER02\SYS:APPS\CASDB would be entered as \\SERVER02\SYS\APPS\CASDB. Press the OK button and the Gateway service will make the connection and the new drive will show up in the drive window.

FIGURE 11.25.

The New Share Dialog Box.

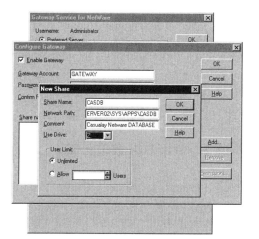

5. Once the drive has been successfully mapped you may administer the share permissions just as you would on any normal share. Keep in mind that the security on the Gateway is very similar to that of the relationship between file and directory level permissions and share level permissions—the lowest level of access will prevail. Be sure that you provide adequate share and directory level protection to your resources.

Once the Gateway drive is fully configured, your users will have no idea that they're accessing a NetWare server. You may map users to these drives in logon scripts, they may become leaf objects in a DFS structure, or users may NET USE to them at their convenience.

There are some GSNW limitations to keep in mind.

- Not all NetWare utilities run through Gateway Services for NetWare.

- NetWare aware applications do not like to run through the Gateway service. See Microsoft documentation for their required workarounds.

- Response time through a NetWare Gateway can be slower than direct NetWare access.

These limitations are not meant to dissuade you from utilizing the Gateway Service for NetWare. However, you should be aware of them. The Gateway Service for NetWare is an excellent tool when used within its limits.

Using NetWare Printers with GSNW

To attach to and share a NetWare printer, make sure that you have properly installed and initialized Gateway Service for NetWare. Launch the Printers property window just as you would to create a normal printer connection and choose to install a network printer server. Once you have added the Gateway service, you will be able to browse NetWare resources in addition to the default Microsoft resources. Find the NetWare server that serves the printer you wish to use, and select that printer. You will be prompted to install print drivers as normal and installation will complete. In order to share this printer with your users, you must create an additional printer. When you select your port, you will see the captured NetWare printer. Choose this as your port and complete the printer installation. Once you have applied the proper permissions (if you don't plan to use the Everyone default), your users will be able to print to this printer as if it were locally attached to your server.

File and Print Sharing for NetWare

Instead of providing NetWare access to Microsoft clients, File and Print Sharing for NetWare provides Windows NT access to NetWare clients. With FPNW installed, you can mount any volume or directory on your Windows NT server as a NetWare volume so that those users that utilize NetWare as their primary server will also have access to your NT resources. FPNW is an excellent tool to be used when migrating to a Windows NT environment but is in direct conflict with many of the Six Key Design Objectives. If there are users who absolutely cannot play a role in your enterprise strategy, FPNW allows you to bend the rules.

File and Print Sharing for NetWare does not ship with Windows NT Server. However, it can be acquired through your software vendor as a part of the Services for NetWare CD. This CD, which costs only $99, also contains a utility that allows you to synchronize your NetWare 3.*x* and Windows NT directories. While the Directory Service Manager for NetWare utility has its place, it is not recommended as a long term solution and therefore will not be covered in this book.

To install FPNW, go to the Control Panel and select Network. Once the Network properties have launched, select Services and then Have Disk. You will soon be presented with a window requesting the location of the new service. Enter the path for your File and Print Sharing for NetWare CD and select OK. At this time you be prompted to select either the FPNW service or the FPNW administrative tools. Select the FPNW service and the administrative tools will be installed as well.

Files will be copied, and soon you will be presented with a window titled Install File and Print Services for NetWare. This screen is where you will enter the local directory path that will act as your NetWare SYS volume, your FPNW server name, and your Supervisor Password and will also configure your performance settings. If C:\Sysvol is not appropriate for your SYS volume (and in most cases if it won't be), enter a different path. Keep in mind that you will most likely not use the Sysvol directory to store anything other than the default Microsoft enhanced NetWare utilities.

When naming your FPNW server, take into account that it cannot be the same name as the Windows NT name. The default is always %Servername%_FPNW, and, while it is a not a required convention, many people leave it so. In addition to providing a Supervisor password, you must also set your performance configuration. The Balance Between Memory Usage and Performance option is in most cases the best choice.

Once you're satisfied with your initial FPNW configuration, select OK and you will be asked to enter a password for the FPNW service account. This account, which you will never modify, will be constantly logged in behind the scene. Enter the appropriate password and, after more files are copied, you will be brought back to the original Services window. Notice that, in addition to the FPNW service, the SAP agent has been added. SAP is necessary for NetWare clients to see and attach to your FPNW server. Select Close at the bottom of the Network configuration screen, and you will be prompted to restart your server in order to initiate the new service.

Creating NetWare-Compatible Volumes

Once the FPNW service is installed, the management of NetWare-emulated resources is very similar to managing Windows NT shares. Users configured to run Novell's NetWare client software (either ipx/netx or VLMs) will log into or attach to your NT server just as they would a NetWare server. However, it is necessary that they have a NetWare-compatible user ID. In order to make an ID NetWare-compatible, launch the User Manager for Domains and select the user you wish to work with.

Notice in Figure 11.26 that there are now two added options in the User Properties window in the User Manager for Domains. The first option is the Maintain NetWare Compatible Login checkbox and the second is the NW Compat button.

FIGURE 11.26.

The User Manager for Domains, Modified for FPNW Accounts.

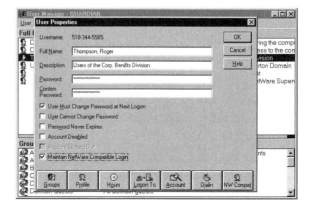

In order for a user to log in to an NT server as a NetWare client, his ID must first be marked as NetWare Compatible ID or he will not be able to access the NT server using the NetWare client software.

The NW Compat button launches the NetWare Compatible Properties window, shown in Figure 11.27, which allows you to configure a user's NetWare environment variables, including the addition of a personal login script. Once you have finished configuring your user's NetWare environment, the user may log in to your FPNW server and access those resources you plan to make NetWare compatible.

FIGURE 11.27.

The NetWare Compatible Properties Window.

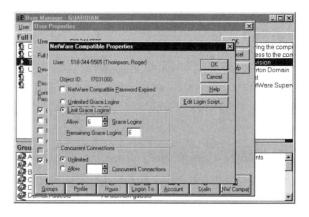

The next step is to create NetWare-compatible resources by designating existing volumes as NetWare volumes. To create these volumes, launch the standard Server Manager and, from the list of available servers, choose one that is running the FPNW service.

FIGURE 11.28.

The Server Manager with FPNW Enhancements.

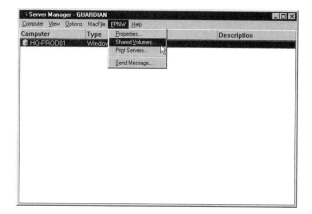

Notice that there is a new menu item added to the Server Manager tool bar: FPNW. In order to create NetWare Shared Volumes on the selected NT server, choose the FPNW menu item, followed by the Shared Volumes option. You will now be presented with a window that looks very similar to the Shared Directories window that launches when you create a standard shared directory. This is due to the fact that FPNW volumes are nothing more than shares that will be presented to your NetWare clients as NetWare volumes. When creating NetWare compatible volumes, keep in mind that the volume level security acts much like share level security and that file and directory level security still applies—allow the two levels to complement one another. As a rule it is helpful to create NetWare-compatible volumes based on your existing shares, so that there will be uniformity between the client types. To create an FPNW volume, select the Create Volume button, and you will immediately be presented with a window that has a Volume Name field, a Path field, a User Limit selection, and a Permissions button (see Figure 11.29). Before entering the volume name and path, keep in mind that you *can* create volumes with names and paths that are identical to your existing shares.

FIGURE 11.29.

Creating a NetWare Compatible Volume.

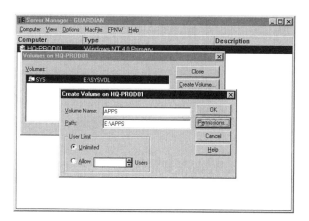

Enter the volume name and path desired, then press the Permissions button. The next window to launch is Access Through Share Permissions, which is the same window you receive when administering standard shares. Select the desired users and/or groups from your domain directory, set the appropriate level of permissions, and select OK until you have returned to the Volumes window. You should now see the NetWare-compatible volume that you just created. Just like when creating normal shares, there is no need to restart you server for these changes to be available to users.

> **CAUTION**
>
> FPNW volumes are not accessible via Microsoft Client for Networks. User's must have the NetWare client installed, whether it is provided by NetWare or Microsoft, in order to access your FPNW drives.

Advanced Features of FPNW

Most of the advanced features of FPNW require a solid NetWare background. With FPNW, you can create a central login script and designate NetWare print servers. All of the utilities that by default exist in the FPNW Public and System folders are fully NetWare-compatible. Programs such as Setpass.exe and Chgpass.exe offer extended functionality in that they synchronize password changes with your standard NT password.

To create a NetWare-compatible login script, simply create a standard login script and store it in the SYSVOL\PUBLIC\ folder as NET$LOG.DAT file. All of the functionality to be gained from a login script on a NetWare server exists on an FPNW server.

In addition to login script compatibility, you may also use many of the familiar NetWare management tools to manage your NetWare-compatible users.

Sharing Printers with NetWare Clients

When you install file and print sharing for NetWare, your printers are automatically made available to those users on your domain that have NetWare Compatible user IDs. As long as you provide your NetWare-compatible users with the appropriate rights, they may print to your printers. Additionally, any time you create a new printer, it will be made available to those users running the native NetWare client, if you provide the appropriate user or group rights.

Macintosh Integration

With the advent of Windows 95 and Windows NT 4.0, many of the classic services offered by the Macintosh have begun to migrate to the Windows platform. Even so, the need for Macintosh connectivity still exists. The following section will cover the Macintosh services offered by Windows NT Server.

Install Services for Macintosh

To install Services for Macintosh, go to the Control Panel and select Network. Once the Network properties have launched, select Services and then Add. You will soon be presented with a list of available services. Select Services for Macintosh, followed by OK, and you will be prompted for the location of your Windows NT server source files. Enter the correct path and again select OK. Files will be copied and your bindings will be reconfigured. At this point Services for Macintosh will be added to the list of installed services in your Services window. To initiate the new service, select Close at the bottom of the Network configuration page and you will be prompted to restart your machine.

Creating and Managing Macintosh-Compatible Volumes

Once Services for Macintosh is installed you may begin creating Macintosh-compatible volumes. Macintosh volumes are created through the Server Manager much like standard shares. However, there are some restrictions to take note of.

1. Unlike standard Windows NT shares, there can be only one Mac volume per directory.

2. Mac volumes cannot be nested: That is, if you create a Mac volume in the Data directory, you cannot create another Mac volume in the Data\Marketing directory.

3. Mac volume security is separate from File and Directory Level security and must be applied specifically for Mac users.

4. Mac volumes can be created only on an NTFS partition.

Macintosh-compatible volumes are very simple to create. Launch the Server Manager and notice that there is a new menu option in the Server Manager tool bar—MacFile. Select this option and select the Volumes option (see Figure 11.30).

FIGURE 11.30.

The MacFile Menu on the Server Manager.

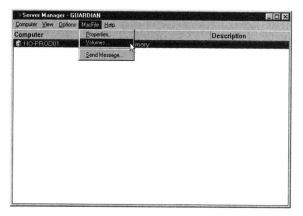

After choosing the Volumes option, a new window titled Macintosh Accessible Volumes will launch that will already include a single default Mac volume—the Microsoft UAM volume. During the initial installation of Services for Macintosh, this volume is created for the sole purpose of storing the Microsoft-provided enhanced network software for Macintosh clients. The enhanced network client is required to access other Mac volumes on your NT server. When a Mac user attaches to the server, he will first see UAM volume and have the opportunity to install this enhanced network client. Once the volume is installed, Mac users will have complete access to those Mac-compatible volumes you have created.

The Macintosh-Accessible Volumes window has three options: Create Volume, Properties, and Remove. To create a new volume, select the Create Volume button, and you will immediately be presented with the Create Macintosh-Accessible Volume window.

Enter the appropriate volume name and volume path. For instance, the administrators of the Horton Domain want to make the \\HTN-PROD01\APPS\MACAPPS directory available to their Macintosh users, so they would enter the full UNC path. Remember that you can create Mac volumes only on an NTFS partition.

After you've entered the volume name and path, you still have four options before moving on to Permissions. First, you may set this volume as being read-only, which will supersede all less-restrictive volume settings. Next, you can choose to limit the number of users who can access your Mac compatible volume. Finally, you can choose whether to allow guests to access the volume. Additionally, you can choose whether to password-protect this volume. If you password-protect this volume, each time a user attempts to access it, he will be prompted for the volume password. Once you have finished configuring the Macintosh-Accessible Volume window, launch the Permissions window by pressing the Permissions button (see Figure 11.31).

FIGURE 11.31.

Mac Volumes Directory Permissions.

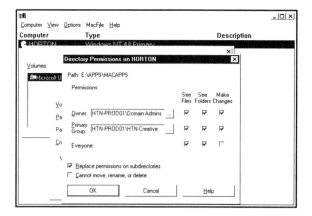

This window is very different from other Permissions windows in NT Server. While you have the ability to assign directory permissions, this window uses only Macintosh access privileges. Permission options on a Mac volume are See Files, See Folders, and Make Changes. These permissions are implemented as follows:

- **See Files.** This setting allows the Owner, Primary group, or Everyone to see and open files in a directory.
- **See Folders.** This setting allows the Owner, Primary group, or Everyone to see and open directories or folders in a directory.
- **Make Changes.** This setting allows the Owner, Primary group, or Everyone to add or delete files and directories and save changes to files in a directory.

In addition to permissions, the following settings are present:

- **Owner.** The Owner field is simply an extension of the Owner field you would normally see in the Security Properties dialog using Windows NT Explorer. An administrator may take ownership of this directory if necessary.
- **The Primary Group**. The Primary group is the group that has primary permissions for this directory. Unless the Everyone option is enabled, only the Primary group will have access.
- **Everyone**. Everyone, as it does elsewhere, means all users in the domain, including guests—however, it is restricted to Macintosh users. If you select this option, all domain users and guests will have access. One caution, however: On Mac-accessible volumes, Everyone overrides all rights, so if you've set more restrictive rights for a specific group than for Everyone, those restrictive group rights will be null.
- **Replace Permissions on Subdirectories.** The Replace permissions on Subdirectories option is identical to this option in standard Directory Level permissions. Checking this box and closing this window will result in copying the new permissions to this directory and all of its subdirectories.
- **Cannot Move, Rename or Delete.** The Cannot Move, Rename, or Delete option prevents the directory and its contents from being moved, renamed, or deleted by users.

Mac volumes act differently than standard Windows NT volumes. With a Mac volume, you cannot set differing levels of access for different groups. For instance, on a standard NT volume you can have a resource granting one user group read access, another group change, and another group list only. A Macintosh volume allows only two groups access: the Primary group, and, if selected, the Everyone group. A user's Primary group is set in the User Manager for Domains (see Figure 11.32) and, unless you enable the Everyone option on a Macintosh-compatible volume, only those users with the designated Primary group as their Primary group will have access. It is important to note, however, that Mac permissions don't affect PC users attaching to the same resources. In this respect, Services for Macintosh truly emulates the Macintosh environment. Furthermore, the Primary group designation allows Macintosh users that are members of a volume's Primary group to grant permissions to folders that they create. In return, when they create a folder, it is automatically associated with the user's Primary group.

FIGURE 11.32.

Primary Group Setting in the User Manager for Domains.

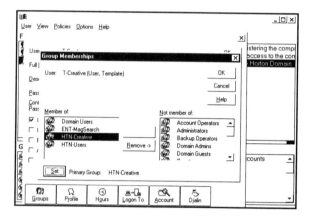

Once the appropriate permissions and options have been selected, press OK until you see the Macintosh Accessible Volumes window. At this point you will see your newly created volume, along with the original UAM volume. Your Macintosh user will now have access to your Windows NT server.

Printing with Services for Macintosh

When Services for Macintosh is installed, an additional service called Print Server for Macintosh is installed as well. This service makes printers connected to your Windows NT server available to Macintosh clients and has the ability to make AppleTalk PostScript printers (with LaserWriter drivers) available to your standard Microsoft clients. Print Services for Macintosh also has the ability to translate all incoming PostScript files for printing on non-PostScript printers. This allows a Macintosh client to send a PostScript job to any Windows NT server printer. (This translation does not work for a standard Microsoft client.) When connecting to any Print Server for Macintosh printer, Macintosh users have the familiar Chooser interface.

Summary

Windows NT Server offers a great number of connectivity options. With tools such as Remote Access, DFS, Gateway Service for NetWare, File and Print Sharing for NetWare, Services for Macintosh, and native OS/2 connectivity, Windows NT Server is keenly positioned as your enterprise anchor. In addition to these options, Windows NT Server can also be made available to UNIX clients on your network. This subject will be covered in Chapter 13, "Basic UNIX Integration."

SNA Connectivity

IN THIS CHAPTER

CHAPTER 12

SNA connectivity is extremely common in today's enterprise environment. Traditional PC-to-host implementations have consisted of the following variety of solutions:

- PC-to-Host Direct Connect (using products such as CM/2 or PC3270)
- Departmental Gateways (such as Attachmate's ZIP gateway)
- Netware SAA
- IBM Communications Manager Servers
- Hardware/Software Emulation Cards

While these types of solutions have provided organizations with the much-needed host connectivity, there is often a high overhead involved in the support of such solutions as well as in keeping track of individual configuration information. Deploying traditional PC-to-host connectivity solutions can be likened to deploying TCP/IP without DHCP, which is to say they can bring with them a support nightmare.

With SNA Server 3.0, Microsoft has provided a PC-to-host connectivity option that eliminates much of the overhead usually associated with such solutions. SNA Server provides a tremendous amount of functionality and an ease of management that brings SNA connectivity into the realm of second-nature. With true BackOffice integration and near zero configuration at the desktop, SNA Server is a fantastic solution for PC-to-host connectivity.

The following is a partial list of SNA Server 3.0's functionality:

- 5,000 concurrent users per server with 15,000 active sessions
- Integrated 3270 and 5250 host print services
- AS/400 Shared Folders Gateway service with the ability to make AS/400 shared folders accesible to all users throughout your enterprise
- Integrated TN5250 and TN3270 service display and print services
- Integration of Windows NT Security with both AS/400 and mainframe host security
- Secure data encryption between SNA Client and SNA Server
- LU 6.2 support including Syncpoint Level 2 for APPC
- Dynamic 6.2 Creation
- Fault tolerant domain design
- Inherent load balancing to provide for increased performance

SNA Server can be an immense benefit to any organization that requires PC-to-host connectivity. While SNA Server management is straightforward, it does, however, require basic SNA knowledge and is not a product that can be deployed with any success without such knowledge due to the tremendous number of configuration and functionality options. The focus of this chapter is not to educate you on SNA Connectivity, nor is it meant to be a technical resource for SNA Server administrators. Instead, the purpose of this chapter is to demonstrate the ease of deployment and management that SNA Server provides through its functionality and BackOffice integration. This demonstration will be made through a sample 3270 deployment using the Guardian Insurance Companies as an example.

Guardian Insurance Companies

Since its inception, the Guardian Insurance Companies has been a mainframe-centric corporation. However, with the advent of client/server development in the early 1990s, Guardian began to look at ways to take advantage of the less expensive distributed PC world. Yet like many companies, they found that it would be extremely difficult to eliminate all mainframe dependencies. Presently at Guardian, there are over 200 OS/2 users using IBM's Communications Manager to directly attach to the mainframe, and approximately 220 Windows users using several fairly old DOS-based gateway systems. As part of their migration to Windows NT Server, the Guardian support organization is moving all desktops from OS/2 and Windows for Workgroups to Windows NT Workstation. At the time of a workstation's reconfiguration, the user is also being moved from his or her current means of 3270 comunications to SNA Server 3.0.

Guardian's SNA connectivity needs are fairly simple when compared to many organizations. While approximately 15 percent of the users will require unique or particular VIPS menus, the great majority of Guardian users have no pariticular configuration requirements, with the exception of a minimum of two 3270 sessions.

While host dependencies are diminishing at Guardian, those that exist are still crucial. Therefore, it is essential that Guardian users have a great degree of fault tolerance built into any host connectivity solution. Thus, Guardian administrators plan to take advantage of many of the fault tolerant features innate to SNA Server. The remainder of this chapater will cover the following subjects in conjunction with the Guardian SNA Server deployment:

- SNA Server Installation
- SNA Server Configuration
- SNA Server Fault Tolerance
- Host Connectivity Configuration
- SNA Server User Deployment

SNA Server Installation

While SNA Server can coexist on a production server without degrading file and print performance too noticably, Administrators of the Guardian Domain have decided to deploy their SNA Servers on dedicated application servers. Doing so, they ensure two things:

- Non–SNA Server-related issues concerning other services or applications on the production server won't interfere with SNA Server availability.
- SNA Server-related issues won't interfere with production server availability.

SNA Server installation is fairly straightforward. To begin the installation of SNA Server, place the SNA Server 3.0 CD-ROM in the CD-ROM drive of your Windows NT Server. After a few seconds you will be presented with the new Autoplay Extension seen on most new Microsoft applications. (See Figure 12.1.)

Figure 12.1.

The SNA Server Autoplay Extension.

The Autoplay Extension offers the following choices:

- **SNA Server Setup.** Selecting this option will launch the SNA Server Setup program.
- **Client Setup.** This option will launch the SNA Client Setup program.
- **Browse CD.** Selecting this option will open a window displaying the contents of the SNA Server CD-ROM.
- **Browse Collateral.** This option will launch your Web Browser and provide access to a great deal of information concerning SNA Server including installation instructions, white papers, deployment guides, and examples of third-party add-ons and solutions.
- **View Release Notes.** Selecting this option will launch release notes concerning SNA Server 3.0.

To begin installation, select the Server Setup button and the SNA Server setup program will begin. Setup will run through the usual Microsoft initialization, including licensing information and searching for previous versions. After this is complete, you will be prompted for an SNA Server location. Be sure not to install the SNA Server program in a shared directory to which users have access. Instead, install the SNA Server in the root of a drive or in a non-shared directory. The default installation directory is C:\SNA; however, you may install it wherever you like. Keep in mind that, like most programs, it is not recommended that you install SNA Server in your system partition due to possible disk limitation; however, if you've planned for enough capacity, the program will present no problems.

The Guardian administrators have chosen to install SNA Server on three dedicated Windows NT 4.0 member servers named GRD-SNA1, GRD-SNA2, and GRD-SNA3. Each server is identically configured with 64 MB of RAM and duplexed 2 GB hard drives. Windows NT Server will be installed on a 500 MB FAT partition in C:\WINNTSRV and SNA Server will be installed in a 500 MB NTFS partition in D:\SNA. The remainder of the storage (approximately 1 GB) has been formatted with NTFS; however, other than housing a virtual memory swap file, it will serve no purpose.

After you've chosen an installation directory, you will be presented with a Select Components button. Click this button and a screen similar to Figure 12.2 will launch a listing all of the SNA Server components that are available for installation.

FIGURE 12.2.

The SNA Server Setup Component Selection Window.

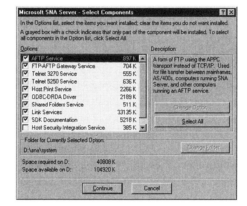

Those components are as follows:

- **AFTP Service.** A service similar to FTP except it allows file transfers using APPC versus TCP/IP. The AFTP Service is used to transfer files between mainframes or AS/400s and other computers running the AFTP service.

- **FTP-AFTP Gateway Service.** This service provides a gateway to hosts running the AFTP to standard FTP clients.

- **Telnet 3270 Service.** This service provides for TN3270, TN3270E, and TN3287 access to hosts and host printers through the SNA Server.

- **Telnet 5250 Service.** This service provides for TN5250 access to AS/400s through the SNA Server.

- **Host Print Service.** This service allows for print emulation to IBM mainframes via LU1 and LU3, as well as LU6.2 print services to AS/400s.

- **ODBC-DRDA Driver.** An ODBC driver that allows for access to relational databases on SNA hosts via DRDA.

- **Shared Folders Service.** A gateway service that will allow domain users to access AS/400 shared folders as if they were standard shared directories.

- **Link Services.** A wide variety of SNA connectivity options.

- **SDK Documentation.** Microsoft SNA Server software development documents.

- **Host Security Integration Service.** A service that can provide for passsword synchronization between your Windows NT domain and an IBM host or AS/400 system.

Because the Guardian Insurance Companies' current requirements only call for standard 3270 Host and Print connectivity, the Guardian Administrators have chosen to install only the following components:

- Telnet 3270

- Host Print Service

- ODBC-DRDA Driver

- Link Services

After the component selection is made, press Continue and Setup will validate that your server has enough disk space. Immediately thereafter, you will be presented with a window titled Server Domain Account Information as seen in Figure 12.3.

FIGURE 12.3.

The Server Domain Account Information Window.

It is here that you will enter the SNA Server service account. This account may either be an existing service account (such as for a Backup service or SQL Server) or may be created from scratch at this time. The Guardian Domain administrators have chosen to create a new service account that will be used by all SNA Servers in their domain, but it will not be shared with any other services.

After you have chosen the appropriate service account, click OK at the bottom of the screen and the service account will either be verified or created in your Domain Directory. Next, you will be presented with the licensing options screen. This window provides the opportunity for you to determine if you plan to license SNA Server on a per seat or per server basis. For SNA Server the licensing translation is as follows:

■ *Per seat* translates to concurrency. If you have 300 SNA Server licenses, you may deploy the SNA client software to as many users as you desire, but only 300 users may access any one of your SNA servers at once.

■ *Per server* means that each server must have an accompanying access license for each user who touches it.

FIGURE 12.4.

SNA Server Licensing Options.

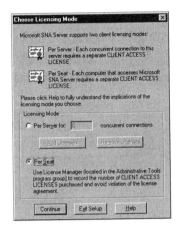

While the per seat licensing option might make sense in a small environment, the Guardian Domain administrators have chosen to go with the per server licensing mode.

After you have chosen the appropriate licensing model, click OK and you will be brought to a window labeled Choose Server Role (see Figure 12.5). SNA Server is deployed in a domain model, much like Windows NT Server. There is always at least one primary SNA Server and there can be as many as 14 other servers acting as backup servers or member servers. Of these servers, only the primary and backup servers can actually host permanent connections, and member servers will act as host backups in case of server failure. The Guardian administrators have chosen to deploy one primary SNA Server and two backup SNA Servers.

FIGURE 12.5.

The Server Role Window.

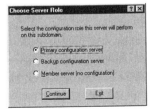

After you have chosen your server's role, click Continue and you will come to the Client/Server Protocols configuration window. Here you will choose what protocols your clients can use to access your SNA Server. You may choose any combination of the following protocols as long as they are installed on your server:

- Microsoft Networking (Named Pipes or NetBEUI)
- IPX/SPX
- TCP/IP
- Banyan Vines
- AppleTalk

Due to the fact that the Guardian administrators are in the process of moving entirely to TCP/IP, they will choose only the TCP/IP option. Keep in mind that this can be modified later.

Following the Client/Server Protocols configuration window, you will be presented with a window titled Network Subdomain Name (see Figure 12.6). Microsoft SNA Servers are organized in subdomains that act very much like Windows NT Server domains, but multiple SNA Server subdomains can exist within a single Windows NT domain.

FIGURE 12.6.

*The Network
Subdomain Name
Configuration Page.*

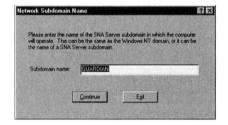

An SNA Server subdomain consists of a single primary server and up to 14 additional backup or member servers. When a user configured for SNA Server client access attempts to initiate an SNA session, that session can be granted from any of the SNA servers in the subdomain, dependent upon your chosen deployment methods. Subdomains can offer a tremendous amount of fault tolerance and load balancing and therefore offer many advantages. However, even though it is very rare that you will find an organization that cannot be served by a single SNA Server subdomain (up to 15 servers each with the ability to provide 5,000 host connections with 15,000 concurrent sessions), there are network concerns to contend with. Due to the fact that SNA Servers in a subdomain will communicate with one another on a regular basis, it is not recommended that you deploy a large subdomain in a routed environment unless the client/server environment uses TCP/IP as the sole protocol. In addition, due to the inherent need for server-to-server communications, it is also recommended that you not deploy a subdomain in a WAN comprised mainly of slow links.

Because the Guardian domain is moving entirely to TCP/IP and has recently implemented an ATM backbone connecting their campus enterprise, the Guardian administrators have chosen to deploy a single SNA subdomain with three SNA Servers.

After you've chosen your subdomain name, select continue and SNA Server will be installed as configured. After files are copied and your registry is updated, your SNA Server installation will be complete. At this time, re-install any Windows NT Service packs that might have been installed previous to your SNA Server installation, or update your server with the most current service packs. Service packs can be found at `http://www.microsft.com` on the home page of the appropriate product. At the time of this writing, Windows NT Server 4.0 was up to Service Pack 2 (but Service Pack 3 is just around the corner) and SNA Server was yet to have a service pack.

After the appropriate service packs have been installed, restart your server. SNA Server installation is now complete.

Installing Link Services

To manage your SNA Server, go to the Microsoft SNA Server common folder in your start menu and choose the application titled Manager.

As you can see in Figure 12.7, the SNA Server Manager looks very similar to the Windows NT Explorer. Services are organized by category and under each service you will find any applicable servers and their current status. As a result, if all three Guardian Domain SNA Servers were in place, all three servers would be listed under the folder titled SNA Servers.

FIGURE 12.7.

The SNA Server Manager.

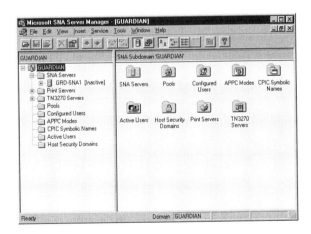

The first step in host connectivity is to choose your *link service*. A link service is the software driver your SNA Servers will use to communicate with the desired host device. The following are available link types:

- 802.2/LLC—Token-Ring, Ethernet, or FDDI connections
- SDLC—leased or switched telephone line connections
- X.25/QLLC—public or private packet-switched networks

- DFT—co-axial or twisted-pair connections via an IBM 3x74 cluster controller
- Twinax—twin-axial connections to an AS/400
- Channel—bus and tag or ESCON connections directly to a mainframe

The administrators of the Guardian Domain have chosen to utilize the 802.2, or network-attached, Link Service. When using the 802.2 Link Service, always take into account that this method requires one link service per host connection (or PU—Physical Unit); however, it is the most convenient connection method for most organizations.

When planning for communications capacity, keep the following information in mind:

- There is a one-to-one relationship between link services and actual host connections with the 802.2 connection type.
- Each host connection, or PU, can contain up to 255 simultaneous display and printer LUs (sessions).
- Each SNA Server can contain up to 15,000 host connections.
- Much like other services under Windows NT, it is necessary to restart your server to activate a newly created link service.

CAUTION

In order for the SNA Server to communicate with non-TCP/IP-based hosts, it is necessary to install the DLC protocol. This protocol, based on SNA architecture, can be installed though the Network Configuration window from the Protocols tab.

To install an 802.2 Link Service, do the following:

1. Go to the SNA Server folder in the tool bar and launch the SNA Manager.
2. Double-click the SNA Server's folder on the left side of the window, and your SNA Server will appear on the right side of the window.
3. Right-click the SNA Server shortcut and choose Insert from the drop-down menu, quickly followed by Link Service (see Figure 12.8).
4. From the list of available link services, choose DLC 802.2 Link Service. Files will be copied and the Link Service Configuration window will appear as in Figure 12.9.
5. From the Link Service Configuration window, you can change the title of the link service, determine which network card the link service will be dedicated to, configure the SAP number (which must be unique to this link), and determine whether the link service can be distributed (which means that other SNA Servers may use the service for host connections). Other than the SAP address, most connections will utilize default settings. Click OK after your configuration is complete and you will be brought back to the Available Link Services window. Install as many link services as necessary.

FIGURE 12.8.

Installing a Link Service in SNA Manager.

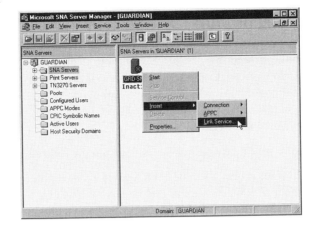

FIGURE 12.9.

The DLC 802.2 Link Configuration Window.

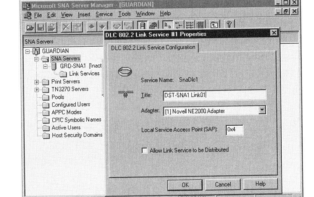

6. After you have finished installing your link services, click the Finish button on the Available Link Services window. Files will be copied, and your server's bindings will be reviewed. After the review is complete, it will be necessary to restart your server before you may configure your link services for host connectivity.

NOTE

For increased SNA Server performance, bind DLC to one network card and your Client/Server protocol to another. All SNA traffic then will be localized to one card and all client/server communication will be localized to the other.

Configuring for Host Connections

PU configuration for the 3270 environment is fairly simple. While there are many configuration options, this section will explore only those settings that are absolutely necessary to make a 3270 PU connection. Consult your SNA Server manual or online help for detailed configuration information. In order to properly configure your SNA Server, you must either be extremely familiar with your company's mainframe configuration or have access to a knowledgeable mainframe operator.

To configure your newly created link service, do the following:

1. In SNA Manager, click the SNA Servers folder on the left side of the window. Almost immediately, the folder will expand, and you will see two sub-folders: Connections and Link Services. The Link Services folder will display your newly created link services and the Connections folder will be empty.

2. Highlight the Connections folder and click your right mouse button. You will quickly be presented with a drop-down menu. Choose the Insert option, followed by Connection, and finally 802.2.

3. You will quickly be presented with a four-tabbed window titled Connection Properties (see Figure 12.10). This is where you will configure your host connection (see Figure 12.11).

FIGURE 12.10.

Installing a Host Connection.

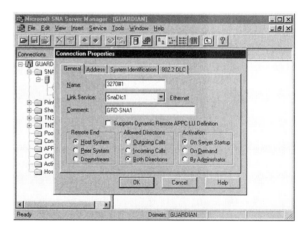

4. To properly configure a 3270 connection, you only need the Remote Network Address (Host TIC) and Local Node ID (for example, MP0054B) as seen in Figures 12.12 and 12.13. After you've input the appropriate information, select OK from the bottom of the window.

5. After configuring a host connection for all desired link services, it is necessary to restart your server for these changes to take effect. Save all changes and restart your server.

FIGURE 12.11.
Configuring a Host Connection.

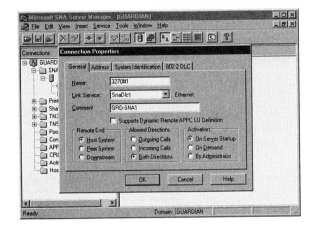

FIGURE 12.12.
The Remote Network Address.

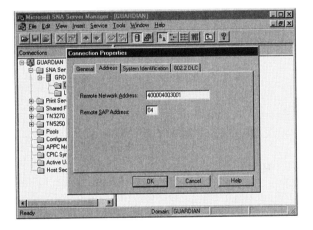

FIGURE 12.13.
The Local Node ID.

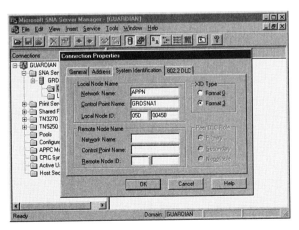

12

SNA
CONNECTIVITY

Creating Display and Printer LUs

After you've configured your host connections, creating and assigning LUs is terribly easy. This section will deal with creating both Display and Printer LUs.

To create a range of Display LUs, do the following:

1. In the SNA Manager, highlight the desired host connection from within the Connections folder, and choose Insert from the text portion of the toolbar. From the drop-down menu, select 3270, followed by Range of LUs as shown in Figure 12.14.

FIGURE 12.14.

Creating a Range of 3270 LUs.

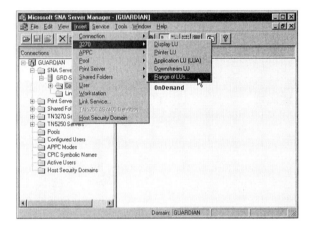

2. You will soon be presented with the LU Creation Wizard as seen in Figure 12.15. This window will display the current SNA domain, the currently chosen server, and the currently chosen connection. If all information is correct, select Next to move on.

FIGURE 12.15.

Configuring an LU Range.

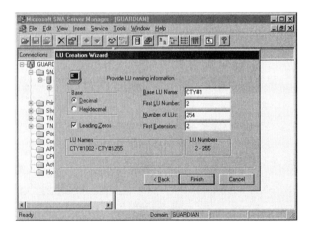

3. The next window is where you will configure your LU Range. Note that you may enter up to 254 sessions. After you've entered the appropriate LU information, select Finish to complete your LU creation.

4. To see your newly configured LUs, double-click the appropriate host connection. The new sessions will not be available until you either restart your SNA Server service or manually start the host connection.

> **NOTE**
>
> Not only is it possible to create LUs one at a time, but you may also modify any individual LU by highlighting it, and then pressing your right mouse button and selecting properties from the drop-down menu.

To create a Printer LU and configure the built-in Host Print Server service, do the following:

1. Highlight the appropriate host connection, and select Insert by pressing the right mouse button, followed by 3270 and Printer LU.

2. Next, you will be presented with the LU Properties page, which is shown in Figure 12.16. Enter an appropriate LU name, followed by a description in the Comment field. Suggested comments include the host printer alias or UID.

FIGURE 12.16.
Printer LU properties.

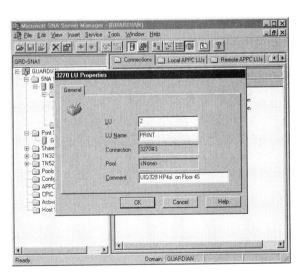

3. After you've finished configuration, select OK and save your changes. Next, to create a host print server, highlight the folder titled Print Servers. (This service does not start automatically.)

4. To configure the Print Server service to start automatically, go to the Control Panel and choose Services. Find the service titled SnaPrint and configure the service to start automatically, as shown in Figure 12.17.

FIGURE 12.17.

Modifying the SNA Print Server Service Startup Value.

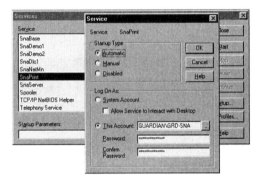

5. Manually start the Print Server service by highlighting the appropriate server and choosing the Start option from the right mouse drop-down menu.

6. Next, using your right mouse button, choose Insert from the drop-down menu, followed by Print Server and 3270 Session. You will quickly be presented with a window titled Print Session Properties. Enter a descriptive name for the print session, followed by a comment. If you wish this printer to be available upon server startup, select Automatic under the heading titled Activation.

7. After you're finished with the General tab, move to the Printing tab, which is shown in Figure 12.18. It is here that you will choose which LAN printer your Print Session will print to. Note that you can print to any printer that your server can connect to, regardless of operating system or printer type.

FIGURE 12.18.

LAN Printer Configuration Page.

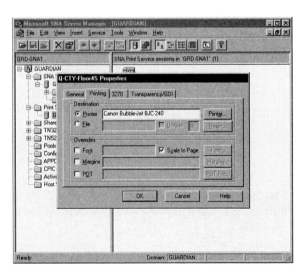

8. After choosing your printer, move to the 3270 tab. Note the text box labeled LU Name (see Figure 12.19) and choose the appropriate printer LU by selecting the drop-down arrow next to the text box. After you complete this processs, make any appropriate configuration changes and save your changes.

FIGURE 12.19.

Selecting the Printer LU.

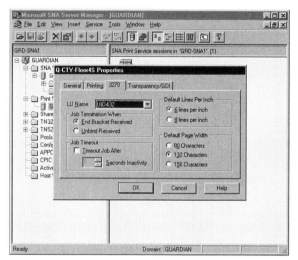

9. After configuration is complete, select OK and save your changes to the SNA domain. Your 3270 printer is now accessible.

Creating LU Pools

LUs can be assigned to users on an individual basis or through the use of LU pools. A *pool*, which can consist of LUs from any like host connection throughout the SNA subdomain, is nothing more than a group of LUs that have been organized to act as a single entity. As long as all sessions in the pool have been configured with identical host access and menu options that meet the users needs, users who have been assigned to a pool experience the same connectivity as those who have been assigned specific LUs.

To create a pool, launch the SNA Manager and follow these steps:

1. On the left side of the SNA Manager, highlight the Pools folder and click your right mouse button. From the drop-down menu, select Insert, followed by Pool and 3270 Display Pool, as shown in Figure 12.20.

2. You will be presented with a window titled Pool Properties (see Figure 12.21). You will enter the pool name and a pool description here.

FIGURE 12.20.

*Creating a New
LU Pool.*

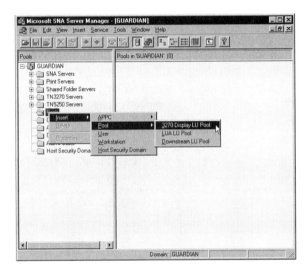

FIGURE 12.21.

*The Pool Properties
Window.*

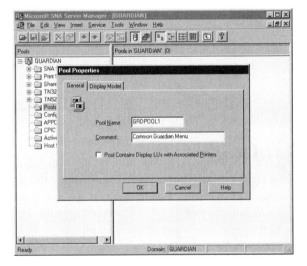

3. After you've named your pool accordingly, choose the Display Model tab, which is shown in Figure 12.22. Here you can predetermine the display model to be used by all users or allow the end user to choose his or her own page size. The Model Can Be Overriden option is, in most cases, chosen by default.

4. After you've configured the display model appropriately, select OK, and your newly created pool will be added to the Pools window (see Figure 12.23).

5. To assign LUs to the pool, click the Connections window and double-click the host connection with the appropriate LUs. Highlight the desired LUs and drag them to the newly created pool. Pool creation is now complete.

FIGURE 12.22.

The Display Model Tab.

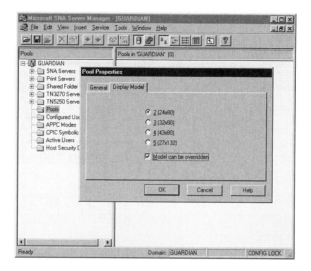

FIGURE 12.23.

The Pools Window.

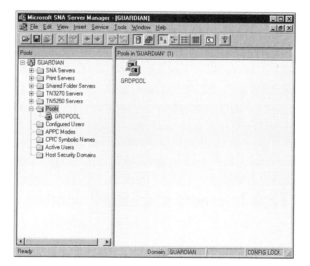

Assigning LUs to Users

With SNA Server 3.0 you can assign both specific or pooled LUs to either an entire group or an individual person. First, however, you must configure the user or group with SNA subdomain rights. To do so, follow these steps:

1. From the text portion of the SNA Manager toolbar, choose Insert, and then choose User.

2. The familiar Add Users and Groups window will appear, as seen in Figure 12.24. Choose the appropriate users and groups and select OK. (Note that these users and groups have previously been configured for basic NT domain connectivity.)

FIGURE 12.24.

Adding Users and Groups to SNA Manager.

3. After your users or groups are added, it is time to assign LUs. To assign a specific set of LUs to a person, go to the Connections window and choose the desired host connection. Double-click until the previously configured sessions are displayed. Select those LUs you wish to assign and drag them to the user. Select Save from the toolbar.

4. To assign a pool of LUs to a user, select the pool and drag it to the desired user or group. To assign more than one configured session to each pool user, repeat the previous procedure.

5. After you've completed assigning LUs and pools, save your changes. LU assignment is now complete.

Server Fault Tolerance and Load Balancing

Due to the fact that an SNA Server by nature must be a high availability server, the administrators at the Guardian Domain have decided to install more link services than are currently necessary. At this time they know that they have a need for a minimum of 600 concurrent sessions, which could easily be handled by a single SNA Server with three PUs, but, due to the geographic distribution of the Guardian campus, they have decided to implement a more fault-tolerant model as seen in Figure 12.25.

As mentioned earlier in this chapter, LUs can be organized in terms of pools that can be assigned to individual users or entire Windows NT groups. Because an SNA Server subdomain essentially acts like a single entity, a pool can consist of LUs from any connection on any SNA Server in the subdomain. With this in mind, the Guardian administrators have decided to implement a design model that requires one and one third times the actual number of required sessions, but will provide for both load balancing and fault tolerance. In essence, each PU will be mirrored on three SNA Servers. These SNA Servers will then be configured to touch alternate entry points. For instance PU A on GRD-SNA1 will be configured to hit a 3174 controller, PU B on GRD-SNA2 will be configured to hit an FEP, and PU C on GRD-SNA3 will be configured to talk directly to the mainframe. These connection types will then be staggered from server to server for each PU set required by Guardian users. Keeping in mind that these SNA Servers are geographically dispersed, a situation in which the end user wouldn't receive a session would be extremely rare.

FIGURE 12.25.
The Guardian Domain's SNA Server Deployment Model.

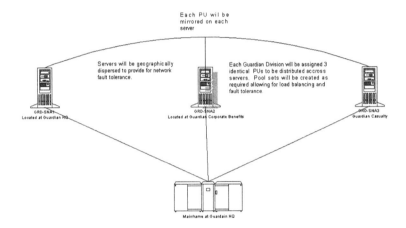

SNA Server User Deployment

Deploying SNA clients is extremely simple. Microsoft SNA Server, much like many client/server applications, requires its own client software. This software, which is very small and is easy to install, drives the connection from the workstation to the server.

Microsoft provides client software for Windows 95, Windows NT, and Windows for Workgroups, but installation is very common among the three versions.

To install the SNA Client for Windows 95, do the following:

1. From the Clients directory of the SNA Server CD-ROM, go to the WIN95 subdirectory and choose Setup to launch the setup program. You will be prompted for the usual licensing information, followed by an installation directory. (The default is C:\WIN95.)

2. After you've chosen the installation directory, you will be prompted for installation components. The options are: 3270 Applet, 5250 Applet, ODBC-DRDA Driver,

AFTP Client, and Host Account Manager (see Figure 12.26). For 3270 access, choose only the 3270 Applet and the ODBC-DRDA drivers, and click Continue.

FIGURE 12.26.

Choosing Installation Components.

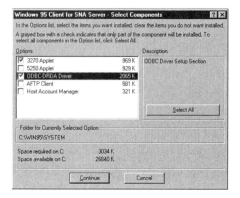

3. The Client/Server Protocols page will appear. Select only the protocol that will be necessary for communication to your SNA Server. TCP/IP is chosen by default (see Figure 12.27).

FIGURE 12.27.

Choosing a Client/ Server Protocol.

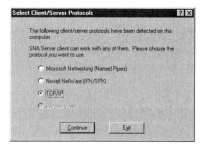

4. After you've chosen your protocol, click Continue and the Client Mode window will appear. Your options are Local and Remote. If you will connect to the SNA subdomain via named pipes (NetBEUI) and the subdomain exists, in your logon domain select Local, and enter the subdomain name. If you connect to the server via TCP/IP, select Remote, and then select Continue.

5. The Remote Server Names page will appear (see Figure 12.28). Here you will enter the names of any servers in your subdomain. Keep in mind that after your clients access any of your subdomain's SNA Servers, they will have access to all accompanying subdomain resources. Enter the appropriate names, and select Continue.

6. Choose OK, and the files will be copied. After installation is complete, you may install your desired 3270 emulation package (such as Extra! For SNA Server) to access your SNA subdomain.

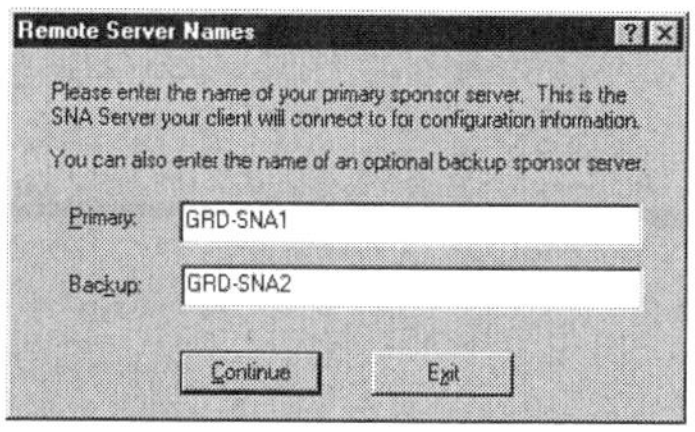

FIGURE 12.28.

Configuring for Subdomain Connectivity.

NOTE

The 3270 and 5250 applets that come with SNA Server are not meant for production use, but rather to test connectivity. In fact, you don't really even need to install the applet in order to connect to your SNA subdomain. These applets are limited to a single session per desktop and offer very little functionality. Companies such as Attachmate, Wall Data, and NetSoft provide rich, full-featured 3270 and 5250 emulators to be used specifically in conjunction with SNA Server.

7. After installation is complete, launch the 3270 Applet (as seen in Figure 12.29) from the Microsoft SNA Server Client folder in your Start bar. In order to test your connection and menu configuration, be sure that you have granted the current user an SNA Session.

FIGURE 12.29.

The SNA Server 3270 Applet.

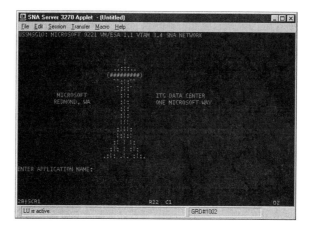

Summary

Microsoft SNA Server 3.0 can be a very valuable asset not only to the network manager, but also to the end user. From its multiple host type and connection options to its inherent fault tolerance and easily navigated Explorer interface, SNA Server is a true enterprise solution.

Basic UNIX Integration

CHAPTER

13

So far in this book, you've learned how your Windows NT Server environment can provide access to Microsoft Clients, OS/2 Workstations, Macintosh Workstations, and even native NetWare clients. While these four client types will make up the majority of all computing workstations in most enterprises, there is a fifth client type—the UNIX Workstation. The UNIX workstation is traditionally considered a more powerful workstation than the other four types and, in most cases, is kept within a UNIX environment. However, Windows NT Server is an extremely open and powerful platform, rivaling even UNIX in stability and strength. Due to these factors, more and more enterprise-dependent applications are moving to Windows NT Server, requiring UNIX workstations to access a non-UNIX server more often. While Microsoft does not provide a UNIX client for Windows NT Server, third-party developers have brought to market a whole slew of UNIX connectivity products. These products, most commonly Telnet Servers, FTP Servers, and NFS Servers (not to mention just about anything having to do with the Internet), allow your enterprise to adhere to two extremely important Key Design Objectives, not only for the classic network client, but also for the UNIX client. These two objectives are as follows:

- **Objective One: A Central User Directory**

  Through the use of BackOffice-compatible Telnet, FTP, and NFS products, your UNIX users will be able to access your Windows NT Server-based resources using their user accounts from within the Domain Directory.

- **Objective Two: An Open and Scaleable Design**

  Due to Windows NT Server's open architecture, it is possible to provide access to your Windows NT Server-based resources to any UNIX workstation throughout your enterprise.

FTP, Telnet, and NFS are just a few of the classic features of the UNIX environment that have been made available for Windows NT Server. This chapter's main focus is not on Windows NT as a UNIX replacement, nor will it be focused on Windows NT as an Internet server. Instead, it will focus on providing FTP, Telnet, and NFS access for UNIX clients throughout your enterprise, as well as some of the advantages your PC users can expect as a result of their implementation.

FTP Service

The FTP service is a platform-independent application used for transferring files from one computer to another. *FTP*, or *File Transfer Protocol*, is a TCP/IP application that was originally used in the UNIX world, but since the mainstream advent of the Internet, FTP has become extremely common in the PC environment as well. FTP is an industry standard, which means that no matter which platform or whose FTP client you use, you can access an FTP server to either download or upload files. FTP is an excellent means of sharing non-secure data on your Windows NT Servers for UNIX clients throughout the enterprise.

There are many third-party FTP servers available for Windows NT, but, with the advent of Windows NT Server 4.0 and the Internet Information Server, Microsoft is now including a BackOffice-compatible FTP server with every copy of Windows NT Server you buy. The advantage of using the FTP server that ships with NT is that it integrates with your Domain Directory, including your existing NTFS permissions, providing an enhanced level of security. FTP, however, is not a highly secure application due to the fact that all FTP clients transport passwords in clear text mode. Even so, FTP is an excellent utility that can add a great deal of convenience for your users when it is deployed properly.

Installing the Windows NT FTP service is extremely easy. When you first install Windows NT Server 4.0, there will be an Internet Information Server (IIS) setup shortcut on your desktop. If you've removed this shortcut, you also can find the IIS setup program (Inetstp.exe) on your Windows NT Server 4.0 CD-ROM in the proper platform installation directory under \Inetsrv (for example, \i386\Inetsrv\). This installation is extremely straightforward and requires no specialized knowledge. After you launch this executable, the IIS installation procedure will begin (see Figure 13.1).

FIGURE 13.1.

The Internet Information Server 2.0 Setup Program.

13

BASIC UNIX
INTEGRATION

After reading the licensing information, click Next at the bottom of the page and you will be brought to a window providing you with component installation options, as shown in Figure 13.2.

This chapter will focus solely on the installation of the FTP service; therefore, select only the following options:

- The Internet Service Manager
- The FTP Service
- ODBC Drivers and Administration

FIGURE 13.2.

*IIS Installation
Options.*

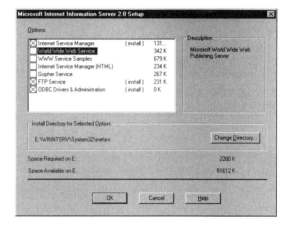

> **NOTE**
>
> If you choose to install all IIS components, you will in no way affect the FTP functionality
> described throughout this chapter.

After you've selected the desired components, you have the option of changing the installation directory. This directory (\%systemroot%\System32\inetsrv) is where the application itself will be stored, but the root of your FTP service—or rather the point at which your FTP users will start—is stored elsewhere. If you do not want to install IIS in your system directory, there will be no repercussions. Keep in mind, in order to enforce NTFS security, you must be sure to install IIS on an NTFS partition.

After you've chosen the desired components and selected an installation directory, click OK at the bottom of the screen to move on. Soon, you will be prompted to confirm the creation of the application directory, followed by a prompt for the path of your FTP publishing directory, as shown in Figure 13.3. The FTP publishing directory acts very much like the root of a DFS structure, in that it is simply the starting point of your FTP directory—where your users attach when they log in to the FTP service. You can store files in this publishing directory if you like, but—as you'll see later in this chapter—you can also set up virtual directories that can exist anywhere on your server or throughout your Windows NT Domain.

After you're satisfied with the path for your publishing directory, select OK at the bottom of the screen. After verifying the creation of directories, setup will begin copying files. After all files are copied, you will be prompted to select an ODBC driver (SQL server is the default), and the FTP service will be started. As stated, the IIS installation process is very simple. It is now time to configure your FTP Server.

FIGURE 13.3.
The FTP Publishing Directory Configuration.

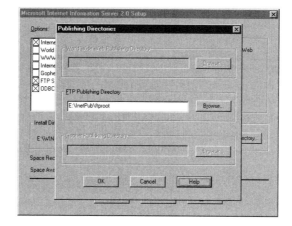

Configuring Your FTP Server

The Internet Service Manager is used to configure your FTP Server. This utility, which is installed during IIS installation, is located in the Microsoft Internet Information Server folder that can be found in the All Users portion of your Start menu. After you launch this application, a screen will appear that displays all of the known IIS servers in your enterprise (see Figure 13.4).

FIGURE 13.4.
The Internet Service Manager.

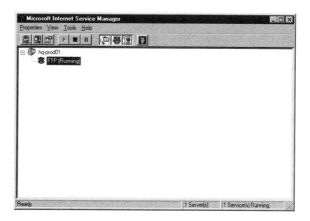

The Internet Service Manager is where you would manage not only your FTP Servers, but also your Gopher and WWW Servers that have been installed as part of IIS. To view what services are installed on a server, simply double-click its icon, and the installed services will be identified, along with their current status. The status meter is a common traffic light: If the traffic light is green, the service is running; if it is yellow, the service is paused; and if it is red, the service has been stopped.

To manage the FTP service properties you may either double-click the FTP traffic light, or use the right mouse click method to launch its properties. Soon, the FTP Service Properties window will open (see Figure 13.5). This window consists of five tabs: Service, Messages, Directories, Logging, and Advanced.

FIGURE 13.5.

The FTP Service Properties.

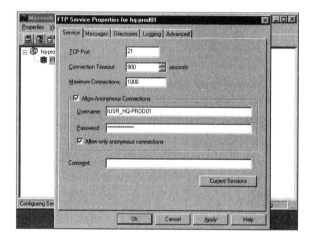

The Service tab default has the following eight options:

- **TCP Port.** This is the default TCP port used for all FTP servers. This setting can be modified, but it is not recommended.

- **Timeout.** This setting, measured in seconds, determines how long the service will wait before disconnecting an inactive user. The default is 900 seconds, which translates to 15 minutes.

- **Maximum Connections.** This setting determines the maximum number of simultaneous connections. The default is 1000.

- **Allow Anonymous Connections.** This setting allows anonymous connections to your FTP root by using the FTP server account. Anonymous connections will have access only to those directories and files that the FTP service account has been specifically granted access to.

- **Allow Only Anonymous Connections.** By deselecting this setting, users will be able to log into the FTP server using their domain user name and passwords. While this sounds like a good idea at first, you should be aware that all FTP passwords are transported across the network in clear text format. Clear text format allows for easy capture by a network sniffer, meaning that domain security could easily be breached. If this setting is left at its default, access will be allowed only to the Anonymous user. If you plan to allow users to log in to the FTP server using their domain accounts, they must either specifically be granted Log On Locally rights (User Manager for Domains under Policies\User Rights) or be a member of a group with such rights.

■ **User name and Password.** During creation, IIS creates a Windows NT service account to be used when users attempt anonymous logons. This account, named IUSR_%computername%, is also used for the Internet Service Manager; however, the random password that was generated for the ISM is not used when users attempt an FTP connection. Instead, users pass along their e-mail address as their anonymous password.

NOTE

The IUSR_%computername% account is an actual user account that will be created for you in the User Manager for Domains. The password that is entered on the Service page of the FTP properties must be the same as that in the User Manager for Domains.

■ **Comment.** Any comment you enter here will appear in the Internet Service Manager.

■ **Current Sessions.** By selecting this, a window with the current FTP sessions will be displayed. From here, you can manage your FTP connections.

After configuring the Service options (usually the default settings are fine), select the Messages tab. This page (as shown in Figure 13.6) is where you will enter a connection message to be viewed by users upon successful logon, as well as where you will go to set an exit and maximum connections message.

FIGURE 13.6.
The Messages Tab of the FTP Service Properties.

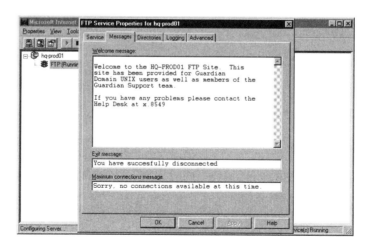

Following the Message tab is the Directories tab, as shown in Figure 13.7. This tab is where you go to configure those directories (other than the FTP Publishing directory) that will be accessible to FTP users. This page provides four options: Add, Remove, Edit Properties, and Directory Listing.

FIGURE 13.7.

*The Directories Tab of
the FTP Service
Properties.*

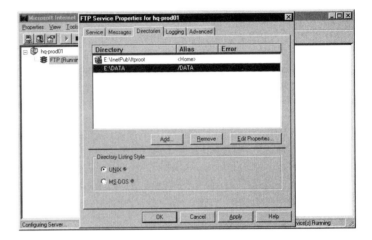

The Add option, shown in Figure 13.8, is where you will define virtual FTP directories that
will allow your FTP users to access resources or servers that don't actually exist in the FTP
Publishing directory.

FIGURE 13.8.

*The Directory
Properties Window for
a Virtual Directory.*

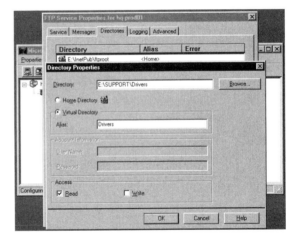

Be aware that even though you have the ability to create virtual directories, they will not show
up in the directory listing when connected to the FTP root. In order to change to virtual drives,
the end user must know that they exist. To make a local directory available, simply type its
path in the Directory text box and a directory alias in the Alias text box. For instance,
E:\Support\Drivers might be named Drivers. Thus, if a user connected to the FTP root needed
access to the E:\Support\Drivers directory, he or she would simply type **CD Drivers** at the command prompt.

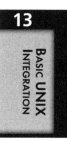

> **CAUTION**
>
> If you plan to publish virtual directories and make them accessible to all users, either the IUSR_%computername% or the Everyone group must have file and directory level access. If not, access will be denied unless the user logs in using an actual domain account that provides access.

It is possible to make a remote directory available as a virtual directory. To do this, simply enter the UNC path of the drive you wish to publish. Keep in mind that you will have to provide a user name and password that has rights to the remote directory. Anyone connecting to this virtual drive will have no more or no fewer rights than this user, but you can set two levels of permissions—read and/or write—on each virtual drive. These permissions will interplay with file and directory level permissions much like share level permissions, which means that the more restrictive permissions will prevail.

After you've finished configuring your virtual directories, select the Logging tab. This page is where you will configure your FTP event logging (see Figure 13.9).

FIGURE 13.9.

FTP Server Log Settings.

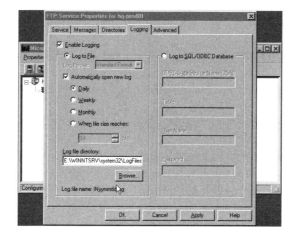

The final configuration page, the FTP Advanced Properties page (see Figure 13.10) allows you to restrict access to specific IP addresses. This type of security, which unfortunately wouldn't work well in an environment using DHCP, provides a slight enhancement to the clear-text password issue. This page also allows you to set the maximum network bandwidth to be utilized for outbound traffic.

After you've configured any desired options on this page, your FTP server configuration is complete.

FIGURE 13.10.

FTP Server Advanced Properties Settings.

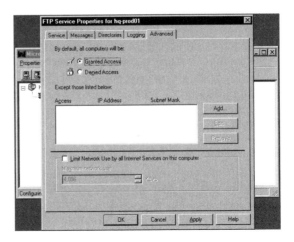

Practical Uses of an FTP Server

In most cases, FTP is used as a means of transferring files that will be moved to a secure location after they have been received. While FTP does not provide a great deal of security, it can be utilized safely in even the most security-minded environments. Users in the UNIX world are sensitive to the clear-text password issues and, in most cases, utilize FTP services to transfer files to a common place and quickly move them to a secure directory. If you are in a security-minded environment, the following tips will allow you to maintain security while still retaining a great deal of functionality. (These tips assume you are providing Anonymous access only.)

- The FTP service does not take a major toll on a server's resources. If you have more than one department requiring FTP access, create more than one FTP server and tell only the necessary users of their existence.

- Provide read-only access to your virtual directories and create a different write-only departmental directory in the FTP root for each department. These directories can be used to upload files that can be moved to the proper directories by a secure client at a later time.

- Because users cannot see virtual FTP directories, they must know the directories exist before they use them. Don't utilize classic directory names such as DATA or UTILS. Instead, name one department's DATA directory something like Zulu and another department's Platinum. Change these directory names on a monthly basis and only tell the users about it on a need-to-know basis.

In addition to providing connectivity to your UNIX clients, with a little ingenuity, the IIS FTP service can become a very useful tool to your support environment as well. For instance, how many times have you visited a desktop experiencing a problem, only to find that the fix requires an updated network card driver, service pack, or print driver? In many cases, these drivers can be accessed only by logging off of the workstation as the end user and back on as the PC Tech. Unfortunately, this scenario can take an inordinate amount of time—especially if you're in a do-or-die situation, meaning that if you don't get to the required resource now, you won't be getting back on the network without it.

Due to the fact that an FTP client is installed on each Windows 95 or Windows NT computer, whenever TCP/IP is installed, this situation can be easily eliminated. By going to a command prompt and typing `FTP HQ-PROD01.guardian.com`, your support personnel can attach to the FTP server without logging the current user off of the network. By changing to a virtual drive that provides access to a directory containing drivers, files, and utilities required for daily support activities, the PC Tech would be able to copy the necessary files on-the-fly.

Telnet Service

Telnet allows your UNIX users to connect to a server via terminal emulation (such as VT100, VT220, and ANSI terminal types) to access data and run character-based applications using the processing power of the remote machine. Unlike an FTP server, a Telnet service running on your Windows NT Server will allow remote users to move throughout the volumes and directories located on the remote server as if they were actually at the server's console. Most Telnet servers for NT simply offer a command-line interface, as if the user were simply at a Windows NT command prompt. While this may not sound very attractive at first, the majority of users accessing your Windows NT Server from a UNIX workstation won't be expecting to run applications.

The major drawback to a Telnet service running on your Windows NT Server is that, like FTP, Telnet passwords are passed along as clear text. If you're in a network with little security concerns, or, as in most organizations, if your UNIX users will only be accessing non-secure data on a regular basis, Telnet is an excellent service to offer.

There is no native Telnet Server for Windows NT, but there are several third-party add-ons that can be implemented. Among these third-party applications is Seattle Lab's SLnet. SLnet, a BackOffice-compatible service, allows Telnet users (regardless of whether they're Microsoft, MAC, OS/2, or UNIX clients) in your existing Domain Directory to access your NT Server and run character-based OS/2, POSIX, and DOS applications. Nearly all command- line functions available through a Windows NT command prompt are available through an SLnet terminal session—as long as the user has the appropriate rights. Furthermore, any OS/2-, POSIX-, or DOS-based application can be run using a Telnet client regardless of the client workstation. SLnet recognizes and adheres to all Windows NT security policies, including NTFS security.

Installing SLnet's Telnet Server

SLnet 2.0 is available for download on the Seattle Labs Web site at `http://www.seattlelab.com`. The file, named SLNET20x.exe, is a self-extracting executable, which, after it is downloaded and launched, will begin the SLnet installation process. This process is terribly simple. After reading the usual licensing screen, you will be brought to a window requiring you to choose an installation type: Typical, Compact, or Custom. Choose the Custom installation option and you will be brought to a component selection screen, as seen in Figure 13.11. Notice that not only does SLnet come with a Telnet server, but also with a Telnet client; the Telnet client must be licensed separately.

FIGURE 13.11.

The Component Selection Window of the SLnet 2.0 Installation Program.

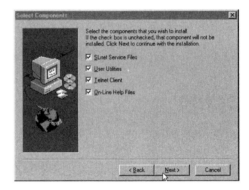

Choose Next at the bottom of the screen, and you will come to a window prompting you for an installation directory for the SLnet utility files. In most cases, you'll want to install the service where no users can access it, such as in your system root or in a secured, non-shared directory. After entering the directory path, select Next again, and you'll be prompted for a location for the Telnet client (if you selected this option). Choose an appropriate directory, followed by Next in the lower portion of the screen. After files are copied, you will be prompted with more licensing information, and the service will be installed and initiated. After installation is finished, your SLnet Telnet Server will be active.

Configuring the Telnet Service

SLnet places its management interface as an extension in the Control Panel and as a shortcut in the SL Products folder in your Start menu. Launch the SLnet Maintenance utility either way, and you'll be presented with the management interface as seen in Figure 13.12.

As you can see, this interface has six tabs: Service, Console, Users, Control, Registration, and About.

The Service tab allows you to configure the following options:

■ **Maximum Connections.** This is a function of your SLnet License, unless you've purchased the Enterprise version. The Demo version limits your Telnet server to 16 connections.

■ **Maximum Logon Attempts.** This is where you would set the maximum number of times a user can attempt to logon before entering a valid user name and password.

■ **Telnet Socket.** This is where you select the TCP/IP socket that the application resides on. The default for Telnet is 23.

■ **Allow Users to Wait for Connection.** By selecting this option, you allow your users to wait in a queue for Telnet connectivity if your maximum connections have been reached.

■ **Create Private Desktop.** This option in essence creates a private DOS window for each user that logs in to the SLnet service. All connections and services utilized in each session run in a separate memory space.

■ **Logon Banner.** This text box allows you to specify a logon banner that will be presented to each user after he or she Telnets in.

■ **Current Status.** This options tells you how many users are in session and how many, if any, users are waiting for a session.

FIGURE 13.12.
The SLnet Telnet Server Management Interface.

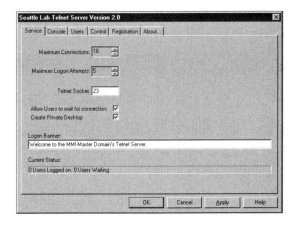

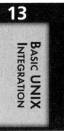

The Console tab allows you to set internal parameters used in the virtual consoles created when users connect to the SLnet service. There is no need to adjust these parameters in most cases. Be sure you know exactly what you're doing if you do make adjustments; changes affect the performance and throughput of SLnet and your Windows NT system as a whole.

> **CAUTION**
>
> While the FTP service provided with IIS is not a major resource drain, Seattle Lab recommends that you account for 1 MB of RAM for each Telnet session to your Windows NT Server. This is a very conservative estimate, but nonetheless should be considered. If you plan to install SLnet on a server, at a minimum increase the RAM by 16 MB.

The Users tab (see Figure 13.13) allows you to set environment variables for specific users who log on to your Telnet server. While it is not apparent at first, you should realize that the user must exist in your Domain Directory for him or her to be able to log on. To set environment variables for a user, simply press the New button on the right side of the Users window. You will be prompted for a name, and after you enter a name, the User Configuration window will appear (see Figure 13.13). This window allows you to control the user's environment as follows:

■ **Default Shell.** By default this is set at a Windows NT DOS shell, but you can set the default shell to be any OS/2, POSIX, or DOS character-based application, such as a menu system or mail program.

FIGURE 13.13.

The User Administration Configuration Window.

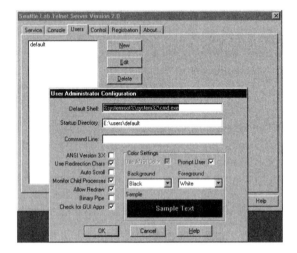

■ **Startup Directory.** This is where you set the user's initial directory. By default, this is set at your server's \users\default directory. This directory could be the user's own home directory or, in case of Anonymous access, a secured common directory much like the root directory in the FTP service.

■ **Command Line.** This option allows you to add any command strings or run any command-line programs upon initial connection.

■ **ANSI Version 3.*x*.** This options allows you to set whether the user's session will comply with ANSI version 3.*x*.

■ **Auto Scroll.** This options allows you to determine whether or not the user's session will automatically scroll.

■ **Monitor Child Processes.** If selected, this option will close any services or applications running at the time when the user logs out. If this option is not selected, users can log in and kick off batch jobs, services, and so on.

■ **Color Settings.** This option allows you to predetermine the user's session colors, but in most cases the user can adjust his or her own color settings at the Telnet client.

The Control tab is where you go to start, pause, or stop the SLnet service; the Registration tab is where licensing information is entered; and the About tab provides legal information concerning SLnet and Seattle Lab.

Overall, the configuration of SLnet is terribly easy. SLnet adheres to your Domain's security settings, including NTFS permissions and domain policies, making it a low-maintenance add-on service that can be utilized to provide another means of easy access for your UNIX users. Much like the FTP service, in order for a user to be able to log on to your SLnet Telnet Server, he or she must be granted Log On Locally rights within the User Manager for Domains under Policies\User Rights.

Practical Uses of Telnet

Telnet, much like FTP, can be utilized for quick access by your UNIX users, and can be utilized by your support personnel to access resources from any TCP/IP desktop regardless of who has logged the machine onto the domain. The following similar security precautions taken for your FTP server can be utilized for your Telnet Server:

- Create specific User IDs and dedicated groups for your Telnet users and provide these groups read-only access to common data.

- Create a common Telnet root directory that can be accessed by your Telnet users as well as your secured clients for easy sharing of non-secure data.

- Create specific departmental directories for your Telnet users that can be accessed only by your Telnet users and their secure (non-UNIX) departmental counterparts. Your Telnet users can then deposit departmental-specific data that can be moved to the secure directories by a non-Telnet user at a later date. Additionally, documents can be copied to this directory from the secured departmental directory for access by your Telnet users.

- Make your Telnet user's Telnet service–specific User Group his or her Primary Group, and remove him or her from the Domain Users group. Thus, if you've followed the suggestions in this book and removed the groups Everyone and Domain Users from all Share and File and Directory Level Permissions, a compromised Telnet user's password will cause only limited concern.

In addition to UNIX connectivity, SLnet offers one more bit of functionality. From an SLnet Telnet session, an administrator can perform any command-line function such as starting and stopping services, managing users and access permissions, and starting and stopping shares. SLnet can also be utilized by an ISP using Windows NT as a commercial Internet server. With the addition of a menu system, each user logging in can be presented a variety of Telnet options.

Telnet is an excellent means of providing access to your UNIX clients. If you're not in a high-security environment, it provides ease of access for all client types. If you are in a high-security environment, it can be a very functional service with the proper precautions.

13

BASIC UNIX
INTEGRATION

NFS Service

NFS, or the Network File System, has long been the standard for sharing files and printers in the UNIX environment. NFS allows computers to "mount" drives that exist on UNIX servers in order to share files with the various types of UNIX clients. Drive mountings are very much like drive mappings in the Netware and Windows NT world; as long as a user has the correct access, he or she can mount and access an NFS drive.

As Windows NT Server has become more pervasive in environments traditionally reserved for UNIX servers, so has the need for UNIX workstations to access NT Servers. Even though FTP and Telnet are very convenient, NFS takes computer-to-computer connectivity one step further. By allowing UNIX workstations to access drives on a remote computer as if they were actually a part of the workstation, NFS makes resource navigation more accessible. There are several NFS servers available for Windows NT. Netmanage, Integraph, and Hummingbird are just a few of the companies that provide enterprise-level NFS services. All of these services offer the same basic NFS functionality, but all with differing levels of convenience in administration.

As of the writing of this book, there seem to be no mainstream NFS solutions that integrate fully into your NT environment. The available solutions today offer varying degrees of NTFS integration and Domain Directory integration, but oddly enough no solution seems to offer the complete integration package. There are, on the other hand, many solid NFS client packages for Windows NT Server and Workstation that will allow clean connections to other NFS servers.

TCP/IP Printing

Microsoft natively supports TCP/IP printing in the form of the classic UNIX LPD/LPR relationship. In this relationship, the LPD service (Line Printer Daemon) on the TCP/IP-based print server receives documents from a client running Line Printer Remote (LPR) client software. LPR and LPD relationships are more common in the UNIX world, but have been adapted to almost all platforms. Windows NT in essence acts as the LPR client to attach to LPD devices. After this attachment is made, the LPD printer can be shared with any user connecting to the Windows NT print server regardless of whether or not the user is using the TCP/IP protocol. In order to use these services, it is necessary to install the Microsoft TCP/IP Print Service through the Network Properties configuration under Services. Note that upon installation, the Microsoft TCP/IP printing services are set to start manually. It's an excellent idea to set this service to an Automatic Startup if you plan to use it to provide TCP/IP print services on a daily basis.

Attaching to LPD Print Servers

TCP/IP printers are created in the same way that standard Windows NT printers are created.

1. Launch the Printers folder, select the Add Printer Wizard, and select My Computer when you have the option to create a local printer or connect to a Network Printer Server.

2. To connect to a TCP/IP-based printer, select Add Port in the Available Ports window. To connect to the LPD device, select the LPR port option and choose New Port.

3. You will immediately be prompted for the Name or Address of the LPR print server you wish to connect to, as seen in Figure 13.14. The name referred to is the fully qualified DNS of the device. For instance, if the Print Server were named MMIPRT01 and it existed in the mmi.com domain, the DNS would be mmiprt01.mmi.com. If you do not know the print server's full name, the TCP/IP address will suffice. Note, that this print server can be either a computer or a network-attached device such as a JetDirect card. Additionally, you must provide the printer name as it is named on the LPD print server. If this is a printer NIC, the printer name will most likely have been supplied by the manufacturer.

FIGURE 13.14.

Adding an LPR Printer Port.

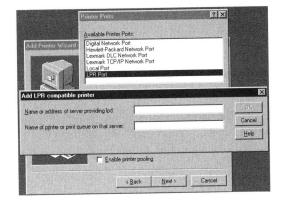

4. After this information is entered and the connection is made, you will install the print driver and have the option to share the printer. After these steps are complete, printing may begin immediately.

Serving LPR Clients

The Microsoft TCP/IP printing service not only provides the ability to attach to LPD devices, but also allows LPR clients to attach to it. For an LPR client to attach to your LPD printer, it simply needs to know your server's DNS name or TCP/IP address and the printer's actual name. Do not provide the LPR client with the printer's share name unless it is identical to the printer's true name. Otherwise, simply provide the LPR client with the actual name of the printer that shows up in the Printers window. After the LPR client has this information, he or she will be able to print to your Windows NT printer as if it were a native UNIX LPD printer.

Summary

Windows NT Server is an extremely open and powerful platform, rivaling even UNIX in stability and strength. Due to its robustness and stability, the number of enterprise solutions usually associated with UNIX are growing. This encroachment into the UNIX enviornment has created a demand for products to allow UNIX workstations to access Windows NT Server. Even though Microsoft does not provide a UNIX client for Windows NT Server, Telnet, FTP, and NFS services are readily available to meet your requirements. While products such as Slnet and Microsoft's FTP server provide complete BackOffice integration, there are a variety of NFS solutions that provide differing levels of BackOffice compatibility that in most cases meet your enterprise needs.

V

PART

IN THIS PART

Advanced Deployment

WINS, DHCP, and DNS

IN THIS CHAPTER

This chapter is not provided as a history, a primer, or a technical white paper on TCP/IP, nor does it pretend to answer all of the questions concerning the deployment of TCP/IP in your enterprise. The goal of this chapter is to give an overview of the TCP/IP tools provided with Windows NT Server and some of the challenges that they address and in some cases even present. This chapter assumes that you have an intermediate-level knowledge of TCP/IP and at the very least have some intimacy with network infrastructure and its relationship to network communications. TCP/IP can be a very large and demanding component of your enterprise, encompassing much more than simple client/server communications. However, in today's environment, the move toward cross-platform standards has made the deployment of TCP/IP nearly mandatory. Unfortunately, even with an industry standard like TCP/IP, each network will have its own unique challenges to overcome. When considering the implementation of TCP/IP in your Windows NT environment, there are some important facts that you should know up front:

- **Fact Number One:** Up to and including Windows 95 and Windows NT 4.0, Microsoft Windows has been and is a NetBIOS application that requires the NetBIOS interface for network communication.

- **Fact Number Two:** In order for Microsoft clients and servers to communicate with one another across networks (subnets) in a TCP/IP environment, you must either employ a NetBIOS Name Server such as WINS, or utilize impractical hosts files.

- **Fact Number Three:** At this time, DNS does not provide for Microsoft-to-Microsoft communication in a TCP/IP network, and, in fact, is only used by Microsoft clients to access more traditional TCP/IP services.

These facts, which may be obvious to some, are oftentimes major stumbling blocks for organizations when they first begin the implementation of TCP/IP in a Windows environment. TCP/IP brings with it a knowledge prerequisite that can be almost as challenging (if not even more so) than that required by the implementation and management of your Client\Server deployment itself. Luckily, Microsoft has done a reasonable job at providing services that minimize the high overhead oftentimes associated with managing a TCP/IP network.

As part of the Windows NT Server operating system, Microsoft provides the basic services you will need to deploy your TCP/IP network: a stable TCP/IP Stack, a sound DHCP service, WINS as a NetBIOS Name Server, and DNS for traditional TCP/IP communication.

Basic TCP/IP Components

Before moving forward with a discussion of the Microsoft TCP/IP services, it is important that you have a base understanding of some of the more common TCP/IP concepts. The following high-level overview has been provided for the person with an intermediate-level knowledge of TCP/IP, or as a light overview for those people with a prior understanding of basic TCP/IP concepts. This overview covers only the components of TCP/IP that are required for client-to-host communications, namely the IP Address, the Subnet Mask, the Default Gateway, the Domain Name Server, NetBIOS Name Servers, and the TCP/IP Node Type.

The IP Address

In an IPX or NetBEUI network, client addressing is dynamic and requires very little, if no, administrative maintenance or intervention. TCP/IP, on the other hand, is not inherently dynamic and requires that your entire enterprise be manually addressed in such a manner that every device, every host, every client, and every network have a unique TCP/IP address. To ensure that all of these entities will have a unique but locatable value, a single TCP/IP address is comprised of two components that combine to provide a single resolvable address: the Network Identification and the Host Identification.

Network and Host Identification

The Network Identification portion of a TCP/IP address identifies what portion of your network a device resides on, while the Host address portion of the address identifies a device as unique. Because there are varying sizes of networks, and a limited number of IP addresses, TCP/IP address schemes have been categorized into three address classes. Since the advent of the Internet, these address classes have been administered by an organization called InterNIC. The InterNIC maintains a list of available IP address schemes and assigns them to organizations in an effort to ensure that no two networks have the same network ID. This is done to prevent conflicts if a network decides to become part of the Internet (which is happening more and more often in today's environment). To effectively distribute these IP addresses, the InterNIC has defined three address classes based on the number of octets that are used to make up a Network ID. These address classes are known as Classes A, B, and C. Table 14.1 provides a breakdown of the three IP address classes, and the number of Host addresses available per class.

Table 14.1. Address Classes and Host Numbers Available.

IP Address Class	Octets used for Network ID	Octets Used for Host ID	Octet A Values	Available Host Addresses
Class A	A	B.C.D	1-126	16,777,214
Class B	A.B	C.D	128-191	65,534
Class C	A.B.C	D	192-233	254

An IP address is made up of four octets, represented as A, B, C, D in the previous table. In all cases, a single IP address is made up of a Host ID and a Network ID. For instance, if a machine had the Class C address of 199.23.232.17, the machine would have a Network ID of 199.23.232 and a Host ID of 17. On the other hand, if a machine had a Class B address of 142.55.39.121 it would have a Network ID of 142.55 and a Host ID of 39.121.

The Network ID portion of the IP address should directly relate to a logical network in your enterprise. These logical networks, also known as subnets, generally relate to a specific port on a router; however, there are cases where these logical networks or subnets refer to virtual or secondary subnets that are associated with the original physical router port. It is in these cases that the Subnet Mask becomes a crucial element in network communications.

The Subnet Mask

Even though your TCP/IP stack is inherently aware of the three TCP/IP classifications and therefore will automatically break down the Host ID and Network ID of any given address, it is necessary to assign each logical network a Subnet Mask. This Subnet Mask assists each client in determining the Host and Network IDs of any packets coming in and any packets going out. A Subnet Mask assigns 1s to the Network ID bits and 0s to the Host ID bits of an IP address providing for quick translation of an IP address. Table 14.2 provides the default Subnet Mask for each network classification.

Table 14.2. The Default Subnet Mask for Each Address Class.

IP Address Class	Network ID	Subnet Mask	Binary Translation
Class A	A.X.X.X	255.0.0.0	11111111.00000000.00000000.00000000
Class B	A.B.X.X	255.255.0.0	11111111.11111111.00000000.00000000
Class C	A.B.C.X	255.255.255.0	11111111.11111111.11111111.00000000

While it might seem redundant to assign a Subnet Mask to a computer when the TCP/IP stack is inherently aware of the network classifications, it can actually be used to further segment your network. Imagine that you're the network administrator of a 100-person company. If you were to use the default Subnet Mask of 255.255.255.0 on a network with two physical subnets, but only one Class C address, you would not be able to address both network segments. However, if you were to apply a Subnet Mask of 255.255.255.192, you could apply a range of 60 addresses to each subnet. While you would lose 130 usable addresses, you would have the ability to address your two physical subnets with only one Class C address. For instance, the Class C address of 195.112.220 used in conjunction with the Subnet Mask of 255.255.255.192 would be divided into the following address ranges:

| First Range | 195.112.220.65 to 195.112.220.127 |
| Second Range | 195.112.220.129 to 195.112.220.191 |

If you've done the math, you'll realize that both of these ranges actually have 62 addresses available; however, there are truly only 60 addresses that can be used for host assignment. This is due to the fact that the first address of each range is reserved for the Default Gateway and the last address is reserved for the Broadcast Address. The Default Gateway will be covered later in this chapter.

NOTE

Several companies provide what are known as Subnet or TCP/IP Calculators. These programs will do automatic translations of Subnet Mask to address range, or vice versa. One such program, TCP/IP Network Assistant, can be acquired by contacting csolder@cisco.com. This program is shareware and can be had for a small fee. It is a highly recommended tool.

Subnet Masks can be an extremely complicated subject. If you are responsible for administering TCP/IP on your network and are not highly familiar with TCP/IP concepts, it is strongly recommended that you receive advanced TCP/IP training. In addition, *Teach Yourself TCP/IP in 14 Days* by Timothy Parker, is an excellent start.

The Default Gateway

The Default Gateway, often simply called the Router, is a device that has knowledge of other Gateways on the network and is used as first contact by devices that need to communicate outside of their own network. In other words, any time a host sends a packet to a device with a different Network ID, the packet is first sent to the Default Gateway. The Default Gateway then forwards the packet to the next logical gateway until the packet reaches the final gateway, which is in most cases dedicated to the Network or Subnet of the destination device. The Default Gateway is in most cases associated with either a physical router port or a logical router port and is independent of any of the TCP/IP tools provided with Windows NT Server. Without a Default Gateway, the client will never be able to access resources outside of its own subnet.

The Domain Name Servers

The Domain Name Server provides a user friendly interface to your TCP/IP network by providing a method for resolving IP Addresses to easy-to-remember Host Names. Take a corporation with a Class B address of 179.55.C.D. Remember that a Class B address has over 65,000 Host IDs available. Without a Domain Name Server, if a user on one subnet needed to access a host on another subnet, not only would the user have to know the Network ID of 179.55, but also the subnet number that the host resides on and the actual destination Host ID. Needless to say, this would be an impossible situation for most corporations as users would have a hard time remembering the destination addresses of all of the resources required on a daily basis.

The Domain Name Server is used to eliminate the need for every user to know not only your network addressing scheme, but also the Host ID of every server or host on your network. The first step in alleviating this situation is to provide a Domain Name to act as an alias for the Network ID. For instance, using a Domain Name Server 179.55.C.D can be translated to GUARDIAN.COM. (Bear in mind that at this time in Windows NT development this

Domain Name bears no relation to your Windows NT Domain.) Next, every common host can be entered into your Domain Name Server with a Host Name and equivalent IP address. Thus, if a user needed to access a Telnet server named GRD-TELNET01.GUARDIAN.COM, the Domain Name Server would be consulted, the address would be resolved, and the user would be forwarded to the requested resource without having to know the subnet or destination address of the host.

In basic terms, the Domain Name Server (DNS) contains a database that maps Host Names to IP Addresses for static devices. When a network host needs to access another host, the DNS is consulted for Host Name to host address resolution. The packets are then sent through the gateway to the appropriate network and finally to the host. While this sounds easy enough, it is actually a fairly complicated service that requires intimate knowledge of TCP/IP and internetworking in general. While Windows NT Server provides an RFC-compliant Domain Name Server, it will not be covered in any detail in this book. What will be covered, however, is the relationship between the Microsoft DNS and the Windows Internet Name Server, also known as WINS.

While Microsoft clients and servers will utilize a DNS for traditional TCP/IP address resolution, at this time they are incapable of using DNS for Domain communications due to their inherent NetBIOS Dependencies. Even though your Windows NT Servers might be configured as Hosts in your DNS table and your Microsoft Clients might be configured to use your DNS for address resolution, your clients will be unable to perform the following using just DNS:

- Log in to a Windows NT Domain across a subnet
- Browse Microsoft computers across a subnet
- Communicate with Microsoft hosts across a subnet
- Attach to shared directories across a subnet

To address these issues, Microsoft designed the Windows Internet Name Server, also known as WINS. WINS is a non-RFC-compliant NetBIOS Name Server that provides NetBIOS name to IP Address resolution for Windows clients, therefore making Domain communication across subnets possible.

WINS/NetBIOS Name Servers

Microsoft clients (as do OS/2) require the NetBIOS interface for client-to-server/client-to-client communication. Unfortunately, the TCP/IP protocol does not inherently provide for this interface. In result, when a NetBIOS-dependent machine attempts to communicate across a subnet with another NetBIOS-dependent machine using only IP, it will fail miserably. Even though Machine A can ping Machine B and vice versa, unless the NetBIOS interface is available, there will be no communication. To resolve this issue, the Internet community at large defined RFCs 1001/1002 (Requests For Comment) providing design details for an IP-friendly NetBIOS interface. This interface, commonly known as a NetBIOS Name Server, acts very much like a standard Domain Name Server; however, instead of providing a flat Host Name to IP address resolution, it provides NetBIOS name to IP address resolution allowing for standard NetBIOS-dependent communication.

At this time, there are only three known NetBIOS Name Servers. The first is Microsoft's WINS, which provides complete NetBIOS-dependent services for all Windows clients—but is not completely RFC-compliant. The second is SAMBA, a shareware-based UNIX service that not only acts as a NetBIOS Name Server, but also allows UNIX hosts to act like Windows for Workgroups workstations and share files with Microsoft clients. The last known NetBIOS Name Server is provided by a relatively small company named Network TeleSystems. IPcentral is an RFC-compliant NetBIOS Name Server that provides NetBIOS Name services to both OS/2 and Microsoft clients, as well as integrated DHCP and Dynamic DNS services.

WINS, Microsoft's NetBIOS Name Server offering, is a fully dynamic NetBIOS Name Server that provides for

- Logging in to a Windows NT Domain across a subnet
- Browsing Microsoft computers across a subnet
- Communicating with Microsoft hosts across a subnet
- Attaching to shared directories across a subnet

The WINS service will be discussed in detail later in this chapter.

Node Type

The IP stack included in Windows 95, Windows NT, and Windows for Workgroups is not only a completely standard TCP/IP stack, but is also compatible with RFCs 1001 and 1002, which define NetBIOS over TCP/IP. NetBIOS over TCP/IP provides for the NetBIOS interface in a TCP/IP environment without the ugly broadcasts of traditional NetBEUI. This functionality is had through the processes of Registration and Resolution.

- Registration is the process used to register a unique Host Name for each computer on the network. A NetBIOS over TCP/IP client will generally register with a NetBIOS Name Server upon startup.
- Resolution is the process used to determine the specific address for a NetBIOS computer name. When a NetBIOS over TCP/IP host needs to communicate with another NetBIOS over TCP/IP host it will both consult with a NetBIOS Name Server and Broadcast if necessary.

Not only do RFCs 1001 and 1002 define the standard for NetBIOS over TCP/IP (NetBT), they also define the name resolution process. Inherent to NetBT are modes that specify how network resources are identified and communicated with. These NetBT modes are defined as follows:

- B-Node: A B-Node client uses broadcast messages to resolve names. B-Node traffic will not cross a subnet unless the node has been supplied with a broadcast list. It is then limited to broadcasting to known subnets only.

14

WINS, DHCP, AND DNS

- **P-Node:** A P-Node client uses point-to-point communication by referring to a NetBIOS Name Server (NBNS) to resolve names. A P-Node client will never broadcast.

- **M-Node:** M-Node clients default to B-Node (Broadcasting) and then move into a P-Node process to resolve names if the desired host is not found through broadcasting.

- **H-Node:** An H-Node client is the exact opposite of an M-Node client. It first defaults to P-Node and consults the NBNS to resolve names. If the desired host is not registered, it then goes into B-Node mode and begins broadcasting on the local subnet. H-Node is the desired mode due to the fact that it drastically reduces broadcasting.

> **NOTE**
>
> While it is possible for a NetBT client to communicate over subnets using an LMHosts file, it is an impractical solution in a large environment. Furthermore, the low administrative functionality offered by WINS gives little reason to use anything else.

Table 14.3 is provided as a TCP/IP basics summary.

Table 14.3. TCP/IP Basics Summary.

Concept	*Description*
Subnet Mask	A Subnet Mask is a 32-bit number that among other things allows the recipient of an IP packet to distinguish the Network ID portion of the IP address from the Host ID.
Router (Default Gateway)	The Default Gateway, often simply called the Router, is a device that has knowledge of other gateways on the network and is used as first contact by devices that need to communicate outside of their own network.
DNS (Domain Name Server)	The Domain Name Server (DNS) contains a database that maps Host Names to IP Addresses providing name resolution for TCP/IP hosts.
NetBIOS Name Server /WINS	The NetBIOS Name Server acts very much like a standard Domain Name Server, however instead of providing a flat Host Name to IP address resolution, it provides NetBIOS Name to IP address resolution allowing for standard NetBIOS-dependent communication.

Concept	Description
NetBT Node Type	The NetBT Node Type identifies how a NetBIOS over TCP/IP Node communicates with other NetBT resources. Available Node types are B-, P-, M-, and H-Nodes. H-Node is the preferred Node Type in a Windows NT Environment.

Client Configuration

For TCP/IP-based clients to communicate with other TCP/IP machines across subnets, they must at minimum be configured with the following information:

- IP Address
- Router Address (Default Gateway)
- Domain Name Server Address
- Subnet Mask

If advanced functionality is desired, including NetBIOS over TCP/IP connectivity, the client may also need to be configured with the following information:

- Host Name
- NetBIOS Name Server/WINS Server
- TCP/IP Node Type

In a traditional environment, it would be necessary to manually configure each of these options (basic and enhanced) for every host on the network. This manual configuration has been a tremendous roadblock for most corporations when considering the implementation of TCP/IP due to such factors as tracking TCP/IP addresses, the changing scheme of the internetwork as a whole and sheer man hours required to not only install the protocol but configure it as well. It was not until the advent of DHCP that the possibility of deploying TCP/IP as a network's primary protocol became a mainstream focus. DHCP, which is an acronym for Dynamic Host Configuration protocol, is a service that dynamically allocates TCP/IP addresses and key configuration options to a workstation upon initial boot up. With DHCP the deployment of TCP/IP as a standard protocol becomes a much less daunting task. As luck would have it, Windows NT Server 4.0 comes with a fully functional DHCP Server in the box.

The Microsoft DHCP Server

DHCP, or Dynamic Host Configuration Protocol, offers the chance to make the deployment of TCP/IP almost as seamless as the deployment of the ipx/spx or NetBEUI protocols. The key word here, however, is almost. Using a DHCP Server, you can dynamically assign your network clients any combinations of 68 standard options; however, Windows clients only need and accept 10 out of the 68 available options. Those accepted by Microsoft clients are

- The Subnet Mask (Option 1)
- The Router, also known as Default Gateway (Option 3)
- The DNS Server (Option 6)
- The Domain Name (Option 15)
- WINS/NBNS Servers (Option 44)
- WINS/NetBT Node Type (Option 46)
- NetBIOS Scope ID (Option 47)
- Lease Time (Option 51)
- Renewal (T1) Time Value (Option 58)
- Rebinding time Value (Option 59)

DHCP is a relatively simple service to administer, but requires intimate knowledge of your network—especially if you have multiple subnets. The remainder of this section will cover the installation of TCP/IP and DHCP on your Windows NT Server, the configuration of the Windows NT DHCP Server, new DHCP Server features found in Service Pack 2, and basic client configuration.

Installing TCP/IP on Windows NT Server

Installing TCP/IP on Windows NT Server is a relatively simple task; however, before doing so it is helpful to have the following information:

- A valid, static TCP/IP address
- The address of your Domain Name Servers
- The address of your WINS Servers
- Your Subnet Mask
- Your Default Gateway

Installing TCP/IP is extremely simple. Either go to the Control Panel and launch the configuration dialog by double-clicking on the Network extension, or use the right mouse button Properties method on the Network Neighborhood shortcut found on your desktop. Either way, you will be presented with the familiar Network configuration window as seen in Figure 14.1.

To install TCP/IP, go to the Protocols tab and select the Add button. You will soon be presented with a list of available protocols. Choose TCP/IP and select the OK button at the bottom of the window. At this point you will be asked if you would like to use the DHCP protocol. Due to the fact that this is a server it is highly recommended that you not use a Dynamic address—especially if this will be your DHCP Server. Select No, and you will be prompted for the location of the Windows NT Server CD. Enter the correct path and select

OK. Files will be copied, and the TCP/IP protocol will be added to your list of installed protocols (see Figure 14.2). Select Close at the bottom of the screen, and the TCP/IP protocol will
be bound to your adapter.

FIGURE 14.1.

*The Network
Configuration
Window.*

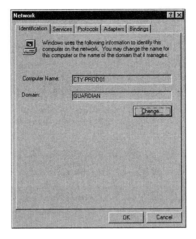

FIGURE 14.2.

*The Protocols Tab of
the Network Configu-
ration Window.*

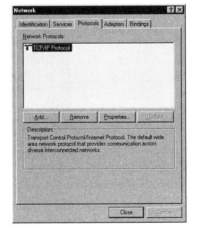

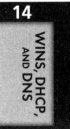

Once bindings are complete, the Microsoft TCP/IP Properties window will launch as seen in
Figure 14.3. This window has five tabs: IP Address, DNS, WINS Address, DHCP Relay, and
Routing.

The first tab, IP Address, is where you will enter your Server's IP Address, the appropriate Subnet
Mask, and the Default Gateway. There is also an Advanced tab on this page that allows you to
configure multiple network cards with IP Address information if you so desire.

The next tab, as seen in Figure 14.4, is the DNS tab. This tab is where you will enter the Host
Name (which is automatically the same as the NetBIOS name you gave your server upon

installation), the Domain name and the address of the DNS Server(s) on your network. If you operate in a multi-Domain environment, you may also enter a Domain Suffix search order. (Again, this Domain has no relation to your actual Windows NT Domain.)

FIGURE 14.3.

The TCP/IP Properties Window.

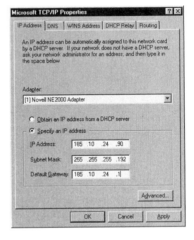

FIGURE 14.4.

The DNS Configuration Tab.

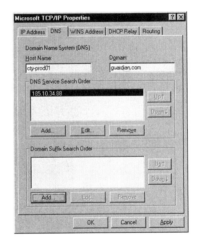

Following the DNS tab is the WINS Address tab, shown in Figure 14.5. This tab is where you input the WINS Server addresses that service your network. You may also instruct your server to enable DNS for Windows Resolution at this point as well—but don't be deceived by this option—the DNS Server must be a Microsoft DNS Server that is configured to interact with a WINS server that holds static addresses for all domains and servers, and is used by clients for dynamic registration.

FIGURE 14.5.

The WINS Address Tab.

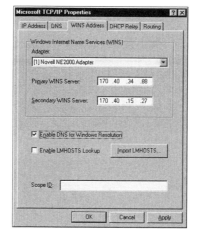

> **NOTE**
>
> DNS for Windows Resolution will allow your H-Node clients to log in to your domains and access your servers using DNS only when the DNS Server is a Microsoft DNS Server that is configured to refer to a WINS Server for name lookups. When a client attempts to log in to a Domain or access a dynamic workstation, the DNS Server queries the WINS Server which then passes the information to the client through the DNS Server. Theoretically, this should work with any H-Node-compatible client; however, the author has not yet tested this functionality in an OS/2 environment and will not endorse this as Gospel.

Under the DNS for Windows Resolution you will also find two other options:

- Enable LMHOSTS Lookup
- NetBIOS Scope ID

Of these options, LMHOSTS is used only in small environments and the NetBIOS Scope ID is hardly used at all. Neither of these options will be covered in this book.

The DHCP Relay option, shown in Figure 14.6, is useful in an environment without routers that will pass DHCP relay requests or in an environment with a DHCP Server that does not support secondary subnetting or Superscopes as found in the NT 4.0 DHCP Server with Service Pack 2 installed. This page will allow you to configure your server to forward DHCP requests to your DHCP Server by simply adding its address.

The final tab, Routing, is applicable only on a multi-homed server (see Figure 14.7). A multi-homed server is the one that has two or more network cards that have addresses on two or more networks. This option will allow you to route traffic from one network to another using your Windows NT Server. If you are in a fully routed environment, this option is not necessary and may cause undue traffic.

FIGURE 14.6.
The DHCP Relay Tab.

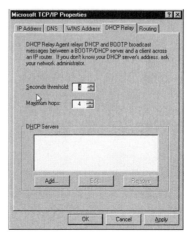

FIGURE 14.7.
The Routing Tab in the TCP/IP Configuration Dialog.

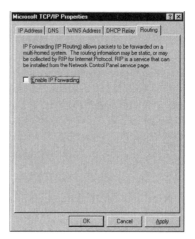

Once you've finished configuring TCP/IP for all network cards on your machine, select OK at the bottom of the window, and bindings will be reset. Once complete, you will be prompted to restart your computer. Upon reboot you will have a fully functioning TCP/IP-based server.

NOTE

If you have a mix of TCP/IP and NetBEUI resources throughout your network, you can increase performance by installing two network cards and binding only TCP/IP to one card and NetBEUI to the other. This would provide two distinct avenues for network traffic to travel and assuming that your clients won't have both protocols installed may also help reduce network traffic.

Installing and Configuring the Windows NT DHCP Server

Installing Windows NT Server's DHCP Server is very simple. The following procedure outlines the necessary steps:

- Launch your server's Network Properties window.
- Go to the Services tab and choose Add.
- Select Microsoft DHCP Server from the list and choose OK. After files are copied you will be prompted with a message informing you that you are required to have a static IP address in order to run the DHCP Server.
- Select OK, and close the Network configuration window. At this time, you will be required to restart your server for the service to take effect.

To take advantage of recent DHCP enhancements, once your server has been restarted you must install Service Pack 2 (or the most current Service Pack, as it will include the DHCP Server enhancements found in SP2). Even if you've already installed the most current Service Pack you must reinstall it in order for these changes to take effect.

Once you've completed the Service Pack installation, you must once again restart your machine. At this time, the Windows NT Server DHCP Server will have been successfully installed.

CAUTION

Service Pack 2, like many corrective service packages, addressed several issues and even added new functionality as seen in DHCP Superscopes discussed later. Unfortunately, SP2 also caused some issues. If you install SP2, be sure that the source files are on your server—do not run SP2 over the network or you will have multiple problems. In addition, copy \System Root\System32\drivers\NETBT.SYS to your desktop before installing SP2 and then copy it back to the same location once the SP update is complete. The NETBT.SYS that ships with SP2 has a confirmed bug that will be addressed in SP3. As with all Service Packs, be sure and read any documentation before performing an installation.

14

WINS, DHCP, AND DNS

After the DHCP Server has been installed and the server has been updated with the latest Service Pack, you can begin configuring the DHCP Server. Launch the Microsoft DHCP Manager (see Figure 14.8) which can be found in the Administrative Tools folder in your Start menu. The DHCP Manager consists of a text-based tool bar and a window split into two views: DHCP Servers and Option Configuration. To manage your server, click on the Local Machine icon in the DHCP Servers window.

The first step is to configure your DHCP Server's basic properties. To do so, go to the Server option on the tool bar and select Properties from the pull-down menu. Figure 14.9 shows the Properties dialog which consists of two tabs, General and BootP Table. The first tab, General, allows you to turn on DHCP Logging (which is highly recommended), as well as configure your DHCP Server for conflict detection, which is also highly recommended.

FIGURE 14.8.

The DHCP Manager.

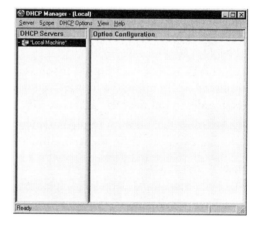

FIGURE 14.9.

The DHCP Server Properties Window.

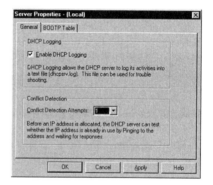

If you configure your sever for DHCP logging, it will maintain a log (in addition to the events your DHCP Server will log in the Event Log) to help in diagnosing any DHCP problems.

Conflict detection is an extremely useful setting. This option allows you to configure your DHCP Server to ping an IP address before it is handed out to a DHCP client. With this option configured, when a client requests an IP address, the DHCP Server will refer to the appropriate DHCP scope, choose the next available IP address, and ping the network to see if it is currently in use. If the DHCP Server determines that the address is not in use, the address will be assigned. If the address is in use by another machine, the address will be marked as BAD_ADDRESS and will not be assigned to any clients. This option is extremely useful due to the fact that no two machines may have the same IP address. If a machine comes up attempting to use an address that is currently in use, chances are that both machines will be unable to register on the network.

The second tab on the DHCP Properties window is labeled BootP Table. This table allows you to reserve TCP/IP addresses for legacy BootP devices. BootP is a predecessor to DHCP, but it does not provide as much functionality as DHCP. Unlike DHCP, BootP does not support the allocation of address leases. When a BootP client accepts an IP address granted it assumes that it has received the address for an infinite lease period. The Microsoft DHCP Server will only respond to a BootP request from hosts for which you have explicitly reserved an address. BootP reservations, which are extremely rare necessities in today's environment, require the boot image, file name, and server name of the BootP client.

Once you've configured the DHCP event logging and conflict detection policies it's time to set up your first DHCP scope. Each DHCP scope is directly correlated to a specific subnet. Therefore, if you have 30 subnets on your network, your DHCP Server will have 30 scopes.

Before configuring a DHCP Scope you must have at minimum the following information for the correlating subnet:

- A valid range of TCP/IP Addresses
- A Valid Subnet Mask
- The Default Gateway

To create a scope, go to the Scope option on the tool bar and select the Create Scope option from the pull-down menu. Very soon you will be presented with the Create Scope window as seen in Figure 14.10. This window is broken down into three sections: the IP Address Pool section, the Lease Duration section, and the identification section.

FIGURE 14.10.

The Create Scope Window.

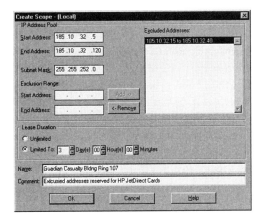

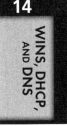

The IP Address Pool section of this window is where you go to configure a scope's

- TCP/IP address range
- Subnet Mask
- Address exclusions

To enter an IP Address range simply input the first address in the scope's range in the text box labeled Start Address and the last address in the range in the text box labeled End Address. At this time if there are any addresses that you wish to exclude from this range you may enter them in the Exclusion Range. Addresses can be excluded at any time, however if you know of any addresses in your range that are currently in use as static addresses, now is a good time to enter them. Once you've entered the Address Range and any exclusions, make sure that you also enter the appropriate Subnet Mask.

CAUTION

The Windows NT DHCP Server requires that any address range be consecutive. For instance, if you have a range of addresses with the Host IDs of from 5 to 75, but 20, 23, and 65 are in use by static devices, you cannot enter three different ranges. Instead, you must enter the entire range and exclude 20, 23, and 65 using the facility provided on the Create Scope page. You may also edit a scope's properties at any time to exclude more addresses or reintroduce previously excluded addresses back into the range. In addition, you may not add addresses to a previously configured range (that is, take a range of from 5 to 75 and expand it to 5 to 95. Instead, you must first delete the existing scope and recreate it with the new range.

After configuring the IP Address Pool portion of this window it is now time to consider the IP Lease Duration. The Lease Duration, which is actually DHCP Option 58, has the potential to be an important setting. When a DCHP address is assigned to a host, the DHCP Server also assigns a lease duration for that host. For instance, if your lease setting for a particular scope was 1 minute (this is a bad idea) and Client A received 185.10.24.6 at 6:00 pm, the IP address lease duration would end at 6:01 pm. At 6:01 pm Client A would then make another DHCP request to make sure that its address was still valid. As long as the request was made within a minute and the DHCP Server had not reassigned the address, Client A would retain its previous address. Obviously, a lease duration of one minute would constantly saturate your network with DHCP requests, defeating the purpose of moving to a clean protocol like TCP/IP. After studying the topic of lease duration, Microsoft set the DHCP Server to default to a duration of three days. Therefore, if Client A were assigned 185.10.24.6 at 6:00 pm on Monday, it would not request verification until 6:00 pm on Thursday of the same week. Likewise, the server would not reassign the address until 6:00 pm on Thursday of the same week. Keep in mind that duration is in a sense also a reservation—as long as Client A were on the network at 6:00 pm on Thursday to re-request its address, it would receive the previously assigned address. If Client A were not on the network at 6:00 pm on Thursday it is possible that the address would be assigned to another client. If that were the case, the next time Client A comes onto the network it will release its previous address and request a new one.

> **NOTE**
>
> Setting the Lease Duration to unlimited is not recommended. The dynamic nature of the lease duration provides a flexible infrastructure in case of address scheme changes.

Following Lease Duration is the identification portion of the Create Scope window. Here you have the option to provide a descriptive scope name that consists of any combination of 128 characters, as well as a scope comment. Keep in mind that a scope directly correlates to a Subnet and will be identified as such by the DHCP Server. The Name option allows you to provide more descriptive information that might be helpful to others who administer the DHCP Server. Information such as building name, floor name, Ring number, segment number, and so on is very helpful in this field. The Comment text box can only be seen when viewing a scope's properties and simply provides more opportunity to describe or document a scope.

After you are satisfied with your scope's configuration, select OK in the lower left-hand corner. You will be notified by the DHCP Manager that the scope has been created but not activated. At this time you may choose to activate the newly created scope. Once activated, the DHCP Server will begin to respond to DHCP requests from the given subnet. If you do not activate the scope now, you may do so at any time.

Once you've configured the basic scope information, it is time to address the DHCP options, such as

- The Router, also known as Default Gateway (Option 3)
- The DNS Server (Option 6)
- The Domain Name (Option 15)
- WINS/NBNS Servers (Option 44)
- WINS/NetBT Node Type (Option 46)

The Windows NT DHCP Server provides two types of Scope Options: Scope-specific and Global. In addition, you also have the ability to edit default values for any DHCP option available.

Scope-specific options can be configured by highlighting the newly created scope, selecting the DHCP Options option from the tool bar, and choosing Scope from the pull-down menu. This window, as seen in Figure 14.11, allows you to choose and edit any of the 68 standard DHCP options. For instance, to configure the Router (also known as the Default Gateway), choose Option 3 followed by Add. The screen will immediately expand to include a window that will display the configured Router address as well as a button titled Edit Array.

FIGURE 14.11.

Scope-Specific Options.

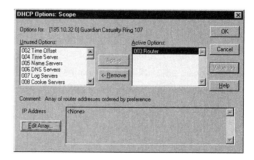

To input the Default Gateway, select the Edit Array button and you will be presented with the IP Address Array Editor as seen in Figure 14.12. It is here that you will enter the address of your Default Gateway. Once complete, press the OK button, and you will be brought back to the standard DHCP Manager window. In the event that your network has multiple subnets, the Default Gateway is often the only Scope-specific option you will configure. Items such as Domain Name, DNS Servers, and WINS Servers are generally universal and will most likely be configured in the Global Options portion of your DHCP scope configuration.

FIGURE 14.12.

The IP Address Array Editor.

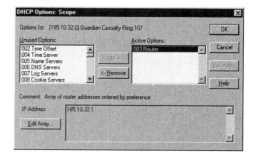

To configure Global Options, simply go to the DHCP Options selection on the tool bar and choose Global from the pull-down menu. This window looks identical to the Scope-specific configuration window and is utilized as such. To enter any global option, simply select it from the list of options and enter the appropriate information.

NOTE

Most scope settings have a default setting, whether it be a blank command string such as Option 12 (Host Name) or a NetBT Node Type such as Option 46. It is possible to edit these default settings by choosing Scope Options on the tool bar, followed by default. At this point you edit the default settings of any of the 68 available DHCP Options. In addition, you may also add new options as required by either changes in TCP/IP standards or proprietary client software.

> **NOTE**
>
> A note on DHCP Option 15: Domain Name. By passing this option along, your IP clients will be able to attach to standard IP resources such as Telnet Servers or FTP servers by simply entering the Host name. The client will then automatically append the remainder of the fully qualified domain name, thus simplifying the use of TCP/IP even further.

Once you've finished configuring a scope's Subnet-specific and Global Options, highlight the scope in the DHCP Manager. All configured scope options will now appear in the Option Configuration window, as seen in Figure 14.13. Note that all Global options are identified with a globe icon and all Scope-specific options are tagged with an icon in the shape of a computer.

FIGURE 14.13.

The Fully Configured DHCP Manager.

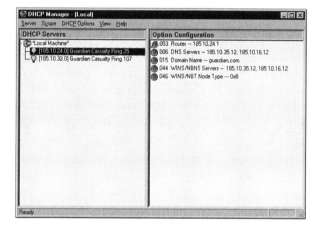

Scope Management

Once a scope has become active and begins receiving requests you may view all active assignments on a scope-by-scope basis. By simply choosing an active scope and double-clicking your right mouse button, you will produce the Active Leases window, as shown in Figure 14.14.

FIGURE 14.14.

DHCP Scope Management.

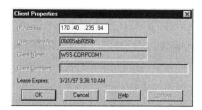

At this point you may do one of the following:

- View a host's properties (MAC address, client name, lease expiration)
- Delete an address assignment
- View the number of active assignments
- View the number of excluded addresses
- Sort by IP Address
- Sort by Host Name

In addition to viewing scope properties, you may also reserve specific addresses for specific hosts. To do so, go to the Scope option on the tool bar and choose Add Reservation from the pull-down menu. To add a reservation, you must have the following information:

- Host Name
- Desired IP Address
- MAC Address (Unique Identifier)

Input the above information and choose OK. Once complete, you have essentially assigned a static IP address with the exception that a reservation can be revoked without visiting the desktop, while a static IP address must be manually reconfigured.

> **NOTE**
>
> To manage remote DHCP Servers, simply go to the Server option on the DHCP Manager tool bar and select Add. At this point you will be presented with a window requesting the name or address of the DHCP Server you wish to manage. Simply enter the appropriate information and the DHCP Server will be permanently added to your list of available DHCP Servers. To remove a DHCP Server from your list of available DHCP Servers simply highlight the desired server, go to the Server option on the tool bar, and select Remove.

Advanced Functionality: The Superscope

With the release of Windows NT Server 4.0 Service Pack 2, Microsoft introduced a new feature to its DHCP Server: the Superscope. The Superscope allows you to configure not only a primary subnet for DHCP address allocation, but also multiple logical subnets as well. This functionality, sometimes referred to as Multi-net, is a key tool in overcoming address scheme limitations.

For example, McMac Mineral deployed TCP/IP eight years ago for the sole purpose of managing infrastructure devices. Even though it legally owned a Class B address at that time there seemed to be no need to fully address every subnet. Unfortunately, McMac utilized a Subnet Mask of 255.255.255.192, which limited each subnet to a maximum of 62 addresses.

Presently, the McMac enterprise has 78 subnets in place, most of which have well over 62 devices including Hubs, Routers, Printers, and workstations. In order to change the subnet mask to a more expansive design, a great deal of static hosts would need to be modified and all Routers would need to support VLSM (Variable Link Subnet Masks). Even though the Windows NT DHCP Server supports VLSM, most of the McMac routers do not. To replace the Routers and readdress all of the static hosts would require a tremendous amount of time and effort. Unfortunately, as is the case with most support organizations, McMac does not have the manpower or the budget to replace over a million dollars in routers. While most routers will support the ability to assign multiple logical subnets to a physical router port thereby overcoming the lack of addresses per physical subnet, most DHCP Servers do not know how to "address" the logical subnet. The traditional method of addressing this issue has been to either place a DHCP Server in each logical subnet, or to install multiple network cards in each DHCP Server. These issues are easily overcome through the Superscope.

The Superscope provides a simple yet tremendous functionality to the DHCP Server. By creating a Superscope you are simply pairing a physical subnet with as many logical subnets as required to address your client needs. Once the addresses in the original physical Scope have been completely utilized, the DHCP Server will begin assigning addresses from the next Scope in a Superscope. Assuming that the logical scope (or scopes) has been defined on the router, Superscope's functionality is seamless.

Creating a Superscope is simple:

- Ensure that any logical subnets you plan to utilize have been defined on your routers.
- Launch the DHCP Manager. In the DHCP Servers window, highlight either Local Machine or the address of the DHCP Server you wish to manage.

From the DHCP Manager tool bar, select Scope followed by Superscope from the pull-down menu. You will immediately be presented with a window titled Superscopes (see Figure 14.15).

FIGURE 14.15.

The Superscopes Window.

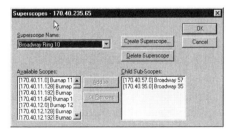

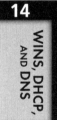

Select the Create Superscope button, and you will be prompted for a Superscope name. Be sure to provide a good descriptive name at this point. Select OK.

Next, highlight the desired physical and all appropriate logical scopes in the Available Scopes window (see Figure 14.15) and select Add. The selected scopes will now become part of the larger Superscope.

Once complete, your Superscope will be created. Note that there is no Superscope designation to be found anywhere else in the DHCP Manager.

Name Resolution: Microsoft's WINS Server

WINS provides a fault tolerant and dynamic database for the registration and resolution of NetBIOS name to IP address mappings in the internetwork. The Windows Internet Name Service can either compliment or replace a DNS Server depending on your network needs; however, it is at this time necessary for the following functions:

- Domain Login across subnets
- Browsing across subnets
- Attaching to resources across subnets
- Domain communication

Installing WINS is extremely easy:

- Launch your Server's network properties by using the right mouse click Properties method on the Network Neighborhood shortcut on your desktop.
- Once the Network properties window opens, go to the Services tab and select Add. Choose Windows Internet Name Service from the list of available services, followed by OK.
- Once the service has been installed, choose Close from the main configuration page. Your bindings will be configured and you will be prompted to restart your server.
- Before continuing, be sure to reinstall the last service pack that was added to your server and restart your server once complete.
- After your server has restarted, you may manage your WINS Server by going to the Administrative Tools program group in your Start menu and choosing the WINS Manager.

Understanding WINS Management

Other than the initial configuration and the occasional addition of a static address, WINS is one of those few network services that you can put in place and very rarely think of. WINS not only provides NetBIOS name to IP Address resolution, it also provides dynamic name registration and resolution, unlike traditional TCP/IP services. When a WINS client comes up on the network it will register itself with the WINS Server. If the client is a DHCP client and had a previous registration with another IP address, the older registration will be overwritten, thus keeping the WINS database both current and dynamic. If the machine has the same address as it did the last time it registered with the WINS server, its entry will simply be validated.

Windows 95, Windows NT, and Windows for Workgroups all come with WINS-compatible TCP/IP stacks. WINS addresses can be entered manually on each of these platforms, or can be assigned dynamically through your DHCP service (Option 44 on your RFC standard DHCP Server). Note that in order to use WINS servers for name resolution your workstation must be configured in either H-Node or P-Node mode as discussed earlier in this chapter (again, this option can be configured via DHCP).

FIGURE 14.16.
The WINS Manager.

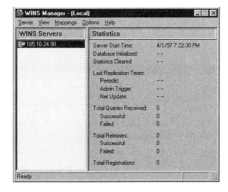

There are certain WINS concepts that you should be familiar with before implementing your WINS servers. Those concepts are

- Basic and Advanced WINS Configuration
- WINS Server Replication
- Static Mappings

Basic and Advanced WINS Configuration

Basic and Advanced WINS Server Configuration is where you define intervals for managing your WINS database and your WINS Server's relationships with replication partners. The WINS server dialog, shown in Figure 14.17, can be launched from the WINS Manager by going to the Server option on the tool bar and selecting Configuration.

FIGURE 14.17.
The WINS Server Configuration Window.

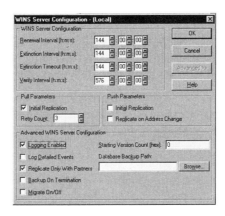

14

WINS, DHCP, AND DNS

The top half of the WINS Server Configuration window deals with client registration intervals. These options—Renewal Interval Extinction Interval, Extinction Timeout, and Verify Interval—are defined as follows in Table 14.3.

Table 14.3. WINS configuration options.

WINS Option	Option Configuration
Renewal Interval	This setting specifies how often a client will reregister its name with the WINS server. The WINS server default setting is 144 hours (six days).
Extinction Interval	This setting specifies the interval between the time an entry is marked as released and when it is marked extinct—the default setting is six days. If after six days an entry has not reregistered, it will be marked extinct.
Extinction Timeout	This setting specifies the interval between the time an entry is marked extinct and when it is removed from the database. Like the Renewal Extinction Intervals, the default setting is six days.
Verify Interval	This setting specifies the interval in which a WINS Server must verify that entries that do not exist in its database are no longer active. The default value is 24 days.

The default settings for these options are in most cases more than adequate. These settings minimize network traffic and at the same time keep the database current. The only time that you might need to modify these settings is if you have a very migratory client base.

The next section of the WINS Server Configuration window deals with replication. WINS Server replication provides two services: load balancing of client registration and resolution and fault tolerance. WINS Servers replicate in two manners: Push and Pull. A WINS Pull partner will pull new and modified WINS entries from its replication partner on a predetermined interval or upon administrator initiation. A WINS Push partner, on the other hand, will send a message to its pull partner when its database has changed. When the Pull partner acknowledges the Push request, the Push partner will begin sending database changes. The Push and Pull Parameter configurations on this page determine whether or not the server will attempt to push or pull changes from its replication partner upon server restart.

The final section of the WINS Server Configuration window deals with advanced configuration. These settings are defined as follows in Table 14.4.

Table 14.4. WINS Configuration Options.

WINS Configuration Option	*Option Description*
Logging Enabled	This option specifies whether or not database changes will be logged in the jet.log.
Log Detailed Events	Choosing this option will cause your server to log significant detail. Depending on how much registration and resolution activity your network experiences this option can cause a resource drain on your server.
Replicate Only with Partners	This option prohibits your server from replicating with any other server that is not specifically configured as a replication partner.
Backup on Termination	This option causes your WINS Server to back up its database whenever the WINS service is stopped.
Migrate On/Off	This option designates static unique and static multi-homed addresses as dynamic. In other words, if a new client registers with these addresses, these records will be overwritten. This option is turned off by default.
Database Backup Path	This option allows you to determine where WINS database backups should be stored.

WINS Server Fault Tolerance and Replication

If you move to a complete TCP/IP environment, Microsoft WINS Server will become a crucial element in the success of your enterprise. With this in mind, Microsoft has designed WINS with inherent fault tolerance through both database replication and client-side primary and secondary configuration options.

Due to the importance of this service it is always a good idea to deploy at least two geographically diverse WINS servers—therefore, if one server goes down, or one area of the network experiences difficulties, WINS services will still be available. When configuring your DHCP Server, you can pass both WINS addresses to the client. The client will attempt to utilize the first address in the array, and if that server is not available, will move to the next.

To configure a WINS Server as a replication partner, do the following:

■ Go to the Server option on the WINS Manager tool bar and choose Replication Partners from the drop-down menu. You will quickly be presented with a window titled Replication Partners, shown in Figure 14.18.

FIGURE 14.18.
*WINS Replication
Partners.*

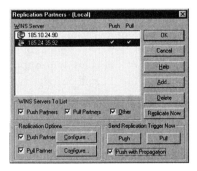

■ Select the Add button on the right side of the Replication Partners window, and you will be presented with a prompt asking for the name or IP address of the desired WINS Server. Enter the name as requested and select OK. You will now be brought back to the Replication Partners window.

At this point the WINS Server you just added will appear in the Replication Partners list configured as both a Push and Pull server.

Note that replication is configured to occur only when a replication partner queries a server for replicated information which is based on a predetermined number of updates. You can also trigger replication from within the Replication Partners window by selecting the Replicate Now window.

In most cases replication will run smoothly and your clients will always have a consistent database of NetBIOS name to IP addresses.

Adding Static Entries

Even though WINS is completely dynamic it is a good idea to provide static entries for all Windows NT Servers. There are six types of static entries in WINS:

■ Unique: A unique host is a unique host with one network card. The majority of all static WINS entries will be unique.

■ Group: A group is a group of computers (such as a workgroup). By configuring a group packet broadcasts are sent to an entire group instead of single users.

■ Domain Name: The Domain Name is the name of a Windows NT login domain. The Domain Name option would also be applicable to LAN Manager and IBM LAN Server Domains.

■ Internet Group: An Internet Group is very similar to a Group, however you can sort devices such as printers into an Internet Group for easy browsing.

■ Multi-homed: A Multi-homed machine is one that has a single Host Name, but several network cards.

To add a static entry, follow the ensuing procedure:

- Go to the Mappings option on the tool bar and choose the Static Mappings option from the drop-down menu.
- From within the Static Mappings window, select the Unique option and enter the client name and associated IP address. Select OK once finished.
- Once complete, the machine will have a static mapping in the WINS database.

NOTE

To manage a remote WINS Server, simply go to the WINS Manager tool bar and select Server. From the pull-down menu, choose Add WINS Server and either input the server's IP address or NetBIOS name. If the server does not have NetBEUI loaded you must use the IP address. The WINS Server will then be added to your list of available servers.

A Note on OS/2 Interoperability with WINS

As stated many times throughout this book, Windows, Windows 95, Windows NT, and OS/2 are applications with inherent NetBIOS dependencies resulting in a required NetBIOS interface. Without the NetBIOS interface, communication between client and server would not be possible due to the fact that (among other things) the NetBIOS interface provides name and address resolution for network communications. Since TCP/IP is fast becoming a requirement in the enterprise, network managers are faced with deploying TCP/IP to all of their servers and clients. While this is no issue in the UNIX world (nor the pure Microsoft world), it is not all that easy to deal with in the mixed Microsoft/IBM networking world due to the differing implementations of the NetBIOS dependency, as well as the fact that TCP/IP does not inherently support this dependency. This quandary leaves the network manager with two choices:

- Stay with NetBEUI as the standard protocol (which is ugly in a large, routed enterprise) and use IP for UNIX and traditional TCP/IP services only.
- Move completely to TCP/IP, which does not natively provide for the NetBIOS interface, and find a supportable alternative to this interface.
- Due to this lack of inherent support for the NetBIOS interface, moving to TCP/IP in the mixed Microsoft/IBM environment requires that either some very ugly alternatives to the NetBIOS interface be implemented (such as manual OS/2 configuration or the maintenance and implementation of Hosts files), or that a NetBIOS Name Server be put into place. The NetBIOS Name Server acts very much like an industry standard DNS server, however instead of translating FQDN (fully qualified domain) names to IP addresses and vice versa, it translates NetBIOS names to IP addresses and vice versa, providing for a non-chatty streamlined replacement for the NetBIOS interface

without the network burden often presented by NetBEUI. Unfortunately, due to the lack of foresight or care, IBM does not provide a NetBIOS Name Server for OS/2, while Microsoft provides one that works only with Microsoft clients (WINS). Since the NetBIOS Name Server is an industry standard, one would think that multiple corporations would be providing such a beast—however this is not the case.

Within the last year or two, a small company named Network Telesystems (http://www.nts.com) has developed a NetBIOS Name Server that works not only with OS/2 but also as a replacement for WINS in the Windows NT environment. IPCentral, formerly known as Shadow Server, not only provides a NetBIOS Name Server, but also a fairly solid DHCP and DNS solution along with an address management interface. If you are in a mixed OS/2–Microsoft environment, it is definitely worth your while to contact this company. On the other hand, if you are in a Microsoft-only environment, WINS is sufficient—especially when considering the fact that the next generations of Windows and Windows NT will no longer have the NetBIOS dependency that exists today.

Client Configuration Issues

As seen earlier in this chapter, your Windows NT DHCP Server will automatically configure your Microsoft workstations for TCP/IP connectivity. This section will cover client-side configuration for Windows for Workgroups, Windows 95, and Windows NT, as well as a brief synopsis of OS/2 and NetBIOS over TCP/IP.

Configuring Windows for Workgroups for DHCP Connectivity

Installing TCP/IP in Windows for Workgroups is not as complicated as people have historically made it out to be.

1. In Windows, launch the Windows Setup program from the Main program group. Select Options followed by the Change Network Settings option.

2. Once the Network Setup window has loaded, press the Drivers button. Select the Add Protocols button, and a list of available protocols will load.

3. Select the Unlisted or Updated Protocol and provide the path to the WFW TCP/IP files.

4. Once the files are copied, you will be presented with a Microsoft TCP/IP configuration window. To configure your Windows for Workgroups machine for DHCP you need to select only the Enable Automatic DCHP Configuration box.

5. Once complete, select OK and close out of the Network Settings dialog. Restart the machine, and you will receive a DHCP address.

6. To ensure you've received an address, go to a DOS window and type **IPCONFIG**. You should very quickly be presented with your host IP address, subnet mask and default gateway. To view more detailed information type **IPCONFIG /ALL**.

7. Once you've verified that you've received an address, your DHCP installation will be complete.

> **NOTE**
>
> TCP/IP for Windows for Workgroups is included on the Windows NT 3.51 and 4.0 server CD-ROMs in the \Clients\TCP32WFW\NETSETUP directory.

Windows 95

Before beginning the installation of TCP/IP for Windows 95, ensure that you have access to the Windows 95 installation CD-ROM or a network distribution of Windows 95. TCP/IP installation and DHCP configuration are terribly easy under Windows 95 as evidenced through the following procedure:

1. Go to the Control Panel and double-click on the Network icon or right mouse click on the Network Neighborhood icon on the desktop and choose Properties. Choose the button labeled Protocols.

2. You will soon be presented with a list of protocols categorized by manufacturer. Go to the Microsoft option and choose TCP/IP. Press OK, and you will be brought back to the Network properties page.

3. Upon initial installation of TCP/IP, DHCP is selected by default. At this point simply press OK to close the Network Properties box.

4. You will soon be prompted to restart the machine in order for the changes to take effect. Save any open documents and restart the machine.

5. Once your Windows 95 workstation has restarted, you should verify that you received an IP address. To do so, go to a DOS window and type **Winipconfig**, then press Enter. You will immediately be shown your TCP/IP address as well as any other setting that was passed along by your DHCP Server.

6. At this point, DHCP has been successfully installed.

Windows NT 3.51

To install TCP/IP and DHCP on a Windows NT 3.51 computer ensure that you have access to the Windows NT Workstation 3.51 installation CD-ROM and follow these steps:

1. Go to the Control Panel and double click on the Network icon. Once the network configuration window launches, choose the Add Software option and select TCP/IP Protocol and related components from the available choices.

2. Next, you will be presented with a window labeled Windows NT TCP/IP Installation Options. Choose only Connectivity Utilities and Enable Automatic DHCP Configuration, then select OK.

14

WINS, DHCP, AND DNS

3. Once you are brought back into the Network Properties window, select OK. Windows NT will go through a binding process, and then you will be given the message that you must shut down and restart your machine in order for the changes to take effect. Restart the machine.

4. To verify that you have been assigned an IP address upon restart, go to a DOS window and type **ipconfig**, then press Enter. You will then be shown your IP address, default gateway, and subnet mask.

5. At this point, DHCP has been successfully installed on your workstation.

Windows NT 4.0

Installing TCP/IP and DHCP on a Windows NT 4.0 computer is very similar to a Windows NT 3.51 computer. Ensure that you have access to the Windows NT 4.0 Workstation installation CD-ROM and follow these steps:

1. Go to the Control Panel and double-click on the Network icon or right mouse click on the Network Neighborhood icon on the desktop and choose Properties. You will soon be presented with the Network configuration window. Choose the tab labeled Protocols, followed by the Add button.

2. Very soon you will be presented with a list of available protocols. Choose TCP/IP Protocol. Within seconds you will be asked if you wish to use DHCP. Select Yes. You will then be prompted for the location of the Windows NT Workstation 4.0 CD-ROM. Enter the path and press enter.

3. Once files are copied to your computer you will be informed that you must shut down and restart your machine in order for the changes to take effect. Ensure that all necessary data has been saved and restart the machine.

4. Upon reboot, to verify that you have been assigned an IP address, go to a DOS window and type **ipconfig**, then press Enter. You will then be shown your IP address, Subnet Mask, and default gateway.

OS/2 Warp 3.0 and Greater

At this time IBM does not provide a clean NetBIOS over TCP/IP solution for OS/2 nor will OS/2 operate in conjunction with Microsoft WINS Servers; however, it is possible to configure an OS/2 workstation to interoperate in a pure TCP/IP environment. Once configured properly, OS/2 will use NetBIOS over TCP/IP broadcasting or resource connectivity, but do not be alarmed: NetBT broadcasting does not present anywhere near the network load that true NetBIOS does. In reality, NetBT broadcasting is comparable to IPX broadcasting in terms of network traffic.

The following steps are required before OS/2 DHCP will work properly in a NetBIOS over TCP/IP environment:

■ MPTS must be updated to WR08213 or greater

■ TCP/IP must be version 3.1 or greater

■ TCP/IP must be updated to UN00959 or greater

■ The OS/2 workstation must have a properly defined DHCP configuration file (DHCPCD.CFG)

The following steps walk you through OS/2 configuration:

1. Ensure that your MPTS has been updated to WR08213 or later.

2. Install TCP/IP version 3.1 and immediately update it to UN00959 or greater. Reboot your machine as required.

3. Upon restart, go to the OS/2 window and launch the TCP/IP configuration utility by typing TCPCFG.

4. Under Configuration Options, select Automatically, Using DHCP. Do not select the DDNS option.

5. Remove any name server or gateway addresses and close out of TCP/IP Configuration. At this time it may be necessary to reboot your machine.

6. Once TCP/IP is installed and configured, launch MPTS and add NetBIOS over TCP/IP as found in the Protocol window in the upper right corner.

7. If NetBEUI is also installed, change the LAN number for NetBIOS over TCP/IP to 1. After installation make sure that your IBMLAN.INI reflects this change.

8. Next, Edit NetBEUI over TCP/IP and select Configure Broadcast List. Add the Fully Qualified Domain name of your Windows NT Primary Domain Controller (make sure that your PDCs exist in your DNS Server). Close the Broadcast list configuration and continue to close windows until you exit MPTS.

9. Next, edit the DHCPCD.CFG file to reflect the following information (the DHCPCD.CFG file can be found in your \MPTN\ETC directory):

```
# Basic options required
clientid   MAC
interface lan0
option 1                      # Subnet Mask
option 3                      # Router
option 6                      # Domain Name Server
option 12                     # Host name
option 15                     # Domain Name
option 28                     # Broadcast Address
option 44                     # NBNS/WINS Server
option 46                     # NetBIOS over TCP/IP Node Type
```

10. Notice that this DHCP configuration file allows for the assignation of WINS server addresses. This option is rather optimistic due to the fact that at this time the OS/2 DHCP client does not seem to accept Options 44 or 46 from a DHCP Server.

11. Once you've edited your DHCPCD.CFG, restart your machine and you should have full NetBIOS over TCP/IP connectivity. Note that if you frequently log in to more than one domain you must enter the FQDN name of each Domain's PDC.

14

WINS, DHCP, AND DNS

Summary

In today's environment, the move toward cross-platform standards has made the deployment of TCP/IP nearly mandatory. Unfortunately, even with an industry standard like TCP/IP, each network will have its own unique challenges to overcome. While Microsoft provides an easily managed TCP/IP infrastructure through WINS and DHCP, it is still highly recommended that those people responsible for the deployment and management of TCP/IP in your environment receive advanced training in TCP/IP, as well as have a firm understanding of NetBIOS over TCP/IP and the requirements inherent to Microsoft internetworking.

Providing Fault Tolerance

IN THIS CHAPTER

CHAPTER 15

Key Design Objective Five is simple and to the point: fault tolerance. The enterprise today is becoming both the heart and the brain of a successful corporation, therefore the Network Administrator often takes the heat when a disaster strikes—even when it might have been out of his or her control. To be prepared for disaster, it is important to have a solid tape backup system in place, and to build as much fault tolerance into your servers as possible. Through a solid backup system such as Seagate's Backup Exec and the deployment of a standard RAID 5 solution throughout your environment, you can prepare and even avoid disaster in your enterprise. This chapter will cover the topics of software-driven fault tolerance, hardware-driven fault tolerance and the implementation of Seagate's Backup Exec.

Backing Up Your Servers

The main thrust of this book is to help you deploy enterprise-level solutions that will play in a scalable, well-managed and fault-tolerant environment. To serve these purposes, this book will not cover the backup software built into Windows NT other than to say that it exists and it will back up your files in a crunch. Further than that, Windows NT Backup is only slightly better than the solution that ships with NetWare—neither one are meant to fit in a true enterprise environment.

There are many key features to look for in a server backup solution. The following features are those to look for when deciding upon your backup solution:

- Remote monitoring and administration
- Centralized administration
- Integrated BackOffice support
- SNMP support
- Multiple backup methods (Full, Copy, Differential, Copy, and so on)
- Windows NT Registry protection and restoration
- Open and Skipped File Processing
- File Version Control
- An easily searched disk-based catalog
- The ability to maintain a tape-based catalog
- A wide variety of tape drive support
- Support for multiple platforms

While there are many backup solutions available for Windows NT, none is so successful as Seagate's Backup Exec for Windows NT. Formerly by Arcada, Backup Exec has become the de facto standard for backup solutions in the Windows NT arena. An evaluation copy of Backup Exec for Windows NT can be obtained from the Seagate Web site at

```
http://www.smg.seagatesoftware.com/winteval.htm
```

The remainder of this section will cover some of the features found in Backup Exec, and provide examples as to the functionality this product offers.

Backup Exec Installation

Backup Exec can be installed directly on the server you plan to back up, or can be installed on a Windows NT Workstation and used to back up multiple servers across the network. What's more is that Backup Exec has the ability to run multiple backup jobs, backing up to multiple tape drives at once (although no more than three concurrent jobs are recommended). To install Backup Exec it is recommended that you place the expanded files in a directory named BEINSTALL under a subdirectory titled BEV611. Once the files are expanded, run the Setup program that can be found in the root of the BEV611 structure. You will immediately be presented with the screen shown in Figure 15.1. Notice that this screen has four installation choices: Backup Server, Remote Admin, ExecView Only, and Cancel.

FIGURE 15.1.

*The Initial Backup
Exec Installation
Program.*

Backup Exec has two methods of monitoring and controlling backup and restore operations. ExecView can be used locally on your backup server or remotely from a Windows NT computer to monitor the success and failure of the past, current, and future backup and restore jobs. Additionally, it is possible to install remote administration tools that will allow you to both monitor job status and remotely manage backup and restore jobs.

To install the Backup Exec service, select Backup Server. You will next be prompted for a serial number and installation directory. If you do not enter a serial number at this point you will have 60 days to evaluate the product. If after evaluation you decide to purchase this product you will have the opportunity to enter a valid serial number, thereby keeping all of your configuration information. After selecting an installation directory and selecting Next, an installation status bar will appear and files will be copied. At approximately 90% completion you will be prompted for the User ID and Password of a Backup Exec Service ID account. This account will be used to allow the Backup Exec service to log on to your servers behind the scenes and back up data. This account must be a member of the Backup Operators group and the Administrators Group, as well as be granted Log In as a Service right within your domain.

FIGURE 15.2.

The Service Account Window.

> **NOTE**
>
> Your Backup Exec Service Account must also be granted membership in the Administrators and Backup Operators groups, and Log In as a Service right in any member server or Resource Domain you plan to back up. If you do not do so, even though you will be able to connect to these resources during job setup, when the service account attempts to attach to these servers and back them up, access will be denied.

If an appropriate service account does not already exist, you will be prompted to verify the new ID's password. Once complete, Backup Exec will grant the user membership in the Administrators group and ensure that the user has Log In as a Service right in your Domain.

Once your Service Account is configured, you will be prompted to enter the server name of any previous Backup Exec installation throughout your enterprise. If you do enter a name, the installation program will automatically add the existing backup server to the list of servers you can manage and monitor.

> **NOTE**
>
> If you do not enter the name of an existing backup server at this time, there are no further implications. At a later date, you can choose to remotely manage any Backup Exec installation as long as you are authorized to do so.

Once you've determined whether or not to enter the name of an existing installation, setup will be complete. At this point you may begin configuring Backup Exec.

> **NOTE**
>
> Seagate provides agents that will allow you to back up NetWare Servers, Windows 95 workstations, OS/2 workstations, and UNIX-based computers. In addition, Backup Exec will natively back up Windows NT Workstations and OS/2 LAN Servers, the latter requiring user-defined shares.

Backup Exec: An Interface Overview

Backup Exec utilizes the tape drive device drivers built in to Windows NT. If you have not already done so, install your tape drive(s) by going to the Control Panel and selecting the Tape Device shortcut. After your tape drive(s) has been installed, it will be necessary to reboot your machine.

> **NOTE**
>
> In most cases if your backup server has multiple drives that utilize the same driver there will be no need to install the driver more than once. Upon reboot Windows NT will find and configure all of the tape drives.

> **CAUTION**
>
> When installing multiple tape devices, whether they be internal or external, be sure that the SCSI IDs of each device are unique. If you do not configure them as such, chances are your tape drives will encounter problems—if they work at all.

Once your drives are configured, launch the Backup Exec management interface, shown in Figure 15.3, that can be found in the Backup Exec folder in your Start menu.

FIGURE 15.3.

The Backup Exec Management Interface.

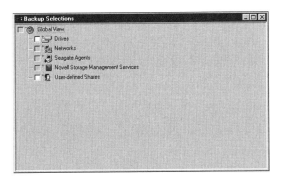

15

PROVIDING FAULT TOLERANCE

As you can see, this utility is made up of a fairly comprehensive tool bar and four management windows. The tool bar consists of the following selections:

- **File.** This menu item can be used for printer setup or to exit the application.
- **Tree.** This option will allow you to manage the expansion level of any given directory tree.
- **View.** This option is most pertinent when viewing storage media or remote volumes. It allows you to determine whether you will view simply the directory tree or a directory tree on the left side of the screen, followed by the actual files and directories on the right side of the screen (see Figure 15.4).

FIGURE 15.4.

Viewing Files and Directories.

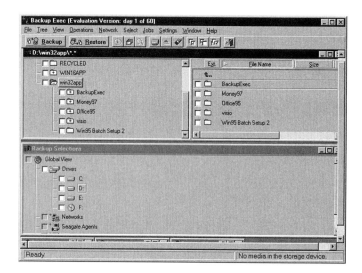

- **Operations.** This option allows you to determine if you are going to: archive, back up, restore, or verify files; catalog media; erase media; or format tapes. In addition, it is from here that you can search catalogs for files and directories.
- **Network.** Under this selection, you can connect to additional Backup Exec Servers, create User Defined Shares (UNC Paths to resources), set the Default Attach information to be sent to all Microsoft-compatible resources, and attach as a different user to selected devices.
- **Select.** This option allows you to select multiple files for back up and restore them using wild cards and advanced variables. Additionally, it is in this menu item that you will create and manage the backup selections that will be included in your Backup Jobs.
- **Jobs.** This menu item allows you to select pre-configured jobs for automatic kick-off, or to set up and schedule jobs for on-going or special services.
- **Settings.** This drop-down menu contains several settings pertinent to configuration preferences, network settings, hardware settings, catalog settings, and so on. The options in this menu are all very crucial.

- ■ **Window.** This option allows you to select which window to view as your primary.
- ■ **Help.** This option provides access to Backup Exec help files.

The management windows within Backup Exec are the Backup Selections window, the Storage Media window, Scheduled Jobs, and the Job History window.

The Backup Selections window, shown in Figure 15.5, is where you will go to select those devices and their shares that you wish to back up. This window provides an easily navigable interface to the resources within your enterprise. With a similar look and feel to the Network Neighborhood, this window categorizes available resources by local drives, networks, Seagate agents, user-defined shares and, if the NetWare component is installed, NetWare SMS resources.

FIGURE 15.5.

The Backup Selections Window.

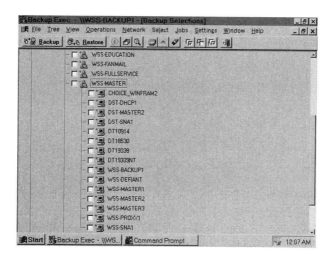

You can customize what resources you will be able to see or attach to using the Settings menu on the tool bar. For instance, by going to the Settings menu, followed by Network, you will be presented with a figure similar to Figure 15.6. This window allows you to determine whether you will be able to select and back up user-defined shares, default Windows NT shares, SQL and Exchange Servers (with the proper agents installed), and AppleTalk zones.

FIGURE 15.6.

The Network Settings Configuration Window.

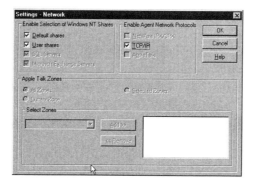

The Scheduled Jobs window is where you will go to view your scheduled jobs. As seen in Figure 15.7, this window allows you to view and modify previously configured job settings.

FIGURE 15.7.

The Scheduled Jobs Window.

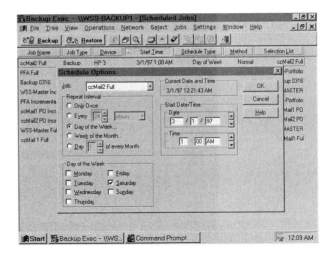

The Job History window allows to view a job's history (see Figure 15.8). Depending on how much detail you've configured your server to log, history logs can give you varying degrees of information from a log containing a success audit of each file and a directory to a log containing failures only.

FIGURE 15.8.

The Job History Window.

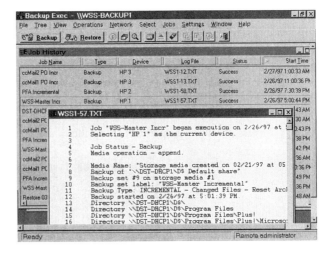

> **NOTE**
>
> If a job was unsuccessful for any reason, it will show up in the Job History window in red for easy identification. It is very rare that you will not be able to glean what went wrong with a particular backup or restore job from the Job History log.

Following the Job History window is the Storage Media window, shown in Figure 15.9. This window will maintain a list of all the media sets that have been used with Backup Exec for as long as you desire. Backup Exec will maintain a catalog for each of these tape sets providing for easy file and directory searching and restorations.

FIGURE 15.9.

The Storage Media Window.

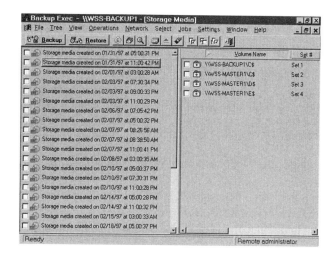

Common Configuration Issues in Backup Exec

This section will cover some of the more common configuration issues in Backup Exec, beginning with Event Settings and ending with Auto Loader configuration.

Event Settings

Even though Backup Exec maintains its own job history, it also fully integrates with your Windows NT Event log. In conjunction with Windows NT Alerts (covered in Chapter 5, "Server Standardization, Installation, and Implementation"), this feature means that you will be notified in case of a failed job without having to constantly monitor progress. Additionally, you can browse the Applications portion of the Event Viewer for notices of job success and/or Backup Exec service issues (see Figure 15.10).

To configure the Event settings, go to the Settings menu item and choose Events. You will be presented with the window shown in Figure 15.11, titled Settings–Events.

15

PROVIDING FAULT TOLERANCE

FIGURE 15.10.

Backup Exec Integration with the Event Log.

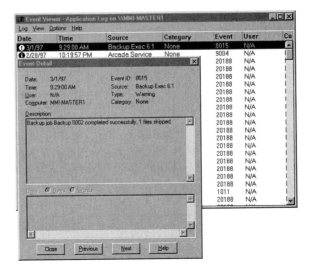

FIGURE 15.11.

The Settings–Events Window in Backup Exec.

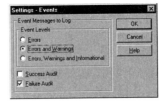

Notice that you have the opportunity to monitor both failures and successes through your Event Viewer. In addition, you can choose to integrate the following types of messages into your Event Viewer:

- Error messages
- Error messages and warnings
- Errors messages, warnings, and informational messages

In most cases, the Errors and Warnings selection is more than sufficient. Keep in mind that if you choose the Errors, Warnings and Informational option your event log size settings will need to be adjusted—Backup Exec will send a great deal of information.

Job History Settings

Job History settings can be configured by going to the Settings menu and selecting Job History. This will bring up the window shown in Figure 15.12 that will allow you to determine the level of Job History logging that will be maintained.

FIGURE 15.12.
*The Job History
Settings Window.*

Your choices are

- Summary information only
- Summary information and directories processed
- Summary information, directories, and files processed
- Summary information, directories, files, and file details

In most cases, the Summary information and directories processed option is enough to allow an administrator to sleep at night. This option will show which directories have been processed as well as provide summary information concerning any files that were not backed up. The third and fourth options will not only provide a listing of the directories that were backed up, but also each file and quite a bit of detail. The Job History log is not only an excellent tool for maintaining historical information, it also provides excellent troubleshooting information in case of backup issues.

Setting Up a Backup Job

A complete backup job is made up of three components: the Backup Selection, the Job Setup, and the Job Scheduler. The following procedure will details the steps necessary to set up a backup job:

1. Using the Backup Selections window, select the servers and drives that you wish to back up. Next, go to the Select tool bar item and choose Save Selections from the drop-down menu. Name the selection appropriately. For instance, if you plan to configure a job containing just your SNA servers, name the job SNA Backup.

2. Next, move to the Jobs menu item and choose Setup. You will be presented with a window titled Jobs–Setup that lists the default jobs Differential, Full, Incremental, and Skipped Files. Select the Create Window, and you will be brought to a Window titled Create a New Job (see Figure 15.13). It is here that you will choose the selection list of resources, name the job for future reference and determine whether the job is to be one of the following types: Back up, Restore, Verify, Archive, Catalog, Retention, Format, or Erase. Keep the default setting, Backup, and select the Options button.

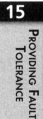

15

PROVIDING FAULT TOLERANCE

FIGURE 15.13.

The Create a New Job Window.

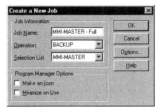

3. You will next be presented with a window titled Backup (see Figure 15.14). It is here that you will determine whether you will perform a Full, Incremental, or Differential backup. It is also here that you will determine which tape device you will back up to. Remember, it is possible to perform multiple backups at once—as long as they don't all require the same tape device. Choose the appropriate backup type and configuration options and close this window.

FIGURE 15.14.

The Backup Configuration Window.

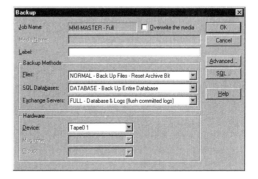

4. Next, close this window, and then close the Create window, until you're back at the Jobs–Setup window. To schedule your job choose the Schedule button, and you will be presented with a window listing all the scheduled jobs that have been previously configured. To schedule a new job, select the Add button and you will launch the Schedule Options window, shown in Figure 15.15. It is here that you can schedule a job for ongoing service or for simply a run-once situation. Simply select the correct job from the Job: text box, choose the scheduling features necessary, and select OK. Your job will now be added to the list of scheduled jobs. At this point, you will have successfully configured a job.

CAUTION

In the Settings menu under Hardware, you have the option to save a particular tape drive as the default device. Doing so will select this device as the default drive for every job you create. While this is a nice feature, it is also a major drawback. For instance, whenever

Backup Exec is open, even if it is processing nothing, it has control over the default device. If a job requiring the default device is scheduled to kick off when Backup Exec is open, it will not start until you've closed Backup Exec. Unless you're using an Autoloader, it is recommended that you do not choose a default device.

FIGURE 15.15.

Creating a Scheduled Job.

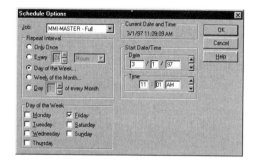

Restoration Methods with Backup Exec

Restoring files in Backup Exec can be as easy as navigating the Storage Media window and choosing the files or directories you wish to restore, or can include a detailed search of all storage media maintained.

Simple Restorations: Files and Directories

To back up files and directories to their default destinations, perform the following:

1. Choose the storage media that contains the directory or files that you wish to restore. Storage media is categorized by date, so make sure you're selecting the correct set. Once you've expanded the media, you will be presented a list of all the shares and drives that are contained on the media set you've chosen. Remote resources will be listed by UNC path while local resources will be listed by drive letter. These resources will further be broken down by the date they were backed up and the type of backup job that was processed (Normal for a full backup, Incremental or Differential for their respective types). Choose the resources you wish to restore and select the Restore button from the tool bar.

2. You will now be presented with a window titled Restore Job. This window allows you to choose whether to restore the server's Registry, restore directory security, or preserve the directory's tree structure. Do not select to restore the Registry unless you want your current hardware and Domain Directory information to return to the state as it existed when the backup was made.

3. Select Run Now, and the files will be restored. If Backup Exec requires another tape, it will inform you of which tape you need (by date) and wait for you to insert it.

15

PROVIDING FAULT
TOLERANCE

4. Restoration in Backup Exec is a very fast process, having the ability to restore over two gigabytes over a 16MB network in a little less than an hour.

Advanced Restoration: Searching for Files and Wild Card Selections

Many times a user will lose a file or delete a file and have no idea where he or she stored it. Luckily, Backup Exec provides a simple way to find those files:

1. To search for a file, go to the Operations option on the tool bar and select Search Catalogs. You will be presented with a screen shown in Figure 15.16, titled Catalog Search Criteria.

FIGURE 15.16.

The Catalog Search Criteria Window.

2. It is here that you can select the storage media you wish to search, determine to search all storage media, select whether you wish to search all subdirectories, and enter a file name. Note that you can use wild cards in the File text box.

3. Enter the file (and if desired, the path to that file) that you're searching for and select OK. Backup Exec will now begin searching for the file.

4. Once the search is complete, Backup Exec will present you with a complete version listing of the file you searched for, allowing you to restore any version of the file you wish—as long as the tape set hasn't been erased. By selecting the desired file and pressing the Restore button on the tool bar, you can restore the file to its original location.

Backup Exec will also allow you to make wild card selections from directories within the storage media, allowing you to restore all files of a certain type or containing a certain name. To do so:

1. Find the storage media that contains the files you're looking for and select the proper drive or resource. If you know exactly which directory the files are in, go to that directory. If not, remain at the root.

2. From the Select drop-down menu, choose Advanced, and you will be provided with the Advanced Restore File Selection window, shown in Figure 15.17. This window provides a great deal of selection criteria including dates, backup sets, paths, file selections, and subdirectories. Enter the appropriate information and select OK.

FIGURE 15.17.
*The Advanced Restore
File Selection Window.*

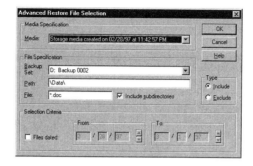

Backup Exec will now select all of the files adhering to your selection criteria.

NOTE

By selecting the Exclude check box in the lower right side of the screen you can choose to de-select any selected files from a previously chosen directory structure.

3. After files are selected, simply press the Restore button on the tool bar, and files will be restored as directed.

Redirecting Files

Files may be redirected during any restore job. To do so, when in the Restore Window simply select the File Sets option. This will add a File Set Destination portion to the Restore Job window, allowing you to enter an alternate destination for the files. Unless the files exist on the local machine, a path must be entered using UNC pathing.

To Restore the Registry in Backup Exec

Backup Exec has the ability to back up a server's Registry during every backup job. You can restore a server's Registry at any time by simply selecting any file to restore and choosing the Restore Registry option in the lower left corner of the Restore Job window. If you do so, the next time you boot your server, the Registry will revert to the version that you restored.

This is an excellent tool to use in case you've added a driver or a piece of software that has impacted your server in a negative manner. It's quite a bit quicker than using the Emergency Repair process to return your computer to its previous state—if you have an Emergency Repair disk, that is.

It's important to note that when you select the Restore Registry option, Backup Exec will restore the entire Registry, including the Domain Directory, hardware settings, software settings, and the elements of user profiles that exist in the Registry. Be certain that you need to restore the Registry before you do so.

NOTE

It is also possible to restore a server's Registry by simply selecting the `\%systemroot%\` `config` directory from your backup set. The files contained within this directory are, in fact, your Registry.

Restoring an Entire Server

To restore a server using a locally attached tape drive and locally installed version of Backup Exec, follow these steps:

1. Install Windows NT and Backup Exec on the target machine. Be sure to configure the hard drives using Disk Administrator and format them using the same file system as before the failure. Next, load the correct drivers for the tape drive. Do not worry about any further advanced configuration as you will be restoring all such information over the new installation.

2. Reboot the machine and launch Backup Exec. Insert the latest Full backup set of the downed computer and fully catalog it. If there exist subsequent Differential or Incremental backups on different media, be sure to catalog them as well.

3. Select each set from the Full and Incremental backups that contains the drives that need to be restored. Select the Restore button on the tool bar and choose to restore the registry and security. Click OK to start the restore. If prompted, be sure to restore over existing data.

4. Change tapes as necessary, and after the restore is finished, shut down and restart the computer. The recovery process is now complete, and you should have a fully operational server.

To restore a server over the network, use the following procedure:

1. Install Windows NT on the target machine. Be sure to configure the hard drives using Disk Administrator and format them using the same file system as before the failure. Aside from getting the machine back on the network, don't worry about any further advanced configuration, as you will be restoring all such information over the new installation.

2. From remote Backup Exec server, insert the latest Full backup set of the downed computer and fully catalog it if it hasn't been already done. If there exist subsequent Differential or Incremental backups on different media, be sure to catalog them as well.

3. Select each set from the Full and Incremental backups that contains the drives that need to be restored. Select the Restore button on the tool bar and choose to restore the Registry and security. Click OK to start the restore. If prompted, be sure to restore over existing data.

4. Change tapes as necessary, and after the restore is finished, shut down and restart the remote computer.

5. Next, to ensure that the proper Registry information has been restored on the remote computer, select the `\%systemroot%\system32\config` directory from the last full and all subsequent differential backup sets and click Restore. Select the Restore Registry switch and ensure that the Destination options, Restore to, and Restore to path are correct for your situation. If the target drive is an NTFS partition, select Restore File Permissions as well.

6. After the Restore is complete, restart the machine. The recovery process is now complete.

> **NOTE**
>
> When restoring a server that acts solely as a Domain Controller, it is much faster to simply remove the computer account from the domain using Server Manager and bring up a new Backup Domain Controller. Likewise, when restoring member servers that act as simple application servers, such as SNA Server, it is often times faster to reinstall Windows NT, followed by the application, and simply restore the Registry and any application configuration files.

Recommended Deployment Method

Backup Exec is by far one of the most solid backup systems available for Windows NT. The only feature that Backup Exec is truly missing is an advanced tape management system. While this is somewhat of a drawback, most systems (such as Palindrome) that do have advanced tape management features suffer from a major loss in performance.

Backup Exec has the ability to process multiple jobs at once; therefore, it is possible to break up your backup jobs by tape drive and schedule them accordingly. The following list contains suggestions for a successful implementation of Backup Exec:

■ Create two jobs for each Backup Selection set: Full and Incremental. Schedule them so that the Full backup resides on its own tape and the subsequent incrementals reside on a single tape. This provides a sort of safety net in case one of the tapes is damaged.

■ Pull a complete tape set every quarter and store it in a safe place. This will provide an archival source to be drawn on throughout the year.

■ If your backup server will process multiple jobs at once, install multiple network cards and stagger the start times at least an hour apart.

■ Label your tapes according to the date they were created and the backup sets they contain. This will correspond to the Storage Media catalog contained within Backup Exec.

- If performing remote backups, install Backup Exec on a dedicated Windows NT Workstation. This will minimize the operating system cost and ensure that your Backup Exec server will always be available to perform disaster recovery.

- Back up your Backup Exec catalogs with every backup job. This takes a minimum amount of tape space and will alleviate the need to catalog each tape in case of a hardware failure.

- Document your backup selections and scheduled jobs and include instructions for simple and disaster recovery. You will not only find this to be an aid to all support personnel in your corporation, but also to yourself.

Disk Fault Tolerance

No matter how solid your backup system is it is important to have some type of online fault tolerance. Through such technologies as RAID, Disk Mirroring, or Disk Duplexing you can equip your servers with differing levels of disk fault tolerance that will ensure a quick restoration of service in case of disk failure and in some cases, in case of a complete server failure as well.

Through the Windows NT Disk Administrator, you can configure varying levels of software-driven disk fault tolerance, and through server vendors and third-party vendors you can deploy third-party hardware-driven solutions, either of which will increase your level of fault tolerance. This section will first cover the Windows NT Disk Administrator and the software-driven fault tolerance solutions included, and will also cover some of the available hardware-driven solutions that have been designed to increase your server availability.

Windows NT Disk Administrator

The Windows NT Disk Administrator can be used to perform the following tasks:

- To create logical and extended disk partitions
- To create and extend Volume Sets
- To create Stripe Sets (RAID 0)
- To create Stripe Sets with Parity (RAID 5)
- To regenerate failed disks in RAID 5 Stripe Sets
- To initiate disk mirroring (RAID 1)
- To break disk mirroring
- To format drives
- To assign alternative drive letters to physical and logical drives
- To determine existing drive properties

This tool, shown in Figure 15.18, which is very infrequently used when compared to other tools such as the User Manager for Domains and the Server Manager, has a fairly intuitive interface except where advanced disk management is concerned. Due to their more advanced features, the following sections will detail the creation of Volume Sets, Stripe Sets, Stripe Sets with Parity, and Mirror Sets.

FIGURE 15.18.

The Windows NT Disk Administrator.

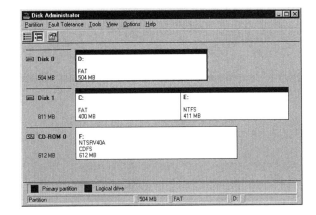

Creating a RAID 0 Stripe Set

RAID 0, or striping without parity, is a set of from two to 32 disks that have been configured to act as one physical drive. Different from a simple Volume Set, a RAID 0 Stripe Set stripes data from disk to disk, spreading files in 64K blocks at a time across all of the disks in a Stripe Set. This striping of data maximizes disk performance by utilizing each drive to read or write the same file at the same time. The performance is fantastic; however, there is one major drawback—if one of the drives in the Stripe Set fails, all data throughout the Stripe Set is lost. RAID 0 offers absolutely no fault tolerance and should be used with extreme caution.

> **NOTE**
>
> A Windows NT Boot or System partition cannot take part in a software-driven Stripe Set. If you wish to include your Boot or System partition in your Stripe Set, you must utilize a hardware-driven solution.

To create a RAID 0 Stripe Set, you must start with at least two hard disks containing comparable amounts of free, unpartitioned disk space. This disk space can reside on disks that are currently in use without affecting their existing configuration; however, to achieve the performance gains granted by RAID 0, it is highly recommended that you dedicate drives to a Stripe Set.

NOTE

Each disk that participates in a Stripe Set should be of comparable size due to the fact that each disk in a Stripe Set will be sized identically. For instance, if you have four disks that are to participate in a Stripe Set, two containing 810 MB and two others containing 540 MB, your Stripe Set would be sized as if you actually had four 540 MB drives. While the unused space on your 810 MB drives would be available for use outside the Stripe Set, if used, it will degrade performance.

CAUTION

For a disk to participate in a Stripe Set, it must not be partitioned or formatted. Before proceeding with your Stripe Set creation, be sure you delete existing configuration information on those disks you wish to use.

To create a Stripe Set, do the following:

1. Launch the Disk Administrator.

2. Highlight the unconfigured space on each drive that you wish to include in the Stripe Set by holding down the Control key and clicking once on each disk. If using new drives, do not partition or format them.

3. Still holding down the Control key, select the Partition option on the tool bar, followed by the Create Stripe Set menu item.

4. The system will confirm your selection. Once confirmed, the Disk Administrator will create a Stripe Set consisting of evenly sized partitions on each disk; that is, if the first disk had 300 MB of free space, the second had 275 MB of free space, and the third had 450 MB, the Disk Administrator would utilize only 275 MB on each disk, resulting in a Stripe Set of 825 MB.

5. Once the Stripe Set has been configured, go back to the Partitions menu and select the Commit Changes Now option.

NOTE

In order for any disk configuration changes to take place in the Disk Administrator, you must select the Commit Changes Now option found in the Partitions drop-down menu.

6. Once the configuration is saved, highlight the newly created Stripe Set and move to the Tools option on the tool bar. From the drop-down menu, select Format and you

will be presented with a screen, shown in Figure 15.19. Select the desired file system, followed by the Quick Format option, and press Start. Soon, your Stripe Set will be formatted.

FIGURE 15.19.

Formatting a Drive through the Disk Administrator.

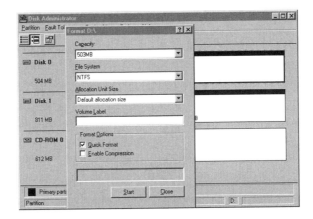

7. Update (or create) your Emergency Repair Disk by running **RDISK.EXE** using the Run option on your Start menu. You will be required to reboot your server before the Stripe Set can take effect.

While RAID 0 does provide excellent performance, it is important to note that if any of the drives in a RAID 0 Stripe Set fail, the only way to recover the data is to re-create the Stripe Set and restore the data using your Backup solution. RAID 0 provides no fault tolerance and should be used very sparingly.

Creating a Stripe Set with Parity (RAID 5)

RAID 5, or Striping with Parity, spreads files in blocks across all disks much like RAID 0, but also uses an algorithm to stripe parity bits for each file across each disk. This parity bit contains enough information to not only rebuild any given disk upon a single disk failure, but also continue to provide complete access to data on the RAID 5 Stripe Set even after a disk failure. Using the parity information striped across each disk, files are re-created in memory upon demand.

> **NOTE**
>
> RAID 5 requires a minimum of three disks to create a Stripe Set.

Through striping, RAID 5 is fairly similar to RAID 0; however, the similarities stop very quickly. If you were to create a Stripe Set with RAID 0 using four 300 MB disks, you would end up

15

PROVIDING FAULT
TOLERANCE

with a single striped Volume Set containing 1200 MB disk space. In RAID 5, using the same four 300 MB disks you would end up with a Volume Set containing only 900 MB of usable disk space. This loss of storage space is due to the additional data bits being striped across each disk with each file. To determine how much usable storage a RAID 5 Stripe Set will contain, use the formula of N-1, N being the number of total disks, 1 being one total disk. In other words, if you have five equally sized disks, once you've configured a RAID 5 Stripe Set your usable storage would be equal to the total of only four of those disks. (Four 9 GB drives in RAID 5 will give you 36 GB of usable disk space, while four 9 GB drives in RAID 0 will give you 45 GB of usable disk space.)

It is possible to create a RAID 5 Stripe Set in Windows NT using disks that are partially partitioned and formatted without harming the existing configuration. While it is heavily recommended, those disks that will participate in a Stripe Set are not required to be the same size or the same type of disks. Remember, three or more disks are required to create a Stripe Set with Parity.

> **CAUTION**
>
> For a disk to participate in a RAID 5 Stripe Set it must not be partitioned or formatted. Before proceeding with your Stripe Set creation, be sure you delete existing configuration information on the disks you wish to utilize.

To create a Stripe Set with Parity, you must do the following:

1. Launch the Disk Administrator.

2. Highlight the un-configured space on each drive that you plan to include in the Stripe Set by holding down the Control key and clicking once on each disk.

3. Still holding the Control key, select the Fault Tolerance option on the tool bar, followed by the Create Stripe Set with Parity menu item.

4. The system will confirm your selection. Once confirmed, the Disk Administrator will create a Stripe Set consisting of evenly sized partitions on each disk. Remember, if you have four 500 MB hard drives, you will have a Stripe Set with 1500 MB of usable disk space, not 2000 MB.

5. Once the Stripe Set has been configured, go back to the Partitions menu and select the Commit Changes Now option. This is required before you go any further.

6. After the configuration is saved, highlight the newly created RAID 5 Stripe Set and move to the Tools option on the tool bar. From the drop-down menu, select Format. Select the desired file system, followed by the Quick Format option, and press Start. Soon, your Stripe Set will be formatted and fully functional.

7. Either create or update your Emergency Repair Disk by running RDISK.EXE from the Run option on your Start menu. You will be required to reboot your server before the Stripe Set can take effect.

One of the nice features of RAID 5 is that if a disk fails, you can regenerate the missing disk once it is replaced. To regenerate a Stripe Set with Parity, do the following:

1. Launch the Disk Administrator. Before continuing, ensure that there is either a new hard drive to replace the dead Stripe Set member or an unaccounted-for amount of free space that equals the size of each Stripe Set member on an existing disk.

2. Select the Stripe Set with Parity followed by the unused area of free space.

3. Go to the Fault Tolerance option in the Disk Administrator tool bar and select the Regenerate option. Your selection will be confirmed and you will be prompted to restart your machine.

4. Upon reboot, the Windows NT System will regenerate the missing disk as instructed. Once complete, the system will come back online, Stripe Set intact.

TIP

Keep an unused drive in your system at all times so that you can minimize the time it will take to regenerate your Stripe Set. This way, you can pull the dead drive out of your system when it is convenient for your end users.

Mirror Sets (RAID 1)

The Mirror Set, or RAID 1, is an extremely common method of providing fault tolerance. Mirroring requires two disks and actually provides what its name suggests—the mirroring of one disk to another. With a Mirror Set, all data written to Disk 0 is also written to Disk 1. Therefore, if Disk 1 fails, the administrator can make a minor adjustment to the Windows NT BOOT.INI, reboot the machine, and all data up to the point of failure will be intact. Much like striping in Windows NT, mirroring can utilize two entire disks, or two equally sized partitions on two physical disks. Unlike striping, however, it is possible to mirror any partition, including the boot or system partitions.

To create a Mirror Set, perform the following steps:

1. Launch the Windows NT Disk Administrator.

2. Select either an existing drive followed by a partition on a separate hard drive with an equal amount of free space or two unconfigured partitions by holding down the Control key and clicking on each partition.

3. From the Disk Administrator tool bar select Fault Tolerance followed by Establish Mirror. Confirm the creation of the Mirror Set. Next, move to the Disk Administrator tool bar and select the Partitions option, followed by the Commit Changes selection.

15

PROVIDING FAULT TOLERANCE

4. After the configuration is saved, highlight the newly created Mirror Set and move to the Tools option on the tool bar. From the drop-down menu, select Format. Select the desired file system, followed by the Quick Format option, and press Start. Soon, your Stripe Set will be formatted and fully functional.

5. Either create or update your Emergency Repair Disk by running RDISK.EXE from the Run option on your Start menu.

It is possible (and encouraged) to enhance Disk Mirroring through Disk Duplexing. Disk Duplexing comes into play when you mirror two disks, but also use two separate disk controllers. In this scenario, if a disk controller fails in your system, you not only have a redundant disk, but you also have a redundant disk controller. Through relatively simple changes to your BOOT.INI (see Figure 15.20), you can have a machine back up in no time. The BOOT.INI, which exists in your boot partition, is used by Windows NT during the boot process to determine which controller, which hard disk, and which disk partition your Windows NT Server Operating System exists on.

FIGURE 15.20.

The BOOT.INI.

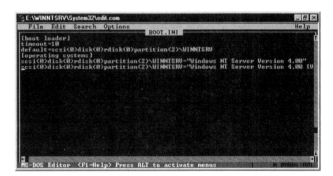

The BOOT.INI conforms to what is known as ARC naming conventions. The following line conforms to ARC naming.

```
default=scsi(0)disk(0)rdisk(0)partition(2)\WINNTSRV
```

It breaks down as follows:

- **Default.** Default informs your system which boot option to default to. If you had OS/2 or Windows 95 installed on your system, you could set either of those operating systems as your default by using the System extension of the Control Panel, on the page titled Startup/Shutdown (see Figure 15.21).

- **SCSI (0).** SCSI indicates that your controller is either SCSI or IDE, followed by the ordinal number of the hardware adapter. For instance, if the drive was hung from the second SCSI controller in your machine, the BOOT.INI would read: `default=scsi(1)`. (The first adapter is always signified as 0.)

FIGURE 15.21.

*The Startup/Shutdown
Page of the System
Properties.*

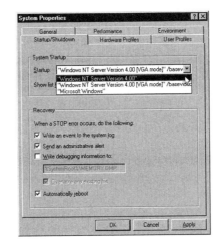

■ **DISK (0).** DISK (0) indicates the actual SCSI ID of the drive. For instance, if a drive configured with a SCSI ID of 3 were hung from the first controller, the line would read: `default=scsi(o) disk(3)`.

■ **RDISK (0).** The RDISK parameter is very rarely utilized. RDISK signifies a non-SCSI or SCSI-compatible drive. If such a drive exists in your machine, this setting will be utilized instead of the SCSI setting in your BOOT.INI.

■ **Partition (2).** This variable indicates which partition the System files actually exist on. Partition numbers start with partition 1, meaning that if the system files exist on C:\ drive the setting will appear as partition (1), and if the system files exist on the E:\ drive, the setting will be partition (4).

If you duplex your system drive and your default load option in your BOOT.INI file was set as

```
default=scsi(0)disk(0)rdisk(0)partition(2)\WINNTSRV
```

and your primary drive were to fail, it would be necessary only to edit the BOOT.INI, as follows:

```
default=scsi(1)disk(0)rdisk(0)partition(2)\WINNTSRV
```

This change signifies that the second SCSI controller will be used on reboot, bypassing the first drive and controller altogether. Upon reboot, your server will default to the mirrored disk and all functionality will stay intact.

It is possible to create a boot disk that can be utilized in case of a drive or controller failure. Instructions are as follows:

1. Format a floppy disk using Windows NT Server. Doing so writes information to the boot disk that will identify the appropriate loader file when the system is booted.

2. Copy the following files from your Windows NT Server to your boot disk:

```
NTLDR
NTDETECT.COMNT
BOOTDD.SYS
BOOT.INI
```

3. Edit the BOOT.INI so that it reflects the SCSI and boot partitions of the mirrored disk.

4. Test your boot disk and store it close to the server.

> **NOTE**
>
> If your system has a DOS-based boot partition, an excellent alternative to the boot disk is a batch file that will replace the existing BOOT.INI with a BOOT.INI that reflects the necessary changes to boot to the mirrored disk. This can be done safely by placing read-only copies of the BOOT.INIs in an alternative directory off of the root of your boot drive.

Volume Sets

Volume Sets provide no fault tolerance, but are often used nonetheless. A volume set is a set of two or more disks, or areas of free space on a disk, that have been combined to create a single logical drive. A Volume Set can consist of up to 32 disks or partitions and offers no fault tolerance whatsoever; however, it is useful for extending an existing drive or partition when storage space is short.

If you are using a hardware-based RAID 5 solution, there are no fault tolerance worries when expanding volumes; however, one of the major drawbacks to a Volume Set with no hardware-driven fault tolerance solution is that if one of the drives in the Volume Set fails, you lose all of your data. Volume Sets should be used with caution.

Much like Stripe Sets, the boot or system partitions cannot take part in a Volume Set. Additionally, only the Windows NT installation used to create the Volume Set can read the Volume Set. DOS, Windows 3.*x*, Windows 95, or OS/2 cannot access a Volume Set.

To create a Volume Set, perform the following:

1. Launch the Windows NT Disk Administrator.

2. Holding down the Control key, select the drive or partition that you wish to extend, followed by an area of free space on any of your disks.

3. From the Disk Administrator tool bar, select Partition, followed by Create Volume Set. Next, you will be asked to size and confirm the creation of the Volume Set.

4. Move to the Disk Administrator tool bar and select the Partitions option, followed by the Commit Changes selection.

5. At this point you will be reminded to update your Emergency Repair Disk and required to reboot your server. Upon reboot, the Volume Set will be formatted during the non-GUI portion of the OS initialization. Once the volume creation is complete, Windows NT will boot once again and come back up with the Volume Set intact.

> **NOTE**
>
> Before creating a Volume Set, Stripe Set, or Mirror Set it is a good idea to make sure you have an updated Emergency Repair Disk. After Volume Set, Stripe Set, or Mirror Set creation, it is also suggested that you create an additional ERD, allowing you to fall back in case an issue might arise.

It is also possible to extend a Volume Set. Instructions are as follows:

1. Launch the Windows NT Disk Administrator.

2. Holding down the Control key, select the Volume Set that you wish to extend, followed by an area of free space on any of your disks.

3. From the Disk Administrator tool bar select Partition, followed by Extend Volume Set. Next, you will be asked to size and confirm the extension.

4. Move to the Disk Administrator tool bar and select the Partitions option, followed by the Commit Changes selection.

5. At this point you will be reminded to update your Emergency Repair Disk and required to reboot your server. Upon reboot, the extended Volume Set will be formatted during the non-GUI portion of the OS initialization. Once the volume creation is complete, Windows NT will boot once again and come back up with the Volume Set intact.

The following summary is a rehash of the guidelines provided in Chapter 5:

- Stripe sets can consist of up to 32 disks or partitions.
- RAID 0, Striping without Parity, provides enhanced performance but no fault tolerance.
- RAID 5, Striping with Parity provides enhanced fault tolerance.
- RAID 5 requires three disks while RAID 1 requires only two.
- RAID 1, or Disk Mirroring, requires two disks.
- RAID 1 can be enhanced by using two disk controllers.
- The boot or system partitions can take part in a Mirror Set.
- The boot or system partitions cannot take part in a Stripe Set.
- In multi-boot configurations, Windows 3.*x*, Windows 95, DOS, and OS/2 are incapable of reading a Volume Set created by Windows NT.
- The boot or system partitions cannot take part in a Volume Set.

15

PROVIDING FAULT TOLERANCE

Hardware-Driven RAID Technology

While software-driven mirroring and striping with parity is an excellent step toward fault tolerance, software solutions still allow for multiple points of failure. For instance, a RAID 0 or RAID 5 Stripe Set are readable only to the Windows NT installation that created them. If for some reason your Windows NT installation were to become corrupt and you had no solid backup or emergency repair disk (while this sounds ugly, it happens!), there would be no way to recover the data in your Stripe Set. The same can be said for a Volume Set. If your installation were to become unrecoverable, your Volume Set would be null and void. Additionally, with software-driven RAID you cannot hot swap failed drives—in other words, if a drive fails you can't simply pull it out of the system and install a new one while the server is still running. For these reasons, it is highly suggested that you consider a hardware-driven RAID system.

All major server vendors today provide RAID solutions. Hardware-driven RAID, which is seamless to your operating system, provides the following advantages:

■ The ability to hot swap failed drives

■ Dynamic growth and regeneration of Stripe Sets

■ The ability to recover failed disks on-the-fly

■ The ability to include your OS in a RAID solution

■ Increased performance

■ Improved server availability

■ Operating system-independent fault tolerance

Most hardware-driven RAID solutions are configured through a BIOS setup program provided from the RAID manufacturer. These solutions allow you to create RAID system drives consisting of multiple physical drives that will appear as a single drive to your operating system. For instance, if you had a Hot Swap RAID cabinet that held seven drives and you installed seven 9 GB drives you could create a single RAID volume that would appear to your operating system as a 63 GB drive. If one of those drives in your RAID set were to fail you would have the ability to pull the dead drive out while the server was running, install a new one, and regenerate the data on-the-fly. The best part is that the user would have no idea!

Windows NT does have limitations as far as drive size is concerned. When utilizing a hardware-driven RAID solution, it is best to create two system drives—one approximately 500 MB for the operating system and another using the remaining space available. Windows NT will install on the first system drive, and once complete, you will have the ability to manipulate the second drive in any manner you please.

> **NOTE**
>
> Creating multiple system drives on your RAID system will not affect RAID performance in any way. Even though you will have two logical drives defined, each volume will still take advantage of all disks in your RAID configuration.

A Case for External RAID

When determining your server design, among the many decisions you will have to make is what type of RAID system you will employ. It goes without saying that if your goal is to provide increased server availability that RAID 5 should be your solution of choice. The question then becomes: Do I purchase the internal RAID solution that my server vendor offers, or should I purchase an external RAID Solution? While the RAID solutions offered by most server vendors will provide the desired effect of increased availability, companies like HP, Compaq, and IBM do not adhere to standard RAID technologies, nor are they in the storage business. Therefore, the following complications can arise:

- Lack of product availability
- Lack of product consistency across lines which results in drive incompatibility from server to server
- Fault tolerant storage unavailable upon server hardware failure
- Incompatibility with other server vendor's solutions
- The inability to reuse your RAID systems upon server redeployment

An external RAID solution can address these issues, as well as provide for increased availability. Companies such as Storage Dimensions that specialize in fault tolerant storage systems provide a consistent product line that will work from server to server, regardless of make or model. Using an external RAID solution provides the following benefits:

- Drive compatibility from model to model.
- Increased product availability.
- A decrease in server cost: All that is required is a processor, memory and network card. External RAID from a third-party vendor usually costs considerably less than those solutions provided by server vendors.
- The ability to reuse your RAID systems upon server redeployment.
- The ability to move your RAID system to a standby server in case of server failure.

Of these benefits, the last is perhaps the most significant. Short of deploying a server clustering or mirroring solution, the ability to move your server's storage from one server to another within a 15-minute period of time is reason enough to deploy an external RAID system. Take the Guardian Domain, for example. Assume that HLT-PROD01 is a Compaq Proliant 800 with

128 MB of RAM and a storage dimensions external RAID solution containing 27 GB of usable disk space. Furthermore, assume that the Guardian Administrators maintain a PCI-based Pentium Desktop with an identical network card as a hot spare server in case of a hardware failure. If at two o'clock in the afternoon the Compaq's power supply were to fail, HLT-PROD01 would be unusable. If the server utilized an internal RAID solution you would have two choices: Maintain an expensive hot spare server (for every different model that you deploy), or wait for your hardware service organization to show up, diagnose the situation, and order parts. Where external RAID is involved, all that will be required to bring the server back online is to pull the RAID card out of the dead server, install it in the hot swap server, plug the external RAID into the hot swap server and turn it on. Within 15 minutes users would be back online and the failed server could be addressed without inconveniencing the users. Alternatively, the hot swap server could have its own RAID card (approximately $1,800.00) and instead of swapping cards, the administrators could simply restore the production server's RAID configuration to the hot swap server using a configuration backup disk. Either way, the server is online within 15 minutes and users are hardly inconvenienced.

Summary

Fault tolerance is a crucial aspect of your enterprise. A solid backup system in combination with server and disk redundancy are important to the success of any environment. While RAID 5 of any kind is a tremendous benefit to your environment, the recommended solution is an external hardware-driven, third-party RAID system that can be standardized on for all servers throughout your enterprise. In addition, while there are many backup solutions available for Windows NT, Seagate's Backup Exec without a doubt meets the needs of your Windows NT–based enterprise.

Advanced Trust Relationships

IN THIS CHAPTER

CHAPTER 16

The trust relationship is one of the few aspects of enterprise networking that can be seen as either an asset to your enterprise or a well-intentioned management nightmare. Competitors such as Novell advertise the complexities of the trust relationship, while extremely large and diverse organizations—which must either interoperate with internal or external business partners, or operate in an extremely diverse environment—have come to view the trust relationship as a much needed tool. The trust relationship is a key player in Windows NT Server's adherence to several of the Key Design Objectives endorsed throughout this book:

- By allowing multiple domains to share the same Domain Directory, the trust relationship adheres to Objective One: A Central User Directory.

- By providing seamless access to outside domains, the trust relationship plays a big part in Objective Three: A Single Logon to All Common Resources.

- As seen in the Master Domain Model, the trust relationship can have a crucial role in Objective Four: An Open and Scalable Design.

The trust relationship has been discussed in brief throughout several chapters of this book and is an integral component in the design and implementation of the intercorporate deployment model. This chapter will explore the trust relationship in detail by providing a definition of the major Windows NT Server domain models, detailing the steps necessary to establish and manage trust relationships, and walk step-by-step through the implementation of the intercorporate domain.

The Domain Models

Before Windows NT Server was introduced, there was only one domain type: the single domain. The single domain provides a way to group users and servers into one directory, allowing users to access multiple resources through a single network logon. While the single domain provides a great deal of functionality for small- to medium-sized organizations, it does not provide a method for users in one domain to access resources in another domain. Traditionally, in order to access resources in an outside domain, the user must maintain multiple logon IDs, which in turn leads to confusion and unnecessary support problems. Through the introduction of the trust relationship, Microsoft has alleviated many of the issues concerning domain interoperability. Through trust relationships, users from one domain can access resources in another domain without requiring an additional logon or the maintenance of multiple logon IDs. Furthermore, through the use of trust relationships, you can design a highly secure enterprise that conforms to the culture and organization of your environment.

There are two types of domains in the trust relationship: trusting and trusted. They are defined as follows:

- The trusted domain is the domain in which the user IDs reside.
- The trusting domain is the domain in which the desired resources reside.

For instance, if through a trust relationship (see Figure 16.1) users from the Mars domain could access resources in the Mercury domain, the Mars domain would be the trusted domain, while the Mercury domain would be the trusting domain.

FIGURE 16.1.

The Trust Relationship.

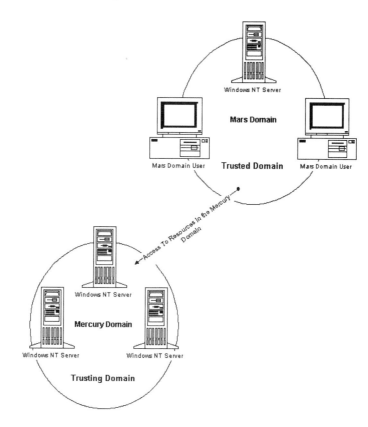

Microsoft has classified four domain types: the single domain, the complete trust domain, the master domain, and the multiple master domain. Of these domain classifications, only the single domain and master domain models are endorsed by this book. However, on a limited basis, the remaining models—the complete trust domain and multiple master domain—do have their place.

Following are definitions for each domain classification:

- **Single domain.** The single domain model, which is the simplest domain model, is the building block for the interdepartmental and the interdivisional domains. In the single domain there is only one domain in which all users and resources exist. There are no trust relationships in the single domain model.

- **Complete trust domain.** The complete trust domain model, shown in Figure 16.2, exists when each domain in the trust relationship is both a trusted and trusting domain. For instance, at this point, users in the Mars domain can access resources in the Mercury domain, but not vice versa. If users in the Mercury domain required access in the Mars domain and another trust relationship were set up, there would be complete trust between the two domains.

Figure 16.2.

The Complete Trust Model.

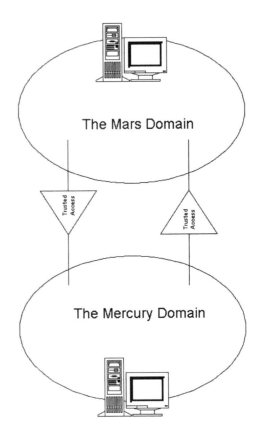

The Mars Domain

The Mercury Domain

■ **Master domain.** The master domain model, which is the basis for the InterCorporate domain, is perhaps the most powerful domain model available. In the master domain model (see Figure 16.3), only one domain maintains a User Directory. All users log into the master domain but access resources in the resource domain. The resource domain, which is nothing more than a trusting domain, maintains divisionally or departmentally specific resources only; no users are defined in these domains. If users need access to resources in other resource domains, there are no additional trust relationships required. Because all user and group accounts are maintained in the master domain, only group membership changes are needed to provide inter-domain access.

FIGURE 16.3.
The Master Domain Model.

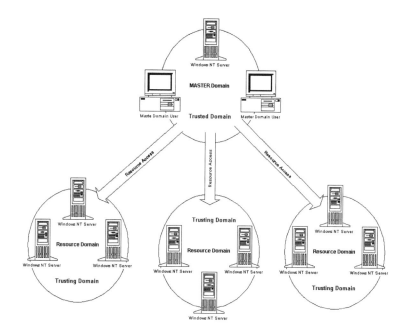

- **Multiple master domains.** The multiple master domains model occurs when resource domains trust more than one master domain. For example, if users defined within the XYZ Corporation's master domain needed access to resources within the ABC Corporation's master domain deployment, it would be necessary for the resource domains within the ABC Corporation to trust the XYZ Corporation's master domain. Therefore, two master domains would now exist for those resource domains. If it became necessary for users in both master domains to access resources in all of the resource domains, each resource domain would have to trust each master domain. Therefore, each resource domain trusts each master domain.

As stated earlier in this chapter and elsewhere in this book, the two most manageable deployments are based on the single domain and master domain models. While it may become necessary to implement a variance of the other domain models, the single and master domain models will offer the greatest functionality. Additionally, when considering the upcoming release of Windows NT Server 5.0 and its new Directory Service, the single and master domain models will provide the most intuitive migration.

Establishing the Trust Relationship

Trust relationships are initiated using the User Manager for Domains. To create a trust relationship, you must first determine which domain is the trusted domain and which domain is the trusting domain. This is generally an easy task. The domain that holds the desired resources is the trusting domain, and the domain that holds the users who need to access the desired resources is the trusted domain.

Part One: Designating the Trusting Domain

Trust relationship creation is a two-part process. While there is no particular requirement, it is easiest to start at the soon-to-be trusted domain when initiating the trust relationship.

1. Launch the User Manager for Domains, and choose Policies in the toolbar.

2. From the Policies drop-down menu, select Trust Relationships to open the Trust Relationships window, as seen in Figure 16.4.

FIGURE 16.4.

The Trust Relationships Window.

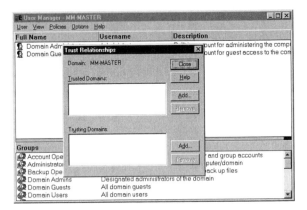

3. Press the Add button next to the Trusting Domains window to launch the Add Trusting Domains window, as seen in Figure 16.5. Here you will enter the name of the domain that holds the desired resources, as well as the password to be used by the trusting domain when it performs its half of the initiation.

FIGURE 16.5.

The Add Trusting Domain Window.

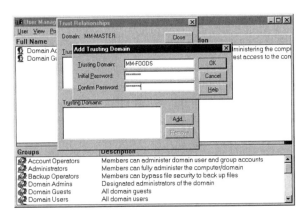

4. Select OK and the domain name will be added to the Trusting Domains window. The first half of the trust creation is now complete.

Part Two: Completing the Trust

1. Using the User Manager for Domains, choose to manage the trusting domain by selecting it from a list of available domains. Once the User Manager is focused on the trusting domain, go to the Policies option of the toolbar and again select Trust Relationships.

2. To finalize the domain's role as a trusting domain, select the Add button next to the Trusted Domains window. You will immediately be presented with a window titled Add Trusted Domain (see Figure 16.6).

FIGURE 16.6.
The Add Trusted Domain Window.

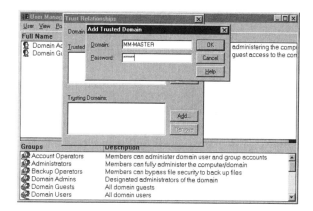

3. At the Add Trusted Domain window, enter the trusted domain's name and the password you determined in the first part of the trust relationship procedure. Select OK, and after a few seconds you will receive a message informing you that the trust relationship has been initiated.

Providing Access to Trusted Users

Creating the trust relationship is just the first part in providing access to trusted users. After the trust relationship has been initiated, users from the trusted domain still cannot get to any resources in the trusting domain. In order for users in the trusted domain to access resources in the trusting domain, one of the following two things must happen:

■ First, a global group from the trusted domain can be added to an existing local group in the trusting domain.

■ Second, a global group from the trusted domain can be directly applied to resources within the trusting domain.

> **CAUTION**
>
> Many people become unnecessarily wary of the trust relationship, believing that after the relationship is initiated, trusted users have full reign over the trusting domain's resources. Other than explicitly granting trusted users access, the only way that users from a trusted domain can access resources in a trusting domain is if the group Everyone has been applied to a resource within the trusting domain. Remember, as stated earlier in this book, the group Everyone really means everyone.

There are generally two reasons that a trust relationship has been initiated. The first reason comes to play when the trusting domain exists as part of a master domain deployment. The second reason, which is slightly more rare, exists when two very separate domains have a specific reason to share resources.

In the master domain scenario, no groups (other than the default) will exist in the resource domains, and therefore global groups will be applied directly to resource domains. In the second instance, chances are that the trusting domain administrator will selectively add trusted users and groups to local groups within his or her domain, and therefore the process will be more time-consuming.

Adding a trusted group directly to a trusting resource is only minutely different from applying rights to users within your own domain. Assume that you need to add a trusted group to the Win32apps share on a trusting server. The following steps must be taken:

1. Launch the Server Manager and select the trusting domain. Select the server you wish to manage and choose Properties from the Shared Directories from the Computer drop-down menu.

2. Next, you will be presented with the Shared Directories window. Select the share you want to add rights to, and click the Properties button.

3. At this point you will be see the Share Properties window, shown in Figure 16.7. Click the Permissions button, and the Access Through Share Permissions Window will launch. To add users from the trusted domain, click the Add button.

FIGURE 16.7.

The Share Properties Window.

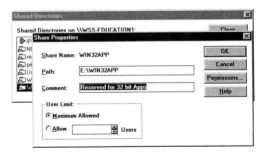

4. You will now be presented with the Add Users and Groups window seen throughout resource management, but there is a difference. Click the List Names From text box at the top of the window and you will see not only the trusting domain listed, but also the trusted domain (see Figure 16.8). Note that the current domain is always specified by an asterisk next to its name.

5. Select the trusted domain, and you will soon be presented with that domain's directory, shown in Figure 16.9. From here, you can apply to the share any specific user or global group that you wish. File and directory level permissions allowing, users from the trusted domain may now access the resources under the Win32app share of the trusting server.

FIGURE 16.8.

The Add Users and Groups Window.

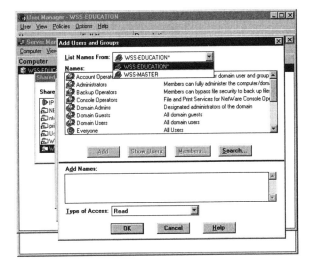

FIGURE 16.9.

The Resource Domain's Directory Listing.

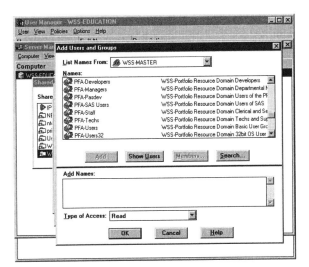

While adding trusted users and groups to local groups within the trusting domain is not terribly difficult, it can be time-consuming. To do so, the following steps must be taken:

1. Launch the User Manger for Domains from within the trusting domain.

2. Select the Local Group to which you wish to add trusted users. Double-click and you will be presented with the Local Group Properties window (see Figure 16.10). Click the Add button to the left side of the Members window and you will be presented with the Add Users and Groups window (see Figure 16.11).

3. From the List Names From text box, select the trusted domain. You will next be presented with a listing of the users and global groups from within the trusted domain. Select the desired users or global group and press Add.

FIGURE 16.10.

The Local Group Properties Window.

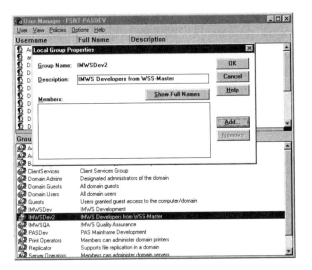

FIGURE 16.11.

The Add Users and Groups Window.

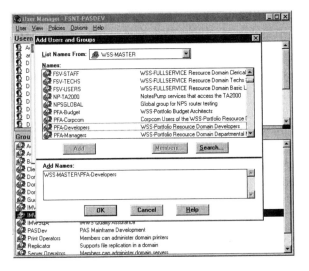

4. Select OK and you will be brought back to the Local Group Properties window. Notice in Figure 16.12 that the global group from the trusted domain is now added to the Members window. At this point, users in the trusted global group can access any resources that your local group has been applied to.

FIGURE 16.12.

The Modified Local Group Properties Window.

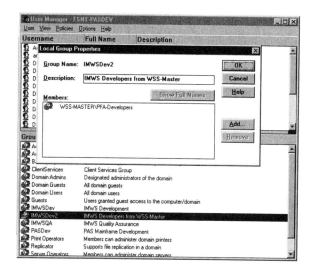

Administering a Resource Domain

In the master domain model, all user accounts are maintained in the master domain, while all resources will reside in the resource domains. When a trust relationship is created, there is no automatic transference of administrative ability from the master domain to the resource domain. In other words, administrators in the master domain do not have automatic authority in the resource domain. After the trust relationship has been created, the following groups must be accounted for:

- Account Operators
- Administrators
- Backup Operators
- Print Operators
- Server Operators

In order to allow users in the master domain to assume the functions represented by these groups in the resource domain, users or global groups from the master domain must be added. For instance, to allow the master domain's Domain Admins administrative privilege in the resource domain, it is necessary to add this group to the local Administrators group as shown in Figure 16.13. After this has been completed, users from the master domain can manage the resource domain without requiring additional authentication.

FIGURE 16.13.

Assigning Administrative Rights in a Resource Domain.

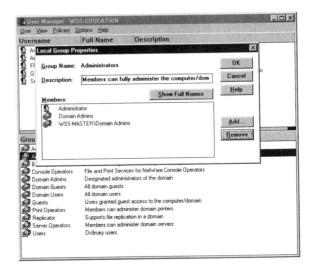

NOTE

A trust can be initiated in any order, but if the trusted domain is added at the trusting domain before the trusted domain initiates its side of the relationship, it could take up to 15 minutes for the relationship to take effect. Additionally, if the trusted domain adds the trusting domain first, when the trusting domain finalizes the trust relationship, the trusted domain's Domain Admins group will automatically be added to the trusting domain's local Administrators group.

Likewise, you must also assign master domain users membership in the resource domain's Account Operators, Backup Operators, Print Operators, and Server Operators groups if you wish to delegate those duties. This process is as simple as adding pre-defined global groups from the master domain to the default local groups in the resource domain. After complete, administration of your resource domains will be seamless.

After you've finished managing group membership, there is still one task to accomplish. Even though your master domain groups have been granted membership in the local groups of your resource domains, no users from your master domain have the ability to log on locally to servers within the resource domain—not even the Domain Admins group. If you wish to allow any master domain groups the right to log on locally to your resource domain servers, you must specifically grant those rights.

To grant a master domain global group the ability to log on locally to your resource domain servers, do the following:

1. Launch the User Manager for Domains.

2. Select Policies from the Policies drop-down menu, followed by User Rights to open the User Rights Policy window.

3. From the text box titled Right, select Log on Locally (see Figure 16.14). Notice that only the Administrators, Backup Operators, Print Operators, and Server Operators have the right to log on locally. Even though you've applied global groups from your master domain to these local groups, you still do not have the right to log on locally.

4. To add global groups from the master domain, click the Add button and open the familiar Add Users and Groups window. Choose the desired global groups from your master domain, and select OK. You will be brought back to the User Rights Policy window with your changes added to the list of users granted Log on Locally rights (see Figure 16.15). After you select OK, those users you selected will have the ability to log on locally to any server within the resource domain.

FIGURE 16.14.
The User Rights Policy Window.

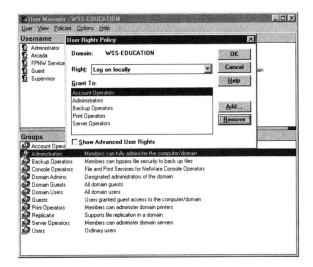

FIGURE 16.15.
The Modified User Rights Policy Window.

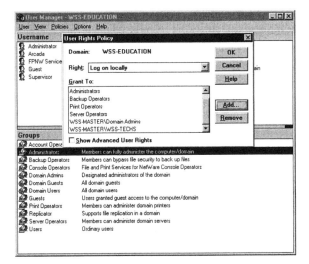

Implementing the InterCorporate Model

Much like the interdepartmental and interdivisional models take the single domain model and build on it by providing guidelines for structure and standardization, the intercorporate model takes the master domain model a step further by providing structure and standardization to an extremely large and diverse environment. Many of the issues concerning the implementation of the intercorporate domain have been dealt with in earlier chapters, but the following issues either bear repeating or have not yet been covered:

- Initiating the Trust Relationships
- Applying Administrative Rights to the Resource Domains
- Managing Servers within a Resource Domain
- Logging into the Master Domain
- Logging into the InterCorporate Domain from an NT Workstation

Creating the Trust Relationships

McMac Industries is made up of a master domain (MM-MASTER) and three resource domains. By nature, each domain will require a primary domain controller, but only the master domain will require backup domain controllers—one in each location. Much like the interdivisional domain, servers will follow group naming conventions. Therefore, the resource domains production servers and primary domain controllers will be named as follows:

Domain	Division	Production Server/PDC
MM-Foods	McMac Foods	MMF-PROD01
MM-Paper	Watterson Paper	WTP-PROD01
MM-Salt	Jansen Salt	JNS-PROD01

Much like the interdivisional domain it is a good idea to dedicate a primary domain controller in the intercorporate's master domain, and there is little choice but to dedicate backup domain controllers in the master domain for each location. The master domain controllers could follow the enterprise naming conventions (MME), but the MM-MASTER administrators have chosen to name their domain controllers MMI-MASTER1, MMI-MASTER2, MMI-MASTER3, and MMI-MASTER4.

After creating the primary domain controllers for each resource domain, as well as for the master domain, the next step in creating the master domain model is the initiation of trust relationships. In the master domain model, only the master domain is a trusted domain, while all other domains are trusting. To initiate the trust relationships within the InterCorporate model, the following steps must be taken:

1. From the master domain, launch the User Manager for Domains and choose Policies in the toolbar.

2. Within the Policies drop-down menu, select Trust Relationships and you will be presented with the Trust Relationships window as seen in Figure 16.4.

3. Click the Add button next to the Trusting Domains window to launch the Add Trusting Domains window as seen in Figure 16.16.

FIGURE 16.16.

Designating Resource Domains.

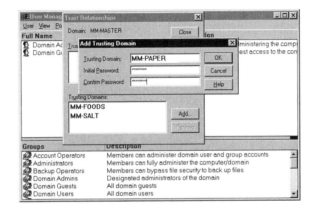

4. To designate the MM-FOODS, MM-SALT, and MM-PAPER domains as resource domains, enter each name and an appropriate password for each. After you've entered the domain name, select OK and the resource domain will be added to the Trusting Domains window.

5. Go to the first resource domain (for this example, the MM-FOODS domain). Using the User Manager for Domains, go to the Policies option of the toolbar and again select Trust Relationships.

6. To finalize the domain's role as a resource domain, select the Add button next to the window titled Trusted Domains. You will immediately be presented with a window entitled Add Trusted Domain (see Figure 16.17).

7. At the Add Trusted Domain window, enter the master domain's name (MM-MASTER) and the password you determined when designating your resource domains. Select OK, and after a few seconds you will receive a message informing you that the trust relationship has been initiated.

8. Repeat steps 5 through 7 for each resource domain.

After you have completed these steps, all required trust relationships will have been initiated. It is now time to delegate administrative authority.

FIGURE 16.17.

Finalizing the Creation of the Resource Domain.

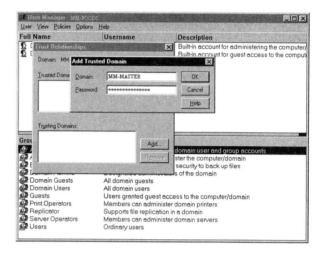

Applying Administrative Rights to the Resource Domains

After your trust relationships have been initiated, it is time to delegate administrative authority. Remember that when a trusting domain finalizes the trust relationship with a trusted domain, the trusted domain's global group, Domain Admins, automatically becomes a member of the resource domain's local Administrators group. Due to this fact, the McMac Standards committee has determined that only one person from each division should become a member of the master domain's Domain Admins group, while the following groups will be created and applied to the appropriate domain's Administrators group:

MMI-Admins	MMI-Master Domain Administrators
MMF-Admins	MM-Foods Resource Domain Administrators
WTP-Admins	MM-Paper Resource Domain Administrators
JNS-Admins	MM-Salt Resource Domain Administrators

Each of these groups will be granted membership in the Account Operators and Server Operators groups in the master domain (see Figure 16.18). Remember that the Account Operators group can manage all domain user account properties (excluding those of users who have membership in the following groups: Administrators, Domain Admins, Server Operators, or Account Operators), and the Server Operators group can manage all domain servers. These groups will provide the resource domain administrators with the ability to manage servers and users in the master domain, but because both of these groups are local, will not provide them any automatic rights in the resource domains. In order to provide these Resource Domain Admins supervisory rights in the appropriate resource domains (see Figure 16.19), they must be added to the respective local Administrators groups as follows:

■ The MMI-Admins group will be granted membership in the Account Operators and Server Operators groups.

- The MMF-Admins group will be granted membership in the MM-Foods Administrators group.

- The WTP-Admins group will be granted membership in the MM-Paper Administrators group.

- The JNS-Admins group will be granted membership in the MM-Salt Administrators group.

FIGURE 16.18.

Applying Administrative Rights in the Master Domain.

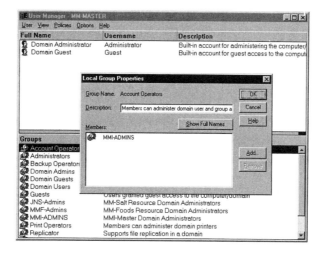

FIGURE 16.19.

Applying Administrative Rights in the Resource Domain.

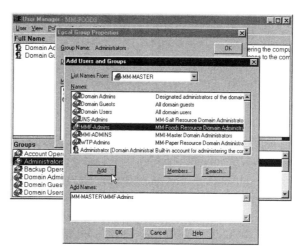

After you have completed these steps, each resource domain's administrators will have enough rights to successfully perform their jobs without comprising security or authority in their companion resource domains.

> **NOTE**
>
> This method of delegating authority in resource domains is very extreme. It is not at all unheard of or antithetical to simply make all resource domain administrators members of the master domain's Domain Admins group and apply that group to each resource domain's local Administrators group.

In addition to domain administrators, each resource domain will have its own group of dedicated network technicians, while all support organizations will share the same help desk. The support groups have been created as follows:

MME-HelpDesk	MM-Master Enterprise Help Desk Personnel
MMI-NetTech	MM-Master Domain Network Technicians
MMF-NetTech	MM-Foods Resource Domain Network Technicians
WTP-NetTech	MM-Paper Resource Domain Network Technicians
JNS-NetTech	MM-Salt Resource Domain Network Technicians

It has been determined that the MME-HelpDesk will be added to the Print Operators group in each resource domain and that each network technician will be added to the Print Operators group in their respective resource domains. Furthermore, each resource domain's Network Technician group will be added as server operators in their resource domains and granted Log On Locally rights. After finished, authority delegation will have been successfully completed.

Managing Servers within a Resource Domain

As you've seen throughout this book, and as you'll see in detail in Chapter 19, "Supporting Windows NT Server," the Server Manager is a key tool in managing your Windows NT Server servers. The Server Manager facilitates the following management functions:

- The creation and management of shared directories including share level permissions
- Service management including starting, stopping, and startup modification
- The management of user connections, shared directory use, and files currently in use
- The addition and removal of Windows NT machines from the domain
- Forced Domain Synchronization

Many of the management features provided by the Server Manager are remote interfaces of those tools that exist locally on servers and workstations. However, all users in the InterCorporate model will utilize the master domain as their logon domain; therefore, each time the Server Manger is launched, they will be presented only with the servers and workstations in the Master Domain. In order to manage a resource domain simply select Computer from the Server Manager's toolbar, followed by Select Domain (see Figure 16.20).

FIGURE 16.20.

*Selecting an Alternative
Domain to Manage.*

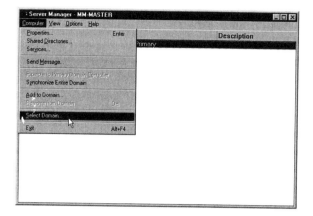

You will soon be presented with a list of available domain's on your network (see Figure 16.21). Choose the resource domain you wish to manage, and assuming that rights have been correctly applied to the Resource Domain Directory, you will have full management functionality.

FIGURE 16.21.

*Viewing the List of
Alternative Domains.*

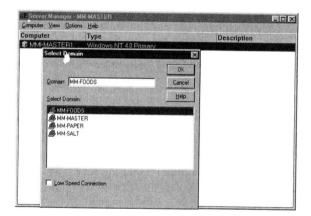

Logon Scripts and Logging On to the Master Domain

Any user that exists in the InterCorporate domain will log in to the master domain. Because there are no user IDs maintained in the resource domains (other than the default Administrator, Guest, and any Service Users), there is no way a user could log on to a resource domain. This confuses some people, and in those cases it is best explained like this: The resource domain is nothing more than an organizational unit designed to organize a department or division's resources into an easily navigated container. The next question usually is "If I log in to the master domain, how do I get to my resources?" And the answer is no different from that in any of the other deployment models: through logon scripts and through navigating the Network Neighborhood.

Logon scripts have common elements throughout all of the deployment models. Much like there are basic elements common to all logon scripts in the InterDepartmental and InterDivisional deployments, there will be common elements in each resource domain's divisional or departmental logon scripts. For instance, all users in the MM-MASTER deployment, regardless of which resource domain they work in, will receive the letter H:\ for their Home Directories, I:\ for their Departmental Directories, O:\ for their Applications Directories and S:\ for their DFS Directories. Additionally, all servers will have the same Directory and Share conventions, leading to a great deal of standardization throughout the deployment.

It is important that all end users receive the same drive mapping for the same resources from resource domain to resource domain. For instance, if a user in the MM-FOODS resource domain calls the Help Desk to inquire about issues with their I:\ drive, that Help Desk representative will know automatically that the I:\ drive is where all applications are stored—regardless of which resource domain the user is from.

Adding NT Workstations to the InterCorporate Deployment

Windows NT Workstations, much like stand-alone Windows NT Servers, must be added to the domain before they will be allowed to logon using an ID from the Domain Directory. In the InterDepartmental and InterDivisional domains, there is only one domain to join; however in the InterCorporate Domain, an NT Workstation can be added to the master domain or to any of the resource domains and still be able to log on to the master domain. It is recommended that you add Windows NT Workstations in their respective resource domains; thus, users will be organized with their proper resources when browsing the network.

After joining the domain, the Windows NT Workstation will be configured to log on to the resource domain by default. To log on to the master domain simply click the down arrow next to the Domain text box, and you will be presented with a drop-down box listing your local workstation name, your resource domain's name, and your master domain's name. Choose the master domain and log on using your Master Domain ID.

Summary

Much like the InterDepartmental and InterDivisional models take the single domain model and build on it by providing guidelines for structure and standardization, the InterCorporate model takes the master domain model a step further by providing structure and standardization to an extremely large and diverse environment. Through the use of the trust relationship, and the master domain model, adherence to the following Key Design Objectives endorsed throughout this book are made possible:

- Objective One: A Central User Directory
- Objective Three: A Single Logon to All Common Resources
- Objective Four: An Open and Scalable Design

Combining the design principles found in the InterDepartmental and InterDivisional groups with the power of the master domain model, the InterCorporate deployment is an easily managed and scaleable enterprise.

Domain
Documentation

IN THIS CHAPTER

CHAPTER

17

Domain documentation is one of the most critical pieces of a successful enterprise environment. Unfortunately, short of fault tolerance, good documentation is also one of the most ignored components of a successful enterprise. Solid Domain documentation can provide the following features:

- Guidelines for On Call Support
- Orientation for New Support Personnel
- A Blueprint for Future Growth
- Guidelines for Disaster Recovery
- Training Material for Employees
- Material for Domain Security Analysis
- Process Documentation

At this time, there are no standards in Domain documentation, so in most organizations it is up to the network administrator to determine what should be documented and in what manner. Unfortunately, in many cases the network administrator doesn't have the time. This chapter will provide guidelines for Domain documentation on a component-by-component basis. If you follow the guidelines laid out in this chapter, the end result should be a network manual customized for your environment. This manual, which should be considered a living document and should be updated on a monthly basis, will not necessarily provide a seamless blueprint of your domain, but will be a step in the right direction.

Server Documentation by Domain

Disaster recovery, capacity planning, and new personnel orientation are just a few of the reasons that your servers should be documented. The biggest dilemma with server documentation are the questions of what information should be included and in what format it should be written.

Server documentation can be broken down into at least six categories:

- Hardware Configuration
- Operating System Configuration
- Disks, Partitions, and Volumes
- Normal Running State
- Primary Contact
- Vendor Support Numbers

As far as format is concerned, what is most important is that the same format be used for each server. Following is an example of the server documentation that will be utilized in the Guardian Domain—the interdivisional deployment example used throughout this book.

Category	*Server Identification*
Server Name	CORP-PROD01
Domain	Guardian
Primary Purpose	Production Server for the Corporate Benefits Division
Server Location	12849 W. 103rd, 4th Floor Computer Room
Client Base	Corporate Benefits Division of the Guardian Insurance Companies

Category	*Hardware Configuration*
Vendor Model	Compaq Proliant 800 Dual Pentium Pro Model One (200MHz)
Memory Config	128 MB of RAM (4 x 32MB ECC SIMMS)
Serial Number	874Y4392
Network Card	HP DeskDirect PCI 100 VG AnyLAN (Quantity Two)
Storage Configuration	Storage Dimensions SuperFlex 3000 External Disk Array (S/N 1780239x7)
	Quantity Five 9 Gigabyte Hot Swap Drives
	Disks 0,1,2, & 3 configured as System Drive
	Disk 4 configured as Hot Spare
	Two System Drives:
	Drive 1 = 500MB
	Dive 2 = 36,384MB
Peripheral Devices	15" Samsung SyncMaster 4ne
	Compaq Keyboard
	Compaq Mouse

Category	*Operating System Configuration*
Operating System	Windows NT Server 4.0 (Service Pack 2)
System Root	C:\WINNTSRV\
Protocols	TCP/IP Address One: 195.102.78.33
	TCP/IP Address Two: 195.102.78.34
Additional Services	Distributed File System
	SNMP Agent
Configuration Notes	Bootable to Windows 95 DOS. Contains Microsoft Network Client that can be used to gain access to TCP/IP resources via DHCP.

17

DOMAIN
DOCUMENTATION

Category	Disks, Partitions, and Volumes
Physical Disks	Two physical RAID 5 volumes
	Drive 1 = 500 MB
	Drive 2 = 36,384 MB
Disk 1	Formatted Fat 500 MB
	Contains Windows NT System Files, Win95 DOS and Microsoft Network Client
Disk 2	Partition One: 2, 096MB NTFS Apps Volume
	Partition Two: 2, 0096 MB NTFS Support Volume
	Partition Three: 16,384 MB NTFS Data Volume
	Free Space: 15,788 MB

Category	Normal Running State
Compaq Proliant 800	Powered on with default Windows NT Screen Saver
SDI RAID Cabinet	Both Power Supplies powered on, five drives in the seven-bay cabinet with one inactive

Category	Support Information
Primary Contact	Dexter Burch
	Pager: 555-6782
	Extension: 55293
	Home Phone: 555-6839
Secondary Contact	Greg Ledom
	Pager: 555-1024
	Extension: 0524
	Home Phone: 555-0817
Vendor Support Numbers	Compaq: 1-800-555-6272
	Storage Dimensions: 1-800-555-3322
	Microsoft: 1-800-555-BILL

This document, which will be created for each server in the Guardian Domain and distributed to all support personnel, can be used as a form of reference for capacity planning, network inventory, and as an on-call reference in case of server failure. It is also an excellent reference for any new support personnel, especially those who will be involved in network administration or engineering.

User Directory Documentation

User directory documentation should be maintained less for disaster recovery purposes and more for personnel orientation and design guidelines. User directory documentation should contain at a minimum the following information:

- Divisional Groups
- Departmental Groups
- Cross-Divisional Groups
- Enterprise Groups
- User Templates

In addition, each of the preceding bulleted items should be provided with a description and any guidelines as far as convention and growth are concerned. The following document, which is an example of user directory documentation, will begin with broad domain coverage of the Guardian Domain, but provide detail for only the casualty division. The Guardian Domain is the interdivisional deployment example used throughout this book.

USER DIRECTORY DOCUMENTATION AND EXPANSION GUIDELINES FOR THE GUARDIAN DOMAIN

Last Modified: February 18, 1997

Document Objective: To provide both a reference for the existing User Directory and guidelines for future user deployment.

Directory Design Basics: The Guardian Domain's User Directory is broken down into four organizational categories:

- Enterprise Groups
- Divisional Groups
- Departmental Groups
- Cross-Divisional Groups

These groups are defined as follows:

Group	Definition
Enterprise Groups	Enterprise Groups are groups specifically dedicated to particular enterprise resources. To be considered an enteprise resource, a resource must not be bound by departmental or divisional ties; rather, it should be a resource that can and will be accessed by any user from any division within the Domain. Each enterprise resource will have a dedicated Enterprise Group.

continues

continued

Group	Definition
Divisional Groups	The Domain is broken down into organizational units called Divisions. A Division directly corresponds to a business unit within the Guardian Insurance Companies, and therefore, the Divisional Group is the base user group for all users within a division. If a user works for Guardian Health, his or her Divisional group will be dedicated to Guardian Health. Likewise, if a user is an employee of Guardian Casualty, his or her Divsional Group will be that dedicated to Casualty. All users, with the exception of support personnel, should be members of the appropriate Divisional group. This group will be granted access to all resources that are common to a particular Division. The Divisional Group is in essence equivalent to an Organizational Unit in X.500 terminology.
Departmental Groups	Departmental Groups are groups that have been dedicated to the individual departments within a Division. Each Divisional department will have its own Departmental group. Departmental groups will be applied to those resources that are specific to its users needs.
Cross-Divisional Groups	Cross Divisional Groups are created when members from one Division need access to resources within another division. If a resource needs to be accessed by more than two divisions, the division should then be considered an Enteprise group. In terms of Cross-Divisional Group deployment, the owner of the resource in question should be the owner of the Cross-Divisional Group.

Group Names should contain both a prefix and a suffix. The prefix should indicate if the group was designed as a Divisional Group (or a departmental group under that) or as an Enterprise Group. Suffixes are defined as follows:

Organization	Prefix	Explanation
Guardian Health Insurance	HLT	This prefix represents all departmental and Cross-Divisional Groups hosted from within the Guardian Health Insurance Division.

Organization	Prefix	Explanation
Guardian Corporate Benefits	CORP	This prefix represents all departmental and Cross-Divisional Groups hosted from within the Guardian Corporate Benefits Division.
Guardian Casualty	CTY	This prefix represents all departmental and Cross-Divisional Groups hosted from within the Guardian Casualty Division.
Guardian Headquarters	HQ	This prefix represents all Departmental and Cross-Divisional Groups hosted from within the Guardian Headquarters Division shall have a prefix of HQ.
Enterprise Group	GRD	Signifies that the group is an Enterprise Group. The suffix should be describe the resource that the group is dedicated to.

The following groups exist in the User Directory as of February 18, 1997:

Enterprise Groups:

Design Note: All Enterprise Groups will be preceded with a prefix of GRD. If you have a resource that will be accessed by more than two Divisions, it should be classified as an Enterprise Resource, and therefore have a dedicated Enterprise Group.

GRD-CBTSystems	Computer Based Training to be provided to all Guardian Personnel
GRD-MGRBenefits	HR Benefits Documentation to be shared with Guardian Managers
GRD-Proxy	Provides access to the Guardian Proxy server for WAN based Internet Access
GRD-EMAIL	Provides access to the Guardian Domain's e-mail system

Divisional Groups:

Design Note: Divisional Groups are to be added only if Guardian acquires an additional operational unit. Divisional Group design should only be modified with the consensus of all Network Administrators. The Divisional Group is the base group for each corporate Division.

HQ-Users	Users of the Guardian Domain from Guardian HQ
HLT-Users	Users of the Guardian Domain from Guardian Health
CORP-Users	Users of the Guardian Domain from Guardian Corporate Benefits
CTY-Users	Users of the Guardian Domain from Guardian Casualty

continues

17

DOMAIN DOCUMENTATION

continued

Divisional Breakdown:

Following is a breakdown of the Guardian Casualty Division by:

- Divisional Group
- Departmental Group
- Cross-Divisional Group

Guardian Casualty's Divisional Group:

CTY-Users   Users of the Guardian Domain from Guardian Casualty

Guardian Casualty's Departmental Groups:

Design Note: These groups are designed to provide secure access to department-specific resources at the NTFS level. Provide membership to these groups only to the appropriate users within the Casualty Division.

CTY-Accounting   CTY-Accounting Users of the Guardian Domain

CTY-Marketing   CTY-Marketing Users of the Guardian Domain

CTY-Admin   CTY-Administrative Users of the Guardian Domain

Guardian Casualty's Cross-Divisional Groups:

Design Note: These groups are designed to provide access to Guardian Casualty resources on a need-only basis. If more than one outside Division needs access to this resource, create an Enterprise Group.

CTY-HQprofiles   Guardian HQ Human Resource users requiring access to Casualty Job Profiles

Guardian Casualty User Templates:

Users in the Guardian Domain have been categorized by user components in order to organize user needs into logical groups. Once this needs categorization is organized, they are then grouped and a Template is created. User Templates provide at least two important roles:

- Templates eliminate the need to create users from scratch each time an employee joins the company
- User Templates enforce security and environment variable conventions

The categories that make a User Template include the following:

- Group Membership
- Logon Script Assignment
- Home Directory Assignment
- Logon Restrictions
- Dialin Permissions

In addition to using User Templates for creation and organizational enforcement, the Guardian Domain has also set User Naming standards. Naming standards are as follows:

Logon ID: All users shall use their Social Security Numbers as their logon ID.

Full Name: All user full names shall be entered in the Last Name, First Name format.

As of February 18, 1997, the Guardian Casualty Division has only three User Templates as follows:

User Name: User Element	Description
Template Created For	Guardian Casualty Users in the Accounting Department
Template Name	T-CTY-ACCTG
Template Full Name	Template, User
Template Group Membership	CTY-Users
	CTY-Accounting
	GRD-EMAIL
Template Logon Script	CTYACCTG.BAT
Template Home Directory Path	\\CTY-PROD01\DATA\USERS\ %USERNAME%
Template Logon Hour Restrictions	Monday through Friday, 9 pm to 2 am
Dialin Permissions	None

User Element	Description
Template Created For	Guardian Casualty Users in the Accounting Department
Template Name	T-CTY-ACCTG
Template Full Name	Template, User
Template Group Membership	CTY-Users
	CTY-Marketing
	GRD-EMAIL
	GRD-Proxy
Template Logon Script	CTYMRKT.BAT
Template Home Directory Path	\\CTY-PROD01\DATA\USERS\ %USERNAME%
Template Logon Hour Restrictions	Monday through Friday, 9 pm to 2 am
Dialin Permissions	None

continues

continued

User Element	Description
Template Created For	Guardian Casualty Administrative Users
Template Name	T-CTY-ADMIN
Template Full Name	Template, User
Template Group Membership	CTY-Users
	CTY-Admin
	GRD-EMAIL
	CTY-Hqprofiles
Template Logon Script	CTYADMN.BAT
Template Home Directory Path	\\CTY-PROD01\DATA\USERS\%USERNAME%
Template Logon Hour Restrictions	Monday through Friday, 9 pm to 2 am
Dialin Permissions	None

To create a user using the User Templates, launch the User Manager for Domains and copy the desired User Template. Be sure to adhere to Guardian User Naming conventions.

Design Note: If a new environmental variable which affects User Template components is introduced into the environment be sure to modify the User Template accordingly!

The main thrust of the User Directory documentation presented up to this point has been to serve as both orientation material and a design guideline for new and existing administrative personnel. The next section will provide a format for documenting the application of the users and groups that exist in your User Directory to your Domain resources.

Domain Security

The application of domain security is serious business. It is important to maintain a list of those users with advanced rights, including but not limited to administrators, account operators, service IDs, and backup operators. In addition, it is helpful to maintain a list of shares per server and the groups that have access to them. The following section will provide examples for domain security documentation.

DOMAIN SECURITY DOCUMENTATION FOR THE GUARDIAN DOMAIN

Last Modified: February 18, 1997

Document Objective: To provide a reference for the implementation of Domain Security

This document should be used to document the application of Domain Security equivalencies and Domain Security to server-based shares.

In addition to Share documentation, the following information will be listed for the Guardian Domain:

- Domain Administrators
- Administrators
- Account Operators
- Server Operators
- Backup Operators
- Users with Logon Locally Rights
- Users with Logon as a Service Right

The following table lists users with advanced security equivalencies:

Security Equivalent	User Name	Full Name
Administrator	510451121	Burch, Dexter
	478444930	Kramer, Cosmo
	521429029	Ledom, Greg
	501342234	Rice, Lucy
	498550021	Rutledge, Bill
Domain Administrator	510451121	Burch, Dexter
	478444930	Kramer, Cosmo
	521429029	Ledom, Greg
	501342234	Rice, Lucy
	498550021	Rutledge, Bill
Account Operators	492543331	Trees, Greg
	508984728	Thomas, Mike
	509393939	Plescia, Frank
	509875393	Miller, Linda
	478394505	Donahue, Cheryl
	501293948	Duffy, Peggy
	510394674	Maclandsborough, Russ
	503949589	Riggs, Scott
Backup Operators	BE-611	Exec, Backup
Server Operators	510394674	Maclandsborough, Russ
	503949589	Riggs, Scott
Users with Logon Locally Rights	BE-611	Exec, Backup

continues

17

DOMAIN DOCUMENTATION

continued

Security Equivalent	User Name	Full Name
Users with Logon as a Service Rights	BE-611	Exec, Backup

Design Note: All network technicians are by default given membership in the Account Operators Groups. Additionally, senior Network Technicians are given membership in the Server Operators Group.

Following is a breakdown of shares by server and the rights that have been applied:

HTN-PROD01

UNC Path	Share Name	Groups	Rights
\\CTY-PROD01\APPS	Apps	CTY-USERS GRD-TECHS Domain Admins	Change Change Full Control
\\CTY-PROD01\DATA	Data	CTY-USERS HQ-USERS GRD-TECHS Domain Admins	Change Change Change Full Control
\\CTY-PROD01\SUPPORT	Support$	GRD-TECHS Domain Admins	Change Full Control
\\CTY-PROD01\CTY-DFS1	CTY-DFS1	CTY-USERS GRD-TECHS Domain Admins	Change Change Full Control
\\CTY-PROD01\SUPPORT\ CLIENTS	Clients$	GRD-TECHS Domain Admins	Change Full Control

The remainder of the Domain Security documentation will go on to list each server throughout the domain and list all shares and their permissions. In environments that have deployed the InterCorporate model, servers should be documented in terms of Resource Domains.

NOTE

Somarsoft, Incorporated sells a product titled DumpACL which can be obtained from the Somarsoft Web site at http:\\www.somarsoft.com. DumpACL has the capability to query your server for a wide variety of security settings, including Share permissions, NTFS permissions, User Directory information, Domain Policies, and Domain Service rights, and dump that information into an ASCII delimited text file. Once the file is created, it can be imported into Access (or any such database application) and used for Security documentation purposes, security analysis, and training material. DumpACL is a highly recommended application that at first seems terribly simple, but in reality has a great deal of possibility.

Standards Documentation

In addition to Domain documentation, it is important to document your application and deployment standards, including:

- Applications & Installation Instructions
- Operating Systems & Installation Instructions
- Protocols & Installation Instructions
- Enterprise Resource Documentation

This type of documentation would be an excellent source for training material for new and existing employees. The following document will provide an overview of what brief look at the Standards Documentation in the Guardian Domain.

DOMAIN STANDARDS DOCUMENTATION FOR THE GUARDIAN DOMAIN

Last Modified: February 18, 1997

Application and Operating System Standard:

The following table lists the application, operating system and protocol standards for the Guardian Domain as of February 18, 1997:

Category	Standardization
Network Operating System	Windows NT Server 4.0
Desktop Operating System	Windows NT Workstation 4.0
	Windows 95 for laptop users
Office Automation Application Suite	Microsoft Office 7.0
Enterprise Mail System	cc:Mail (Migrating to Lotus Notes)
Enteprise Groupware Solution:	Lotus Notes
3270 Connectivity Solution	Microsoft SNA Gateway 3.0
	Attachmate Extra! for SNA Server
Internet Browser	Microsoft Internet Explorer
Remote Access Connectivity	Shiva Lan Rover
	Citrix Winframe
User Naming Standards	Social Security Number for User ID
Server Naming Standards	Prefix-Suffix format:
	Prefix = 3 letter code for Guaridan Division
	Suffix = Description of server function
Protocol Standard	Netbios over TCP/IP

continues

continued

Guardian Directory Structure Standards:

Following is a list of standard applications installation directories for all users in the Guardian Domain.

Document Convention: x:\ = appropriate drive letter based on hardware capacity

Operating Systems:

      Windows 95 = x:\Win95

      Windows NT Workstation: = x:\Winntwrk

      Windows NT Server: = x:\Winntsrv

Hard Drive Root Structure:

      16-Bit Apps: = x:\Win16app

      32-Bit Apps: = x:\Win32app

Application Directory Structure:

      Extra! For SNA Server 32-Bit = x:\win32app\Ep!sna32

      Extra Personal Client 32-Bit = x:\win32app\Extra32

      MS SNA Client 32: = x:\win32app\SNA32

      MS Office Pro 7.0 = x:\win32app\MSOffice

      Lotus Notes - 32bit = x:\win32ap\notes

      cc:Mail = x:\win16app\ccmail & x:\win16app\ccmail\data

      Microsoft DOS Client = x:\MSNet

Product Installation Documentation:

The installation procedure for the following software should be the identical from machine to machine:

- Microsoft SNA Server Client
- Attachmate Extra! for SNA Server
- Lotus Notes
- cc:Mail
- Microsoft Office
- NetBIOS over TCP/IP

Procedure # 1: SNA Server and Extra! Installation

In order to access an SNA Server it is first necessary to install the Microsoft SNA Client software. This software is available in the the 32-bit version for both Windows NT and Windows 95 (\\%ServerName%\\Win32App\MS-SNA32\).

Windows NT Workstation 3.51 or 4.0:

1. Go to the appropriate application directory and run Setup.

2. You will be prompted for an installation directory. Type
   `\\%LocalDrive%\Win32app\SNA32` and press Enter.

3. After choosing the installation directory, you will be brought to a screen labled Select Client/Server Protocol for Client Setup. Once here, choose TCP/IP as your protocol.

4. Next, you will be prompted for the SNA Domain type. Your logon domain is the GUARDIAN Domain, but your SNA Server resides in the GRD-SNA1 Domain. Therefore, choose Remote Domain.

5. After selecting Remote Domain, you will be prompted for the name of your Primary and Secondary SNA Servers. These Servers are GRD-SNA01 & GRD-SNA02.

6. You will next be presented with a page titled Optional Components. Please select the ODBC drivers & 3270 Applet only. The other options will lend no functionality.

7. Next, files will be copied to your machine, and upon completion you will be notified that the Client Software was installed succesfully. Even though you are not prompted to do so, reboot your machine. If you do not, your system might encounter serious problems.

Windows 95:

1. Go to the appropriate application directory and run Setup.

2. Next you will be prompted for an installation directory. Choose
   \\%LocalDrive%\Program Files\SNA95.

3. After choosing the installation directory, you will be prompted for the Installation Type - Complete or Custom. Choose Custom and select only the ODBC & 3270 options.

4. After agreeing with the license agreeement, you will be brought to a screen labled Select Client/Server Protocol. Once here, choose TCP/IP as your protocol.

5. Next, you will be prompted for the SNA Domain type. Your logon domain is the GUARDIAN Domain, but your SNA Server resides in the GRD-SNA1 Domain. Therefore, choose Remote Domain.

6. After selecting Remote Domain, you will be prompted for the name of your Primary and Secondary SNA Servers. These Servers are GRD-SNA01 & GRD-SNA02.

7. Next, files will be copied to your machine, and upon completion you will be notified that the Client Software was installed succesfully. Even though you are not prompted to do so, reboot your machine. If you do not, your system might encounter serious problems.

Once the SNA Client Software has been installed, it is necessary to install a 3270 Emulator. The GUARDIAN Standard application for 3270 access is Attachmate's Extra! for SNA Server.

17

DOMAIN DOCUMENTATION

This application is available in both the 16-bit version (\\%ServerName%\Win16App\Ep!sna16) and the 32-bit version (\\%ServerName%\Win32App\Ep!sna32). This application provides advanced functionality and is fully supported by Winchester Support Services. Installation instructions follow:

Windows NT Workstation 4.0 & 3.51 as well as Windows 95:

1. Go to the appropriate installation directory and run Setup. This will install a client/server version of the software, requiring only minimal PC disk space.

2. Continue through the Welcome, License Agreement, and User Name screens until you are requested to input an installation directory. Choose the path \\%LocalDrive%\Win32app\Ep!SNA32. Files will be copied to your machine and you will be told that installation was successful. Please reboot your machine at this point.

3. Once your machine has rebooted, go into the Extra! Program group and launch Extra!. A small screen will appear prompting you to Create or Launch existing sessions. Choose Creating a New Session.

4. A new screen will appear asking you the connection type. Choose Microsoft SNA Server. Next, you will be presented with a configuration screen. On one side of the screen you will see your assigned LUs or LU Pools greyed out. On the lower left-hand side of the screen is a check box labled Connect to Any Resource. Uncheck this box, and select the first of your available resources. Click Add and then Next.

5. You will now be presented with options for File Transfer Type. IND$FILE is recommended. After choosing your transfer type select finish.

6. Once you have finished configuration, Extra! will launch. If you have more than one available LU, you must create a session for each one. To create more sessions, go to File in the upper-left corner, and select New Session. You will then be brought back to the Creating a New Session screen from step 3.

7. Once you have created your sessions, you will be prompted to save them before you exit. Please do so.

8. Next, you will be asked once again if you would like to create a new session or launch an existing session. If you want to place shortcuts to individual sessions on your desktop, simply create a new icon or a shortcut pointing to the session you have created. Upon clicking it, it will launch Extra! directly into the appropriate session.

Installation Procedure # 2: NetBIOS over TCP/IP Installation

Dynamic TCP/IP will automatically configure your workstation to connect to all true TCP/IP resources throughout the Enterprise. As long as the host address of the machine you're attempting to connect to is entered in the Domain Name Server, you will be able to make a TCP/IP connection. Furthermore, with the installation of DHCP you will be able to configure your Notes users for TCP/IP connectivity, alleviating the stress that NetBEUI causes both the Network and the Notes Servers.

Microsoft clients will receive the following information from the DHCP Server:

- Domain Name
- Subnet Mask
- TCP/IP Address
- Domain Name Server Addresses
- Default Gateway
- WINS Server addresses

The remainder of this document will describe the steps necessary to install DHCP Windows 95, and Windows NT 4.0 Workstation.

Windows 95:

1. Ensure that you have access to the Windows 95 installation CD-ROM or a network distribution of Windows 95.
2. Go to the Control Panel and double click on the Network icon or right mouse click on the Network Neighborhood icon on the desktop and choose Properties.
3. Choose the button labeled Protocols.
4. Go to the Microsoft option and choose TCP/IP. Press OK and you will be brought back to the Network properties page.
5. DHCP is selected automatically so there is no need to adjust any properties.
6. Press OK to close the Network Properties box. You will be prompted to restart the machine in order for the changes to take affect. Restart the machine.
7. To verify that you have been assigned an IP address, go to a DOS window and type `ipconfig`, then press Enter. You will then be shown your IP address.

NOTE

If any address fields are currently filled in, erase their contents. All necessary information will be passed along by the DHCP Server.

Windows NT 4.0:

1. Ensure that you have access to the Windows NT 4.0 Workstation installation CD-ROM.
2. Go to the Control Panel and double-click on the Network icon or right mouse click on the Network Neighborhood icon on the desktop and choose Properties.
3. Choose the page labeled Protocols.
4. Click Add and a list of available protocols is presented. Choose TCP/IP Protocol.

5. Within seconds, you will be asked if you wish to use DHCP. Select Yes. You will then be prompted for the location of the Windows NT Workstation 4.0 CD-ROM. Enter the path and press Enter. Files will be copied from the CD-ROM now.

6. Next, you will be given the message that you must shutdown and restart your machine in order for the changes to take effect. Restart the machine.

7. To verify that you have been assigned an IP address, go to a DOS window and type `ipconfig`, then press Enter. You will then be shown your IP address.

Backup Documentation

Another important aspect of good Domain documentation is solid documentation of your backup servers. This documentation should include where your backup servets are located, where tapes are stored, what backup routines are configured, and the location of a reference for restoration methods.

The following is an example of Backup Server documentation form the Guardian Domain.

THE GUARDIAN DOMAIN'S EXISTING BACKUP SCENARIO

The current backup scenario employs Seagate Backup Exec Version 6.11 in conjunction with Storage Dimensions external DLT drives. Each drive has the capacity to hold 60 GB each. Currently the Guardian Domain backups are spread across four Windows NT Workstation 4.0 machines using a total of six DLT drives.

Basic Configuration:

The Backup Exec Service account name is GUARDIAN\BE-611 with a password of 'Tarantula'. This account must be a member of the Backup Operators group in the Guardian Domain, as well as on each member server throughout the Domain in order to properly backup all files. BE-611 has been configured with workstation logon restrictions, enabling it only to logon to the four backup servers. These workstations are named as follows:

Server Name	Location	Division Serviced
GRD-Backup1	The Guardian Building, Lower Level Computer Room	Dedicated to Guardian HQ
GRD-Backup2	Guradian Casualty, Fourth Floor Computer Room	Dedicated to Guardian Casualty
GRD-Backup3	Guardian Health, First Floor Computer Room	Dedicated to Guardian Health
GRD-Backup4	Guardian Corp. Benefits Third Floor Computer Room	Dedicated to Guardian Corporate Benefits

Tape Management:

Each machine, which is configured with a single 60 GB DLT tape drives, has four tape sets associated with it. A tape set consists of one tape for full server backups and one tape for incremental weekly backups. On Friday night of each week a full backup is run, while on Monday through Thursday nights an incremental backup is run. Tape sets are named for the division they back up. For instance, a tape set and its accompanying schedule for the Casualty Domain looks like the following:

Week	Monday through Thursday	Friday
Week 1	Casualty Incremental 1	Casualty Full 1
Week 2	Casualty Incremental 2	Casualty Full 2
Week 3	Casualty Incremental 3	Casualty Full 3
Week 4	Casualty Incremental 4	Casualty Full 4

In addition to a permanent label reflecting a tape name and set number, each tape is also labeled with the date the tape is inserted into the machine. For instance, Casualty Full 1 would also bear the label 3-7-1997. This date will correlate with the naming conventions used by Seagate Backup Exec.

On Monday of each week, all drives are cleaned and the incremental tape set for the week is inserted and erased. These tapes remain in the drive until after the Thursday incrementals. On Friday, each drive is cleaned again, and the full backup tape set is inserted and erased.

Data Archival:

Tapes that are not currently in use are kept in the Data Safe in each computer room. At the end of each quarter the last complete tape set is removed from rotation and stored off site with Data Guard Data Services. Data Guard can be reached at 555-7272.

Backup Jobs:

The following tables show the current distribution of backup jobs throughout the Domain:

The Casualty Division:

Job Name	Casualty Incremental	Casualty Full
Device	DLT1	DLT1
Model	SD67583	SD67583
Bios Rev.	19608	19608
Schedule	Monday through Thursday at 9:00 PM	Friday at 9:00 PM
Backup Type	Incremental	Normal (Complete)
Currently protected	CTY-PROD01\C$	CTY-PROD01\C$

continues

17

continued

Job Name	Casualty Incremental	Casualty Full
Servers	CTY-PROD01\D$ CTY-PROD01\E$ CTY-PROD01\F$ GRD-BACKUP2\C$ GRD-BACKUP2\D$ GRD-SNA03\C$ GRD-SNA03\D$ GRD-SNA04\C$ GRD-SNA04\D$ GRD-EWS03\C$ GRD-EWS03\D$ GRD-DHCP03\C$ GRD-DHCP03\D$ GRD-BACKUP2\C$ GRD-BACKUP2\D$	CTY-PROD01\D$ CTY-PROD01\E$ CTY-PROD01\F$ GRD-BACKUP2\C$ GRD-BACKUP2\D$ GRD-SNA03\C$ GRD-SNA03\D$ GRD-SNA04\C$ GRD-SNA04\D$ GRD-EWS03\C$ GRD-EWS03\D$ GRD-DHCP03\C$ GRD-DHCP03\D$ GRD-BACKUP2\C$ GRD-BACKUP2\D$
Selection Name	Casualty Incremental (1 through 4)	Casualty Full (1 through 4)
Approximate total bytes of full backup	38 GB	38 GB

Emergency Contact Information:

Category	Support Information
Primary Contact	Dexter Burch Pager: 555-6782 Extension: 55293 Home Phone: 555-6839
Secondary Contact	Greg Ledom Pager: 555-1024 Extension: 0524 Home Phone: 555-0817
Vendor Support Numbers	Compaq: 1-800-555-6272 Storage Dimensions: 1-800-555-3322 Microsoft: 1-800-555-BILL Seagate: 1-800-555-5493

Backup Procedures:

The Backup Exec Restoration Procedures have been printed off and placed in a clear plastic folder and attached to the side of the Computer Rack holding the Backup Server. In addition, Backup Exec Help provides detailed information on restoring files, directories, and entire servers.

Summary

Domain documentation is serious business. The guidelines and ideas presented in this chapter are by no means meant to cover all of the important areas of your Domain documentation, but at least to provide a head start in the right direction. Other areas of your Domain that might warrant documentation are

- Logon Scripts
- Automated Installation Processes
- Support Delivery Methods
- Change Management Procedures
- NTFS Permission Application

The importance of documentation cannot be overstated. Remember Domain Documentation should be considered a living document and be updated on a monthly basis. While documentation may not necessarily provide a seamless blueprint of your Domain, it will at least put you a step in the right direction.

17

DOMAIN
DOCUMENTATION

VI
PART

Supporting Your Domain

CHAPTER 18

Systems Management and the Support Organization

IN THIS CHAPTER

The success of a support organization hinges on a number of things, including the following:

- The manner and efficiency in which support is delivered
- The proficiency with which resources are managed
- Information dissemination to support personnel
- Proactive communication with the end user
- Successful process management

This chapter will explore these issues in two sections: systems management and the support organization. The first section, "Systems Management," will discuss support tools available today as well as the advantages provided, while the second section, "The Support Organization," will discuss process management, workload management, and effective communications.

Systems Management

Although distributed computing has its advantages, it most certainly has its disadvantages. Even though Big Iron is expensive, swapping a terminal, altering a punchdown, or adding a selection to a VIPS menu is a lot quicker and easier than diagnosing many of the problems PC users experience on a daily basis. With the Network Computer (NC) and Microsoft's Zero Administration for Windows (ZAW) on the horizon, it would appear that distributed computing could enter the realm of the mainframe in terms of simplified user support one day, but ZAW is still in an alpha stage, and the NC doesn't seem to be replacing PCs wholesale on any level.

The cost of supporting a PC has been estimated at anywhere between $3,000 to $20,000 a year over a five year period. Regardless of the validity of these estimates, there are a host of support issues that cost time and money. Even though a company might implement and maintain a variety of standards that help reduce the cost of supporting a distributed computing environment, organizations are still faced with the high cost of maintaining industry currency. Luckily, there are several systems management packages that have been developed to specifically address many issues involved in supporting a distributed environment. These packages provide the following functions:

- Automated Software Distribution
- Software Inventory
- Hardware Inventory
- Event/System Monitoring
- Performance Monitoring
- Remote Diagnostics
- Remote Desktop Control

With a well-designed implementation, a systems management package can reduce the time and money that it takes to support a distributed environment. This chapter will explore these features and the impact that they might have on your environment.

Software Distribution, PC Inventory, and Remote Diagnostics

Software distribution and PC inventory are keys to a successful systems management suite. These functions provide the ability to electronically distribute applications to all desktops regardless of OS platform, provide complete hardware and software inventory information, allow for remote workstation diagnostics and remote workstation control, and include complete virus protection in many cases. In addition, the asset data collected through the inventory piece could be used for a variety of purposes including license control, accounting information, trend analysis, and so on. Four practical examples follow.

Example One: Hardware/Software Inventory

The accounting department needs exact numbers on how many PCs are in the building, what their model and hardware configurations are, and what software is loaded. Through the use of server-initiated inventory agents, the network manager is able to configure the server to query each network workstation to gain configuration information. This information is then dumped into a table so that custom or predefined reports may be generated.

Example Two: Company-Wide Software Upgrades

A new version of Microsoft Office is released, and the corporation decides that it offers many benefits to the end user. The traditional method for distributing upgrades is for a support technician to visit each workstation and install the software manually. This method can cause the end user great inconvenience and take an extended amount of time. With a solid software distribution/asset management system, a network administrator can use workstation inventory figures to group all workstations of similar types into categories. Next, the administrator can develop (usually within one or two hours) a distribution package that is tailored to each workstation category. That day, a message is distributed to all users that instructs them to leave their workstations powered on that night. The network administrator then schedules these software distribution packages to be sent to each workstation beginning at 7:00 p.m. When the employees come in the next morning, the new version of Microsoft Office is installed and they've lost no work time. With this method, user inconvenience is minimized, and the company saves money by preventing lost work hours.

Example Three: Priority Service Response

A user calls the support center and mentions that his or her workstation is no longer printing properly. After entering a problem ticket in the priority support tracking system, the technician utilizes the remote control application built into the network administration suite and takes control of the user's desktop. Within seconds, the technician realizes that the printers have been set up properly, but that something has become corrupt within Microsoft Word. Instead of going to the user's desktop and spending a great deal of time attempting to troubleshoot the issue, the technician sends the end user a predefined MS Word Distribution package that removes the existing installation of MS Word and installs a fresh version. While this

18

distribution package is running, the technician can work on other support-related issues, effectively maximizing work time. After completion of the distribution package (perhaps 15 to 20 minutes later), the technician once again takes remote control of the workstation and attempts to print from within Word. The document prints, and the problem is solved.

Example Four: New Workstation Purchase

Five new workstations are purchased for immediate use. Traditionally, a support technician would be required to spend a great deal of time configuring the workstation for network connectivity and installing all standard applications. With a solid distribution package, the technician can simply insert a network boot disk that logs onto the network and loads the software distribution agent. The technician would then send a complete workstation distribution package to each new workstation, and the configuration would be complete within two hours. In the meantime, the technician can perform daily support duties, once again maximizing work time.

Performance Monitoring/Early Warning Systems

How many times have you had a server fail or experienced difficulties that could have been avoided if only you had known that the telltale signs were there? So many times we lock our servers away in well-conditioned rooms and very rarely visit them to make sure that the hard drives aren't clunking. We even avoid browsing the Event Viewer as long as no one complains about anything. Yet, unless you've had an unexpected hardware failure, such as a power supply dying or a controller failing, most system crashes can be avoided.

Performance monitors and early warning systems are excellent tools to utilize not only to help you sleep better at night, but also to aid in capacity and performance planning. In addition, these systems can play a big role in Key Design Objective Five: Fault Tolerance.

While Windows NT Server provides a performance monitor of its own, this tool is not proactive nor does it provide for any rules-based scripting or advanced notification features. There are many performance monitors and early warning systems available on the market today, but most are bundled with complete management systems (such as Tivole TME10 and CA Unicenter TNG). No matter which product you deploy, they all offer similar funcitonality. The following are common examples of an EWS at work:

- **Example One:** One of your main production servers suddenly has less than 10 percent of its disk space available, which can lead to an uninitiated server shutdown. Having been detected by your EWS, the system pages the previously configured support personnel and notifies them of the pending emergency.
- **Example Two:** Early Sunday evening, a server hard drive fails, but the server continues to run. The early warning/performance monitoring system makes its monitoring sweep 15 minutes later and realizes that the drive is no longer available. Support personnel are immediately paged with the message, and an appropriate support response is initiated long before the users arrive Monday morning.

■ **Example Three:** Several users are added to a production server, and there is no noticeable resource impact at first. Within three weeks, support personnel begin receiving messages from the EWS system that server memory is being consumed more readily. In response, support personnel add more RAM to the server and effectively avoid user inconvenience through slowed performance or server down time.

Enterprise Virus Protection: Server and Workstation

Workstation and server virus protection is crucial in today's environment. At the server level, virus protection should be a service that continuously scans data areas in an attempt to intercept, clean out, and destroy any viruses, including macro viruses that attack office automation applications. On the workstation level, you should at a minimum configure each workstation to scan at boot, but a continuous service that scans memory and data at system power-on as well as provides continuous detection services during the day would be preferable. Virus protection is often overlooked and unfortunately can account for many disasters.

The Support Organization

Without a solid support-delivery system and a well-trained, well-organized support staff, the enterprise cannot function properly. Unfortunately, next to fault tolerance, one of the most overlooked features of the enterprise is the support organization. The success of the first five Key Design Objectives hinge on the implementation of Key Design Objective Six: A Solid Support Organization. Without a mean to maintain your enterprise infrastructure, all of your hard work and strategic planning have a high potential to end up as wasted time.

A solid support organization is dependent upon the following three important factors:

■ Effective Communications Management
■ In-depth Process Management
■ Realistic Workload Management

The remainder of this chapter will briefly explore these subjects, but one book cannot hope to provide the in-depth look these topics deserve. These topics, much like your enterprise strategy, require real expertise, whether it be acquired in-house or from outside consultants.

Effective Communications Management

Communications management must start at the top and work its way down. For a support organization to be successful, all members must have a basic understanding of what the departmental goals are, what methods are being used to attain those goals, and how members can be supportive in achieving those goals. Furthermore, there must be a communications process in place through which pertinent information is distributed throughout the organization, such as current and future projects, standards information, technical and personnel directions, and changes in any previously announced information. And finally, there must be a method in place to keep the end user informed and participative in future direction.

A good place to start when designing a communications model is the departmental mission.

Development of an Information Systems Departmental Mission Statement

Even though users will know that a network support organization exists to develop and support the enterprise, a departmental mission statement can further develop the support and customer service focus needed by all support organizations. A published informations systems (IS) departmental mission statement that covers the services that are currently provided, the manner that those services should be provided, a customer service focus, and the goals and vision for the future of the department are helpful not only to the support associates, but also to the end-user community which might not be aware of the breadth of services available.

> **NOTE**
>
> The following is a good example of an IS departmental mission statement:
>
> To provide an enterprise foundation for the organization that fosters corporate and associate growth, non-invasive data processing, customer support–oriented service, a high level of service availability, and a flexible, scalable enterprise that is prepared for industry and corporate change.

A departmental mission statement should be a living document that reflects the needs of the organization and provides goals for the support organization. In order to help your employees realize that they are important to your organization, it is often a good idea to let them participate in the design and definition of a departmental mission statement.

Internal Information Distribution

No matter how good your IS strategy is or how important you feel your standards are, your department will have a difficult time achieving its goals unless there is a consistent flow of information to all support team members. The following information is crucial to an organization's success:

- Departmental Initiatives
- Corporate Initiatives
- Application Standards
- Process Flows
- Project Updates
- Personnel Assignments

- Technical Updates
- Progress Roadblocks
- Departmental or Project Successes
- Departmental or Project Failures

The question is how to disseminate this information. Weekly team meetings, discussion databases in Lotus Notes, e-mail, and intranet newsgroups are all viable means of communications. The manner of delivery is not as important as the fact that the data is deliverd.

Communicating with the End-User Community

Even though you might think you're doing a good job of supporting the end user, the end user could (and often does) have a different perspective. Communicating with your end-user community is just as important as communicating with your internal organization. End-user communication should not only include information about your current sevices and initiatives, but should also be investigative in nature to ensure that you, as a support organization, are meeting all the needs that might be found in the user community. Quarterly meetings and monthly projct updates are just a few of the efforts that could be made to improve the working relationhip between your support organization and your end-user community. Occasional surveys and questionnaires are also put to good use when they are tailored for specific projects.

Development of Support Level Agreements

A support level agreement is a written or verbal contract with either the entire company or individual departments that covers the company's or department's expectations of the IS department in the delivery of IS support, as well as the IS department's expectations of the end users' role in acquiring support. Support level agreements (SLAs) should be developed in conjunction with the end user and should include such items as a well-defined support severity stratification, including such detail as deadlines for the delivery of a resolution to each severity level.

For instance, a non-critical issue such as RAM installation or software upgrades would have an expected maximum of a three-working-day response, whereas a user down would have a maximum of a two-hour response. These SLAs must be developed in a realistic manner based on personnel availability and customer need.

In-depth Process Management

Process management seems to be the buzzword of the 1990s, but there is a tremendous amount of value in well-defined and utilized process management. At a minimum, the following items should have well-defined procedures in place:

- The acquisition of support by the end user
- Problem and problem-resolution tracking

The Acquisition of Support by the End User

A support acquisition system should be implemented in order to alleviate the disorganized and dysfunctional methods used by most shops for support acquisition. This method, often known as the "Hey you" method, is based on the user, finding a support technician when something breaks and expecting that support technician to drop everything and solve the problem. Instead, a network-based, user-friendly dispatch system could be used to enter and track non-critical service requests (for example, software upgrades, memory installation, addition or augmentation of user IDs, new workstation installations, and so on). Such a system should be accessible by all users or accessible by key personnel in obvious groups. This system should be capable of producing various reports including average time to respond to requests, trend tracking, request types, and so on. This system could be used not only to streamline the delivery of support, but also to measure the performance of the IS staff, help in personnel capacity planning, and aid in the measurement of SLA success.

While the use of an existing support acquisition system is highly recommended, such a system could be developed using an existing mail system or even a common Web server. The following is an example of an in-house support acquisition system developed using Novell's GroupWise:

> The support acquisition system (SAS) is represented by an icon on each user's GroupWise toolbar. User A needs Office installed on his workstation, so he clicks on the SAS icon and a predefined GroupWise form is launched. The user's name is automatically entered into the ticket, along with his floor number, phone extension, and whether he is a PC or Mac user. He goes to the form field titled Service Type and selects the Install Software option. Next, the user enters MS Office in the Software Type field and clicks the Send Ticket button. The ticket is then sent into the SAS inbox, which has a predefined set of GroupWise rules that move the ticket into the appropriate folder based on the field entries. Via e-mail, support personnel will then be notified that a new ticket has entered the system. When a new ticket comes in, a technician will take ownership of that ticket and his or her name will be entered into the Tech field. Once the work is complete, the technician will close the ticket, and the ticket will then be moved into the appropriate folder as defined in the inbox rules. There will be a logical set of folders and rules defined so that tickets may be monitored based on age, type, and so on.

Problem Tracking and Resolution

In addition to a common support acquisition system, a problem tracking database should be developed to track and dispatch support emergencies. Such a system could be used to track critical service requests, which can be those requiring immediate attention such as a user who can't print, hardware failure, software failure, network not responding, and so on. Such a system should support full text searching and should require that a problem resolution be entered to allow for future reference for easier resolution. In addition, a problem-tracking database should be fully capable of delivering customizable reports to measure trends, IS performance, personnel requirements, and so on. It is not uncommon for an organization to develop a problem-tracking database in Microsoft Office. The following is an example of how a problem-tracking system might be used:

> A user working at her workstation is suddenly unable to access network resources, so she calls the IS support center. A support center tech sitting at a workstation with the problem-tracking database already loaded answers the phone. As the user begins to describe her problem, the tech logs the issue in the database and either resolves the issue over the phone, immediately visits the end user, or assigns the ticket to a more appropriate associate. Once the issue is resolved, the resolution is entered into the database, and at the end of each month, reports will be run categorizing the number of priority incidents, whether they involved hardware or software, which hardware and software specifically, and how many tickets of each type were handled by each tech. Such information could be used to track support trends, hardware/software patterns, end-user training needs, and so on.

Effective Workload Management

Workload management is one of those concepts that seems to elude many organizations, so it's often easiest to define what effective workload management is *not*:

- The tactical duties of supporting 300 desktops take up a minimum of 85 percent of your weekly time, and you are arbitrarily assigned an additional 90 desktops to support.

- 85 percent of your time is committed to administrative and management duties, yet you are given additional projects and assignments two days before they're due on a consistent basis.

- Your group spends 90 percent of its time supporting the 1,500 users in your existing infrastructure, and you are suddenly tasked with not only continuing daily support of that infrastructure, but also with migrating each desktop to a new operating system in six months, and you are given no additional staff.

Workload management begins with matching your current staffing level and their existing workload to your anticipated workload, and ends in maintaining a consistent level of productivity. While this might sound like magic, it can be done. Workload management is critical to keeping your employees happy. There are many tools that can assist in managing your workload such as Project Workbench, Microsoft Project or Team Leader, and Platinum's Enterprise Project Manager. These tools are extremely useful in analyzing staffing and resource trends, managing daily workload, and planning for upcoming projects.

Summary

Communications, workload management, and process management are all important to the success of a support organization while systems management utilities can be key players in the success of your enteprise. The prosperity of the first five Key Design Objectives hinges on the implementation of Key Design Objective Six: A Solid Support Organization. Without a mean to maintain your enterprise infrastructure, all of your hard work and strategic planning have a high potential to end up as wasted time.

Supporting Windows NT Server

IN THIS CHAPTER

Supporting any advanced operating system has the potential to become a challenge, and Windows NT Server is no exception. However, through a combination of many of the built-in diagnostic support tools and several valuable external support resources, the support challenges presented with Windows NT Server are, in most cases, easy to overcome.

While Windows NT provides such advanced support utilities as the Performance Monitor and the Network Monitor (in conjunction with SMS), these tools are usually a last resort to be used once all other resources have been exhausted. For a quick diagnosis of issues, Microsoft also provides the following tools:

- The Event Viewer
- The Task Manager
- Windows NT Diagnostics

These diagnostic tools will, in most cases, provide enough insight to point you in the right direction when you're experiencing difficulties. However, what do you do with the information that you've gathered using these tools? Luckily, there are several resources to turn to when outside support is needed—and many of these resources are absolutely free. The outside support resources to be covered in this chapter are:

- Internet Newsgroups
- The Microsoft Web Site
- The Microsoft Knowledge Base
- Microsoft Technet

The Built-In Tools

Windows NT is a fairly complicated system and, unfortunately, things will go wrong from time to time. Due to the fact that in most cases your organization and your users cannot afford down time, Microsoft has provided three tools to be used in the quick diagnosis of problems. The Event Viewer, the Task Manager, and the Windows NT Diagnostics utilities have been designed to provide real-time performance and configuration snapshots, a history of current events, and diagnostic red flags. These tools should be used in the first stage of problem diagnosis, and will accurately pinpoint system or application problems and issues in most cases.

The Event Viewer

Supporting a network operating system such as Windows NT Server can be a difficult task, especially when that NOS is deployed to perform several diverse functions. To aid in support, Microsoft has provided the Event Viewer. The Event Viewer allows you to view a wide variety of activities and events that have been logged for three significant areas of your Windows NT Server: the Windows NT system itself, Windows NT security, and Windows NT applications.

Events for each of these systems are logged in one of three appropriate logs. These logs, the System log, the Security log, and the Application log are defined as follows:

- The System Log, shown in Figure 19.1, is where all operating system-oriented events are recorded. Events such as the success and failure of services, devices, and network communications issues are logged here.

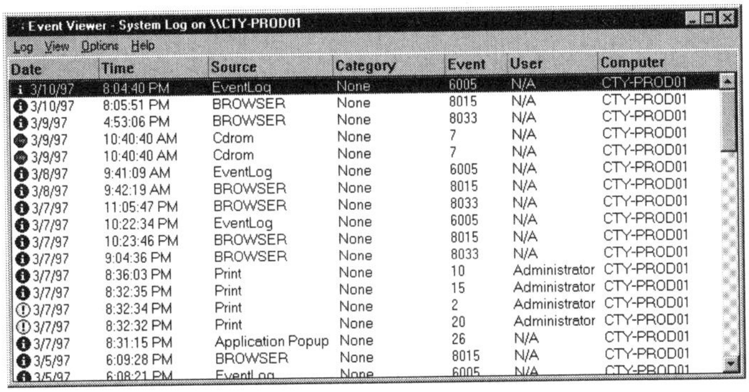

Event Viewer - System Log on \\CTY-PROD01

Log View Options Help

Date	Time	Source	Category	Event	User	Computer
3/10/97	8:04:40 PM	EventLog	None	6005	N/A	CTY-PROD01
3/10/97	8:05:51 PM	BROWSER	None	8015	N/A	CTY-PROD01
3/9/97	4:53:06 PM	BROWSER	None	8033	N/A	CTY-PROD01
3/9/97	10:40:40 AM	Cdrom	None	7	N/A	CTY-PROD01
3/9/97	10:40:40 AM	Cdrom	None	7	N/A	CTY-PROD01
3/8/97	9:41:09 AM	EventLog	None	6005	N/A	CTY-PROD01
3/8/97	9:42:19 AM	BROWSER	None	8015	N/A	CTY-PROD01
3/7/97	11:05:47 PM	BROWSER	None	8033	N/A	CTY-PROD01
3/7/97	10:22:34 PM	EventLog	None	6005	N/A	CTY-PROD01
3/7/97	10:23:46 PM	BROWSER	None	8015	N/A	CTY-PROD01
3/7/97	9:04:36 PM	BROWSER	None	8033	N/A	CTY-PROD01
3/7/97	8:36:03 PM	Print	None	10	Administrator	CTY-PROD01
3/7/97	8:32:35 PM	Print	None	15	Administrator	CTY-PROD01
3/7/97	8:32:34 PM	Print	None	2	Administrator	CTY-PROD01
3/7/97	8:32:32 PM	Print	None	20	Administrator	CTY-PROD01
3/7/97	8:31:15 PM	Application Popup	None	26	N/A	CTY-PROD01
3/5/97	6:09:28 PM	BROWSER	None	8015	N/A	CTY-PROD01
3/5/97	6:08:21 PM	EventLog	None	6005	N/A	CTY-PROD01

FIGURE 19.1.
The System Log of the Event Viewer.

- The Security Log, shown in Figure 19.2, directly correlates to your domain or local auditing configuration. All audit information will be recorded in this log.

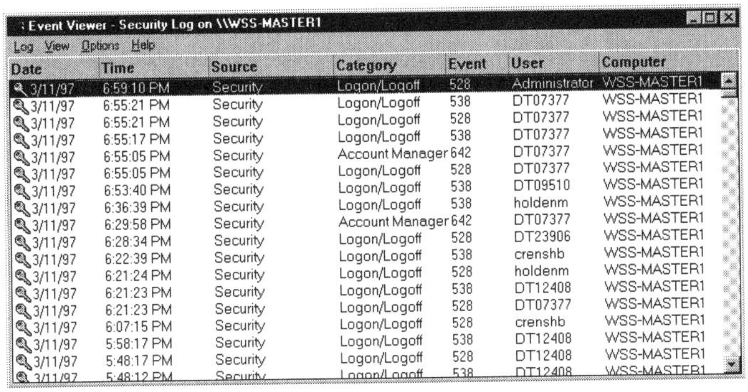

Event Viewer - Security Log on \\WSS-MASTER1

Log View Options Help

Date	Time	Source	Category	Event	User	Computer
3/11/97	6:59:10 PM	Security	Logon/Logoff	528	Administrator	WSS-MASTER1
3/11/97	6:55:21 PM	Security	Logon/Logoff	538	DT07377	WSS-MASTER1
3/11/97	6:55:21 PM	Security	Logon/Logoff	528	DT07377	WSS-MASTER1
3/11/97	6:55:17 PM	Security	Logon/Logoff	538	DT07377	WSS-MASTER1
3/11/97	6:55:05 PM	Security	Account Manager	642	DT07377	WSS-MASTER1
3/11/97	6:55:05 PM	Security	Logon/Logoff	528	DT07377	WSS-MASTER1
3/11/97	6:53:40 PM	Security	Logon/Logoff	538	DT09510	WSS-MASTER1
3/11/97	6:36:39 PM	Security	Logon/Logoff	538	holdenm	WSS-MASTER1
3/11/97	6:29:58 PM	Security	Account Manager	642	DT07377	WSS-MASTER1
3/11/97	6:28:34 PM	Security	Logon/Logoff	528	DT23906	WSS-MASTER1
3/11/97	6:22:39 PM	Security	Logon/Logoff	538	crenshb	WSS-MASTER1
3/11/97	6:21:24 PM	Security	Logon/Logoff	528	holdenm	WSS-MASTER1
3/11/97	6:21:23 PM	Security	Logon/Logoff	538	DT12408	WSS-MASTER1
3/11/97	6:21:23 PM	Security	Logon/Logoff	528	DT07377	WSS-MASTER1
3/11/97	6:07:15 PM	Security	Logon/Logoff	528	crenshb	WSS-MASTER1
3/11/97	5:58:17 PM	Security	Logon/Logoff	538	DT12408	WSS-MASTER1
3/11/97	5:48:17 PM	Security	Logon/Logoff	528	DT12408	WSS-MASTER1
3/11/97	5:48:12 PM	Security	Logon/Logoff	538	DT12408	WSS-MASTER1

FIGURE 19.2.
The Security Log of the Event Viewer.

- The Application Log, shown in Figure 19.3, is where all true Windows NT applications will record application events. For instance, Backup Exec records the successes and failures of backup jobs and SNA Server records communications issues.

As you can see in Figures 19.1 through 19.3, each logged event has seven classifications: Date, Time, Source, Category, Event, User, and Computer. Additionally, each event has an associated symbol. These symbols are used to signify the importance of the event.

FIGURE 19.3.

The Application Log of the Event Viewer.

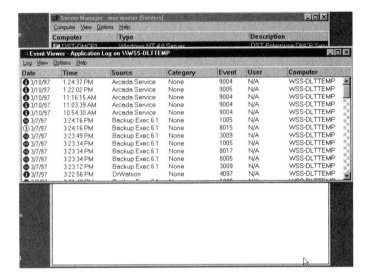

- **The Stop Sign.** This icon represents an error in a device, a service, or an application. It can also represent the inability to perform a function or initiate a device.

- **The Exclamation Point.** This icon represents a warning. Warnings are usually tell-tale signs of events to come such as a DHCP scope with 90% utilization or a disk with a bad block.

- **The Padlock.** This icon, seen only in the Security log, represents a failed attempt at object access or security management.

- **The Key.** This icon, also seen only in the Security log, represents the successful use of an object or security management.

- **The lowercase i.** This icon represents an informational message such as the election of a Master Browser, the successful start or stop of a service, or the processing of a print job.

The Event Viewer can be accessed by going to the Start Menu, followed by Programs and Administrative Tools (Common). The Program will default to whichever log you were in the last time you had the Event Viewer open. For instance, if you were in the Security log the last time you closed the Event Viewer, that is the log you will be presented with upon launching the program.

The Event Viewer is a fairly simple support tool consisting of only a single drop-down menu (no tool bar) and a window displaying recorded events. The drop-down menu consists of four selections—Log, View, Options, and Help—while each event is classified by Date, Time, Source, Category, Event, User, and Computer.

The Log Menu Option

As seen in Figure 19.4, the first menu option, Log, has several options to choose from: System, Security, Application, Open, Save As, Clear All Events, Log Settings, Select Computer, and Exit.

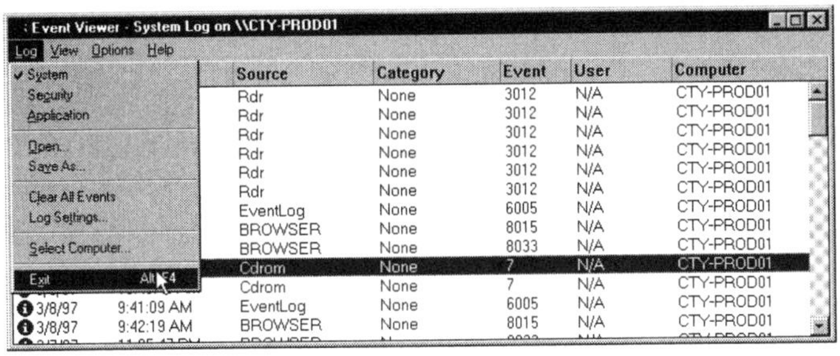

FIGURE 19.4.

The Log Pull-Down Menu.

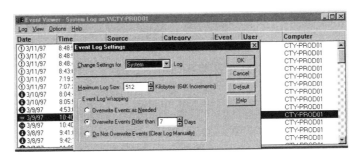

The first three choices—System, Security, and Application—allow you to choose which part of the log you wish to view. For instance, if you're having an issue with an SQL server or your IIS server, you would choose the Application log. On the other hand, if you wished to view security information, you would choose the Security option.

The next two options—Save As and Open—allow you to archive an existing Event log, and open it for evaluation at a later date. This option is convenient if you like to keep a history of issues or security events that can be viewed later. It is also useful for external support providers to be able to look at an event log before coming on-site.

Following Save As and Open is the Clear All Events option. Clear All Events allows you to erase an existing log. (Note that you will be prompted to save the log before it is erased.) This option is pertinent only for the log that you're in at the time. In other words, if you're in the System log and you clear all events, you only clear events for the System log. The Security and Application logs will remain intact.

Following the Clear All Events option is the Log Settings option. This option launches a window as seen in Figure 19.5 that allows you to determine the Maximum log size and Event Log Wrapping settings.

FIGURE 19.5.

The Log Settings Option.

19

SUPPORTING WINDOWS NT SERVER

Log size can be set in 64K increments, and can be made as large as you like. Depending on your Event Log Wrapping settings, the standard size of 512K is fine for a typical computer. However, for items such as SNA servers or DHCP servers, it's an excellent idea to set the log for a minimum of 2,048K, so you can have several days' worth of event history to refer to in case of problems or a tremendous amount of use.

Following Log Size are three Event Log Wrapping options: Overwrite Events as Needed, Overwrite Events Older than X days, and Do Not Overwrite Events (Clear Log Manually). The default Wrapping option is Overwrite Events Older than 7 Days, but depending on the nature of the server, this option may not always be desirable. For instance, in a heavily audited environment, the Security log may fill up before seven days ever comes around. Likewise, on a widely used SNA Server, the application log might fill up almost daily. It is best to watch your servers and adjust log settings as needed. In most cases, the default settings work just fine.

The next two options are fairly self explanatory. The Select Computer option allows you to view the Event log of a remote computer, and the Exit option will close the Event Viewer.

The View Menu Option

Like the Log menu option, the View menu drop-down menu also has several choices. The View choices all affect the manner in which Event log data will be presented. View menu choices, as seen in Figure 19.6, are as follows:

- All Events
- Filter Events
- Newest First
- Oldest First
- Find
- Detail
- Refresh

The All Events option is the default setting. With this option selected, all events logged in the Event Viewer will be displayed.

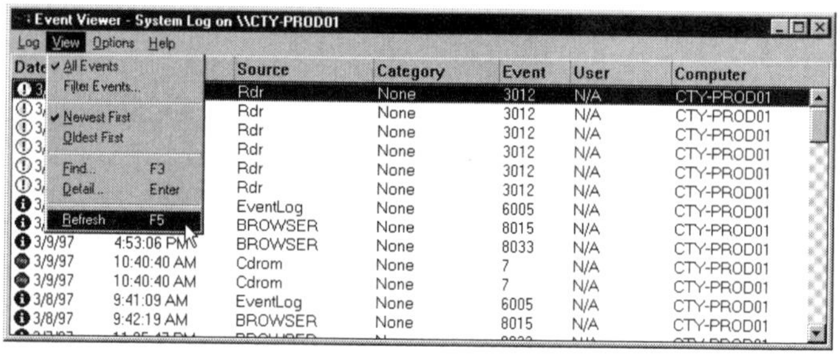

Figure 19.6.

The View Option in the Event Viewer.

The Filter Events option, shown in Figure 19.7, can be quite helpful when trying to isolate a trend. Filter options are listed in Table 19.1.

FIGURE 19.7.

The Filter Events Option of the Event Viewer.

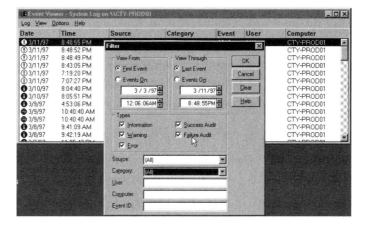

Table 19.1. Event Viewer Filter Options.

Filter Option	*Description*
View From	This option allows you to determine from which date in the Event log you would like to start the event display. The default setting is the day the log was initiated.
View Through	This option allows you to determine the last date for which to display events. The default setting is the date of the last logged event.
Information	This option allows you to determine whether or not you wish to display informational messages.
Warning	This option allows you to determine whether or not you wish to display warning messages.
Error	This option allows you to determine whether you wish to display error messages.
Success Audit	This option allows you to determine whether you wish to display Success Audits (applies only to the Security log).
Failure Audit	This option allows you to determine whether you wish to display Failure Audits (applies only to the Security log).
Source	This option allows you to display events pertaining only to a specific source. This option provides a drop-down menu that lists all devices and services available on your server.
Category	Certain events pertain to specific categories. This option allows you to display only events that pertain to the specific category of your choice.

continues

Table 19.1. continued

Filter Option	Description
User	This option allows you to view events that are specific only to certain users.
Computer	This option is somewhat unnecessary as the event log can display events from only one server at a time.
Event ID	All events are assigned a specific ID. This option allows you to view events that have been logged with a specific ID only.

Following Filter Events are four fairly self-explanatory options: Newest First, Oldest First, Find, and Detail. Newest First and Oldest First enable you to select an event sort order, Find allows you to search for a specific event, and Detail provides you with event detail.

To view a specific event, you can either highlight the event and go to the View menu option and select Detail, or you can double-click the event. All events will provide the date, time, source, category, event, user, and computer associated with the event, as well as a brief description, as shown in Figure 19.8. Depending on the type of event you're viewing, event detail can be extremely detailed (as usually seen in the Security log), or somewhat cryptic as often seen where network communications issues are concerned.

FIGURE 19.8.

Event Details.

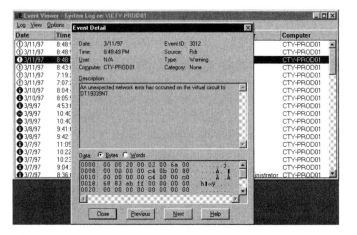

The Event Viewer is a powerful tool, especially when used in conjunction with Technet and the Web-based Knowledge Base, as seen later in this chapter.

Task Manager

The Windows NT Task Manager is a quick and dirty tool that allows you to do the following:

- Gauge your server's current performance
- Terminate applications that are not responding or are causing system difficulties
- Launch new applications
- View and stop running processes
- Set process priority

There are two ways to launch the Task Manager. The first way is to hit Ctrl-Alt-Delete while in a Windows NT session. This will launch the Windows NT Security window as seen in Figure 19.9 that will allow you to not only launch the Task Manager, but also to lock the server, log off the computer, change your password, or shut down your machine.

FIGURE 19.9.

The Windows NT Security Window.

The second way to launch the Task Manager is to choose any free space on your task bar and hold down your right mouse button, as shown in Figure 19.10. You will immediately be presented with a drop-down menu (or more correctly a drop-up menu) that will allow you to run the Task Manager, cascade all open windows, tile open windows both vertically and horizontally, minimize all open windows, and view the task bar properties.

Either way, once you've launched the Task Manager (as seen in Figure 19.11), you will have three tabs to choose from: Applications, Processes, and Performance.

The Applications tab is where you would go to launch new applications or terminate applications that are either not responding or are causing system difficulties.

- **Ending a Task.** To end a task, highlight the task you wish to terminate and click the End Task button at the bottom of the screen. The application will immediately be terminated.
- **Launching a New Task.** To launch a new task, go to the File menu and select the New Task (Run) option. The Create New Task dialog box will launch (as seen in Figure 19.12) and you will have the opportunity to launch a new task or application.

Following the Applications window is the Processes window. Selecting the Processes tab will bring up a list of all of the processes currently running on your server. This is an excellent window to view if you feel that your server is running significantly slower than usual. Notice in Figure 19.13 that along with the active processes you are provided with the CPU that is currently servicing the process, the amount of CPU time that has been dedicated to the process, and how much memory the process is taking up. By viewing this window, you have a good chance of determining what resources are taking an inordinate amount of processor or memory time.

To end a process, simply highlight the process, push your right mouse button and choose End Process from the drop-down menu, as shown in Figure 19.14. A message confirming your selection will pop up. Select Yes, and the process will be terminated.

FIGURE 19.10.

The Task Bar Properties Menu.

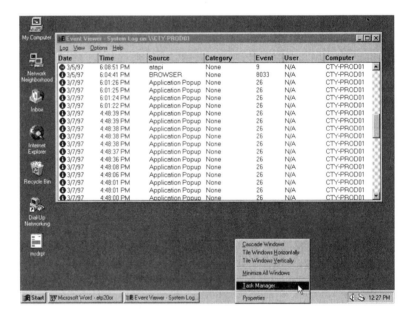

FIGURE 19.11.

The Windows NT Task Manager.

FIGURE 19.12.
Launching a New Task.

FIGURE 19.13.
The Applications Window of the Task Manager.

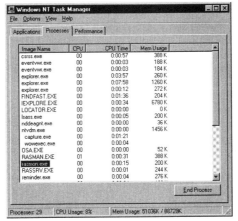

FIGURE 19.14.
Ending a Process with the Task Manager.

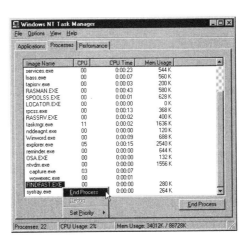

19

SUPPORTING
WINDOWS NT
SERVER

> **CAUTION**
>
> Before ending a process, you should have an idea as to what other processes or services will be impacted once the process is stopped. Process dependencies, much like service dependencies, are very common in Windows NT. By stopping a process, it is very possible to corrupt or even terminate critical services.

Following the Processes window is the Performance window. This window gives you a snapshot of your server's current work level through four separate graph tables.

The first graph on this page is the CPU Usage graph as seen in Figure 19.15. This graph is a real-time graph that shows exactly how much of your CPU is being utilized. To the left of the graph is the CPU Usage History graph that shows the performance spikes your CPU has taken in the last few minutes. These graphs are excellent for determining the current processor load your server is under. If you're having performance issues and your CPU Usage stays under 25 to 35% on a regular basis, you'll know to look somewhere else.

FIGURE 19.15.

The Performance Window of the Task Manager.

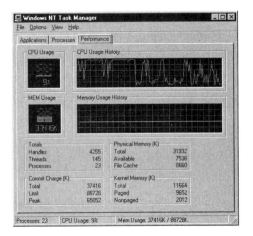

Directly under the CPU Usage graph is the Memory Usage graph, and to its left is the Memory Usage History graph. These graphs, like their CPU Usage counterparts, show both real-time usage as well as a memory usage history. These are also excellent graphs to consult in case of performance issues.

> **CAUTION**
>
> Keep in mind that Windows NT will constantly utilize approximately 85 to 90% of the physical memory installed in your machine, but should the amount of combined virtual and

physical memory in use be more than 65 to 70% on a consistent basis, you most likely need to add more RAM.

Under the CPU and Memory graphs are four telltale tables. These tables—Totals, Physical Memory, Commit Charge, and Kernel Memory—are also very useful in determining whether there is enough physical memory installed on your machine.

The Totals table provides the following information:

- **Handles.** This is the number of system objects, such as files and Registry keys, that are currently open.
- **Threads.** This is the number of execution threads currently open.
- **Processes.** This is the total number of processes currently open.

Next to the Totals table is the Physical Memory table. This table provides the total amount of physical memory installed, the total amount of physical memory available, and the total amount of physical memory currently being used for file caching. The File Cache will vary depending on your server's primary use. For instance, an application server might have a larger file cache than a standard production server, whereas a database server could vary greatly depending on the type of seeks utilized by the clients. Windows NT will generally reserve 10% of your system's physical memory for performance peaks.

The third table, the Commit Charge table, provides information regarding both the physical and virtual memory in use by your server. This table includes the total amount of combined memory in use, the total combined memory available and information on the highest peak in usage. If the total amount of combined memory available is consistently higher than 75 to 85%, you should consider increasing the amount of memory currently installed on your machine.

> **NOTE**
>
> Remember that when creating your paging file, Windows NT will generally set the minimum amount of virtual memory at 100% of the physical RAM installed in your machine, while the maximum amount will be set at one and a half to two times the physical RAM installed in your machine. If the paged memory constantly sits at over 75% utilized, your machine needs more physical RAM.

The final table on this window is the Kernel Memory table. This table shows the amount of memory that is currently in use by the operating system itself. Furthermore, it breaks out what type of memory is being used by providing a row for both Paged (virtual) and Non-Paged (physical) memory. This table gives you a basic idea as to how much of a load the third-party or add-on services are putting on your server.

Any of these tables and graphs can be a problem indicator. The Performance window of the Task Manager is an excellent tool to utilize when experiencing performance issues.

Windows NT Diagnostics

The Windows NT Diagnostic utility provides a tremendous amount of information, but is one of those tools that requires some browsing time before you can understand its value. This utility, which can be found in the Administrative Tools folder on your Start Menu, is a multi-tabbed application, much like the Task Manager, but it has the potential to provide a great deal more information. The Windows NT Diagnostics tool tabs are as follow:

- Version
- System
- Display
- Drives
- Memory
- Services
- Resources
- Environment
- Network

The remainder of this section will briefly cover each of these tabs, but it is highly recommended that you spend some time getting to know the idiosyncrasies of this tool. It is extremely valuable, but is often overlooked.

The first tab of the Windows NT Diagnostics utility is the Version tab, as seen in Figure 19.16. This tab is the easiest place to go when you're not sure of which version or at which Service Pack level your server is currently. This page is the most basic page found in this utility.

FIGURE 19.16.

The Windows NT Diagnostics Tool.

The System tab is where you should go if you're not sure how many processors or which type of processors exist in your computer. Depending on your server hardware, the System tab (as seen in Figure 19.17) can provide a good amount of information concerning the system type, manufacturer, and bios revisions.

FIGURE 19.17.
The Windows NT Diagnostics System Tab.

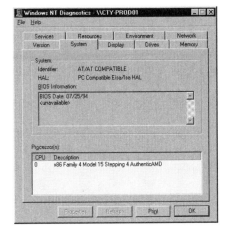

The Display tab, as seen in Figure 19.18, is also a fairly straightforward tab. You can use it to find out what type of video card you have in use, what driver is in use, and the specific files that combine to provide your video driver.

FIGURE 19.18.
The Windows NT Diagnostics Display Tab.

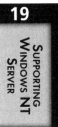

The Drives tab, as seen in Figure 19.19, categorizes your system drives by tape and allows you to view their properties. To view a drive's properties, highlight it and select the Properties button at the bottom of the screen. A dialog box providing general drive information (see Figure 19.20) including storage capacity and current use levels will appear.

The Memory tab (see Figure 19.21) has the potential to be confusing at first, but if you look closely enough, you'll see that it is basically a redraw of the Performance tab of the Task Manager with a few additions.

FIGURE 19.19.

The Windows NT Diagnostics Drives Tab.

FIGURE 19.20.

Viewing a Drive's Properties.

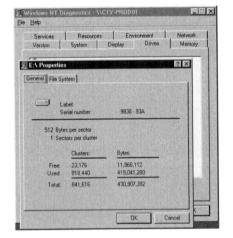

FIGURE 19.21.

The Memory Tab of the Windows NT Diagnostics Utility.

The Services tab, shown in Figure 19.22, offers the ability to list all of the services currently installed on your server as well as all of the devices in place. This tab is easy to view and provides a quick snapshot of what is currently installed on your server. If you double-click any item on either of these lists, a brief description and a list of any other devices (see Figure 19.23) or services that depend upon the select device or service for functionality will appear.

FIGURE 19.22.

The Services Tab of the Windows NT Diagnostics Utility.

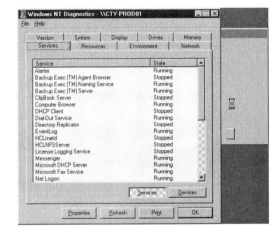

FIGURE 19.23.

The Device Listing Found in the Services Tab of the Windows NT Diagnostics Utility.

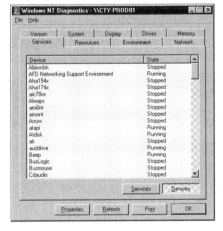

The Resources tab is especially useful when troubleshooting hardware issues. Notice in Figure 19.24 that this tab will provide a list of all IRQ, I/O, DMA, and Memory settings, as well as a list of currently installed devices.

The Environment tab will preview all of the user's currently set environment variables as seen in Figure 19.25. This tab is useful for viewing, especially when you are experiencing difficulties with a product that requires specific environment variables in order to run properly.

Notice in Figure 19.25 that this tab will show information for both the system as a whole and the individual logged-in user.

FIGURE 19.24.

The Resources Tab on the Windows NT Diagnostics Tool.

FIGURE 19.25.

The Windows NT Diagnostics Environment Tab.

The final tab, the Transport Settings tab (see Figure 19.26), provides a great deal of information including:

- Protocol settings and NIC MAC addresses
- General configuration information, including logon domain
- Network configuration settings and network statistics

Again, the Windows NT Diagnostics tool can provide a great deal of information concerning your server. It is highly recommended that you become familiar with this tool through browsing.

FIGURE 19.26.
The Transport Settings
Tab of the Windows
NT Diagnostics Utility.

External Support Resources

In today's world, you can almost always find the information that you're looking for at a minimal cost. There are several ways to obtain outside support for Windows NT, but none that are that much more proficient than the following services:

- Microsoft and Public Domain newsgroups
- The Microsoft Web site, including the Knowledge Base
- The Microsoft Technet CD-ROM

These tools all provide a vast array of information that, if used properly, can help you solve deployment issues, discover new uses for technology, and solve support problems. The remainder of this chapter is dedicated to these support resources.

Newsgroups

If you're not familiar with Internet newsgroups, you should be. Newsgroups provide a place for peer discussion on common support problems and product configuration issues. Newsgroup users are able to post relevant questions to their peers and will be provided with either the solution to their problem or a pointer in the right direction. However, there is an unwritten rule of newsgroups: If you're going to ask for assistance, you should help others as well. In reality, it's not a bad idea to peruse any newsgroups that might be relevant to your enterprise deployment on at least a weekly basis. Often times you will run across users experiencing similar issues or difficulties to those that you might be experiencing, and in many cases you will discover facts and functionality that might assist in delivering services to your users.

Microsoft provides newsgroups for almost every product they currently support and at this time have a minimum of 15 newsgroups dedicated to Windows NT Server alone. As of April 1997, the following Windows NT–oriented newsgroups were available on the Microsoft news server at nntp://msnews.microsoft.com.

- Personal Fax (`microsoft.public.windowsnt.personalfax`)
- Applications, OLE, and NetDDE (`microsoft.public.windowsnt.apps`)
- Domain Administration (`microsoft.public.windowsnt.domain`)
- Domain Name System Server (`microsoft.public.windowsnt.dns`)
- File Systems (`microsoft.public.windowsnt.fsft`)
- General (`microsoft.public.windowsnt.misc`)
- NT Issues on the Macintosh (`microsoft.public.windowsnt.mac`)
- 32-Bit Mail and Schedule+ (`microsoft.public.windowsnt.mail`)
- File and Print Services for NetWare/Directory Service Manager for NetWare (`microsoft.public.windowsnt.dsmnfpnw`)
- Printing (`microsoft.public.windowsnt.print`)
- General Protocol, Networking, and Connectivity Issues (`microsoft.public.windowsnt.protocol.misc`)
- Protocol: IPX (`microsoft.public.windowsnt.protocol.ipx`)
- Protocol: Remote Access Service (RAS) and Other Serial Communication Issues (`microsoft.public.windowsnt.protocol.ras`)
- Protocol: TCP/IP (`microsoft.public.windowsnt.protocol.tcpip`)
- Setup (`microsoft.public.windowsnt.setup`)
- Windows NT Server 4.0 Distributed File System Beta (`microsoft.public.windowsnt.dfs`)

In addition, the following newsgroups are public domain and should be accessible from any news server:

- `comp.os.ms-windows.nt.admin.misc`
- `comp.os.ms-windows.nt.admin.networking`
- `comp.os.ms-windows.nt.admin.security`
- `comp.os.ms-windows.nt.advocacy`
- `comp.os.ms-windows.nt.announce`
- `comp.os.ms-windows.nt.misc`
- `comp.os.ms-windows.nt.pre-release`
- `comp.os.ms-windows.nt.setup`
- `comp.os.ms-windows.nt.setup.hardware`
- `comp.os.ms-windows.nt.setup.misc`
- `comp.os.ms-windows.nt.software.backoffice`
- `comp.os.ms-windows.nt.software.compatibility`
- `comp.os.ms-windows.nt.software.services`

Newsgroups are an excellent source of support, especially when you don't have a readily available consultant, third-party support provider, or product expert in-house.

The MS Web Site

The Microsoft Web Site is an excellent resource for support information. Good, contemporary information and support tools can be can be found at http://www.microsoft.com on a daily basis, seven days a week, 24 hours a day. Some of the resources offered for free by Microsoft are:

- The Microsoft Knowledge Base
- The Windows NT Server Web Page
- The Windows NT Workstation Web Page
- The Windows 95 Web Page

Each of the Web pages, which can be reached by going through the Products page mentioned at http://www.microsoft.com/products provides pointers to documentation, file libraries, and even non-Microsoft Web sites from time to time. It is highly recommended that if you are supporting any of these operating systems, you check them at least once a week for updates.

One of the more powerful tools available on the Microsoft Web Site is the Microsoft Knowledge Base. This tool, found at http://www.microsoft.com/kb, provides quite a bit of the same information that can be found on the Microsoft Technet CD-ROM, but it may not be quite as current. In short, the Knowledge Base is a searchable product history that contains a wide variety of support information including white papers, resolutions to common problems, pointers to hot fixes, bug confirmations, product updates, and support articles. The Knowledge Base is an excellent resource to turn to with questions concerning events logged into your Event Viewer, problems with applications, network connectivity, and so on. Be forewarned, however, that the answers you'll receive are only as good as the queries you enter. Be sure to read the search tips provided with the service.

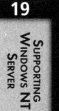

19

SUPPORTING
WINDOWS NT
SERVER

Technet

Microsoft Technet is a subscription service that provides, at a minimum, three monthly CD-ROMs that allow easy access to an extremely comprehensive collection of Microsoft technical information. You'll find the following included on the Monthly Technet CD-ROMs:

- A very current Knowledge Base, including information not found on the Web site
- Technical white papers concerning a variety of Microsoft products
- Support articles and utilities usually only found in Microsoft Resource Kits
- Deployment and planning guides for a vast array of products
- Training material

The Microsoft Technet subscription is an excellent tool that any support organization could use. Even if you don't find yourself running into issues with Windows NT Server in particular, the Technet CD-ROM provides valuable information on almost all Microsoft products and their interaction with other resources throughout the enterprise.

Summary

The time and money spent supporting Windows NT Server can be reduced drastically if you're familiar with the tools available. Through a combination of the built-in diagnostic utilities, newsgroups, the Microsoft Web Site, and the Microsoft Technet service, the time cost of supporting Windows NT Server and your entire enterprise in general can be reduced. It is important to note that for any of these tools to be effective you and your staff must be familiar with the features and options available, but once you begin using any or all of these tools, you'll find that they will provide many support benefits.

I

INDEX

Symbols

A

MACMILLAN COMPUTER PUBLISHING USA

A VIACOM COMPANY

Technical ----- Support:

If you need assistance with the information in this book or with a CD/Disk
accompanying the book, please access the Knowledge Base on our Web
site at **http://www.superlibrary.com/general/support**. Our most
Frequently Asked Questions are answered there. If you do not find the
answer to your questions on our Web site, you may contact Macmillan
Technical Support **(317) 581-3833** or e-mail us at **support@mcp.com**.

Windows NT 4 and Web Site Resource Library

Sams Development Group

This comprehensive library is the most complete reference available for Windows NT and Web administrators and developers. Six volumes and more than 3,500 pages of key information about the Windows NT Registry, Web site administration and development, networking, BackOffice integration, and much more. Contains three bonus CD-ROMs that include networking utilities, third-party tools, support utilities, Web site development tools, HTML templates, CGI scripts, and more! Covers version 4 for Windows NT.

Price: $149.99 USA/$209.95 CDN   ISBN: 0-672-30995-5

User Level: Accomplished—Expert   Pages: 3,200

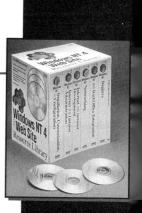

Robert Cowart's Windows NT 4 Unleashed, Professional Reference Edition

Robert Cowart

The only reference Windows NT administrators need to learn how to configure their NT systems for maximum performance, security, and reliability. This comprehensive reference explains how to install, maintain, and configure an individual workstation, as well as how to connect computers to peer-to-peer networking. Includes comprehensive advice for setting up and administering an NT Server network and focuses on the new and improved administration and connectivity features of version 4.0. The CD-ROM includes source code, utilities, and sample applications from the book. Covers Windows NT 4 Server and Workstation.

Price: $59.99 USA/$84.95 CDN   ISBN: 0-672-31001-5

User Level: Intermediate—Expert   Pages: 1,400

Programming Windows NT 4 Unleashed

David Hamilton, Mickey Williams, and Griffith Kadnier

Readers get a clear understanding of the modes of operation and architecture for Windows NT. Everything—including execution models, processes, threads, DLLs, memory, controls, security, and more—is covered with precise detail. CD-ROM contains source code and completed sample programs from the book. Teaches OLE, DDE, drag-and-drop, OCX development, and the component gallery. Explores Microsoft BackOffice programming.

Price: $59.99 USA/$84.95 CDN   ISBN: 0-672-30905-X

User Level: Accomplished—Expert   Pages: 1,200

Peter Norton's Complete Guide to Windows NT 4 Workstation

Peter Norton

Readers will explore everything from interface issues to advanced topics, such as client/server networking, building your own Internet server, and OLE. Readers will master complex memory-management techniques. This book teaches how to build an Internet server and explores peer-to-peer networking.

Price: $39.99 USA/$56.95 CDN   ISBN: 0-672-30901-7

User Level: Casual—Accomplished   Pages: 936

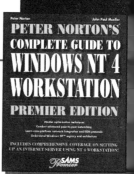

Windows NT 4 Server Unleashed

Jason Garms

The Windows NT Server has been gaining tremendous market share over Novell, and the new upgrade—which includes a Windows 95 interface—is sure to add momentum to its market drive. To that end, *Windows NT 4 Server Unleashed* is written to meet that growing market. It provides information on disk and file management, integrated networking, BackOffice integration, and TCP/IP protocols. The CD-ROM includes source code from the book and valuable utilities. Focuses on using Windows NT as an Internet server. Covers security issues and Macintosh support.

Price: $59.99 USA/$84.95 CDN   *ISBN: 0-672-30933-5*

User Level: Accomplished—Expert   *Pages: 1,100*

Peter Norton's Guide to Windows 95/NT 4 Programming with MFC

Peter Norton and Rob McGregor

Following in the wake of the best-selling *Peter Norton* series, this book gives the reader a "rapid tour guide" approach to programming Windows 95 applications. The reader will learn to use, change, and augment the functions of the MFC library. Readers will use the Microsoft Foundation Class libraries to get the information they need to begin programming immediately. Covers the latest version of MFC for Windows 95 and Windows NT 4.

Price: $49.99 USA/$70.95 CDN   *ISBN: 0-672-30900-9*

User Level: New—Casual   *Pages: 1,200*

Building an Intranet with Windows NT 4

Scott Zimmerman and Tim Evans

This hands-on guide teaches readers how to set up and maintain an efficient intranet with Windows NT. It comes complete with a selection of the best software for setting up a server, creating content, and developing intranet applications. The CD-ROM includes a complete Windows NT intranet toolkit with a full-featured Web server, Web content development tools, and ready-to-use intranet applications. Includes complete specifications for several of the most popular intranet applications, including group scheduling, discussions, database access, and more. Covers Windows NT 4.

Price: $49.99 USA/$70.95 CDN   *ISBN: 1-57521-137-8*

User Level: Casual—Accomplished   *Pages: 600*

Windows NT 4 Web Development

Sanjaya Hettihewa

Windows NT and Microsoft's newly developed Internet Information Server is making it easier and more cost effective to set up, manage, and administer a good Web site. Because the Windows NT environment is relatively new, there are few books on the market that adequately discuss its full potential. *Windows NT 4 Web Development* addresses that potential by providing information on all key aspects of server setup, maintenance, design, and implementation. CD-ROM contains valuable source code and powerful utilities. Teaches how to incorporate new technologies into your Web site. Covers Java, JavaScript, Internet Studio, Visual Basic Script, and Windows NT.

Price: $59.99 USA/$84.95 CDN   *ISBN: 1-57521-089-4*

User Level: Accomplished—Expert   *Pages: 744*

Add to Your Sams Library Today with the Best Books for Programming, Operating Systems, and New Technologies

The easiest way to order is to pick up the phone and call

1-800-428-5331

between 9:00 a.m. and 5:00 p.m. EST.
For faster service please have your credit card available.

ISBN	Quantity	Description of Item	Unit Cost	Total Cost
0-672-30995-5		Windows NT 4 and Web Site Resource Library (6 books/3 CD-ROMs)	$149.99	
0-672-31001-5		Robert Cowart's Windows NT 4 Unleashed, Professional Reference Edition (book/CD-ROM)	$59.99	
0-672-30905-X		Programming Windows NT 4 Unleashed (book/CD-ROM)	$59.99	
0-672-30901-7		Peter Norton's Complete Guide to Windows NT 4 Workstation	$39.99	
0-672-30933-5		Windows NT 4 Server Unleashed (book/CD-ROM)	$59.99	
0-672-30900-9		Peter Norton's Guide to Windows 95/NT 4 Programming with MFC (book/CD-ROM)	$49.99	
1-57521-137-8		Building an Intranet with Windows NT 4 (book/CD-ROM)	$49.99	
1-57521-089-4		Windows NT 4 Web Development (book/CD-ROM)	$59.99	
❏ 3 ½" Disk		Shipping and Handling: See information below.		
❏ 5 ¼" Disk		TOTAL		

Shipping and Handling: $4.00 for the first book, and $1.75 for each additional book. Floppy disk: add $1.75 for shipping and handling. If you need to have it NOW, we can ship product to you in 24 hours for an additional charge of approximately $18.00, and you will receive your item overnight or in two days. Overseas shipping and handling adds $2.00 per book and $8.00 for up to three disks. Prices subject to change. Call for availability and pricing information on latest editions.

201 W. 103rd Street, Indianapolis, Indiana 46290

1-800-428-5331 — Orders   1-800-835-3202 — Fax   1-800-858-7674 — Customer Service

Book ISBN 0-672-31038-4